Encyclopedia *of* Designs *for* Quilting

Phyllis D. Miller

AQS
American Quilter's Society
P. O. Box 3290 • Paducah, KY 42002-3290

Located in Paducah, Kentucky, the American Quilter's Society (AQS), is dedicated to promoting the accomplishments of today's quilters. Through its publications and events, AQS strives to honor today's quiltmakers and their work – and inspire future creativity and innovation in quiltmaking.

Editor – Bonnie K. Browning
Book Design & Illustrations – Whitney Hopkins
Cover Design – Karen Chiles
Photography – Charley Lynch & Richard Walker

Library of Congress Cataloging-in-Publication Data

Miller, Phyllis D.
Encyclopedia of designs for quilting / Phyllis D. Miller.
p. cm.
Includes bibliographical references and index.
ISBN 0-89145-887-5
1. Quilting--Patterns. I. Title.
TT835.M526 1996
746.46'041--dc20 96-39002
CIP

Additional copies of this book may be ordered from: American Quilter's Society, P.O. Box 3290, Paducah, KY 42002-3290 @ $34.95. Add $2.00 for postage & handling.

Dedication

This book is dedicated
to my parents, Joe and Cebah Dutton,
for instilling in their children the idea that work
or chores can be pleasurable and not "work,"
for always letting us know that we could do anything we wished,
and for always being proud of us;

to my husband, Mike, and our sons, Alan and David,
for their support and encouragement,
and for appreciating me, not only as a quilter, but for myself;

to all of my friends
who have so generously shared their knowledge
and time with me over these many years;

and to the quilters and authors before me
who left great quilts and great books
to both inspire and challenge me.

Acknowledgments

Many people contributed to making this book possible and, for that, I would like to sincerely thank the following:

Bill and Meredith Schroeder and the American Quilter's Society for publishing this book;

Bonnie K. Browning for her advice, guidance, understanding, and friendship as my editor;

Karen Chiles for the cover design;

Whitney Hopkins for her computer expertise in drawing my illustrations and designing my book;

Charles R. Lynch and Richard Walker for the beautiful photography;

and Jane Blair, Arleen Boyd, Bonnie K. Browning, June Culvey, Lorraine Dickhaus, Hazel B. Reed Ferrell, Dorothy Finley, Penny Gilmore, Ethel Hickman, Mary Andra Holmes, Starr Kaiser, Anne Oliver, Jenny Perry, Lou Ann Philpot, Karen Riggins, Anita Shackelford, Martha B. Skelton, Cheryl Slaughter, Joyce Stewart, Frances Stone, Leureta B. Thieme, Debra Wagner, and Beverly Williams for loaning their quilts and/or granting permission for photographs of their quilts to be included in this book.

Contents

Introduction 8

Chapter 1 • How to Use This Book 9
- Designs for Quilting Terminology 11
- Tools Needed for Drawing and Marking Designs 11
- Making the Designs Fit 12

Chapter 2 • Straight Lines, Geometrics, and Triangles 15

Chapter 3 • Squares 31

Chapter 4 • Diagonals and Diamonds 51

Chapter 5 • From the Quilt Pattern 69

Chapter 6 • Circles 74

Chapter 7 • Ovals, Crescents, and Curves 93

Chapter 8 • Ropes and Cables 105

Chapter 9 • Hearts and Feathers 125

Chapter 10 • Representational, Naturalistic, and Combinations 145

How to Use the Numerical Index of Designs for Quilting 166

Guide to the Numerical Index of Designs for Quilting 167

Numerical Index of Designs for Quilting 168

Index 194

Bibliography 196

About the Author 197

Introduction

"It's not a quilt until it's quilted" and "How do I quilt it" are often heard phrases. Many times as we look at quilts and are awed by them, we may not be consciously aware that the one thing about a particular quilt that makes it stand out are the stitching lines of the quilting design. The quilting stitches that hold the layers of a quilt together are truly what make a quilt either ordinary or fantastic.

The ***Encyclopedia of Designs for Quilting*** has three purposes: to present a record of traditional quilting designs for use in quiltmaking and for use in quilt documentation; to offer guidance on where to use these quilting designs; and to provide instruction on how quilting designs can be drawn and marked for use in current quiltmaking.

As chairman of the Kentucky Quilt Registry, I have found the need for a comprehensive reference of quilting designs that gives the same mental image to both those doing documentation and the ones reading the information. I have attempted to make this book a reference library of historical quilting designs in addition to being an instructional book.

In the summer of 1968, I decided to make a quilt. Why is still a mystery to me as I was not around another quiltmaker. My paternal grandmother who was a quilter had died when I was twelve so she was not there to influence me. My memories of her are those of a loving grandmother sitting in a rocker sewing small pieces of fabric together into quilt blocks. I have since decided that the desire to be creative through quilting must have been genetic.

In 1968 finding another quilter was not easy and so I had no one to turn to for advice and instruction. My first quilt had everything wrong that is possible to do wrong. Deciding how to quilt that first quilt was probably the easiest part of the whole process.

No one had ever told me that it was hard to quilt across seams and, lucky for me, I have never chosen quilting designs with concern over the stitches crossing the seams. For that first quilt, I had to take inspiration from old quilts and many of those that my grandmother had left were quilted with simple diagonal lines. Since that had worked well in the past, it was good enough for me. After thirty years, I would still choose to quilt my Shoo Fly quilt with the diagonal line design. Sometimes, simple is best.

I am just like most quilters and one quilt was enough to get me hooked. When I started the second one and then another and another, I realized that the quilting, and especially the designs for the quilting, were to me the most important part of the quilt. It was the designs used in the quilting that intrigued me and finding those designs in the size I needed or some instructions on how to do them was usually impossible.

By this time, there were quilt shows to attend with more quilting designs to see and I starting teaching quilting classes. The students in my classes wanted to not only know how to quilt but what design to use for the quilting. So early in my teaching career, one of my classes was "Choosing Quilting Designs" and by the end of every class someone would ask if I was going to put all of the information that I had presented into a book. It has taken a few years to gather the information and to do the research to assemble the traditional designs for quilting that are presented in this book.

When writing the instructions for each of the designs, I have tried to describe the easiest way to draw and mark each of them. There are many ways to accomplish the same end result and my hope is that you will try my way and improve upon it.

My wish is that you, the reader, will use this book as an inspiration to look at quilts with a new eye and to appreciate the beauty that is added to a quilt solely from the design lines used in the quilting.

Phyllis Miller

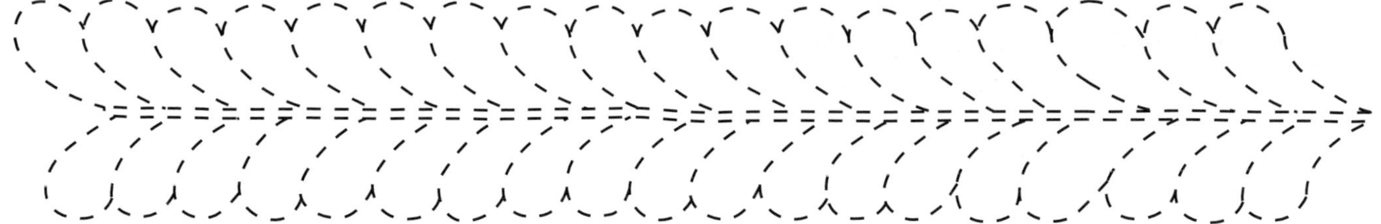

Chapter One
How to Use This Book

Designs for quilting have existed probably since before 200 A. D., although there is little actual proof of the first quilting designs. Since textiles are fragile, it can be assumed that most designs have been passed down from quilter to quilter. Until the last century, patterns or drawings for quilting designs were not printed or sold commerically and therefore, quilters had to mark or draw their own designs by using a handed down design or drawing an original one. Today, many designs for quilting are available but not necessarily always in the specific size that is needed for a specific quilt.

The term "draw" is used loosely and, by no means, requires that you, the quilter, be an artist to be able to "draw" your own designs for quilting. If you can hold a pencil, you can follow the instructions and "draw" the designs for quilting in this book. If generations of quilters before us could "draw" their own designs, so can all quilters of the present.

At the beginning of each chapter, the most often used and most popular designs in that particular grouping will be listed along with any folklore and traditions associated with those designs. Any special tips relating to each category of designs will also be included here. Although quilting designs are not very useful in the dating of quilts, the earliest dates for specific designs will be mentioned when known. Each chapter has a page of color photographs showing quilting designs selected from the designs in that chapter.

The first section of the book contains traditional designs for quilting that have been found on quilts in this country. Chapters 2 through 9 contain designs for quilting that can be drawn using simple tools. The instructions found in this part of the book will give you, the quilter, the basics needed to draw most of the traditional designs for quilting. Because there are as many combinations and variations of designs for quilting as there are quilters, many of the combinations of designs are not included in the book. By studying and dissecting designs, you should be able to put the combinations together to create a design that you may have seen on another quilt. Designs for quilting are like signatures of the quilter. By combining designs, each quilter can make the quilt uniquely theirs.

Representational, realistic, and naturalistic designs will be found in Chapter 10. You will find instructions for drawing only a few of these designs as they are representative of designs that were taken from the surroundings of the quilters. These designs were originally hand drawn by the quilter, and, because of their popularity were used on many quilts over the last century. Any design that can be drawn with a pencil can become a quilting design and the designs in these two chapters have been popular and often used by quilters and, therefore, have joined the ranks of traditional quilting designs. The designs in this chapter are representative and can be and are varied each time they are used.

The second section of the book is an Index to Quilting Designs. The purpose of this section is to present a systematic method of recording the designs used for quilting and to give each design a name. The designs were given the names that were most frequently assigned to them in the past. The designs included in this section are only the traditional designs that were referred to more than once in books about quilting. For example,

Plate 1-1. Marking and drawing tools.

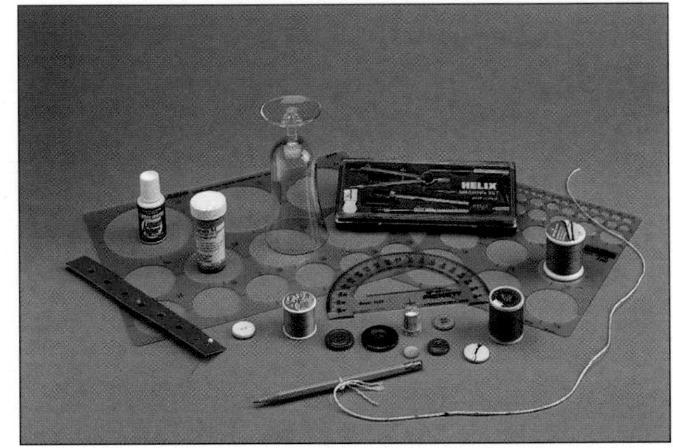

Plate 1-2. Tools for drawing circles.

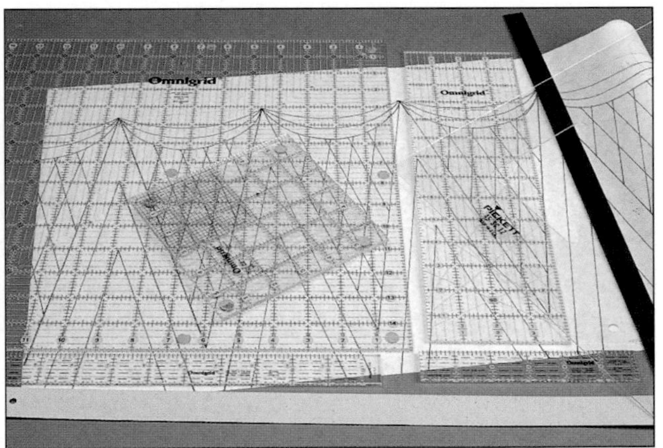

Plate 1-3. Tools for drawing straight lines.

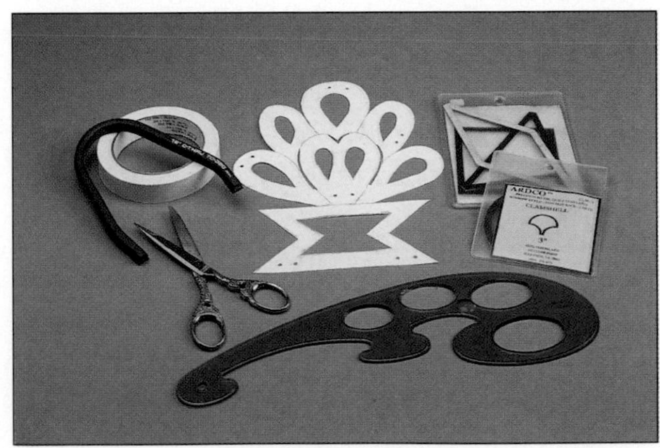

Plate 1-4. Other handy items.

only one tulip is included although there are many variations of the tulip.

The Index to Quilting Designs should prove beneficial to quilt documentors, quilt historians, and to the quilters of today, making it possible for us all to use the same terminology.

In the illustrations or diagrams for drawing each design when a template is shown or a unit of a design is to be traced, those will be indicated in color.

Hopefully, you will be able to take the information provided and draw any design that you see in whatever size will fit your particular quilt. This chapter has the basics needed to use the instructions for drawing the many traditional quilting designs in this book.

DESIGNS FOR QUILTING TERMINOLOGY

The following diagram of a quilt (Figure 1-1) shows the different parts of a quilt that will be referred to in the instructions for drawing the quilting designs.

1. Border – A piece or pieces of fabric that form a framing for the blocks in a quilt top or the center design in a whole cloth quilt.
2. Sashing – Strips of fabric between the blocks in the quilt top.
3. Straight – Refers to being straight or parallel with the edge of the quilt top and not to the grain of the fabric.
4. On-point – Blocks set in the quilt top with the corners of the block up or on point and the block edges on the diagonal.
5. Medallion – A block or design that forms a central focal point.
6. Framing – A strip of fabric or design that is used to emphasize either a block or a design.
7. Diagonal – A line that runs from corner to corner of a square. The square can be a block or the entire quilt top. It also refers to quilting lines that cross the weave of the fabric rather than on the straight of the threads in the fabric.
8. Vertical – Lines that go up and down the length of the block or quilt top.
9. Horizontal – Lines that go across the width of the block or quilt top.
10. Quilt edge – The outside edge of the quilt top.
11. Corner square of the border – If a line were extended from the seams where the blocks or center design of the quilt top are sewn to the border to the quilt edges, a square would result in the corner where the borders join.
12. Blocks – Refers to either pieced, appliqued, or plain fabric squares or units in a quilt top.

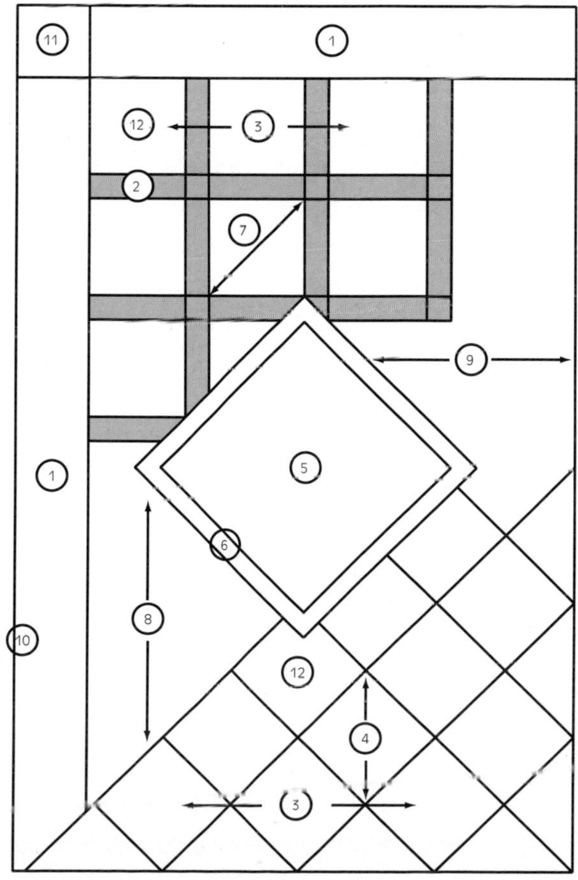

Figure 1-1.

TOOLS NEEDED FOR DRAWING AND MARKING DESIGNS

Paper – White bond paper (8½" x 11") for small designs and for design repeats, butcher paper for large blocks and whole cloth designs; freezer paper for making templates or for large or long designs; and/or clean newspaper paper; graph paper (optional).

Rulers – Always use the same ruler throughout the marking of each quilt or quilt design. Changing rulers in the middle of the game can cause the designs to be uneven. A ruler marked with a grid both across the width and the length and with 45° and 60° markings is the preferred type. Three lengths of rulers (6", 12", and 24") are handy.

Pencil – Use a sharp lead pencil for drawing

designs on paper. For marking directly onto the fabric, use a lead pencil that does not have an oil base or use any of the other fabric marking tools currently available commercially. Test all marking tools by marking on a piece of fabric prior to marking on the actual quilt.

Eraser – Absolutely necessary, especially when drawing the designs on paper. The white erasers are less messy than simple pencil erasers.

Circle Marking Tools – Many quilting designs are derived from the circle. One or more of the following circle objects will come in handy: circle templates (available in office supply stores), compass, protractor, fan/circle marking tool, pencil and string, cup, wine glass, plate, buttons. Remember that in the past most quilters probably had access to only what they had in their homes and those same items will still work.

Black Felt Tip Permanent Marker – Use this marker to go over the designs drawn on a paper pattern to make the design easy to trace onto the fabric. Use a permanent marker on the paper pattern to avoid ink bleeding onto the quilt fabric.

Template Material – Poster board, cardboard or template plastic are all suitable for making quilting design templates.

Other Items That Could Come in Handy – white correction fluid, access to a copy machine, a flexible curve, purchased quilt pattern templates (i.e., diamonds, clamshell, log cabin strips), carpenter's rule or measuring tape, quilter's masking tape, long rule compass, pencil sharpener, a set square or large ruled square.

MAKING THE DESIGNS FIT

Many times the size of the quilting design will be determined by the amount of quilting that is desired or that the quilter is willing to do. With quilting designs, a partial design can end at a seam or the quilt edge. Many of the older quilts were quilted in this manner. To achieve a more symmetrical look, measure and/or fold paper so that the design will fit perfectly into the area to be quilted. Look at each different design to make this decision.

Marking As You Go – Even the most simple of designs will be easier to mark directly on the quilt top if some practice is first done on paper. You can also get an idea of exactly how the design will look on the quilt. When marking as you go, mark a section and quilt that section before moving on to mark and quilt the next section.

Making Templates – For a small area, such as a block design, measure the block with a ruler and divide into equal sections. For example, a 12" block can be divided into 3 sections to make a large design, into 4 sections for a somewhat medium design, into 6 sections (2" each) for a smaller design or into 12 sections (1" each).

Each quilting design has instructions for making a template when one is needed. The template will be shown in the diagrams in color. Use the measurements from dividing the area to be quilted as the basis for making the template.

An easy way to make a template for a quilting design is to draw the design on freezer paper. Iron the freezer paper design onto posterboard using a dry iron. Use paper scissors to cut out the template. Using fluorescent color posterboard (I knew there had to be a use for it) gives a template that is easy to find plus the name of the design and where it was used can be written directly onto the template.

Paper Folding – Cut a piece of paper exactly the size of the area where the quilting design will be used. In other words, for a block cut it exactly the size of the finished block. For a border, the paper only needs to be cut ½ the length of the border and the exact finished width. Include the corner square of the border when cutting the paper. The border may not have an actual square sewn in and, if not, then this is an imaginary square. With a pencil and ruler, draw a line where this square would be. For a rectangular quilt, cut one piece of paper for the border length and another piece of paper for the border width.

For a square, the paper may need to be folded in half diagonally or into four smaller squares. Determine how to fold the paper square by looking at the quilting design.

For a border design, first, fold the paper in half up to the line where a corner square would be. Fold this section in half again. Usually, one more time of folding the paper in half will give a section that is a good size. This will be determined by the design to be drawn. At any rate, one of these sections will be the size that one unit of the design should be drawn to fit.

If the other border is a different length, fold the paper for it in the same manner. The length of the sections of the design will be a little different but the design will fit the quilt perfectly and will also end so the corner design can be drawn in the corner square. Usually the difference will be so slight that the eye will not notice.

Tracing – In designs where one unit of the design is repeated to make the whole design, such as in border designs, only one unit of the design has to be drawn. That unit can then be traced in each of the other sections of the folded paper. In the instructions, when a unit is to be traced, the tracing lines in the diagrams will be indicated by colored lines.

Paper Patterns – The folded paper can now be used for drawing the design for quilting by drawing one unit of the design in one of the sections or cut one section from the folded paper and draw the design on this cut piece of paper. After one unit of the design has been drawn, repeat the design in each section of the paper by tracing. Go over all the design lines on your paper pattern with a permanent black felt tip marker. This makes the design easier to see when tracing the design onto the quilt top.

Since the paper was cut to fit one half of one border, it will be necessary sometimes to flip the pattern over for the other end of the border. If so, trace around the design lines on the back side of the paper with the black permanent marker.

The quilting design can then be traced onto the quilt top by pinning the paper pattern face up to the wrong side of the quilt top. Both the pattern and the quilt top should be facing up. Trace the quilting design, using a fabric marking pencil or pen. It may be necessary to use a light box or another light source to see the design, especially if the fabric is dark.

Move the paper pattern to the next section to be marked, pin, and mark.

Photocopying – Designs for quilting can be enlarged or reduced on a copy machine. Slight distortions from copying are not as noticeable on quilting designs as they are in pieced patterns.

Plate 2-1. Single Parallel Lines (also Tents, By the Piece).
Homespun by Lou Ann Philpot, 1987.

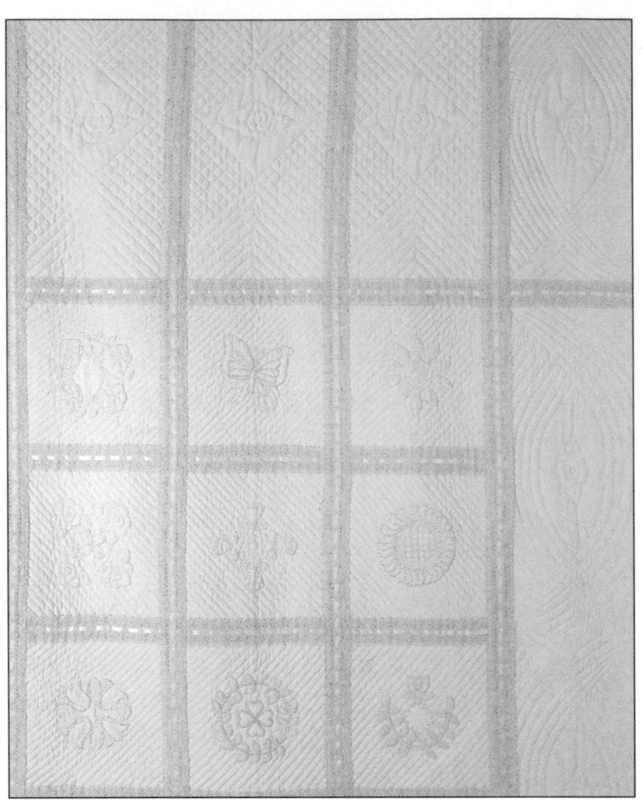

Plate 2-2. Tents (also Squares Crosshatch, Diagonal Lines, Cable).
A Little Bit of Candlewicking by Bonnie K. Browning, 1983. Collection of the Museum of the American Quilter's Society.

Plate 2-3. Bricks.
Night Bloom by Jane Blair, 1985. Collection of the Museum of the American Quilter's Society.

Plate 2-4. Single Parallel Lines (also Squares Crosshatch, Feathered Square Variation)
Bloomin' over Prosperity by Phyllis Miller, 1991.

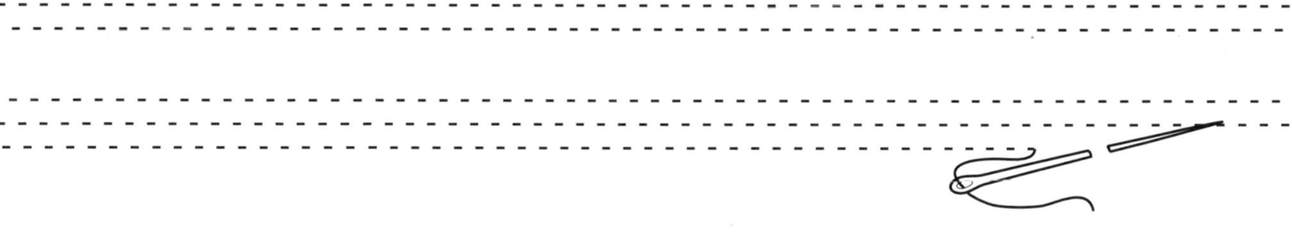

Chapter Two
Straight Lines, Geometrics, and Triangles

The designs for quilting that are formed from using straight lines are some of the easiest designs to mark on a quilt. Straight lines are lines that run either vertically or horizontally with the edge of the quilt. These designs are among the oldest quilting designs and are still frequently used in the individual blocks of a quilt and in borders. Straight line designs are considered good filler designs as well as designs that are suitable for covering the entire quilt surface.

Designs that Zig-Zag are found often in borders and as overall quilting designs. They are easy to mark with a template and are also easy to quilt. The oldest dated quilt using the Zig-Zag design was circa 1840.

The designs that can be classified as being formed from triangles have also been popular and can be used in many variations and in combination with other designs. The triangular designs date from the 1840's. Triangles make good designs to use in borders.

Parallel Lines, Single: also Straight Parallel Lines, Bars, Channel (Figure 2-1)

Figure 2-1.

Recommended Marking: Mark on the quilt top as you go.

How to Mark or Draw: Parallel lines are marked across the straight grain of the fabric or across the quilt surface. They are marked equal distances from each other. Line up a long ruler with a straight line on the quilt. If there is no straight line for a guide, lightly mark one using the ruler. Mark the first line 1" or more, if desired, from the straight edge (Figure 2-2). This line can now be quilted or several lines can be marked before beginning quilting. The second line will be marked one inch (or more) from the first marked or quilted line (Figure 2-3). Continue marking lines the same distance apart until the area

Figure 2-2.

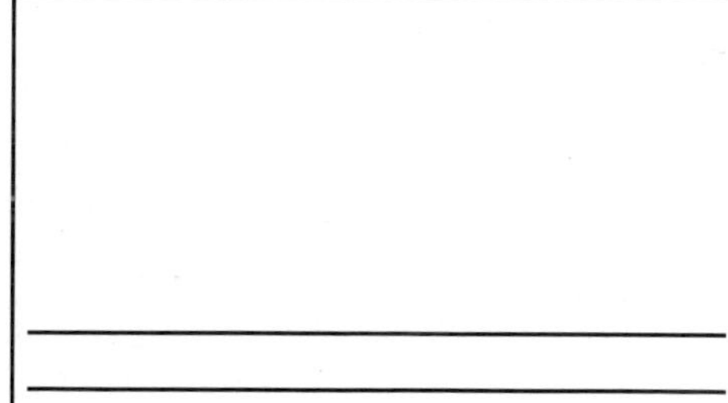

Figure 2-3.

is covered. This quilting design has been found on quilts dating from 1840.

Helpful Note: Always use the same ruler to mark an entire quilt. Rulers do vary. Lines marked across the grain of fabric are harder to hand quilt. When lines are marked across the straight grain of the fabric, the stitches do not show well and it is harder to needle the fabric than when quilting on the diagonal of the fabric grain. Straight Parallel Lines are defined as lines that go across the surface of the quilt. The first line, if it crosses the whole width of the quilt, can be marked using a carpenter's tape measure.

Tools Needed: A long ruler, yardstick, or strip template. A fabric marking pencil or pen.

Where to Use: Use on utilitarian quilts or where parallel lines on the straight are necessary for the effect wanted. Could be used effectively when machine quilting.

Parallel Lines, Double (Figure 2-4)

Figure 2-4.

Recommended Marking: Mark the block or quilt top as you go.

How to Mark or Draw: Double Parallel Lines are found on quilts dating from 1880. Double Parallel Lines are marked the same as Single Parallel Lines. They are marked across the grain of the fabric or the quilt top. A straight line is needed for a starting guide and can be either the quilt edge or a block. Using a ruler, mark the first line across the surface. The second line is marked ¼" from the first line (Figure 2-5). Measure 1" from the second line and mark the third line. The fourth line will be ¼" from the third line (Figure 2-6). Quilt these lines, mark four more lines and quilt those until the area is covered.

Figure 2-5.

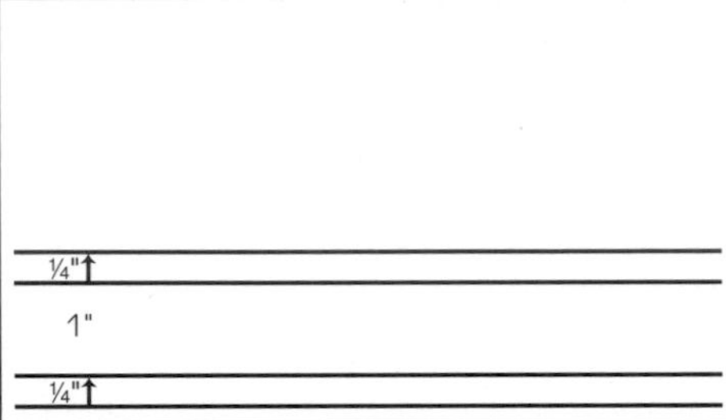

Figure 2-6.

Helpful Note: Check both sides of the quilt top periodically with either a 6" x 24" ruler or a T-square to see that the lines are running parallel with the beginning straight line or edge. The distance given between the double lines gives the best design but can be farther apart, if less quilting is desired.

Tools Needed: A long ruler with markings every ¼". A fabric pencil or pen. Masking tape can be used for a guide if removed and not left on the quilt top for a lengthy amount of time because the glue residue may remain on the quilt.

Where to Use: Good to use in sashings, in plain borders, or horizontally across a quilt where the blocks are set on point. Double parallel lines are easy to machine quilt but difficult to hand quilt especially if the quilting lines are long.

Parallel Lines, Triple (Figure 2-7)

Figure 2-7.

RECOMMENDED MARKING: Mark the block or quilt top as you go.

HOW TO MARK OR DRAW: Triple Parallel Lines are found on quilts dating from 1860. To mark Triple Parallel Lines, follow the same instructions as for the Double Parallel Lines (see Figure 2-4) except this time mark a third line ¼" from the second line. The quilting will follow this sequence: line, ¼" spacing, line, ¼" spacing, line, 1" to 1½" space, line, ¼" spacing, line, ¼" spacing, line, 1" to 1½" space, and repeat across the block or quilt surface.

HELPFUL NOTE: When lines are marked across the straight grain of the fabric, the stitches do not show well and it is harder to needle the fabric than when quilting on the diagonal of the fabric grain. Straight Parallel Lines are defined as lines that go across the surface of the quilt. Blocks set on point can be marked this way and the appearance on the quilt surface is of Straight Parallel Lines but the actual quilting will be done on the bias or diagonal of the fabric.

TOOLS NEEDED: Same as for Single and Double Parallel Lines.

WHERE TO USE: In plain blocks set on point, in borders and as background filler.

Bar: also Plaid, Double Crosshatch, Checkerboard (Figure 2-8)

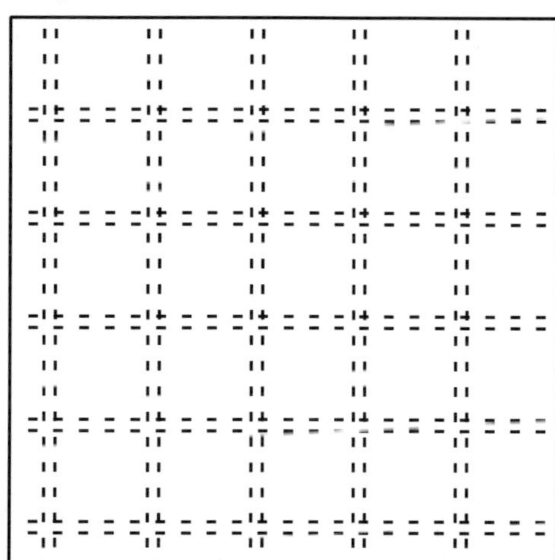

Figure 2-8.

RECOMMENDED MARKING: Mark on the quilt top as you go.

HOW TO MARK OR DRAW: This design is marked on the straight grain of the fabric rather than on the diagonal as is the design traditionally called Plaid. From a straight line that goes across the quilt, line up the ruler and mark the first line along the ruler (Figure 2-9). Quilt this line.

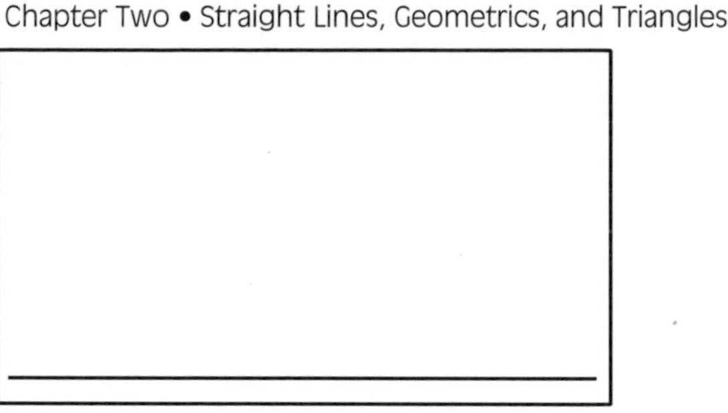

Figure 2-9.

Figure 2-10.

Place the ruler with the first quilted line on the ¼" line mark of the ruler and mark the second line along the edge of the ruler (Figure 2-10). Quilt this second line.

The third quilting line will be marked 2" from the line that was just quilted. The fourth line will be ¼" away from this last line (Figure 2-11) Continue marking and quilting with two lines spaced ¼" apart and then a 2" space across the area to be quilted.

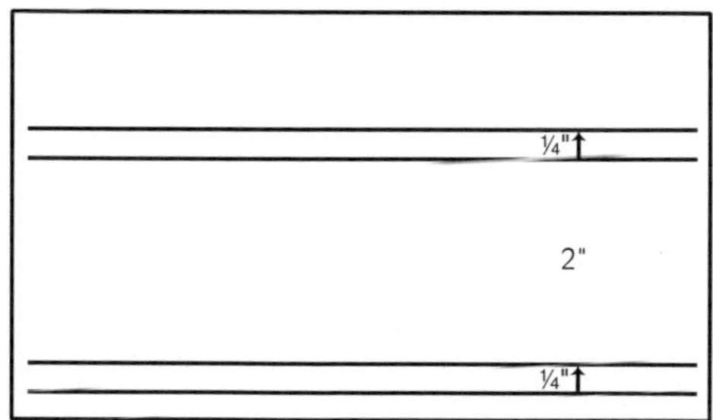

Figure 2-11.

Next, following the same spacing, mark lines running up and down the quilt surface with the same spacing of two lines ¼" apart, a 2" space, two lines ¼" apart, etc.

The Bar design can be spaced farther apart, if desired, i.e. ½" and 3" instead of ¼" and 2" spacing.

HELPFUL NOTE: Check often to see that the lines

are staying parallel and square by checking with either a T-square or a wide ruler to see that your quilting and your marking are staying straight.

TOOLS NEEDED: A long ruler, preferrably 6" x 24", and a fabric marking pencil or pen.

WHERE TO USE: This is a good design to use for filler on plain blocks or over the whole quilt top on simple pieced designs, especially scrap quilts. It is harder to quilt than Plaid which is marked on the diagonal of the fabric.

Bricks (Figure 2-12)

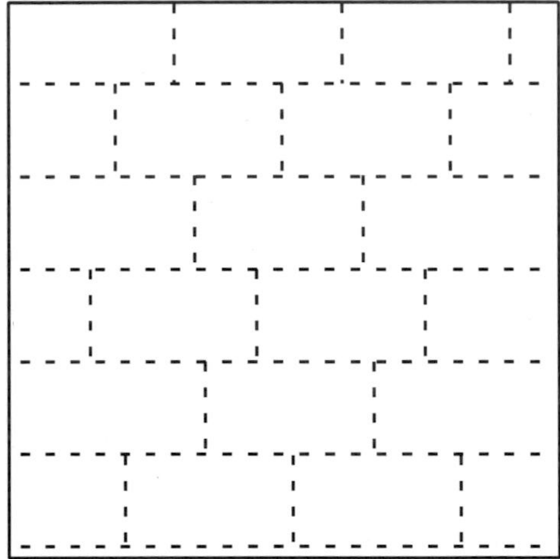

Figure 2-12.

RECOMMENDED MARKING: Can be marked on the quilt top as you go.

HOW TO MARK OR DRAW: This design is marked across the straight grain of the fabric. The first line will be parallel with the straight bottom or top of the quilt or block and will be marked across the entire area that will be filled with the design. The second line will be marked across the top from 2" to 3" from the first line (Figure 2-13). These lines can now be quilted. Continue marking and quilting lines that go across the quilt surface and are spaced evenly apart.

Next, mark lines up and down or vertically between these lines to form bricks or rectangles. You will be making rectangles and these lines should be from 3" to 5" apart (Figure 2-14).

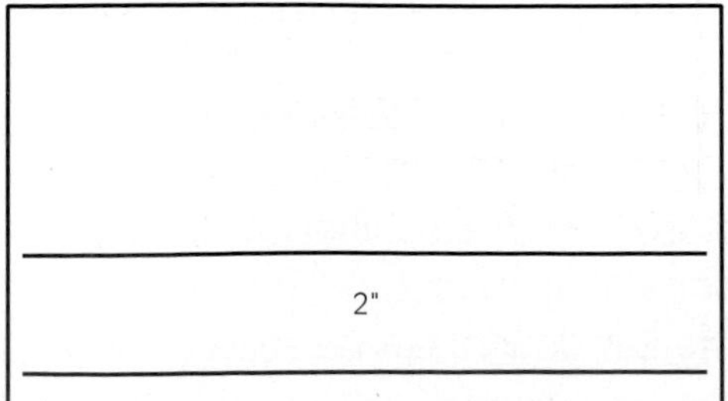

Figure 2-13.

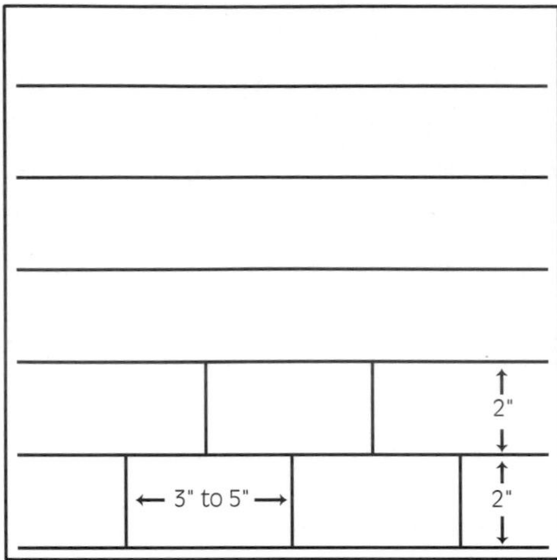

Figure 2-14.

HELPFUL NOTE: Be careful to keep the lines across the quilt straight and parallel. Check with a wide ruler periodically. Note that the vertical lines that form the bricks ***do not*** line up with other brick lines but are placed randomly to look like real layed bricks.

TOOLS NEEDED: A long ruler preferrably 6" x 24" and a fabric marking pencil or pen.

WHERE TO USE: Because this design goes across the straight grain of the fabric, it is harder to hand quilt. Use where the illusion of bricks is desired or when the blocks are set on point and the quilting will actually be diagonally across the grain of the fabric.

Elbow: also Concentric Squares (Figure 2-15)

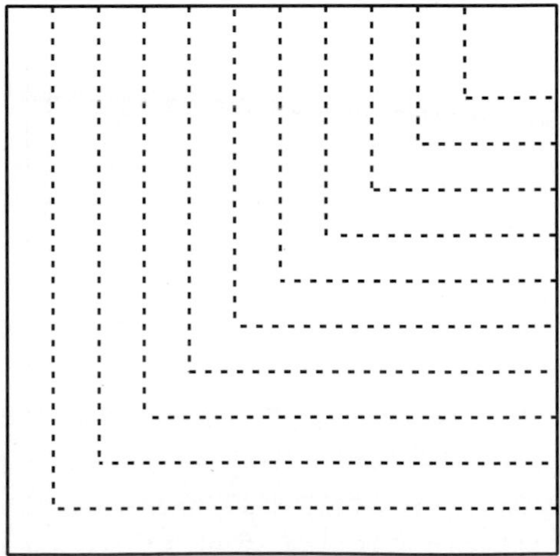

Figure 2-15.

RECOMMENDED MARKING: Mark on the block of the quilt top as you go.

HOW TO MARK OR DRAW: The Elbow design is found on quilts dating from 1875 to present. On the quilt block, draw a faint guide line on the diagonal from corner to corner (Figure 2-16). Using a ruler, mark a line 1" from the lower block edge across the block to the diagonal guide line (Figure 2-17). Turn the ruler and line it up with the side of the block edge and mark a line 1" from the block edge down the block to the guide line (Figure 2-18). This will form the Elbow. Continue marking at 1" intervals until the block is filled.

The whole block can be marked first and then quilted or one Elbow can be marked, quilted, and then the next Elbow marked.

HELPFUL NOTE: Before marking the second part of the Elbow, check to see that the ruler is lined up so that the second part of the Elbow perfectly matches the first part.

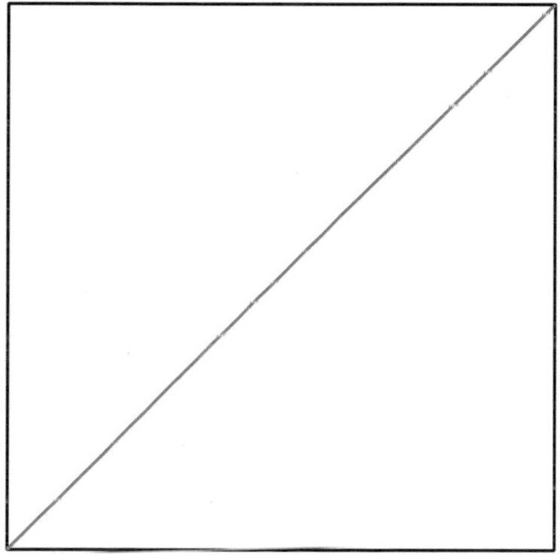

Figure 2-16.

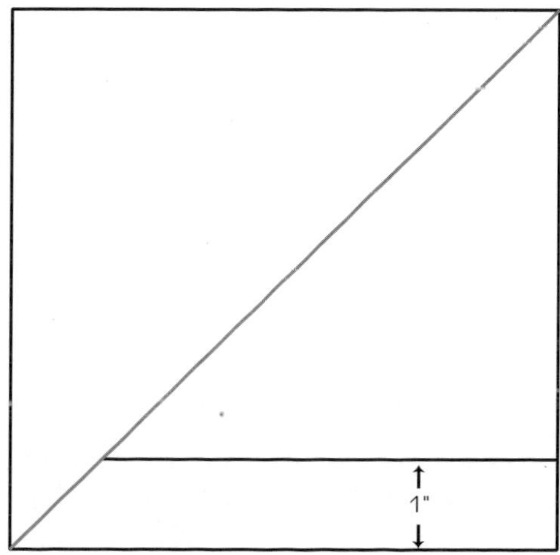

Figure 2-17.

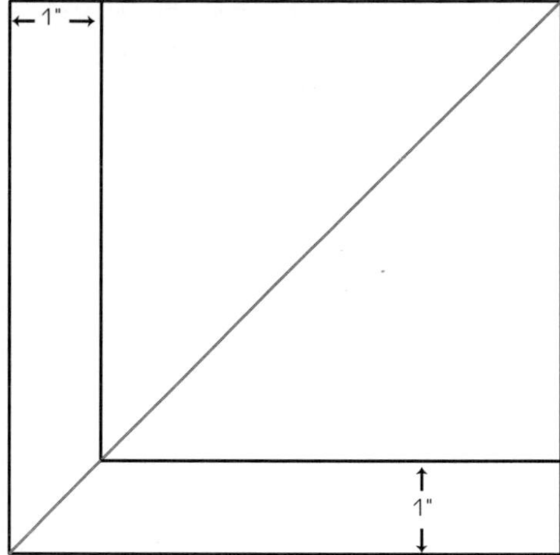

Figure 2-18.

TOOLS NEEDED: A ruler with 1" markings longer than the block. The plastic or metal templates used for cutting log cabin strips work well as a marking tool for the Elbow design. A fabric marking pencil or pen.

WHERE TO USE: Elbow is a good design to use for filler in plain blocks, in corners of borders, and for variety when choosing designs for pieced block quilts. It can be mixed with other geometric designs for a more interesting quilt than where one design only is used.

Zig-Zag: also Streak of Lightning (Figure 2-19)

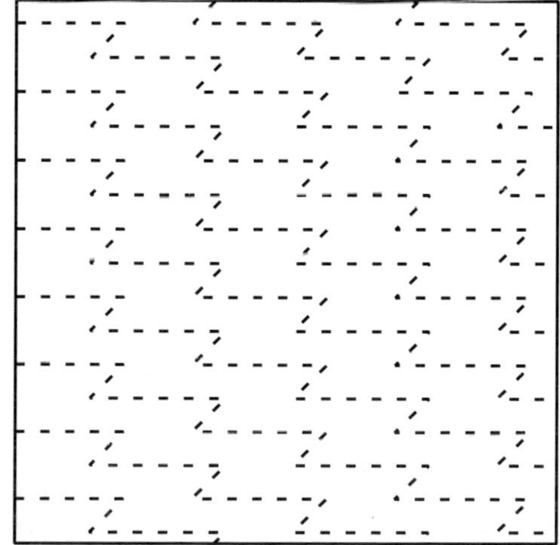

Figure 2-19.

RECOMMENDED MARKING: With a template and mark as you go.

HOW TO MARK OR DRAW: The Zig-Zag design is

more easily marked with a template although it is possible to mark with just a ruler. To make a template, start at the top of a piece of 6" x 12" freezer paper and draw a straight line 4" long. The second line will be 1" below this line and 1" back to the left. The next line is 1" down and 1" back (Figure 2-20). Connect the end of the top line with the beginning of the line below by drawing a line with a ruler (Figure 2-21). To make a useable template, iron this freezer paper drawing to a piece of cardboard or poster board. Cut out the template along the Zig-Zag (Figure 2-22).

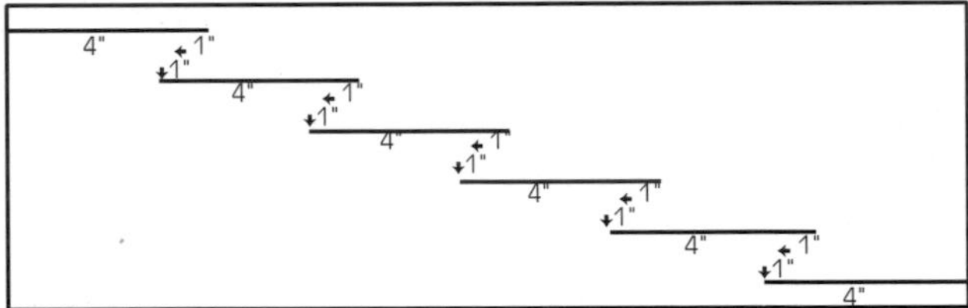

Figure 2-20.

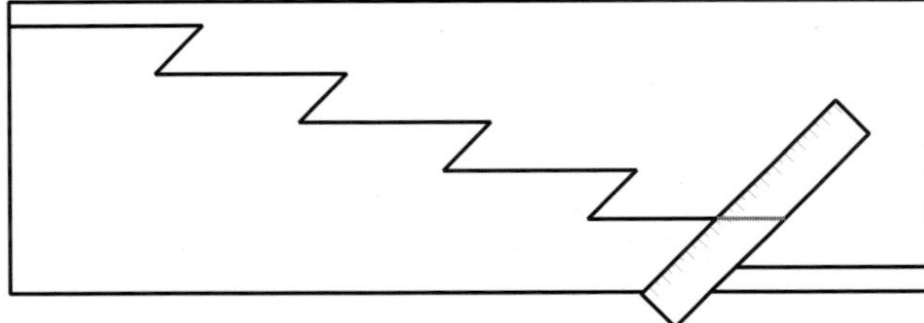

Figure 2-21.

Figure 2-22.

Mark the quilt top by drawing a faint guide line straight across the surface to be covered by the quilting design. Lay the straight bottom edge of the template along this line and mark the Zig-Zag. This can now be quilted or several rows of Zig-Zags marked and then quilted.

To mark the second row of Zig-Zags, mark a faint guide line that is spaced double the distance of the space left between the first and the second line of the Zig-Zag. That distance in this exercise was 1" so the spacing here will be 2" (Figure 2-23). Continue marking and quilting rows of Zig-Zags until the area to be quilted is filled.

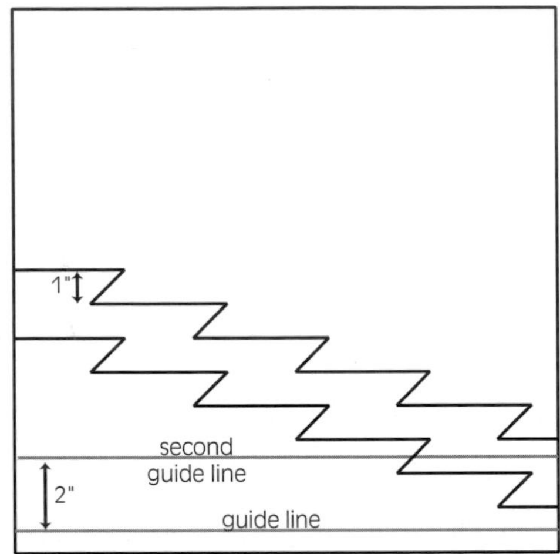

Figure 2-23.

Helpful Note: The look of this quilting design can be varied by making the connecting slant line longer.

Tools Needed: A ruler, template material, and a fabric marking pencil or pen.

Where to Use: As filler for plain setting blocks or over the whole quilt surface disregarding the patchwork pattern. In a pictorial scene, the Zig-Zag design could be used for skies and/or water.

Elongated Z: also Zig-Zag (Figure 2-24)

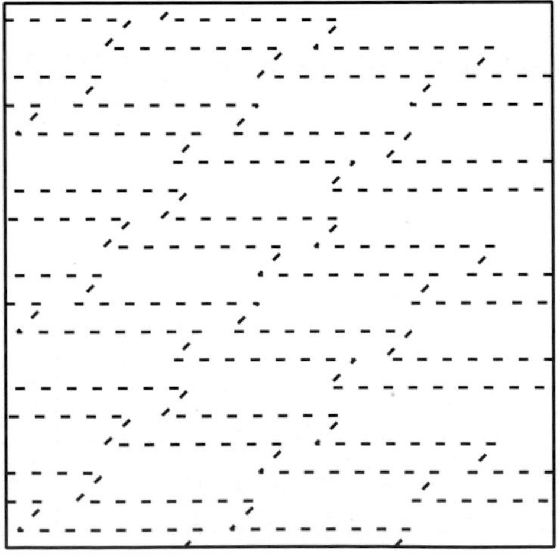

Figure 2-24.

RECOMMENDED MARKING: With a template and mark as you go.

HOW TO MARK OR DRAW: To make the Elongated Z template, start at the top of a piece of paper and draw a straight line (example: 6" long). One inch down from this line and back 1" from the end of the first line, draw another 6" long line and continue until there are at least four lines. (Figure 2-25).

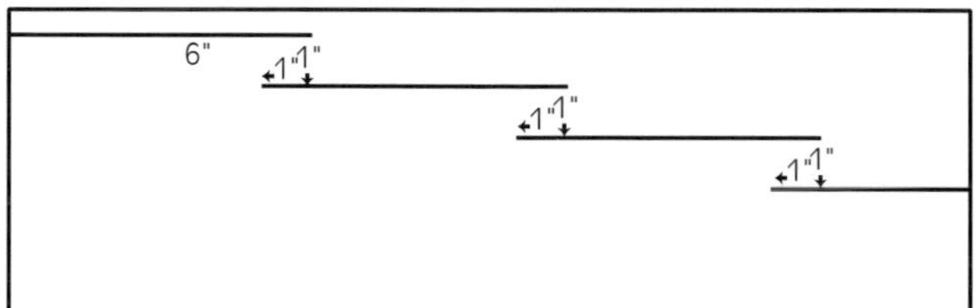

Figure 2-25.

Next, using a ruler, draw a line that connects the end of the top line to the beginning of the line below (Figure 2-26). Using a ruler, mark a second line that will make the Elongated Z 1" wide (Figure-27). Make a template from this drawn Elongated Z.

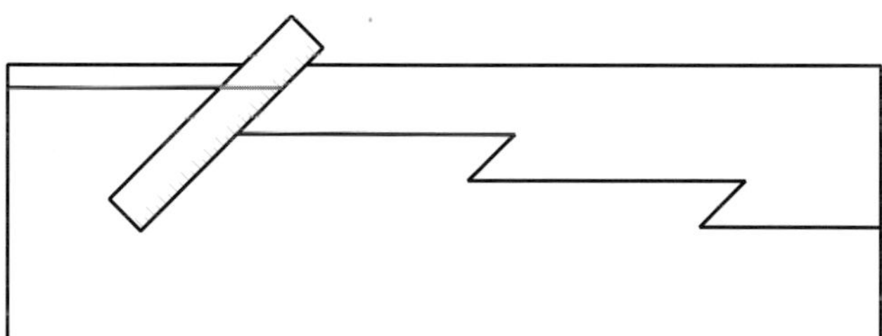

Figure 2-26.

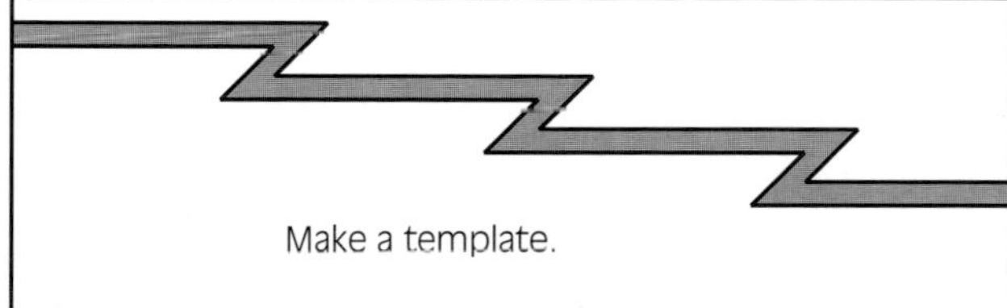

Figure 2-27.

To mark the quilt top, use the template and mark on each side and quilt. Move the template up or down leaving 1" spacing between the angle on the Z and the angle of the Z on the next row (Figure 2-28).

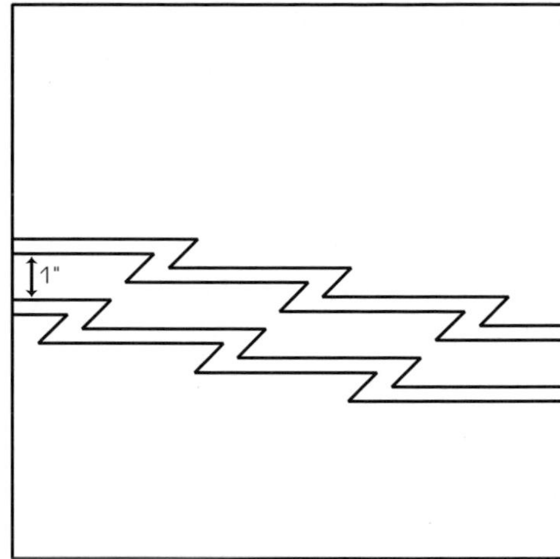

Figure 2-28.

HELPFUL NOTE: The angles on the Elongated Z can be curved to soften the appearance. Changing the line up of one row of Zig-Zags with the previous one will also change the way the design looks. Experiment with the arrangements by drawing the design on paper first and then decide which way you like best.

TOOLS NEEDED: A ruler, template material, and a fabric marking pencil or pen.

WHERE TO USE: As filler for plain setting blocks or over the whole quilt surface disregarding the patchwork pattern. For example, a Rail Fence pattern will take on a very different appearance with this design quilted all over the quilt top.

Pentagon (Figure 2-29)

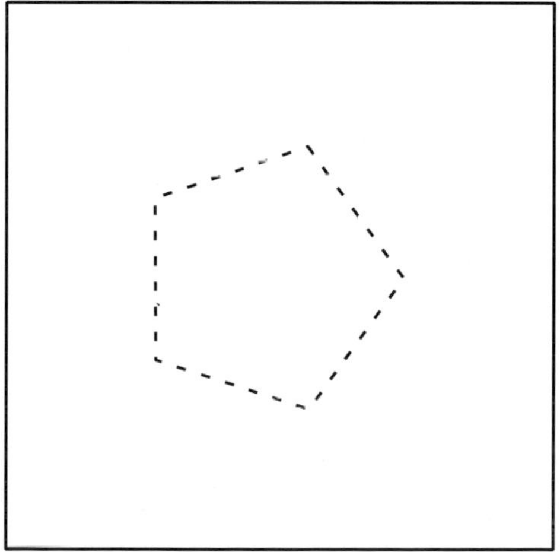

Figure 2-29.

RECOMMENDED MARKING: Using a template and mark the quilt as you go.

How to Mark or Draw: A Pentagon is a five sided figure. This quilting design was found on a quilt of Five-Pointed Stars dated 1898.

To draw a Pentagon for a template, first draw a circle the size of the area you wish to cover. For this example, the circle will be 3". Now, using a protractor, mark the circle off at every 72° (Figure 2-30). Using a pencil and a ruler, draw straight lines connecting the degree marks (Figure 2-31). This is a Pentagon with minimal distortion.

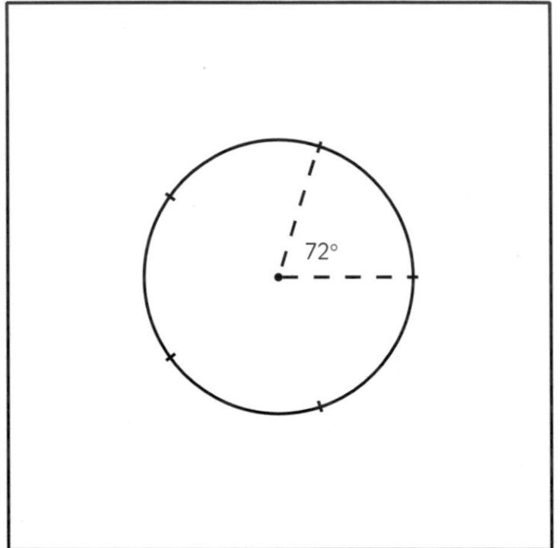

Figure 2-30.

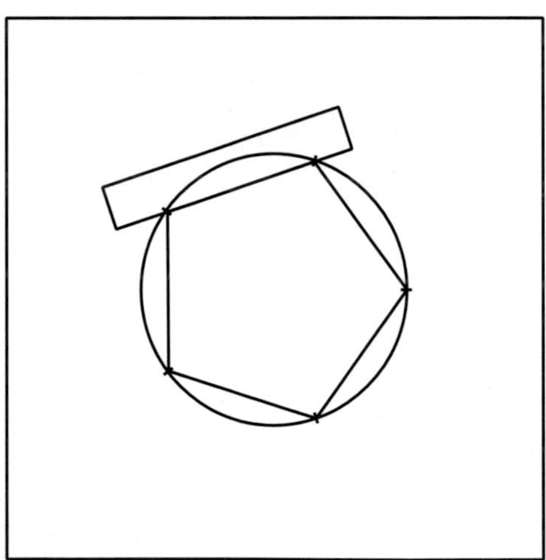

Figure 2-31.

Helpful Note: Draw the Pentagon on the dull side of freezer paper. Iron the freezer paper to poster board or scrap cardboard and cut out. This paper template can be used many times before the edges show wear.

Skip drawing one from these instructions and photocopy the Pentagon (Figure 2-32). Reduce or enlarge the Pentagon to fit the space where it will be used. Quilting designs can be enlarged and reduced successfully on a photocopy machine with minimal distortion.

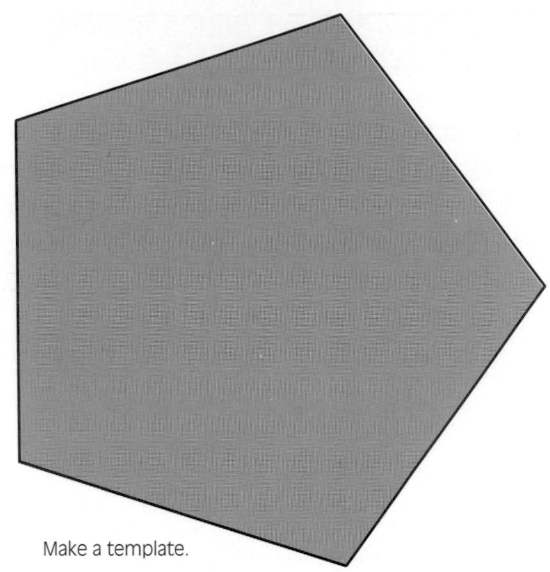

Figure 2-32.

Tools Needed: Regular lead pencil, compass, circle template or saucer, protractor, and cardboard for template making.

Where to Use: In connecting blocks of sashing; in flower centers.

Sawtooth: also Zig-Zag (Figure 2-33)

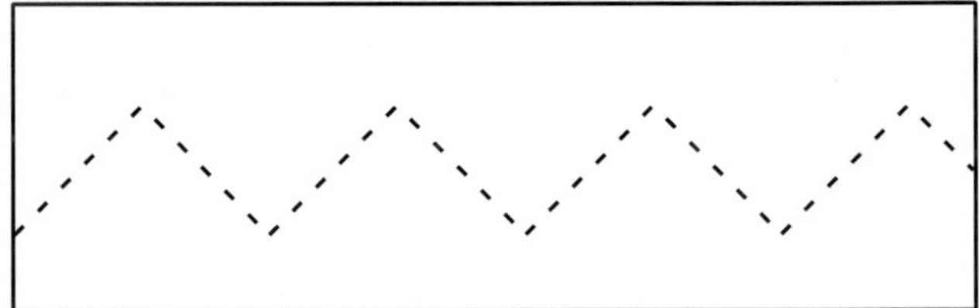

Figure 2-33.

Recommended Marking: Mark on the quilt top as you go using a strip template.

How to Mark or Draw: This simple quilting design used in sashing dates from 1880. All that is needed for marking this pattern is a simple half-square triangle. Draw a square the same as the finished width of the sashing or border. Mark the middle of the square on all sides. Draw diagonal lines across each corner to make a triangle template (Figure 2-34). Mark a faint guide

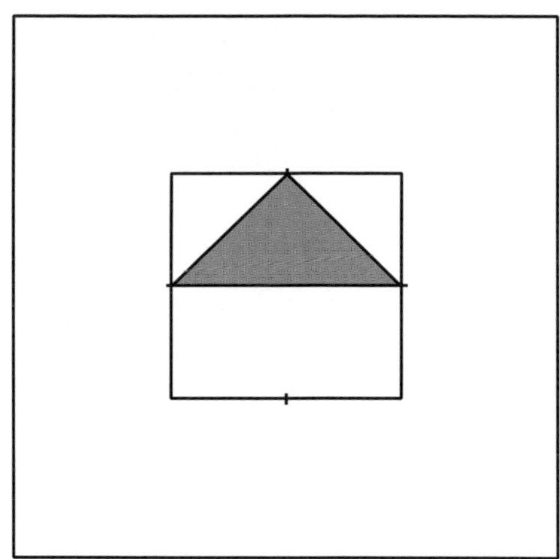

Figure 2-34.

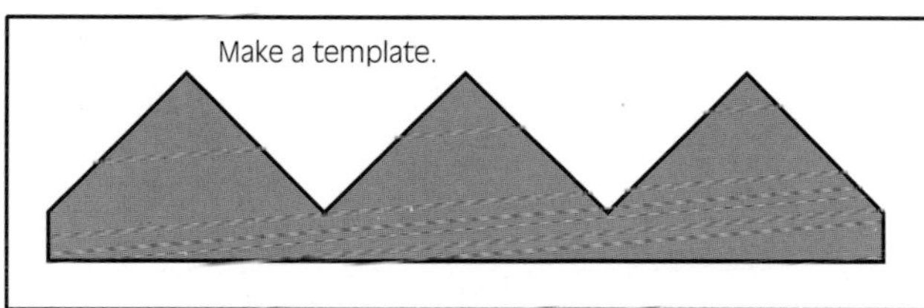

Figure 2-35.

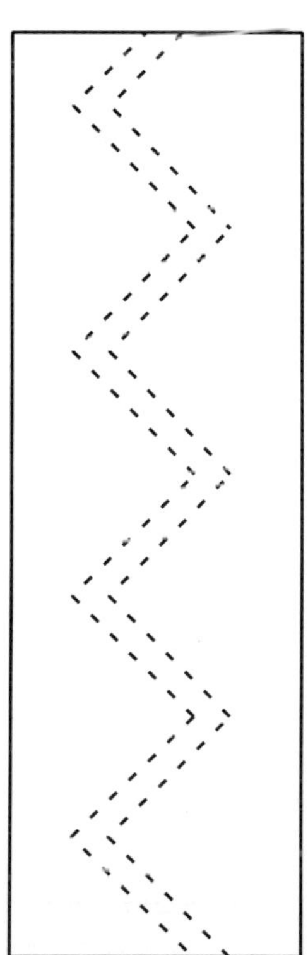

Figure 2-36.

line on the border to aid in lining up the triangles on this line for marking.

HELPFUL NOTE: For easier marking, make a strip template having several connected triangles (Figure 2-35).

TOOLS NEEDED: A ruler, template material, and a fabric marking pencil or pen.

WHERE TO USE: In sashings or borders where a small amount of quilting is wanted. It is an easy design to quilt.

Double Zig-Zag: also Zig-Zag Border Design (Figure 2-36)

RECOMMENDED MARKING: With a template and mark as you go.

HOW TO MARK OR DRAW: This Double Zig-Zag border design dates from 1940. See the instructions for the Sawtooth design on page 22 to determine the triangle size. Draw the one line of triangles (Figure 2-35) and then with a ruler spaced ½" from the first row, draw the second lines. This zig-zag can now be used for making a template (Figure 2-37). Mark on each side of the template.

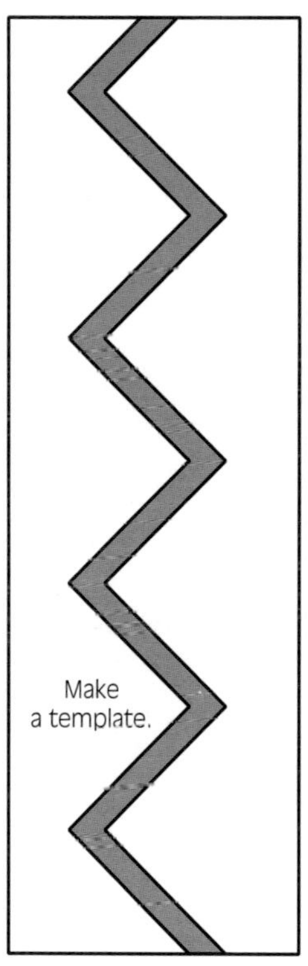

Figure 2-37.

HELPFUL NOTE: Mark a faint guide line across the border to aid in lining up the template as you mark. The width of the zig-zag can be more or less depending on the look you want and the size of the half-square triangle. On the small triangle, a ¼" width is good.

TOOLS NEEDED: A ruler, template material, and a fabric marking pencil or pen.

WHERE TO USE: In borders and in sashings. This design would complement pieced blocks set together with plain sashing strips.

Amish Border Triangle (Figure 2-38)

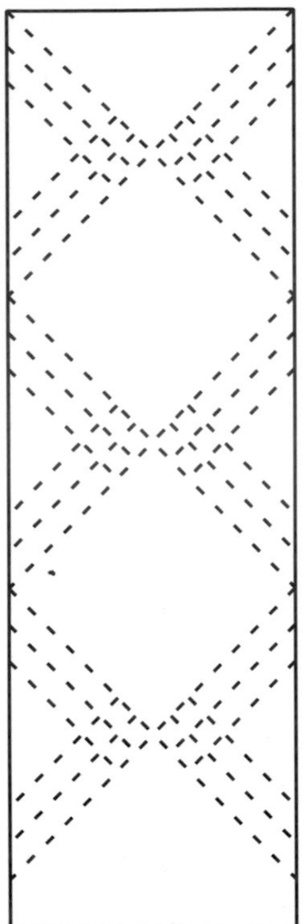

Figure 2-38.

Recommended Marking: Mark on the quilt top as you go.

How to Mark or Draw: The first step is determining the size square needed to fit the border or sashing. Draw a square the size of the width of the border. Mark the middle of the block on all four sides. Now draw lines from center to center to make triangles on each corner (Figure 2-39). Measure the resulting square to determine the distance for marking the squares for the border. Using a 6" wide border as an example, the new square should measure 4¼".

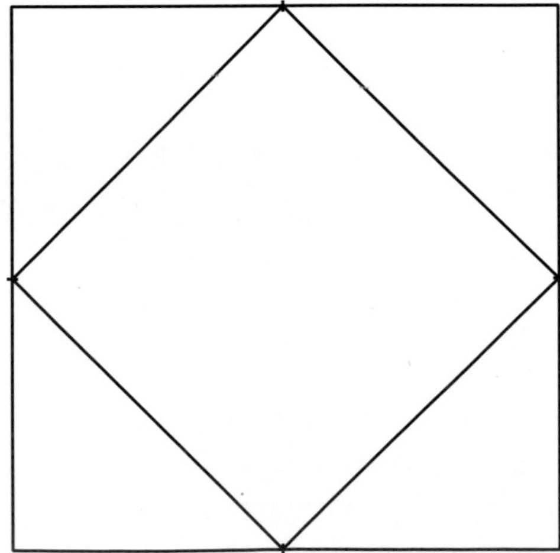

Figure 2-39.

To mark the border, place the 45° line of the ruler along the straight edge of the border and mark a diagonal line from the top of the border across to the bottom. Move the ruler to the left so that the next line will be 4¼" from the first marked line (Figure 2-40). The next step is to turn the ruler over so that the 45° line of the ruler is along the straight edge of the bottom of the border and the edge of the ruler is touching one of the diagonal lines at the top of the border. Mark this diagonal line. Move the ruler to the right 4¼" from this last marking and draw another line (Figure 2-41).

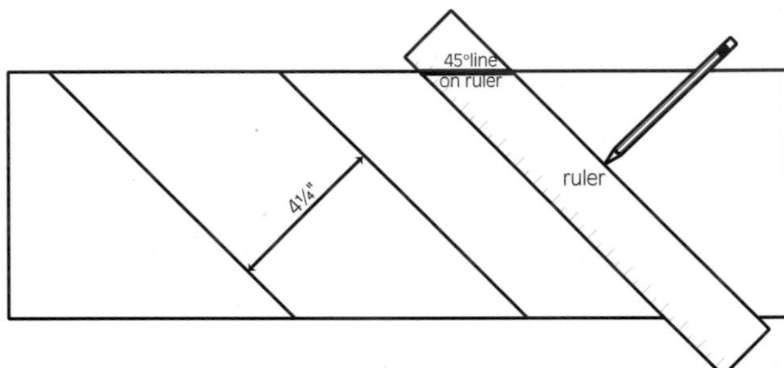

Figure 2-40.

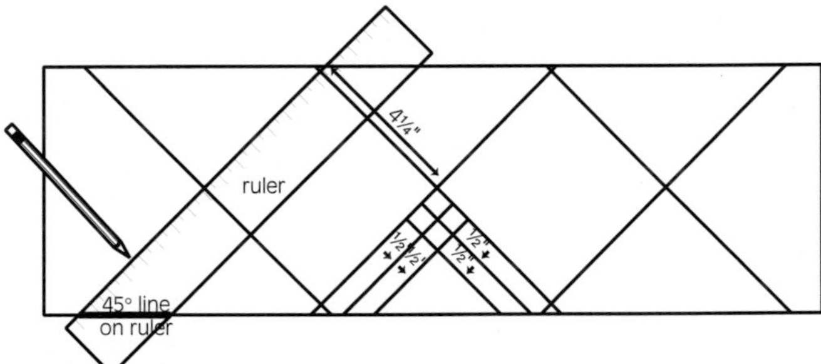

Figure 2-41.

Continue marking until the border is filled with squares on point and triangles at the top and bottom of the border. These lines can now be quilted and the markings and the quilting in the triangles done later. The spacing for the fill-in lines in the triangles is ½" for the 6" border. See Figure 2-41 to see how the triangle fill-in marking is done.

Helpful Note: In the square that results where

the points of the triangles come together, place a flower, heart, or other design that suits your quilt.

The Amish might have a pinwheel or rose in the square.

TOOLS NEEDED: A ruler with 45° mark and a fabric marking pencil or pen.

WHERE TO USE: In borders or wide sashings, especially Amish style quilts, or in the bars on a strippie quilt.

Zig-Zag II: also Parallel Triangles, Wave (Figure 2-42)

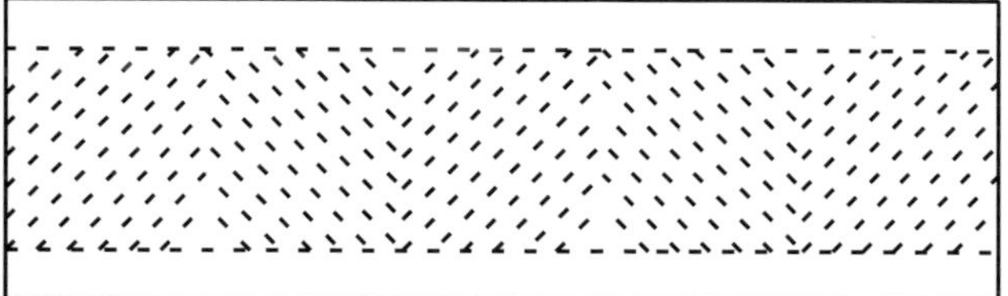

Figure 2-42.

RECOMMENDED MARKING: Mark with a ruler as you go.

HOW TO MARK OR DRAW: Place the 45° mark on the ruler along the bottom edge of the border and mark a line from the top of the border to the bottom edge (Figure 2-43). This mark will be on the left of the ruler. Flip the ruler so that the 45° mark is along the top edge of the border. Line the ruler up so the edge of the ruler touches the previously marked line. Draw a line along the ruler edge (Figure 2-44). This mark will be on the right side of the ruler. This should form a large half-square triangle.

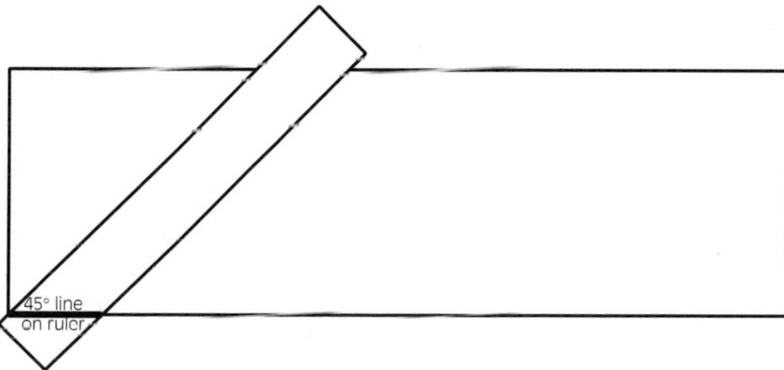

Figure 2-43.

To mark the inside filler lines of each triangle, mark a faint guide line through the middle of

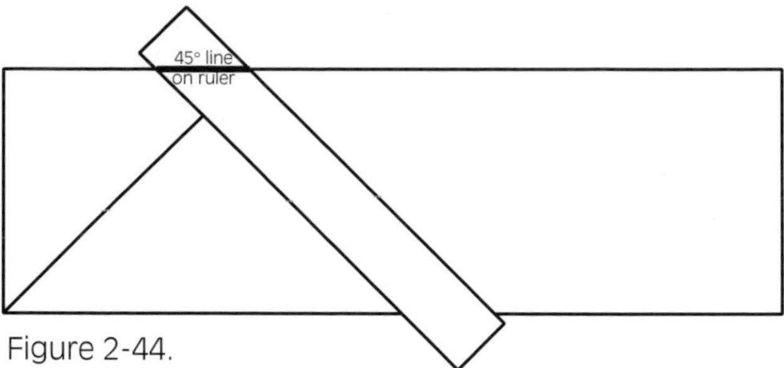

Figure 2-44.

each triangle (Figure 2-45). Using a ruler for spacing, mark triangles inside each triangle. Use the guide line for the peak. Space the filler lines ½" apart or more.

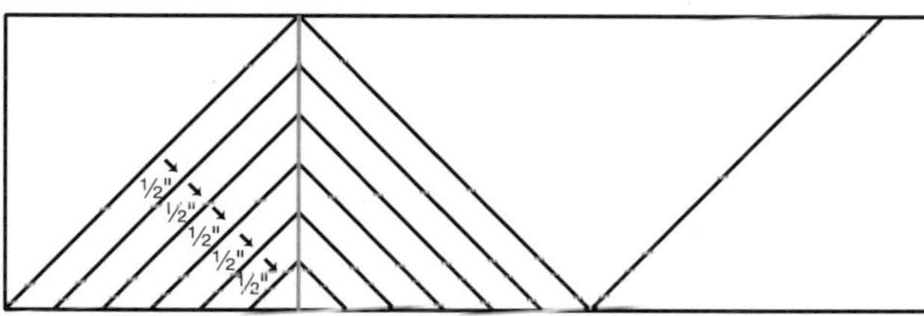

Figure 2-45.

HELPFUL NOTE: Draw two or three triangles and then the filler lines to get a feel for the design before beginning marking on the actual quilt.

TOOLS NEEDED: A ruler with a 45° mark and a fabric marking pencil or pen.

WHERE TO USE: This is a good design to use in borders, especially borders that are fairly wide. It has been used since 1840.

Wave: also Simple Chevron (Figure 2-46)

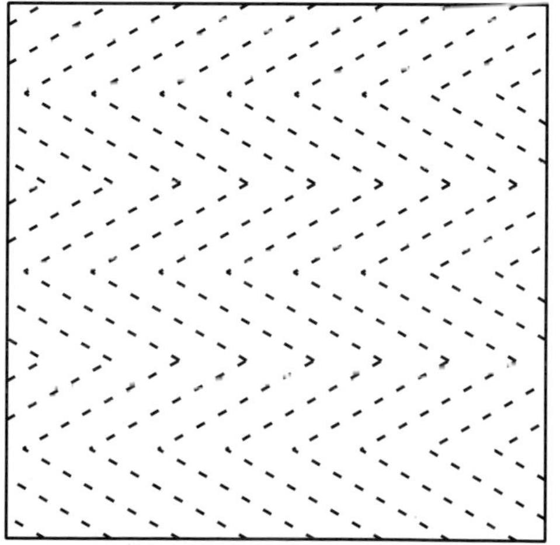

Figure 2-46.

Recommended Marking: Make a template and mark the top and quilt as you go.

How to Mark or Draw: On a piece of paper, draw a 4" long line across the paper and a vertical ruler line exactly in the middle of the 4" line. Take the ruler and place the 4" mark on the end of the first line (4" long line) and the end of the line exactly touching the vertical middle line and draw a line. Repeat for the other side of the triangle. Make a template from this equal-sided triangle (Figure 2-47).

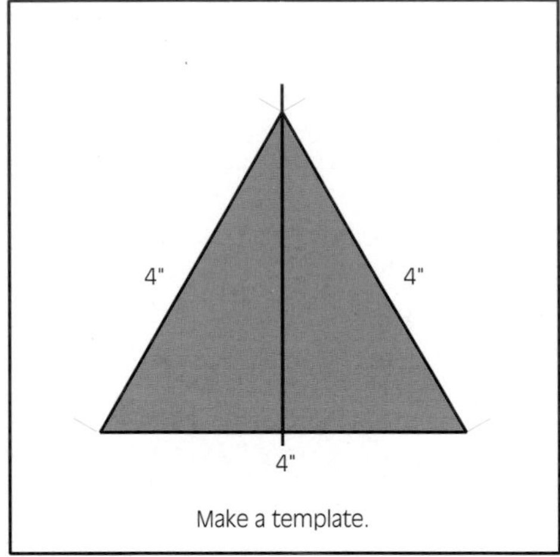

Figure 2-47.

To mark this design on the quilt surface, draw a faint vertical quide line on the area to be filled and place the template against this line (Figure 2-48). Mark on the two sides of the triangle template not touching the guide line. Mark one row of triangles along the guide line.

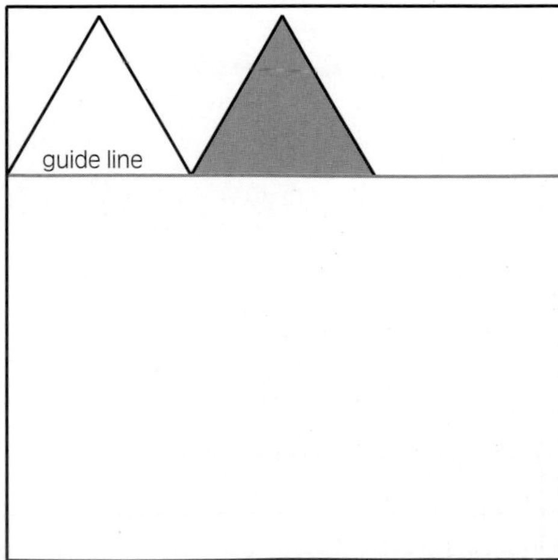

Figure 2-48.

The second row is marked the same by marking a second guide line. For a 4" triangle, 1½" is good spacing (Figure 2-49). Mark several rows, quilt those Waves and then mark several more rows, etc.

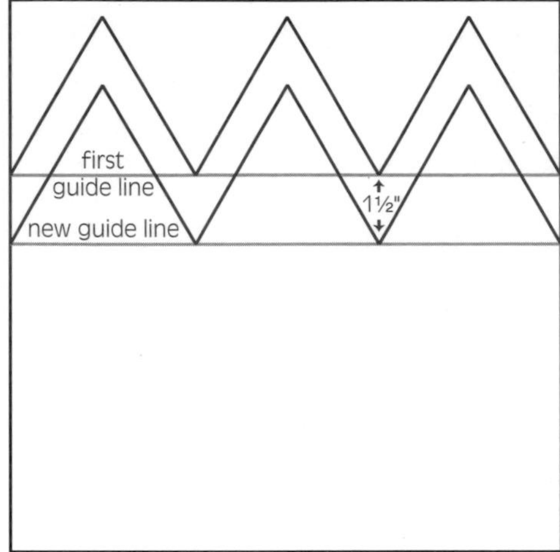

Figure 2-49.

Helpful Note: The Wave design can also be marked horizontally on the quilt. After marking several rows, it will be possible to judge the distance by eye and eliminate marking the guide lines.

Tools Needed: An equal-sided triangle template, a ruler, and a fabric marking pencil or pen.

Where to Use: Simple Chevron pattern was popular on early nineteenth century quilts. The design can be used in plain setting blocks or for an overall design.

Triangle Elbow (Figure 2-50)

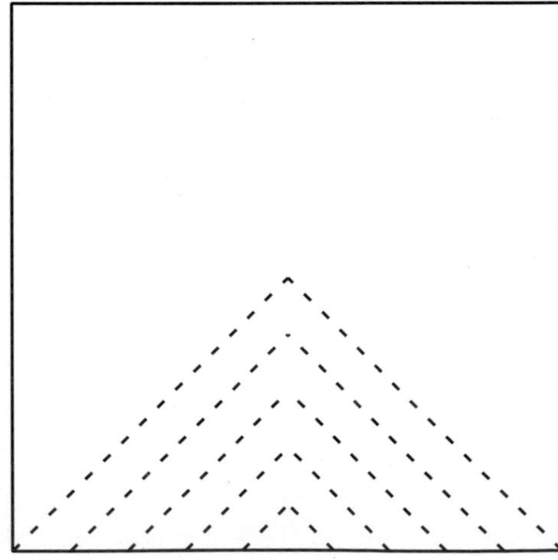

Figure 2-50.

RECOMMENDED MARKING: Mark on the quilt top as you go.

HOW TO MARK OR DRAW: Triangle Elbow is the same quilting pattern as Elbow except it is marked in the large triangles that border a quilt of blocks that are set on point. Faintly mark a guide line down the center of the triangle (Figure 2-51). The first quilting line will be marked 1" from the edge of the half-square triangle to the guide line (Figure 2-52). The second line will be marked on the other edge of the triangle to meet the first line exactly at the guide line (Figure 2-53). Continue marking Elbows until the triangle is filled.

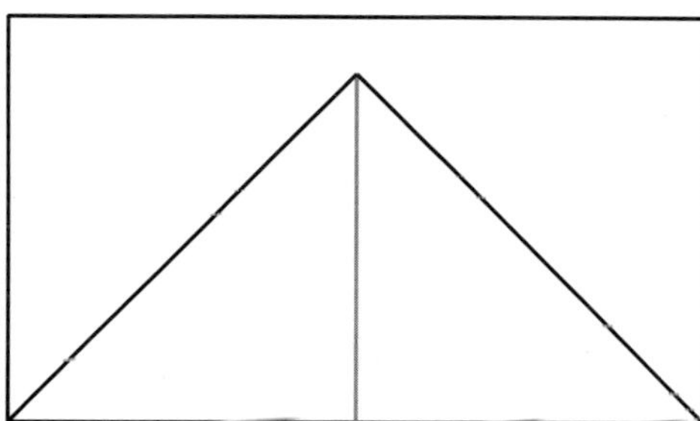
Figure 2-51.

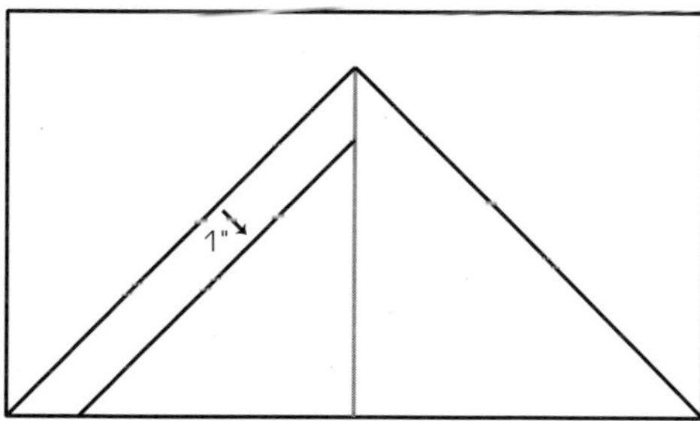

Figure 2-52.

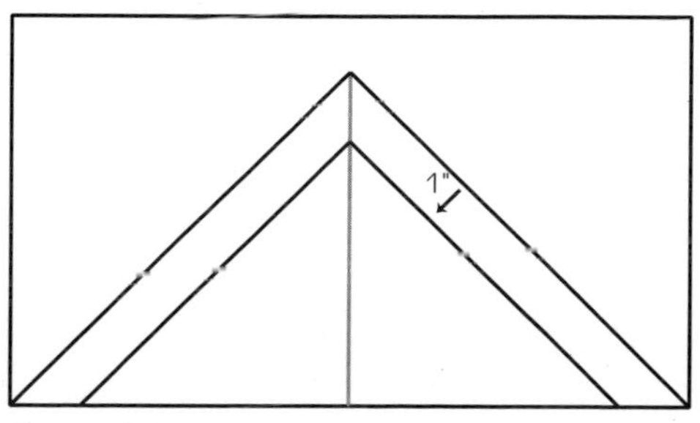

Figure 2-53.

Quilting can be done as each line is marked or after the entire triangle has been marked.

HELPFUL NOTE: The lines for the Triangle Elbow are marked closer together for a small triangle and farther apart for larger ones. The distance between quilting lines will be determined by how much quilting is desired.

TOOLS NEEDED: A ruler with 1" markings that is longer than the side of the triangle. The plastic and metal templates for cutting Log Cabin strips work well for a marking tool. A fabric marking pencil or pen.

WHERE TO USE: This is a good filler for the triangles that border a quilt of blocks set on point. It can also be used in triangles in a pieced block when more quilting is needed to balance either Outline or By the Piece quilting.

The Triangle Elbow could be used in a border. Use a triangle template to mark the triangle shape for the first quilting lines.

Tents (Figure 2-54)

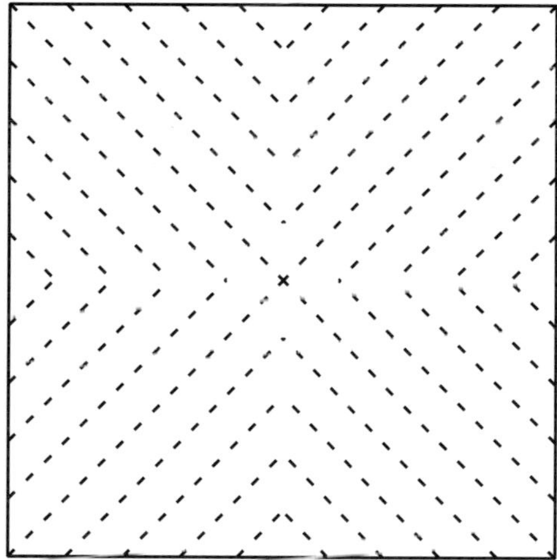
Figure 2-54.

RECOMMENDED MARKING: Mark on the quilt block as you go.

HOW TO MARK OR DRAW: Tents is a block design that echoes quilting lines from an X marked on the diagonal from corner to corner of either a plain or pieced block.

To mark, line up a ruler from lower left corner to upper right corner of the block (Figure 2-55, page 28). Mark this line. The second line will be marked from the other lower corner to the other

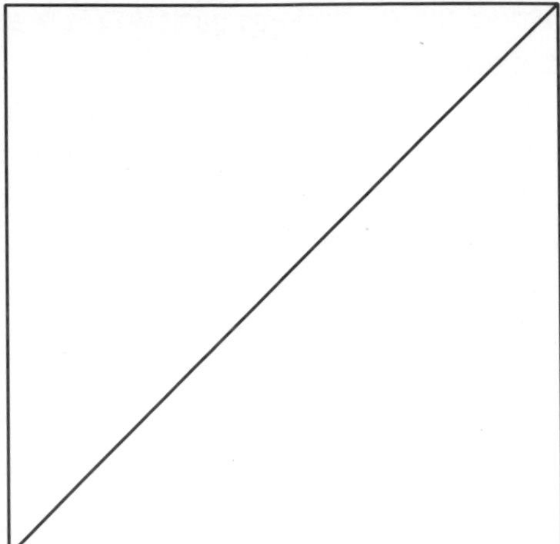

Figure 2-55.

upper corner of the block (Figure 2-56). This X can now be quilted or the entire block marked first.

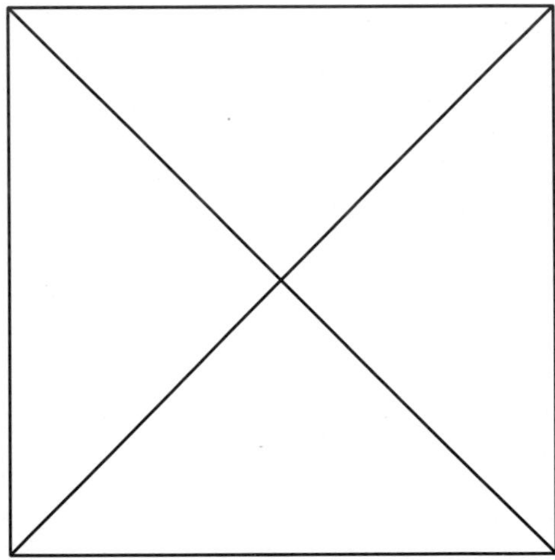

Figure 2-56.

The next step to to mark a faint guide line across the center of the block and down the center of the block (Figure 2-57). Draw lines ½"

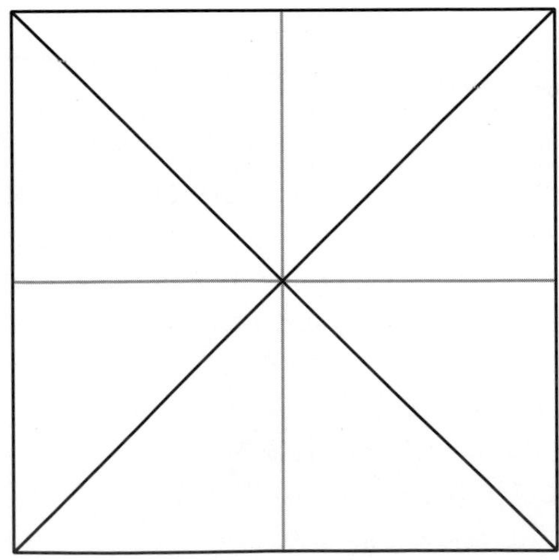

Figure 2-57.

(wider, if desired) parallel to the X line up to the guide line to form a V. Continue drawing lines until the space is filled (Figure 2-58).

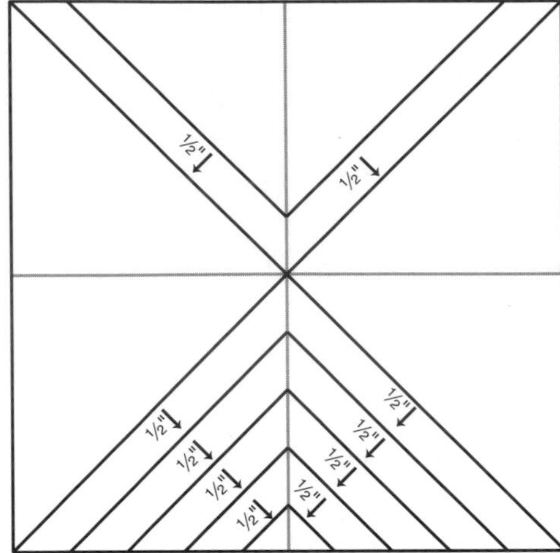

Figure 2-58.

HELPFUL NOTE: Putting a large book or other flat object under the quilt when you mark as you go makes marking the design easier. Be careful that the lines that are drawn to the guide lines meet perfectly.

TOOLS NEEDED: Ruler with ¼" markings that is longer than the diagonal of the block and fabric pencil or pen.

WHERE TO USE: As a filler design in plain setting blocks, in large squares of a patchwork pattern, in combination with other geometric designs such as Single Diagonal Lines.

Triangles: also Basketweave, Zig-Zag (Figure 2-59)

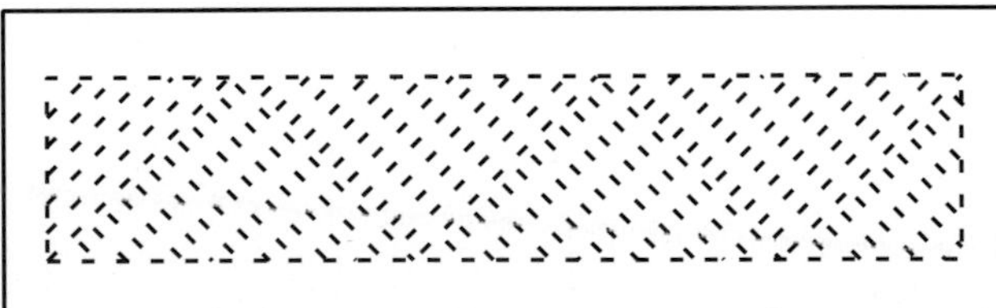

Figure 2-59.

RECOMMENDED MARKING: Mark on the quilt top as you go using a triangle template for the first markings and a ruler and marking pen or pencil for the fill-in lines.

HOW TO MARK OR DRAW: This design was found in the border of a quilt dated 1853. It is based on a

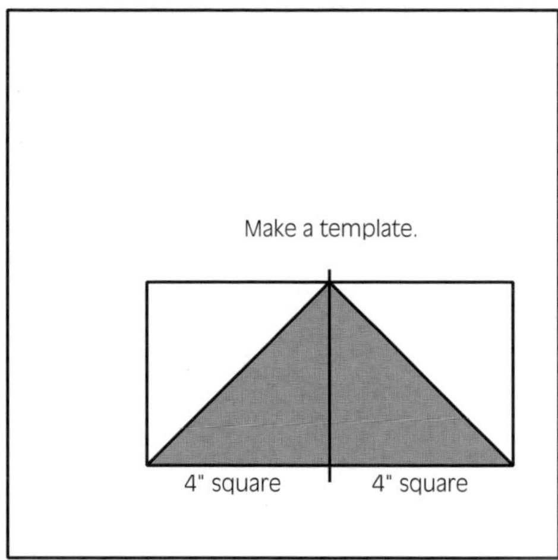

Figure 2-60.

half-square triangle. For this example, the border is 4" wide. To draw the template for the triangles, draw two 4" squares side by side and mark the squares diagonally from corner to corner (Figure 2-60). The triangle formed in the middle can now be used to make a template. Mark the quilt by flipping the template (Figure 2-61). Next, mark the inside of each triangle with parallel lines leaving from ½" to 1" spacing between the quilting lines. Spacing will depend on the size of the triangles. The direction of the parallel lines change from the upper triangle to the lower one. Just mark consistently (see Figure 2-62).

Helpful Note: Drawing this design on paper the size of the area to be filled with quilting first will help to make sure that the design fills the area properly and the corner area can be handled more easily. It may be necessary to reduce the size of the base of the triangle. The triangle does not have to be a perfect half-square triangle for a quilting design.

Tools Needed: A ruler with ¼" markings, pencil, template material (cardboard or plastic), a fabric marking pencil or pen.

Where to Use: Use in a border or wide sashing.

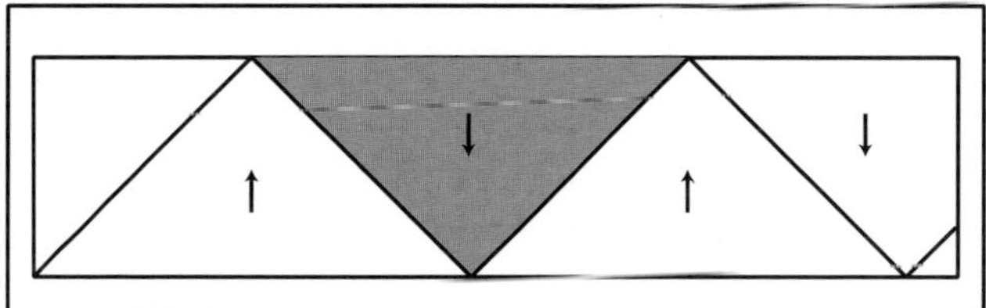

Figure 2-61.

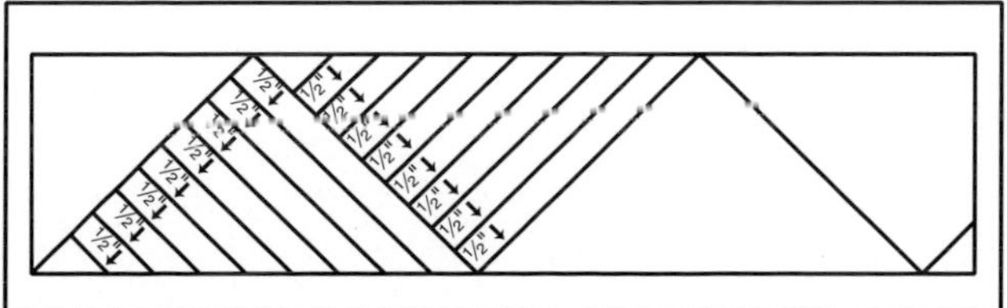

Figure 2-62.

Equal-Sided Triangle (Figure 2-63)

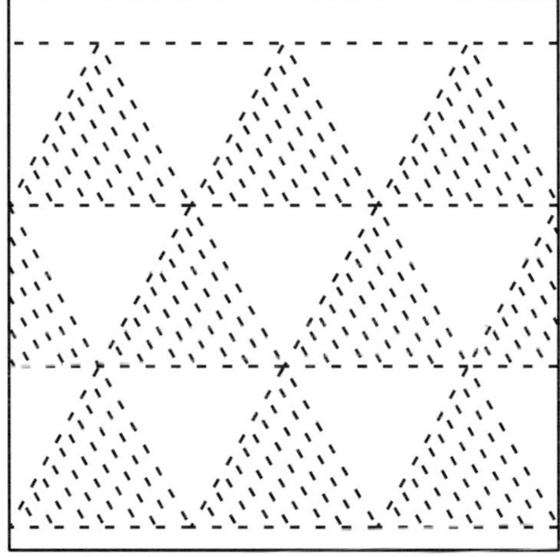

Figure 2-63.

Recommended Marking: Use a template for outline marking of the triangle and mark on the quilt top as you go.

How to Mark or Draw: First, decide what size triangle will be needed to best fill the space to be quilted. If this design is to be used as filler for a plain block, measure the size of the block. For this example, the block will be a 12" square. Divide this by 3. This number should be determined by how large or small the triangle needs to be to look best when quilted. The answer is 4 which will be the size of the equal sides of the triangle.

On a piece of paper, draw a 4" long line across the paper and a vertical line exactly in the middle of the 4" line (Figure 2-64, page 30). Take the ruler and place the 4" mark on the end of the first line (4" long line) and the end of the ruler exactly touching the vertical middle line (Figure 2-65, page 30) and draw a line. Repeat for the other side of the triangle. Make a template from this equal-sided triangle.

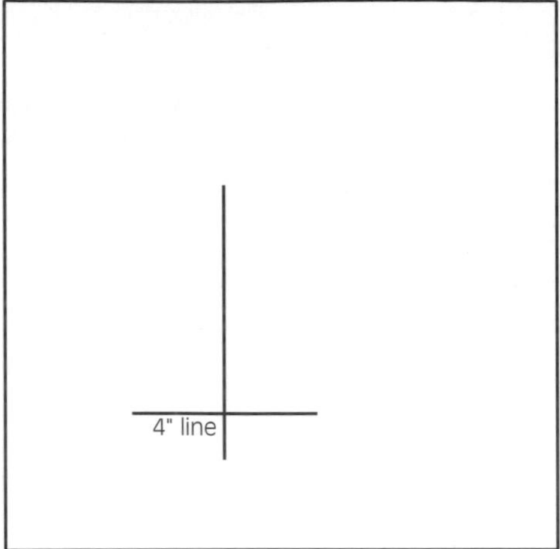

Figure 2-64.

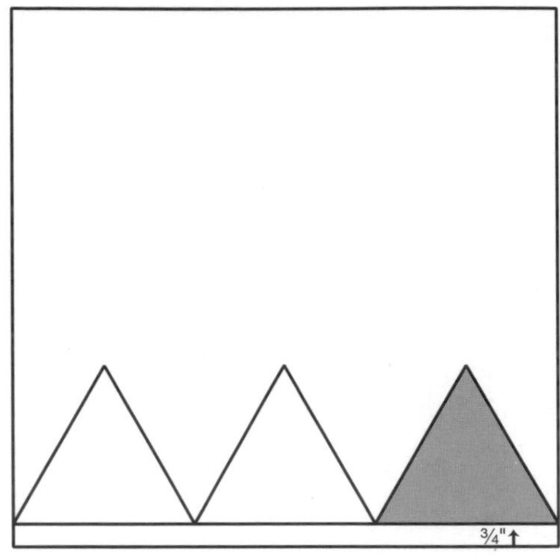

Figure 2-66.

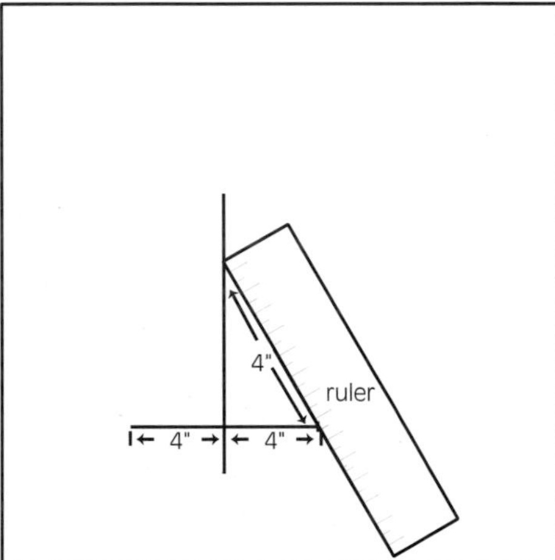

Figure 2-65.

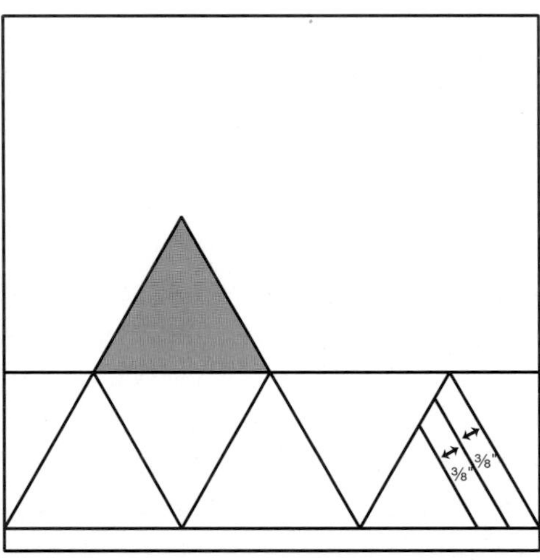

Figure 2-67.

Measure the length of the middle of the triangle. It should measure 3½". For a 12" block, three of the triangles will fit across the block but only 10½" will be used down the block. The difference is 1½" which means the rows of triangles will need to be ¾" from the top and from the bottom.

So, to mark the block, draw a base line across the block ¾" from the bottom. Using the triangle template, draw triangles across the block (Figure 2-66). Repeat the same steps two more times to fill the block. Match the base of the triangle with the triangle below (Figure 2-67). Some of the triangles will not be full triangles.

Mark the inside of the upright triangles with lines parallel to the right side of the triangle. For this size triangle, ⅜" is the best spacing between the quilting lines.

HELPFUL NOTE: This method of drawing an equal-sided triangle would not be acceptable for a pieced block but is acceptable for a quilting design. Quilting designs do not have to fit perfectly like patchwork. This method is perhaps how our ancestors would have made an equal-sided triangle.

TOOLS NEEDED: A ruler, template material (freezer paper ironed on cardboard would work well), and a fabric marking pencil or pen.

WHERE TO USE: This pattern was popular on early nineteenth century quilts. The design can be used in plain setting blocks. If used for an allover quilting design, use the instructions for drawing Diaper on pages 57–58.

Chapter Three
Squares

It will be of no surprise to learn that the most often used and the oldest dated design for quilting is the Squares Crosshatching. It has proven to be a popular design because it is not only easy to mark but also easy to quilt. Squares Crosshatch is marked diagonally across the grain line of the fabric or diagonally on the quilt top and is, therefore, easy to quilt. The dimension that the Squares Crosshatching adds to the quilt surface is pleasing because the stitches lay on top of the fabric, plus when used as a background for more intricate designs it emphasizes the other designs.

Another popular design group found in this chapter are the Plaids. It seems that any design that is double or triple lined makes a good quilt even better.

Consider using any of the Plaid designs for background fillers and for solid setting blocks. The shadows that are created by the double or triple lines allows the light to hit the larger spaces to make a good design.

The Weave and Basketweave are good designs for filling the background of a quilt and also as an overall design disregarding the pattern of the quilt top.

Squares Crosshatch: also Squares, Squares Crosshatching, Diamond, Crossed Diagonals, Cross Bar Quilting, Waffle Quilting, Grid, Simple Grid, Ground Pattern (Figure 3-1).

Figure 3-1.

Recommended Marking: Mark on the quilt top as you go.

How to Mark or Draw: This simple quilting design is one of the oldest (before 1800) and one of the most used designs. It is marked on the bias or diagonal of the fabric.

Using a long ruler lined up across the fabric from corner to corner of a plain block or on the diagonal of the quilt top, mark a beginning line (Figure 3-2). Mark lines parallel with this starting line. The spacing between the lines can vary from

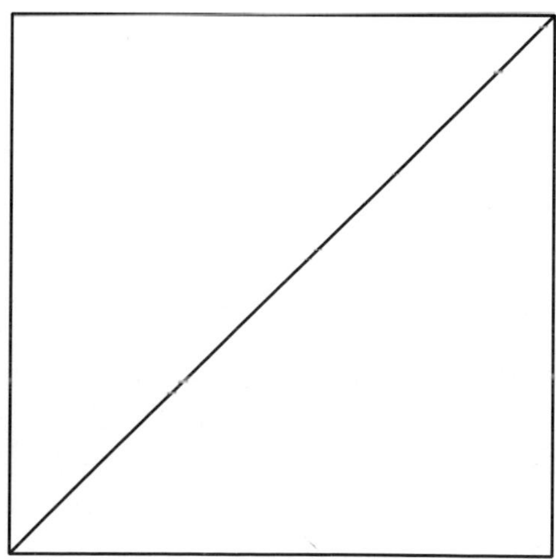

Figure 3-2.

Plate 3-1. Square in a Square (also Squares Crosshatch, Spiral).
Momma's Garden by Anne Oliver, 1992. Collection of the Museum of the American Quilter's Society.

Plate 3-2. Squares Crosshatch (also Outline Quilting, Echo, Feather Swag).
Morning Glory by Phyllis Miller, 1987.

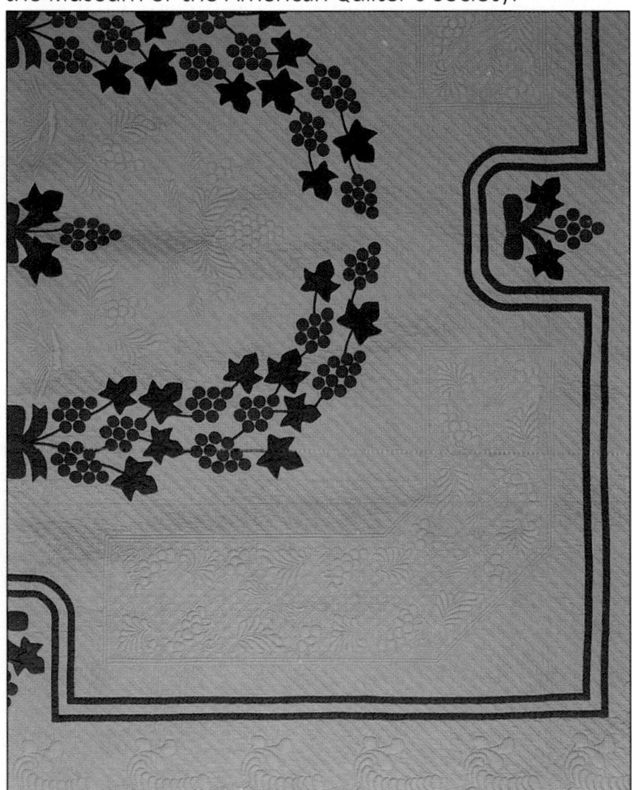

Plate 3-3. Plaid (also Double Diagonal Lines, Grapes and Leaves).
Dot's Vintage 1983 by Dot Finley, 1983. Collection of the Museum of the American Quilter's Society.

Plate 3-4. Swag (also Long Diamond, Squares Crosshatch, Princess Feather, Outline Quilting).
Spring Beauties by Phyllis Miller, 1994.

¼" to 2" depending on the amount of quilting desired. Several lines can be marked and then those lines quilted.

The second step of the crosshatch will make squares. Using a wide ruler, line the 1" mark up with one of the marked or quilted lines and the long edge of the ruler across the bias of the fabric or on the diagonal of the block. Mark this line (Figure 3-3). Continuing marking lines parallel to this first line and the same width as had been marked before.

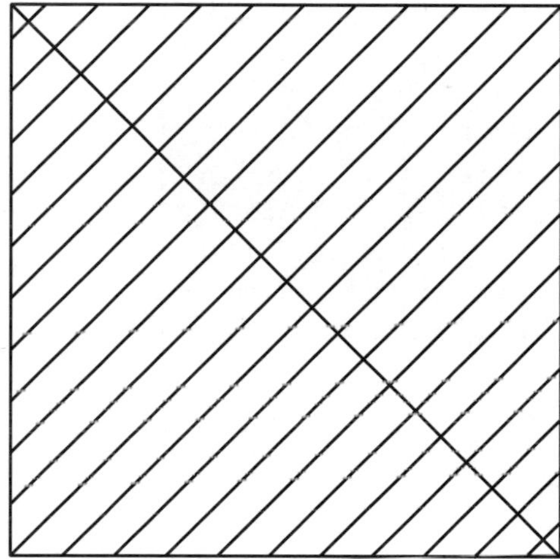

Figure 3-3.

Helpful Note: This is one of the easiest designs to hand or machine quilt. Use the same marking tool to mark an entire quilt. Rulers do vary. The plastic or metal templates for marking Log Cabin strips work well for marking this design. Check often to see that the lines that are crossing are making a square. Check before quilting as it is easier to erase lines than to pick out quilting stitches. Masking tape can be used for marking, if desired.

Tools Needed: A long ruler or other measuring device, a fabric marking pencil or pen, and masking tape, if used.

Where to Use: Squares Crosshatch can be done over the whole quilt surface paying no attention to the appliqué or pieced design. It is best used as background filler for appliqué, as filler for plain setting blocks, and in combination with other linear designs such as plain diagonal lines used in alternating blocks. This design is always successful.

Checkerboard: also Squares, Diagonal Waffle, Diamond, Box (Figure 3-4)

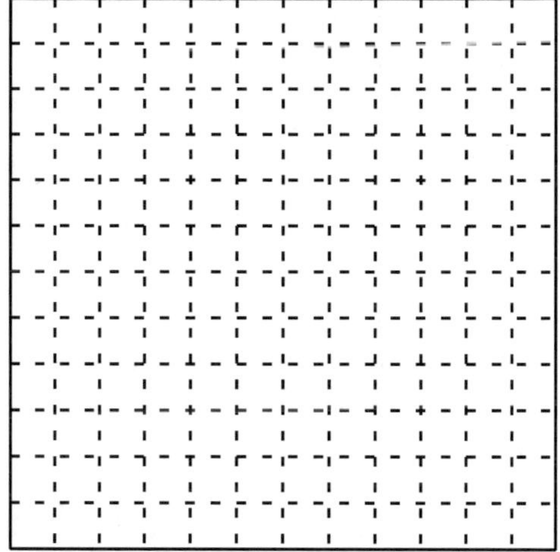

Figure 3-4.

Recommended Marking: Mark on the quilt top as you go.

How to Mark or Draw: Checkerboard is a simple filler design. It is marked on the straight grain of the fabric. The first line is marked by lining up a ruler with a straight edge of either a block, a border, or the grain line of the fabric. Mark consecutive lines spaced from ½" to 2" that are parallel with the first marked line (Figure 3-5). These lines can now be quilted. Next, using one of the marked lines as a guide, place the 1" mark along the marked line and mark along the edge of the ruler so that the lines cross the other lines and form squares (Figure 3-6, page 34). Continue marking and quilting until the surface is covered.

Helpful Note: Check often to see that the lines

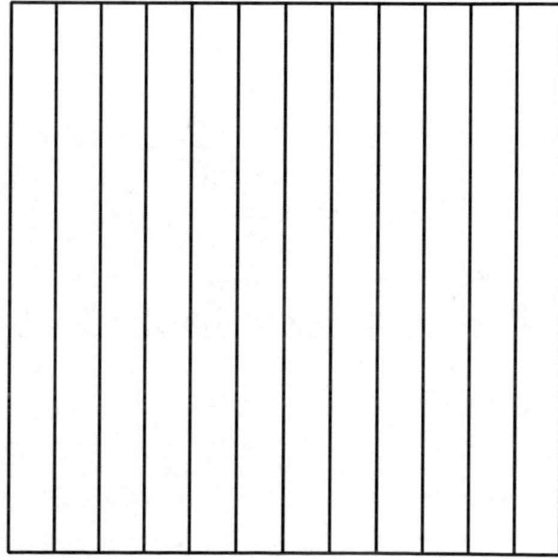

Figure 3-5.

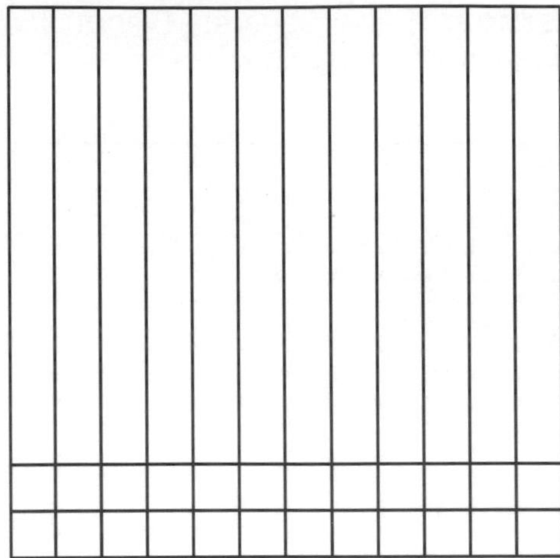

Figure 3-6.

are staying evenly spaced and that a right angle is created where the lines cross. This design is harder to hand quilt than the diagonally marked Squares Crosshatch. It would be a good choice for machine quilting. This design can be marked with masking tape.

Tools Needed: A long ruler, masking tape if used, and a fabric marking pencil or pen.

Where to Use: This design can be used the same as Squares Crosshatch. Blocks set on point and marked on the diagonal will give the appearance of straight marked squares and will be easier to hand quilt.

Crisscross (Figure 3-7)

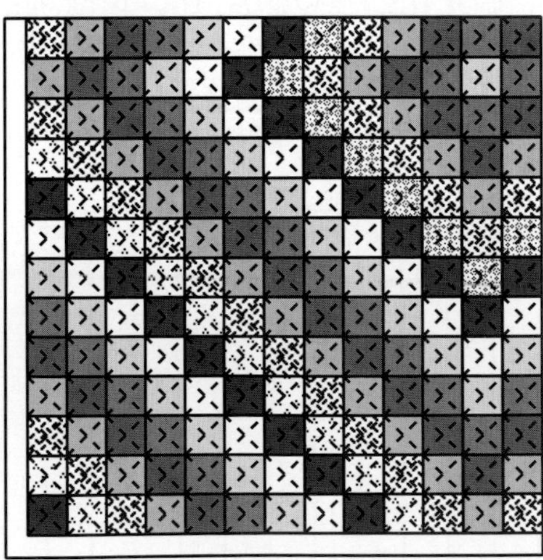

Figure 3-7.

Recommended Marking: Mark as you go.

How to Mark or Draw: Crisscross is a quilting design that dates from 1930 and is used to cross a pieced square design such as Trip Around the World.

The crisscross is formed by quilting lines that cross the small square block to form an X (Figure 3-8). Mark with a small ruler diagonally from corner to corner and then the other corner to corner.

If the crisscross design is marked on a rectangle or across two squares, the resulting quilting will be diamonds (Figure 3-9).

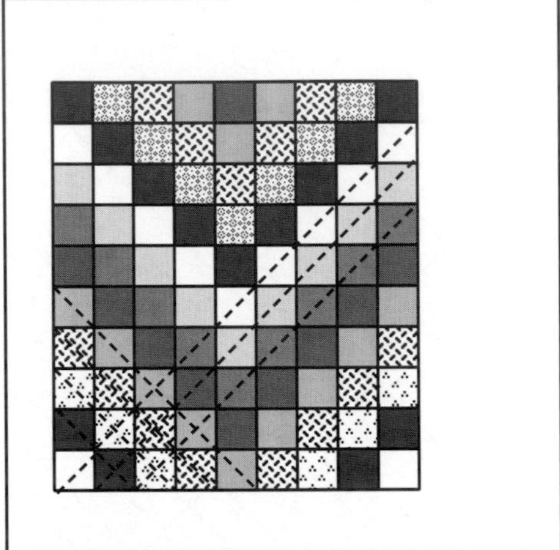

Figure 3-8.

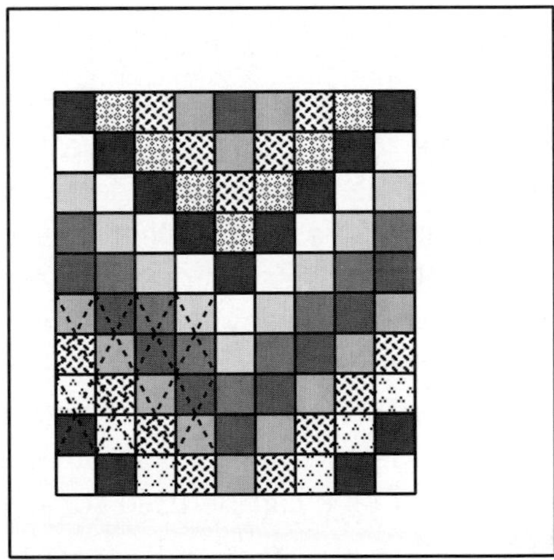

Figure 3-9.

Helpful Note: This easy design can be quilted without marking or by eye. This is one design where marking, if needed, can be accomplished by using masking tape layed corner to corner.

Tools Needed: A small ruler and a fabric marking pencil or pen.

Where to Use: On any patchwork where the pattern is composed of small square blocks.

Plaid: also Double Diamonds, Double Line Crosshatching, Double Line Squares, Double Crosshatching, Simple Plaid, Basketweave (Figure 3-10)

Figure 3-10.

Recommended Marking: Mark on the quilt top as you go.

How to Mark or Draw: Plaid uses the same basic steps as Squares Crosshatch (see page 31). Draw the first diagonal line across the bias of the fabric (see Figure 3-2). The second line should be parallel and spaced ¼" from it (Figure 3-11). The next line should be 1" from this line, the next spaced ¼" from it. Repeat to fill the area to be quilted (Figure 3-12).

To form the plaid, mark another diagonal line that will cross the previously marked lines. Repeat the same spacing – line, ¼" space, line, 1" space – to cover the surface to be quilted (Figure 3-13).

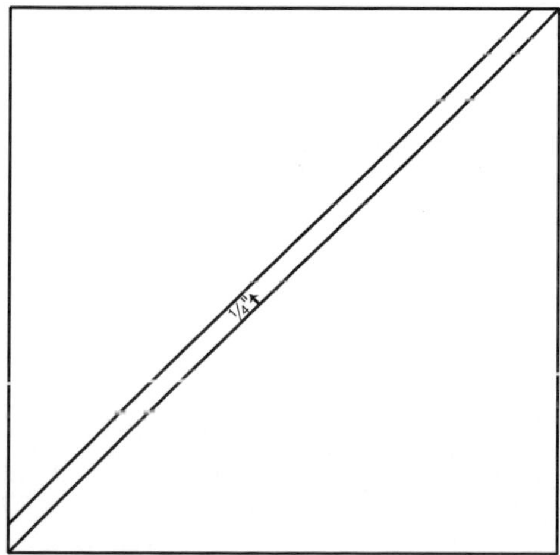

Figure 3-11.

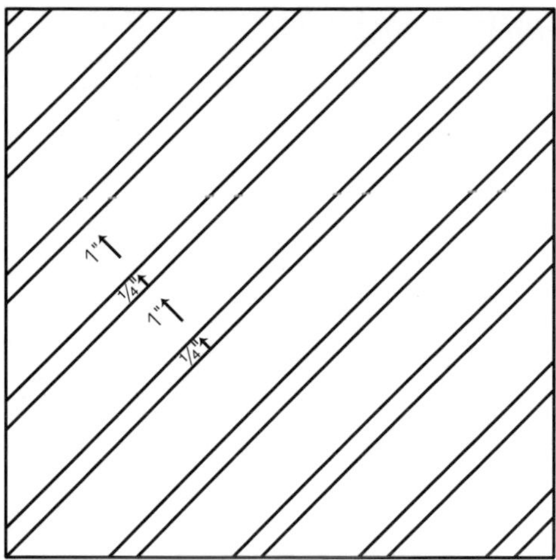

Figure 3-12.

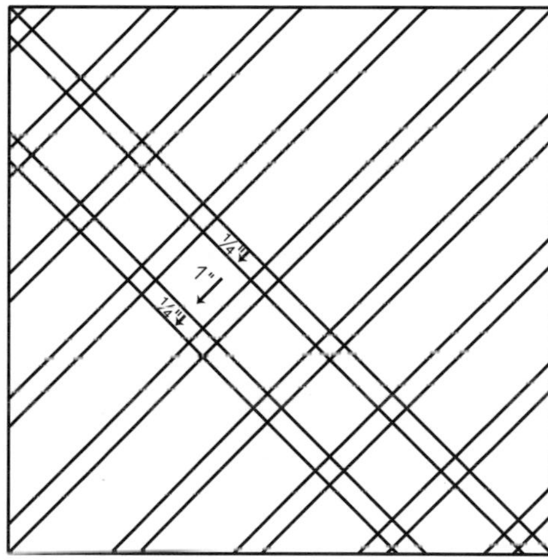

Figure 3-13.

Helpful Note: Check often to see that the cross lines are staying square.

Tools Needed: A long ruler with ¼" markings and a fabric marking pencil or pen.

Where to Use: This beautiful design has been used since the mid-1800's. It can be used as background filler with appliqué, in sashings, in plain setting blocks, or as an overall quilting design. The extra quilting of the second line is well worth the time it takes because of the raised effect it creates. It can be used in combination with other designs such as Single or Double Diagonals. Plaid is very effective when the diagonals cover a pieced block and the Plaid covers plain setting blocks.

Triple Plaid (Figure 3-14)

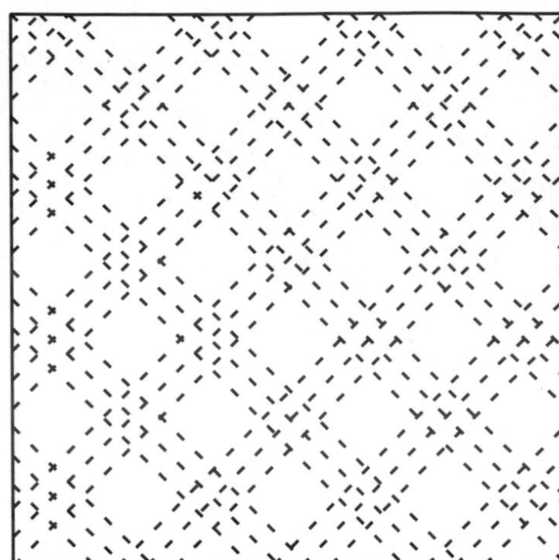

Figure 3-14.

Recommemded Marking: Mark on the quilt top as you go.

How to Mark or Draw: Follow the same directions for marking as for Plaid (see page 35) except the spacing will be line, ¼" space, line, ¼" space, line, 1" space, line, ¼" space, line, ¼" space, line, 1" space, and repeat to cover the area to be quilted (Figure 3-15).

Helpful Note: Take care when drawing this pattern to keep the angles of the intersections square. Check often with a wide ruler or T-square. The 1" spacing between the triple lines can be increased, if desired, and the triple plaid design will still be effective.

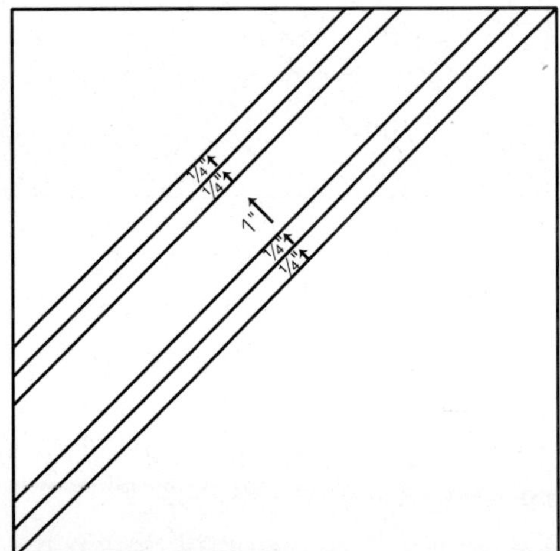

Figure 3-15.

Tools Needed: A long ruler with ¼" markings and a fabric marking pen or pencil. This design can also be marked with masking tape.

Where to Use: Triple Plaid is well worth the extra time involved in quilting because of the look that is achieved. Triple Plaid can be used in the same ways as Squares Crosshatch and Plaid.

Broken Plaid (Figure 3-16)

Figure 3-16.

Recommended Marking: Mark on the quilt top as you go.

How to Mark or Draw: This design is a variation of Plaid (see page 35) and to start follow the same instructions. It is marked on the diagonal of the block or bias of the fabric. The spacing for Broken Plaid will be line, ¼" space, line, 1" space, line, 1" space (Figure 3-17). A wider space can be used instead of the 1" spaces. Mark the lines going on the diagonal in the opposite direction with the same spacing.

Helpful Note: Take care to keep the angles of

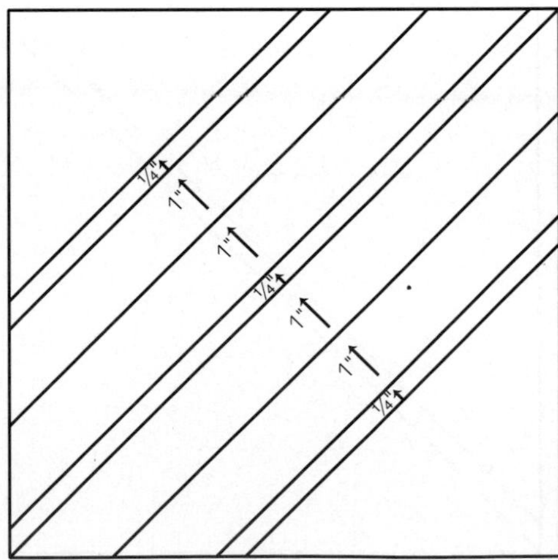

Figure 3-17.

the cross lines square. Also, be alert in marking where there is a single line between the spaces. It is easy to mark double lines here.

TOOLS NEEDED: A ruler with ¼" markings and a fabric marking pencil or pen.

WHERE TO USE: Broken Plaid is a good design to use for an overall pattern disregarding the patchwork design. It also works well as filler or background quilting with appliqué or in plain setting blocks.

Crosses: also Interlocking Squares (Figure 3-18)

Figure 3-18.

RECOMMENDED MARKING: Mark on the quilt top with a template as you go.

HOW TO MARK OR DRAW: The first step for this design is to make a template. Begin by drafting a Nine-Patch block (Figure 3-19). A 3" block makes a good pattern. The template for Crosses is the cross that is formed when the four corner blocks are removed (Figure 3-20).

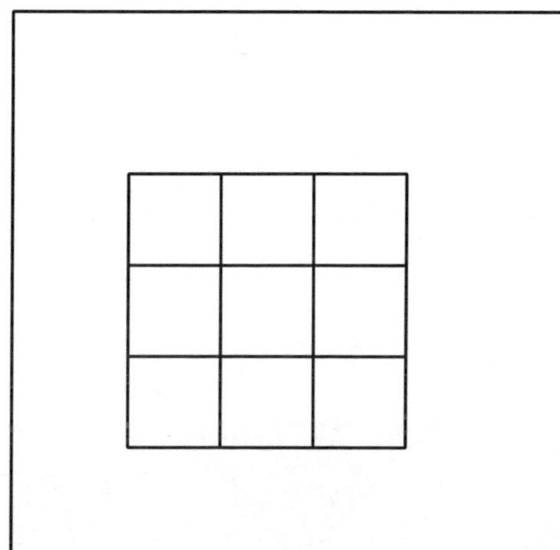

Figure 3-19.

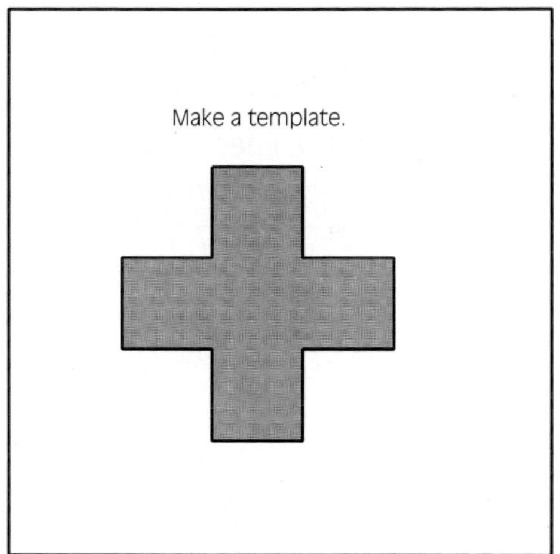

Figure 3-20.

To mark the quilt, turn the template so that it looks like an X when you look at it. Mark a faint guide line up and down the space to be filled. This line should be about the same distance from the block edge as the measurement to the center V of the template. Line the center of the cross template up with the guide line and mark the first cross. Move the template up with the bottom angles of the template touching the top angles of the cross that has just been drawn. Mark several crosses in the row (Figure 3-21).

The next row is marked in the same way but this time the template corners or angles must be touching the one beside it as well as the one

Figure 3-21.

above or below it. Continue marking until the surface to be covered with the design is filled.

Helpful Note: This complicated appearing design is actually fairly easy to mark and easy to hand quilt. Drawing the guide line helps tremendously in matching the crosses. Keep a small ruler handy to straighten the lines.

Tools Needed: A ruler, template material, and a fabric marking pencil or pen.

Where to Use: Crosses is a good filler design for plain setting blocks and could be a good eye teaser quilted overall on patchwork with curves or a circular pattern.

Concentric Squares: also Concentric Lozenge, Elbow (Figure 3-22)

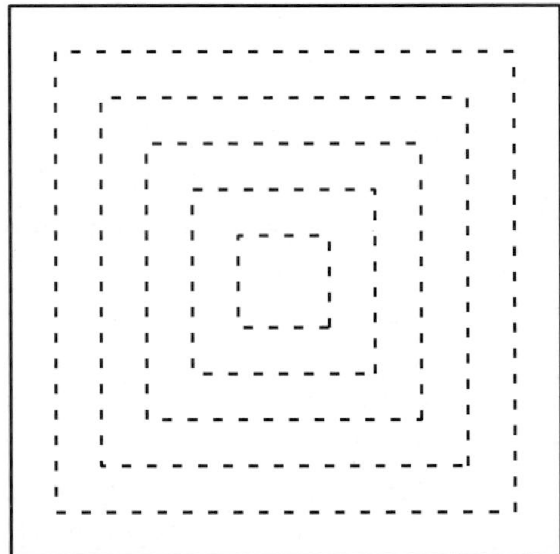

Figure 3-22.

Recommended Marking: Mark with a ruler on the quilt top as you go.

How to Mark or Draw: On the quilt block or square, mark faint guide lines diagonally from corner to corner to form an X on the block. Using the edge of the block as a guide, line up the ruler to be able to mark a line 1" from the outside edge of the block. Start marking from the guide line and mark across the block to the next guide line (Figure 3-23).

Mark around the block to form a square. Move the ruler in 1" and mark another square always being sure to start and stop on the guide line. Continue marking squares until the area is filled and the center square is as small as wanted.

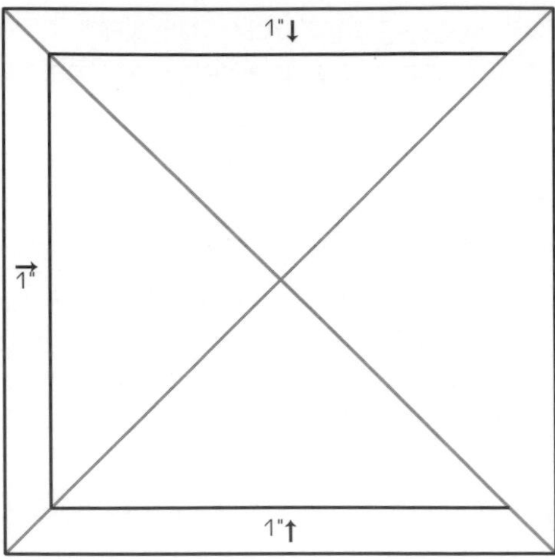

Figure 3-23.

Helpful Note: Be careful that the lines meet precisely at the guide line so that the squares stay square. The space between quilting lines can be more or less than 1" depending on the size square to be filled and the amount of quilting desired. Leave a fairly large square in the center and use that square for a flower or other quilting design.

Tools Needed: A ruler and fabric marking pencil or pen.

Where to Use: This quilting design that has been around since before 1800 can be used in plain setting blocks, in pieced blocks, or both to make an overall design disregarding the patchwork pattern. The design can be varied by drawing the design in a section of a patchwork block such as the Economy Patch (Figure 3-24). Sometimes blocks that need to set on point, such as a

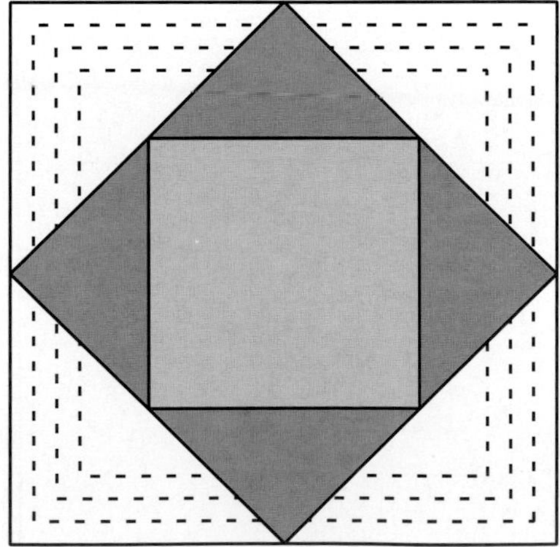

Figure 3-24.

Figure 3-25.

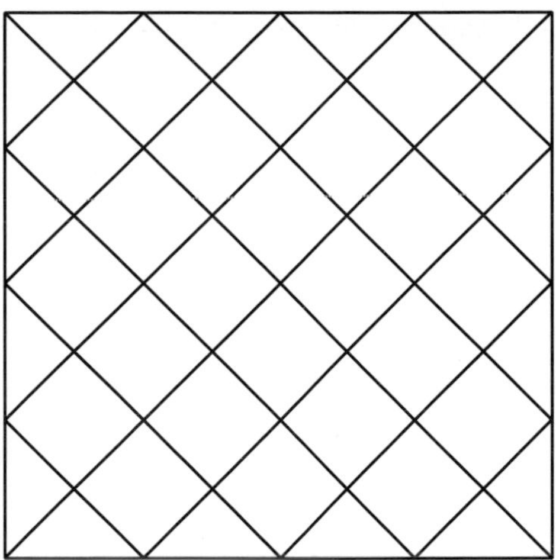

Figure 3-27.

Pieced Lily, have half-square triangles added to make a straight set or to make the quilt top larger. See Figure 3-25 for another variation of Concentric Squares. Both variations make a good framing for a patchwork block.

Weave Pattern (Figure 3-26)

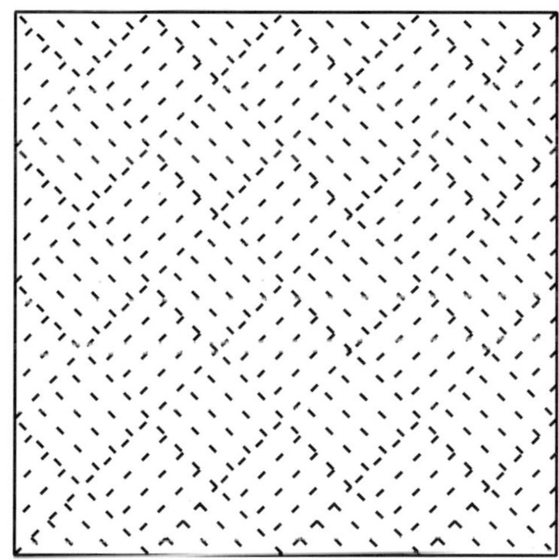

Figure 3-26.

Recommended Marking: Mark on the quilt top with a ruler as you go.

How to Mark or Draw: Start the Weave design by marking a Square Crosshatch design across the block or quilt top. The Crosshatch will be marked diagonally on the block. See page 31 for drawing the Crosshatch (Figure 3-1). Space the lines 4" apart. Fill in the 4" squares with parallel lines spaced 1" apart. Alter the fill-in lines as shown in Figure 3-28.

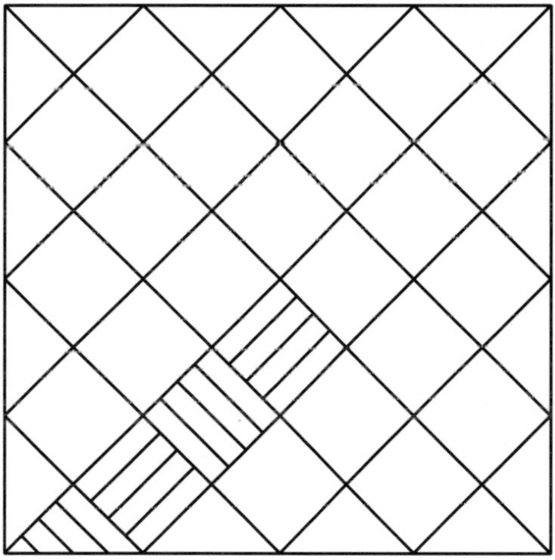

Figure 3-28.

Helpful Note: This quilting design was probably based on the patchwork pattern called Rail Fence and is as easy to mark and quilt as the patchwork design is to piece. A small 1" wide ruler makes filling the 4" blocks easier. Weave looks especially good marking a 2" square and spacing the fill-in lines ½" apart.

Tools Needed: A ruler and a marking pencil or pen.

Where to Use: This design can be used in plain setting blocks, as background quilting with appliqué, in wide sashings, and in borders. It can be marked and quilted over the entire quilt surface disregarding the patchwork or appliqué design.

Weave Variation (Figure 3-29)

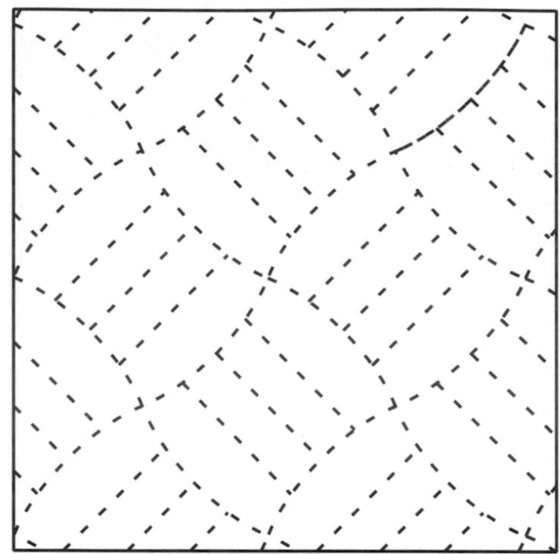

Figure 3-29.

RECOMMENDED MARKING: Mark the quilt top as you go using both a template and a ruler.

HOW TO MARK OR DRAW: Lightly mark a 2" cross-hatch diagonally on the block or surface to be covered. This grid will be used as a guide (see Figure 3-27).

To make the template, draw a 2" square and then draw a slightly outward curved line at the top and bottom and a slightly inward curved line on both sides of the square (Figure 3-30). The arc of the curve should be the same on all sides.

Figure 3-30.

Line up the lines that made the square on the template with the guide line of the grid and mark around the template. Flip the template for every other square and mark to cover the entire surface to be quilted. Fill in with parallel lines following the same instructions given for the Weave Pattern on page 39 and with the spacing between lines of ½".

HELPFUL NOTE: The curves for the template do not have to be perfectly symmetrical. The idea is for the quilting design to look like woven fabric.

TOOLS NEEDED: A ruler, template material, and a fabric marking pencil or pen.

WHERE TO USE: This Weave Variation can be used in plain setting blocks, as background quilting with appliqué, in wide sashings, and in borders. It could also be used as an allover design.

Basket Weave (Figure 3-31)

Figure 3-31.

RECOMMENDED MARKING: Mark with a template and a ruler on the quilt top as you go.

HOW TO MARK OR DRAW: Start by making a template for marking. Draw a bar that is 7" long and 1 inch wide. Across the middle of this bar, draw a bar that is 3" long and 1" wide. Mark the lines for this bar across the long bar (Figure 3-32, page 41). Erase the 7" bar line that is inside the 3" long bar. Mark the 7" long bar in 1" sections. The template should now look like the one in Figure 3-33.

To mark the quilt top, the first step is to mark a faint guide line on the diagonal of the block or area to be marked. Place the Basket Weave template with the bottom of the 7" bar touching the guide line. Mark all the way around the template. Move the template to the right and lay the template so the left part of the long bar covers the right part of the bar that was just marked (Figure 3-34). Move the template to the right overlapping each time until the diagonal guide line is filled.

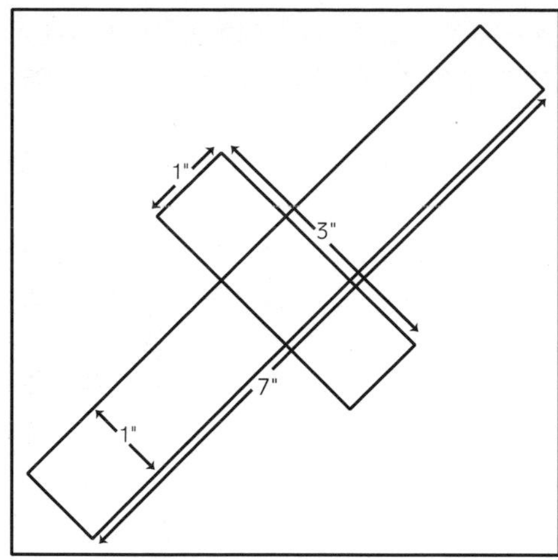

Figure 3-32.

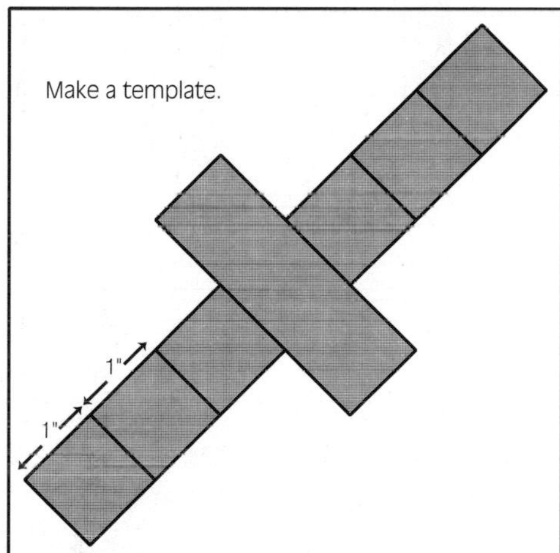

Figure 3-33.

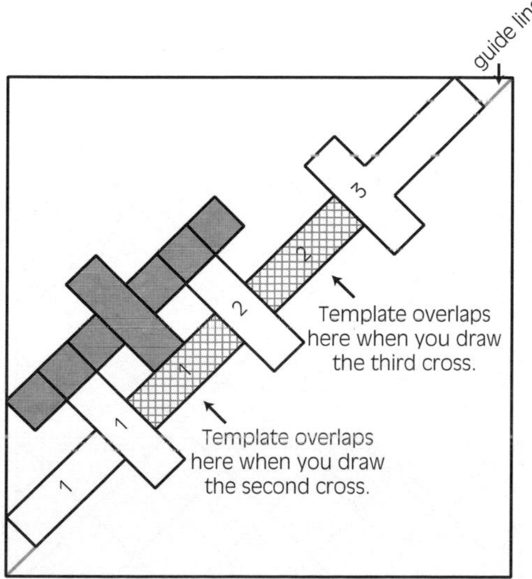

Figure 3-34.

To mark the next row, line the inch marks on the template up with the marked long cross below or above the template. See Figure 3-34. Mark around the template, move it to the right and mark again. Continue until the area to be quilted is marked.

Helpful Note: Practice marking the Basket Weave design on paper first. It is easier than it looks. Notice that in some places it will be necessary to mark the connecting lines of the short 3" bar with a small ruler. Often, mark a new faint diagonal guide line – at least every 6".

Tools Needed: A long ruler, a short ruler, template making material, and a fabric marking pencil or pen.

Where to Use: Basket Weave is an especially attractive design to be used as background for a medallion style appliqué quilt. It can be used in plain setting blocks and as background in appliqué blocks. It also makes a good overall design disregarding the patchwork pattern to create a new design.

Inward-Spiraling Maze (Figure 3-35)

Recommended Marking: Mark with a ruler on the block as you go.

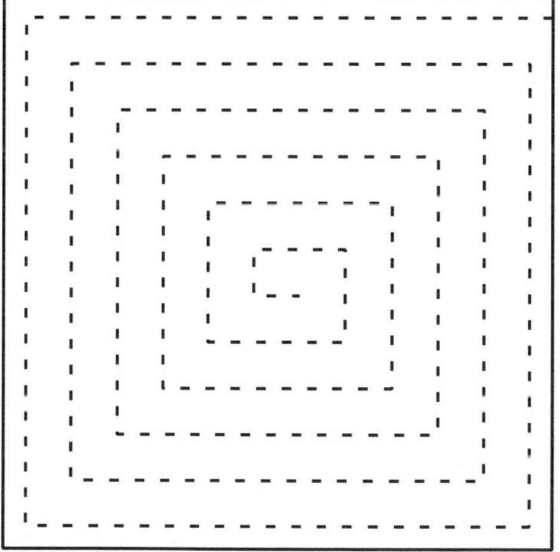
Figure 3-35.

How to Mark or Draw: Start drawing this design by using the block edge as a guide and marking a parallel line 1" from the edge on side #1. For the purposes of this exercise, the block size will be a 12" square. Stop marking the line 1" from side #2 of the block, turn the corner and mark a line 1" from side #2 stopping 1" before reaching side #3 of the block. Turn the corner and mark side #4 from the end of this line back to side 1 stopping 1" from the first drawn line (Figure 3-36). Turn the corner and mark to within 1" of the marked line on side #2. Continue marking in the same order until the center of the block is reached.

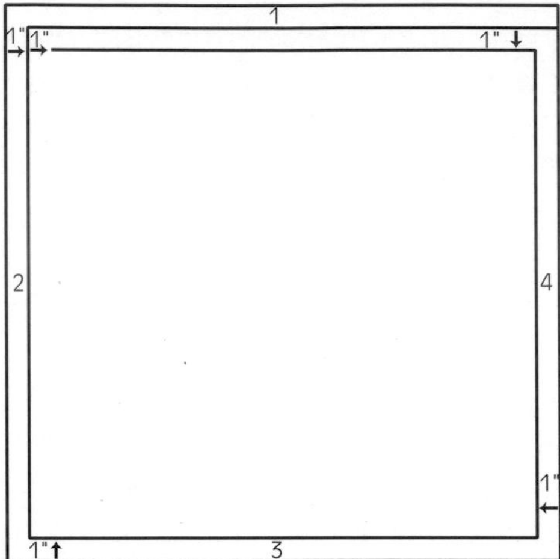

Figure 3-36.

Helpful Note: Practice marking a block on paper before attempting to mark on an actual block. This same Maze can be marked in a rectangle or triangle. It is a little hard to quilt because the quilting lines follow the grain of the fabric.

Tools Needed: A ruler and fabric marking pencil or pen.

Where to Use: In plain blocks or over patchwork designs such as the Nine Patch Checkerboard or other blocks where the pieces in the block are on point. The advantage to using the design with these blocks is the fact that the quilting would be across the bias of the fabric.

Square in a Square (Figure 3-37)

Figure 3-37.

Recommended Marking: Mark with a ruler and a template of the quilt top as you go.

How to Mark or Draw: First, make a template to mark the inner square. For the most pleasing quilting design, draw a 1½" square. Draw another square in the center of the 1½" square that measures 1". This square will be ¼" inside the larger square. Cut out the center square and around the outside of the 1½" square to make a template (Figure 3-38).

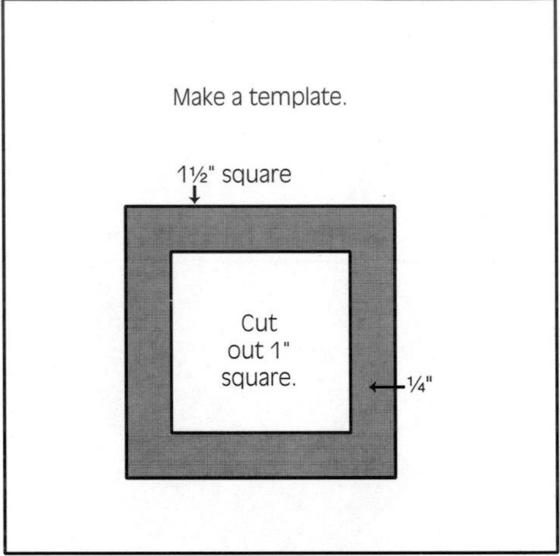

Figure 3-38.

To mark the Square in a Square design on the quilt surface, mark a Squares Crosshatch (see page 31) with line spacing 1½" apart. This crosshatch should be marked on the diagonal of the fabric. Place the template in the marked square of the crosshatch and draw the interior square (Figure 3-39).

Helpful Note: This is a beautiful design and well worth the time given to marking and quilt-

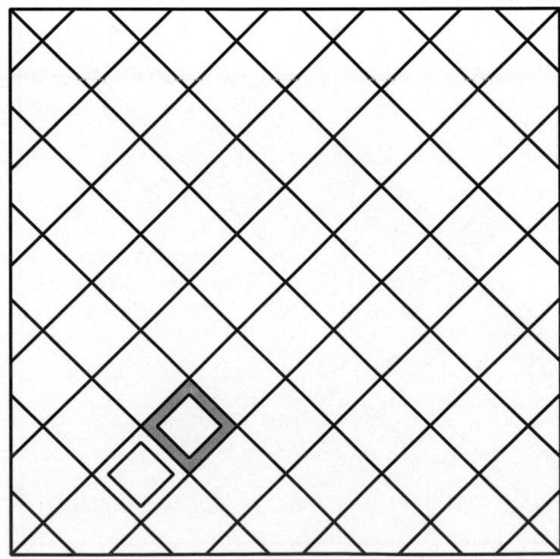

Figure 3-39.

ing it. Draw a few squares on paper first before marking on the actual quilt. All of the design can be marked with a ruler, but using a template is much faster.

Tools Needed: A long ruler, template material, and a fabric marking pencil or pen.

Where to Use: Square in a Square is a good background filler for plain setting blocks, for background in a whole cloth quilt or for a medallion style appliqué quilt.

Linked Squares (Figure 3-40)

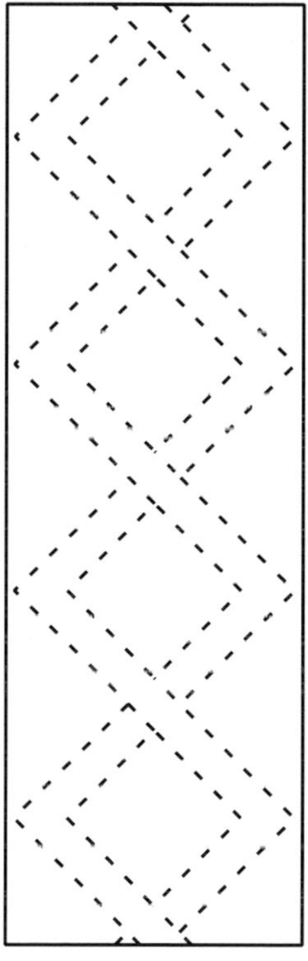

Figure 3-40.

Recommended Marking: Mark with a template on the quilt border as you go.

How to Mark or Draw: The measurements given for a template for this design will fit a 6" wide border. To make the template needed for marking this design, draw a 4" square on paper. Draw a square inside the 4" square that is ¾" smaller on all sides or that measures 2½" square. On the left top of the square, draw an extension that is 2½" long (the size of the inner square) and ¾" wide (Figure 3-41). Erase the pencil lines made when drawing the template except the one line at the bottom right-hand corner (Figure 3-42). The template is now ready to use in marking the Linked Squares design.

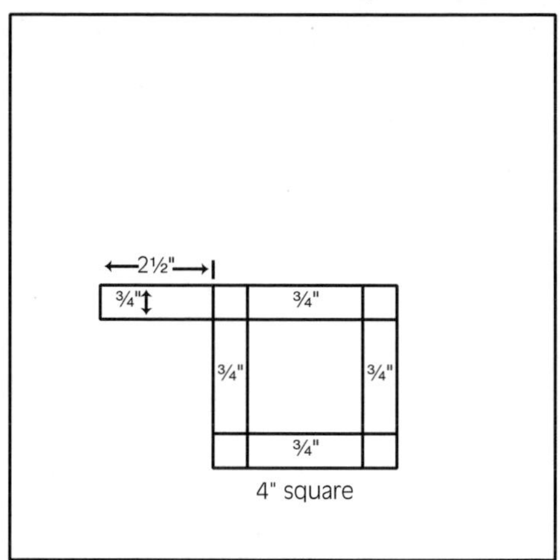

Figure 3-41.

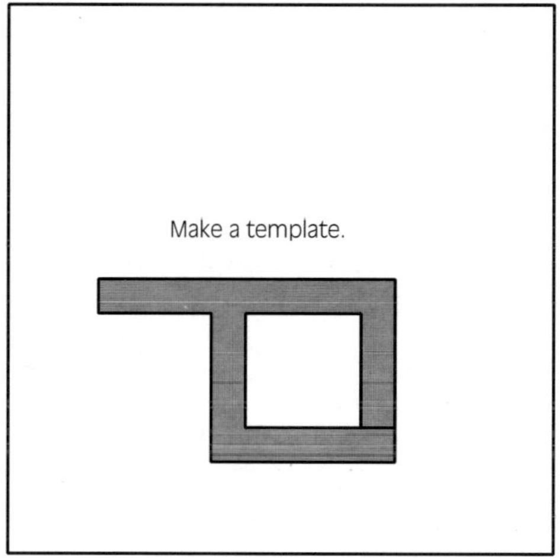

Figure 3-42.

Draw a faint guide line down the center of the border parallel with the border edge. Line the template up by placing the template on point with the corners of the inside square, with the tail or bar of the template down, along the guide line (Figure 3-43). Mark around the template starting with the marked line on the lower right corner and ending at the lower corner. Do

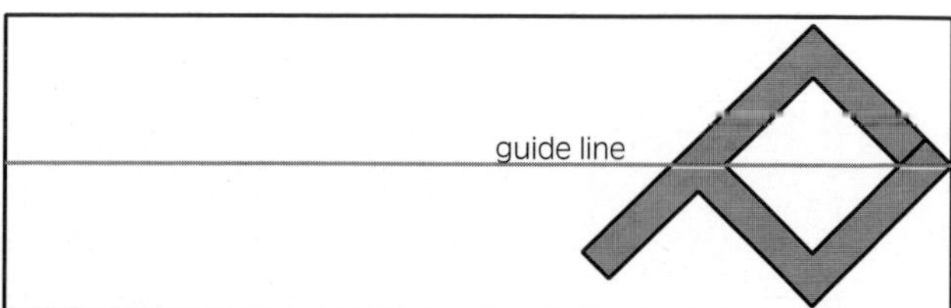

Figure 3-43.

not mark the end of the bar. Move the template to the left with the template overlapping the previously marked bar (Figure 3-44). Mark around the template again starting with the marked line, skip marking the end of the bar and end at the corner below the starting point. Continue moving the template and marking until the border is filled. It will be necessary to add fill in lines and perhaps erase short lines occasionally. The squares should give the appearance of being woven.

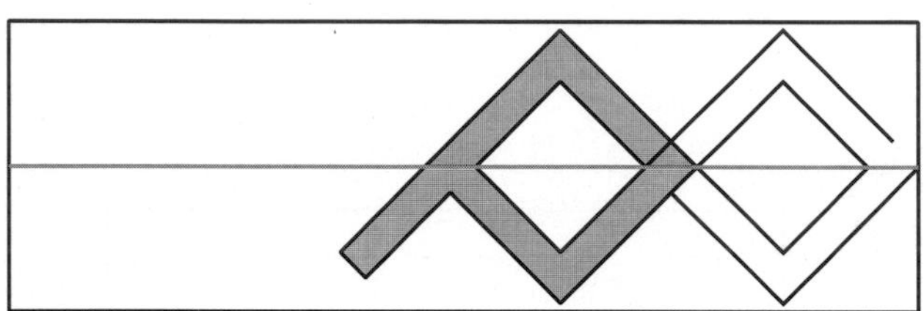

Figure 3-44.

Helpful Note: Mark a practice run of the Linked Squares on paper first to get the feel for overlapping and where to mark and where lines will need to be added.

Tools Needed: A ruler marked with ¼" measurements, template material, and a fabric marking pencil or pen.

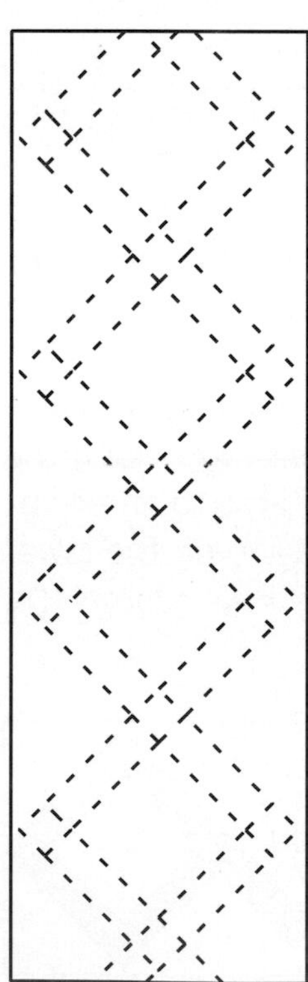

Figure 3-45.

Where to Use: This design is meant for borders but could be used in sashing if it is wide enough.

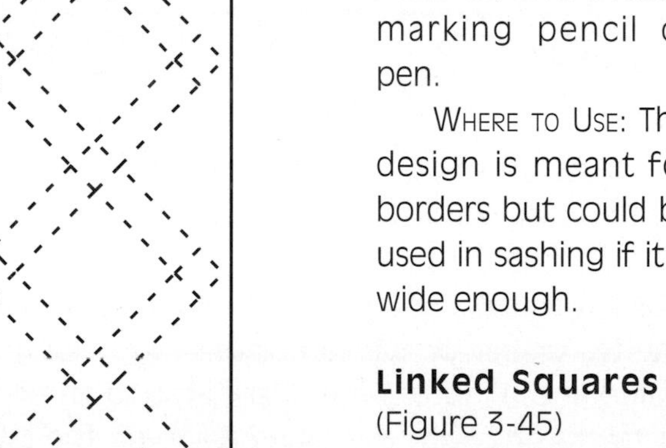

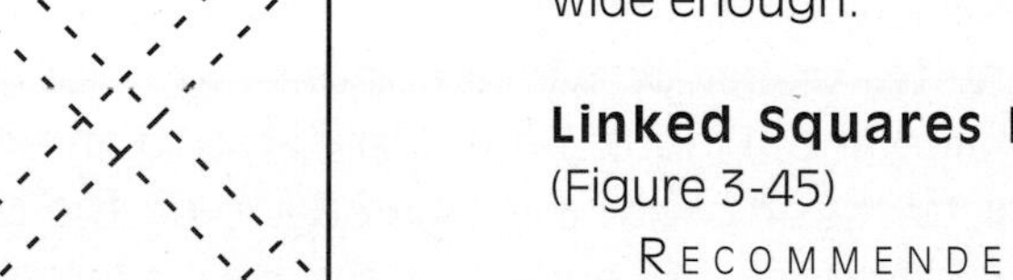

Linked Squares II

(Figure 3-45)

Recommended Marking: Mark with a template on the quilt border as you go.

How to Mark or Draw: To make the template for this Linked Squares design, draw a 4" square on paper.

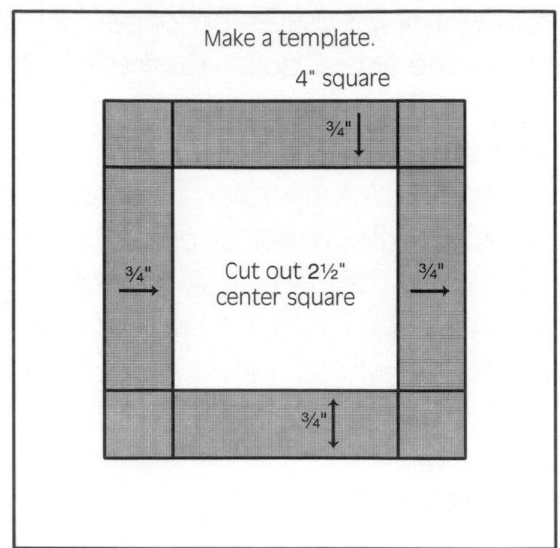

Figure 3-46.

Mark a square inside the 4" square that measures 2½" or spaced inside ¾" (Figure 3-46). Cut out the center small square and the template is ready to use. These measurements are for a 6" wide border.

To mark the border, mark a faint guide line down the center of the border. With the template on point, line up the corner angles on the guide line and mark around the inside and outside of the template. Move the template so that the corner square of the template overlaps the corner of the just drawn square (Figure 3-47). Continue marking until the border area is filled. It will be necessary to go back and fill in the lines that form the squares on the corners of the squares. Look at the first square in Figure 3-47.

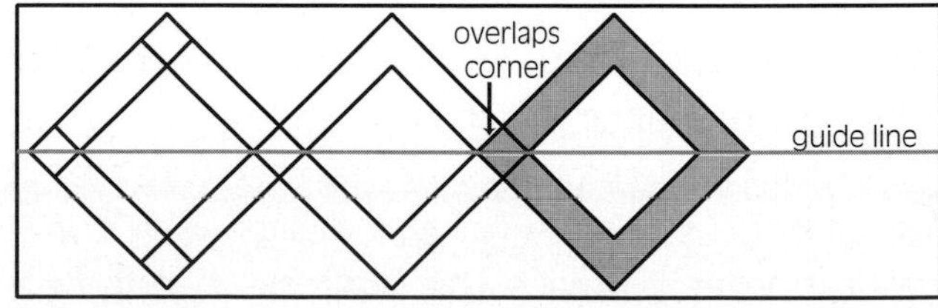

Figure 3-47.

Helpful Note: Practice marking the design on paper before marking on the actual quilt. This design is easy to mark and easy to hand quilt.

Tools Needed: A ruler, template material, and a fabric marking pencil or pen.

Where to Use: This design can be used in borders and in wider sashings.

Woven Squares (Figure 3-48)

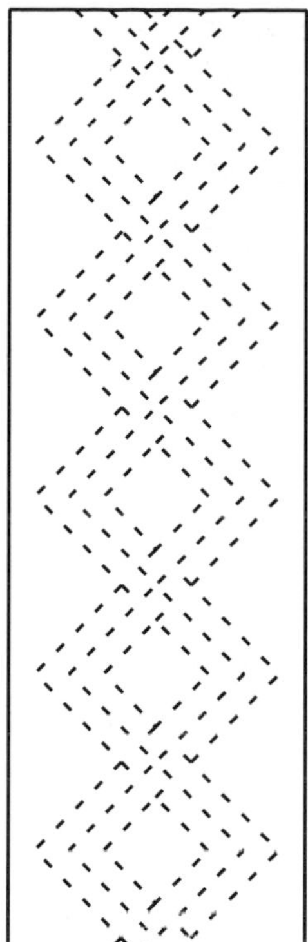
Figure 3-48.

RECOMMENDED MARKING: Draw the design on a paper pattern and transfer to the quilt top before assembling the quilt layers.

HOW TO MARK OR DRAW: To make a paper pattern to use for marking, cut a piece of paper the width of the border and half the border's length. Next, make a pattern of one unit to be used in drawing the full pattern. As an example, for an 8" wide border, a 5" square will fit. Draw a 5" square on a sheet of paper. Mark the first lines ¾" inside the 5" square. Move the ruler in and mark another set of lines ¾" inside the previously drawn lines (Figure 3-49). Erase lines that cross other lines to get a pattern that looks like the drawing in Figure 3-50. Go over the pattern lines with a black felt tip marker so that the design will be easy to trace.

To draw the paper pattern for the border, mark a faint guide line in the middle along the length of the paper that was cut to fit the border. Place the paper with the one design unit under

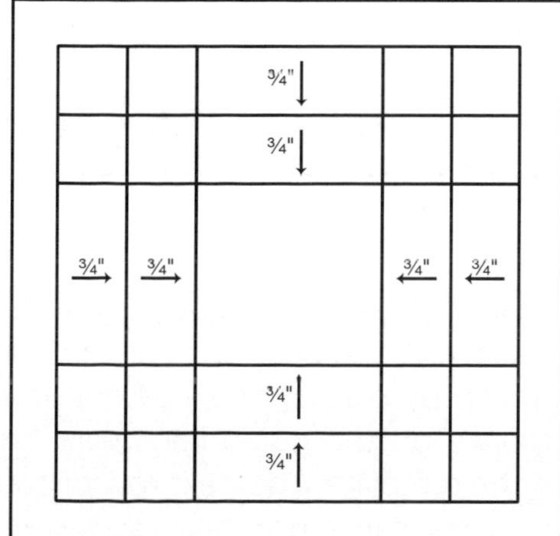

Figure 3-49.

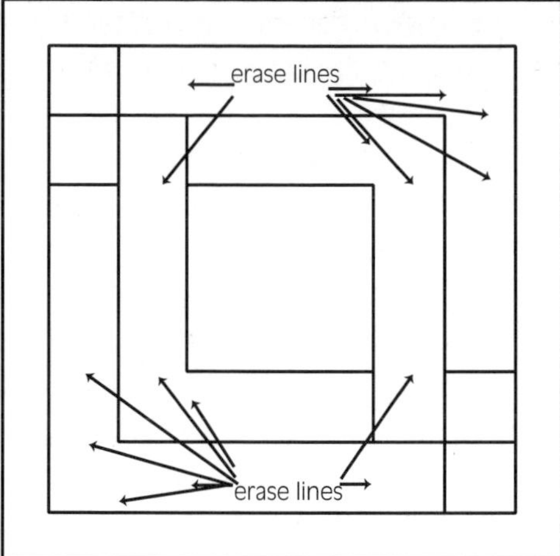

Figure 3-50.

the pattern paper and line it up, on point, with the corners of the square on the guide line. Start so the Woven Squares design will be at the end of the paper that is the center of the border. Using a pencil, trace the design onto the paper pattern, move the design, overlap with the just drawn square and trace one more unit onto the pattern paper (Figure 3-51). The unit with 1 has been drawn and 2 is the design unit showing through the paper pattern and ready to be traced. Trace

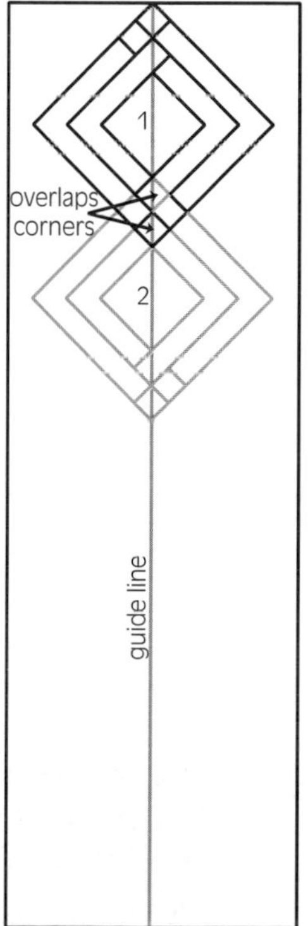

Figure 3-51.

another unit, move the design under the paper, trace the next unit, and continue until the border paper pattern is filled.

After the whole paper pattern has been drawn, erase the unwanted lines. Using a ruler, go over the whole design with a black felt tip pen. This will make the design easy to see through the fabric and therefore easier to transfer to the quilt border.

To transfer the Woven Squares design to the quilt top, pin the paper pattern on the underneath side of the quilt top, with both the pattern and the quilt top up. Pinning will keep the pattern from slipping as you mark the top.

Helpful Note: Dark fabric may require the use of a light box. Usually, just placing a piece of white poster board underneath will help to make seeing the design possible.

Tools Needed: Freezer or butcher paper, pencil, ruler, and felt tip pen for making the pattern. A fabric marking pencil or pen and perhaps a ruler for marking the quilt top.

Where to Use: Woven Squares is a border design but could be used in fairly wide sashings.

Herringbone: also Chevron, Steps (Figure 3-52)

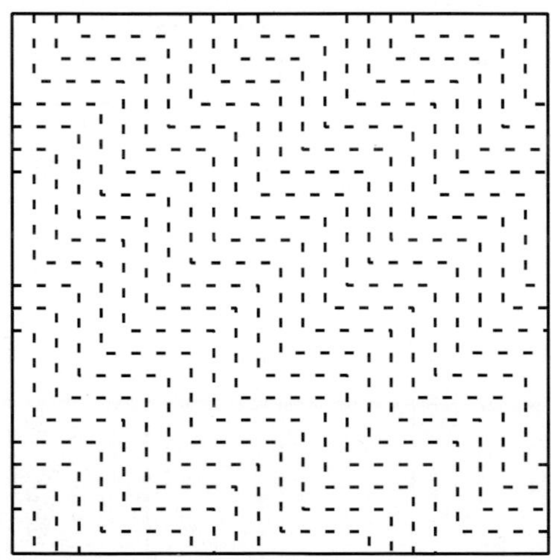

Figure 3-52.

Recommended Marking: Mark with a template and a ruler on the quilt top as you go.

How to Mark or Draw: Since Herringbone is easier marked with a template, make a template by first drawing a long diagonal line (18" long) on paper.

Using a ruler, draw half-square triangles along the diagonal line. Either a 2" or 3" half-square triangle is a good size. The half-square triangles should be drawn so that they touch along the diagonal line (Figure 3-53). Move the ruler away from the steps that have just been drawn and draw a second set of steps. The spacing should be ½" for a 2" half-square and 1" for a 3" half-square (Figure 3-54). Cut the template out along the lines that make the steps.

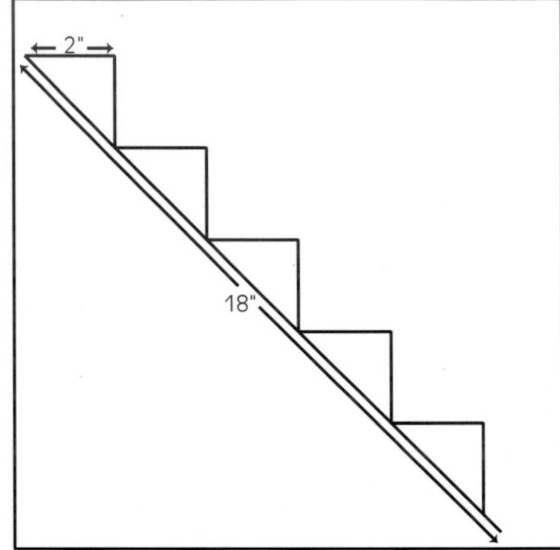

Figure 3-53.

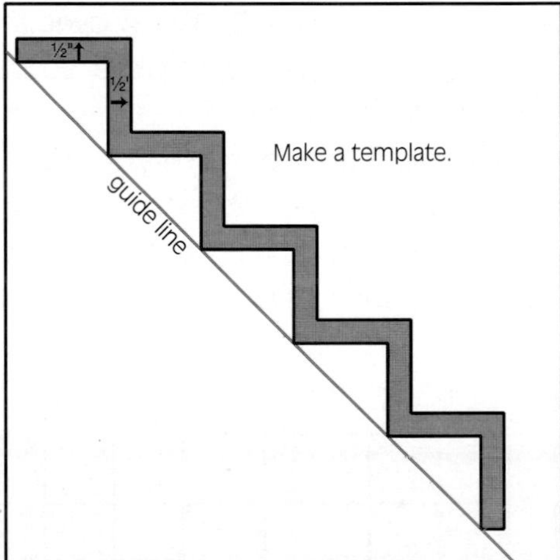

Figure 3-54.

To mark the quilt top, draw a faint diagonal guide line across the block or quilt top. Line the template up by placing the bottom angles of the template on the guide line. Mark on both sides of the template. The next row of steps will be spaced the same distance as the width of the steps.

The template can be used to measure by laying the template along the last drawn lines or another faint diagonal guide line can be used. A large area can be marked and then quilted or one set of steps can be drawn, quilted, and then the next lines marked and quilted.

HELPFUL NOTE: Even though this design is marked with a diagonal guide line, the quilting stitches will be on the straight grain of the fabric. This makes the design a little harder to quilt. Using a half-square triangle ruler makes this a very easy design to draw and to mark. Larger half-squares with wider spacing between steps can be used if less quilting is desired.

TOOLS NEEDED: A long ruler, a small ruler, template material, and a fabric marking pencil or pen.

WHERE TO USE: Herringbone can be used in plain setting blocks, in an overall pattern disregarding the patchwork design, and as background filler.

Box Links (Figure 3-55)

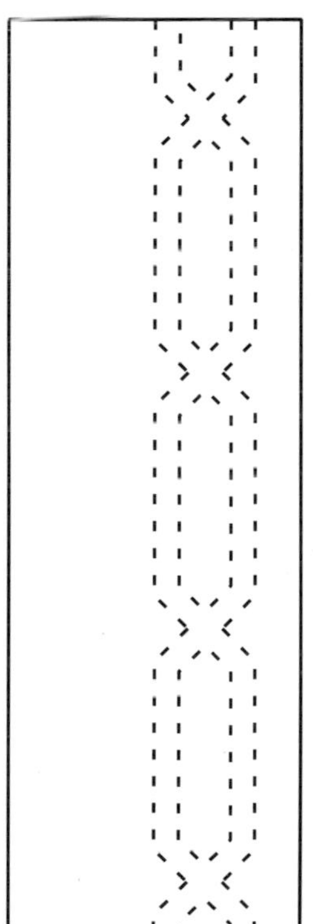

Figure 3-55.

RECOMMENDED MARKING: Mark with a template on the quilt top as you go.

HOW TO MARK OR DRAW: First, make a template by drawing a rectangle that is as wide as the border area to be filled and twice as long (example: 4" width and the length would be 8"). On each end of the rectangle draw squares the same as the width (example: 4"). With a ruler, draw lines from corner to corner in the squares to form an X (Figure 3-56). Draw a line spaced 1" inside the rectangle and the triangles that touch the rectangle (Figure 3-57). This will form one of the links. To get the boxes to link, the point of the end of the link must overlap the next link by having the triangle point touch the marked X (Figure 3-58). Draw at least three of these links for the template (Figure 3-59). The center must be cut out of the template.

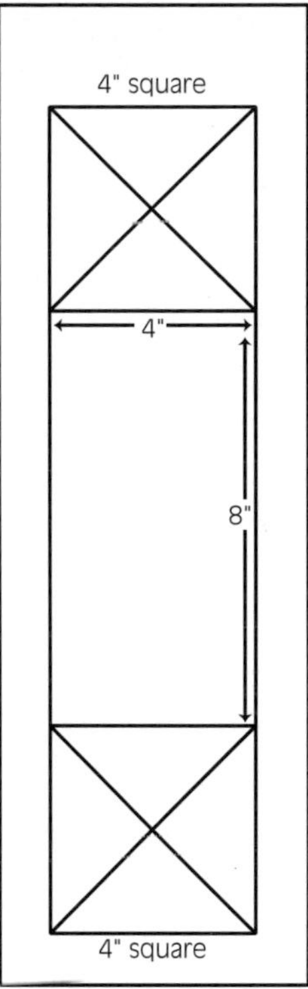

Figure 3-56.

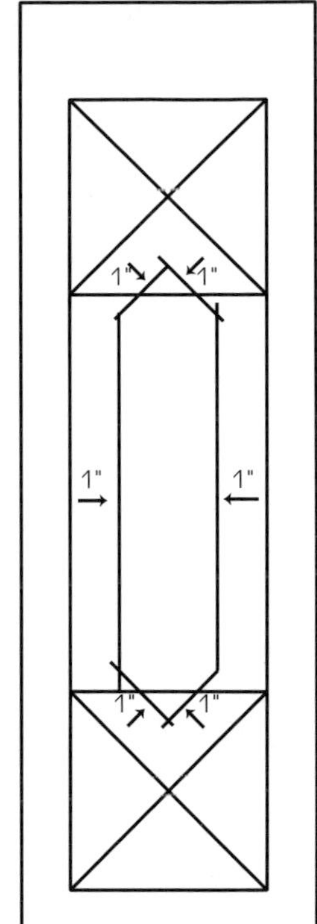

Figure 3-57.

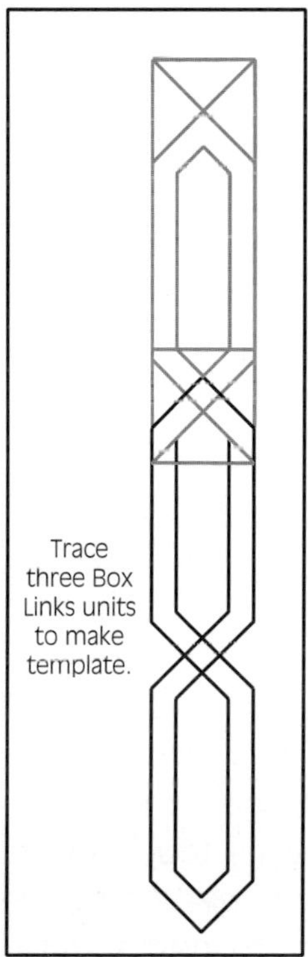

Figure 3-58.

Figure 3-59.

Mark Box Links on the border of a quilt by always lining the template up the same distance from either the border edge or the border seam and mark around the outside and the inside of the template until the border is filled. Remember to overlap the end of the template with what has been drawn when moving the template to the next position.

Helpful Note: It is much easier to mark and quilt this design than to make the template.

Tools Needed: A ruler, template material, and a fabric marking pencil or pen.

Where to Use: Box Links is designed for borders but could also be used in sashings.

Diamond-Set Squares (Figure 3-60)

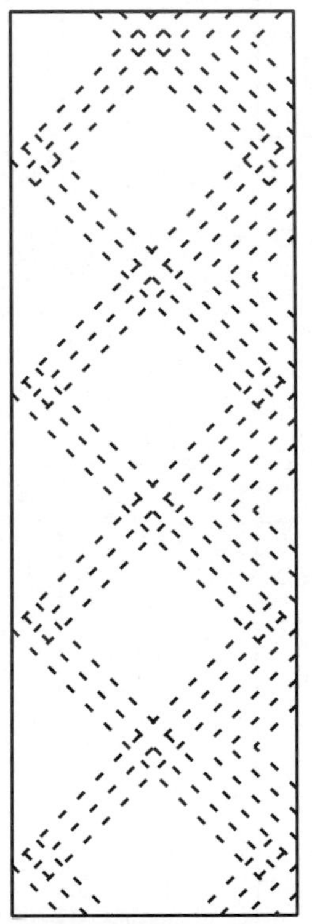

Figure 3-60.

Recommended Marking: Mark with a ruler on the quilt top border as you go.

How to Mark or Draw: Use a long ruler with a 45° mark and line the 45° mark up with the edge of the border. Mark along the edge of the ruler. Flip the ruler with the 45° mark lined up with the border seam and the right ruler edge touching the diagonal line that was just drawn. Mark along the edge of the ruler (Figure 3-61). The next step will be fill in lines that will be marked inside this triangle. These fill-in lines will be ⅜" apart. For this example, the measurements are for a 6" border. Mark two lines with this ⅜" spacing, move the ruler (line up the 45° mark again) over 2½" and mark another line from the border seam to the border edge. Flip the ruler and mark two lines spaced ⅜" apart (Figure 3-62). Move the ruler 2½" and mark another line. Continue marking until four or five squares have been formed (Figure 3-63).

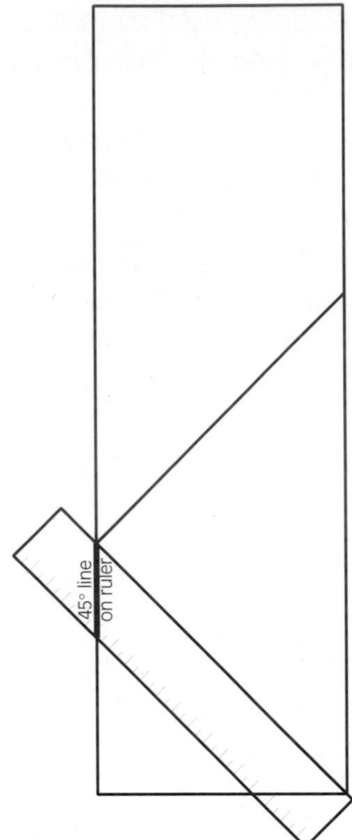

Figure 3-61.

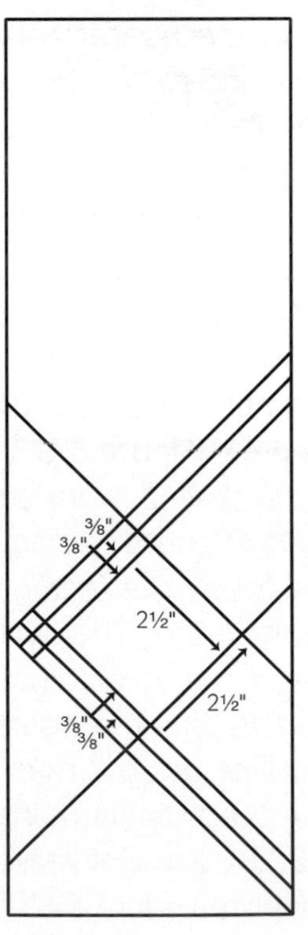

Figure 3-62.

Mark the fill in lines in the bottom triangles by marking a faint guide line down the center of each triangle. Mark these fill-in lines the same width (⅜") by marking to the guide line (Figure 3-64). Some of the lines that extend into this area will need to be erased or ignored when quilting.

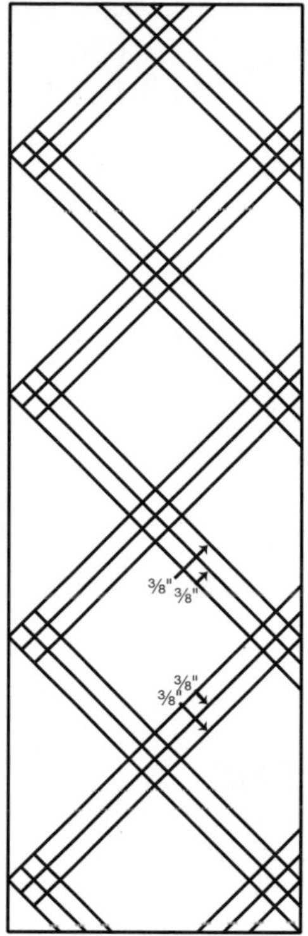

Figure 3-63.

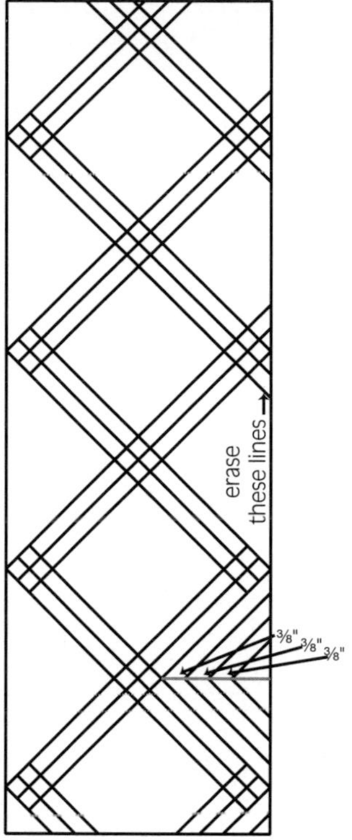

Figure 3-64.

Helpful Note: This design can also be marked using a template. See Figure 3-46 on page 44 for directions for making a template that can be used for Diamond-Set Squares. The empty triangle at the top of the border would be a good place for a design such as a leaf. Inside the square would be a good place for a flower or a heart.

Tools Needed: A long ruler with a 45° marking, template material (if used), fabric eraser, and a fabric marking pencil or pen.

Where to Use: Use for a fairly wide quilt border. This design is especially suited to an Amish style quilt, a strippie quilt, and could be successfully used in bars or sashings.

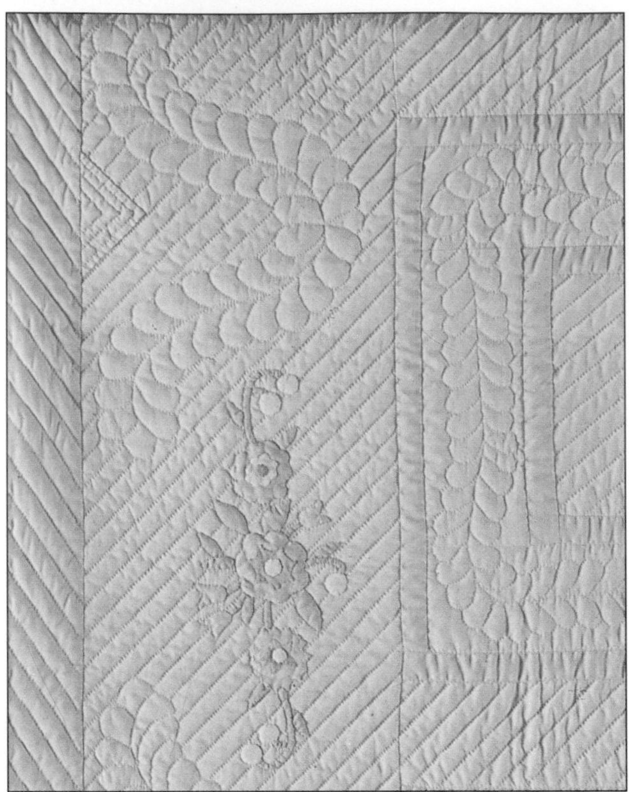

Plate 4-1. Diagonal Lines (also Feathers).
Anne Orr's "Ye Olde Sampler" by Ethel Hickman, 1985. Collection of the Museum of the American Quilter's Society.

Plate 4-2. Diagonal Lines (also Echo).
Chips and Whetstones by Martha B. Skelton, 1987. Collection of the Museum of the American Quilter's Society.

Plate 4-3. Diamond (also By the Piece, In the Ditch, Ovals).
Celebration by Joyce Stewart, 1988. Collection of the Museum of the American Quilter's Society.

Plate 4-4. Double Line Diamond (also Single Parallel Lines)
Double T by Sarah C. Dutton, author's grandmother, ca. 1910.

Chapter Four
Diagonals and Diamonds

Of the designs found in this chapter, the most popular and often used designs are the diagonal lines. They run a close race with the Squares Crosshatching in frequency found on quilts dating from the early 1800's to the present. Single, Double and Triple Diagonal Lines were found on both pieced and appliquéd quilts. The lines are easy to mark and easy to quilt which probably explains their popularity.

Because the Hanging Diamond is an easy to mark and fairly easy to quilt design, it has been the favorite from the Diamond family of design. It is found as an overall design on both pieced and appliquéd quilts, and is used as background filler and in plain setting blocks.

The Diamond (based on the 45° diamond) has also been a favorite design especially to be used as background filler and in plain setting blocks. Both the Hanging Diamond and Diamond can be single, double or triple line.

Diagonal Lines: also Diagonal Pipe Line, Diagonal Parallel, Diagonal Crosshatching, Diagonal Background, Diagonal Herringbone (Figure 4-1)

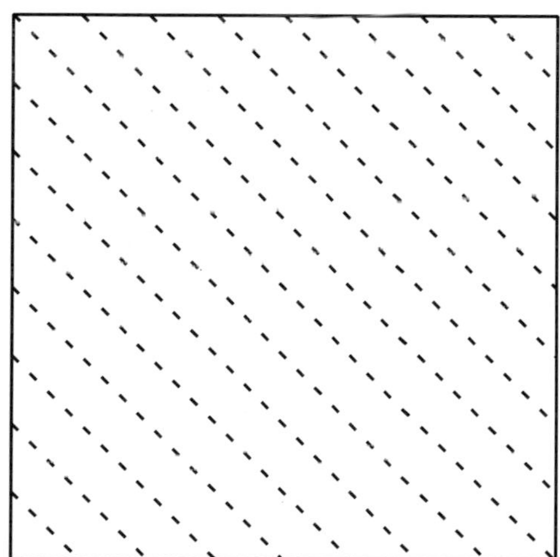

Figure 4-1.

RECOMMENDED MARKING: Mark on the quilt top as you go.

HOW TO MARK OR DRAW: Diagonal Line quilting has been found on quilts dating from the very early 1800's. It is marked on the bias or diagonal of the fabric.

To start, use a long ruler that is placed from corner to corner of a block or on the diagonal of the quilt top. Mark a diagonal line along the ruler edge (Figure 4-2). Mark parallel with this starting line across the block or surface of the quilt. The spacing between quilting lines can vary from ½" to 1½" depending on the amount of quilting desired or the look that is wanted. The direction of the diagonal lines is strictly personal preference. They can be marked from lower left to upper right or from lower right to upper left (see Figure 4-2).

Diagonal Line marking is referred to as Diagonal Herringbone when it is used in a quilt made of

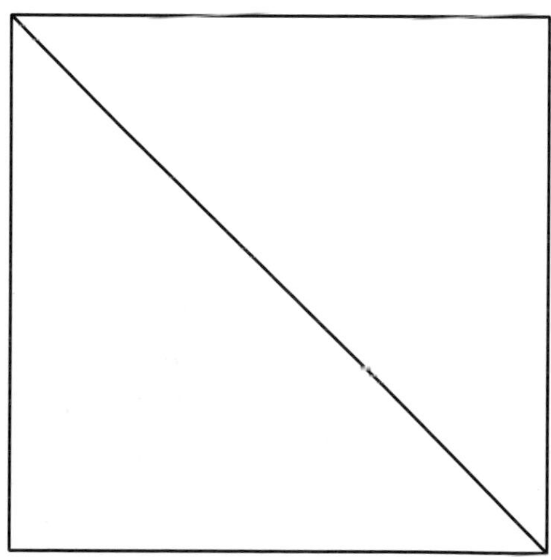

Figure 4-2.

blocks. The direction of the diagonal lines alternate from one block to the next block across the quilt top.

HELPFUL NOTE: Always use the same ruler or marking device for a whole quilt top. Using a long ruler with a 45° mark makes getting the diagonal marks truly on the bias much easier. If the whole quilt surface is to be marked, a carpenter's tape measure makes marking a very long line easier. If you have no one to help, the carpenter's tape can be held to the quilt with a clothespin. Strip templates used for marking Log Cabin strips work well to mark this design, especially in blocks.

TOOLS NEEDED: A long ruler and a marking pencil or pen.

WHERE TO USE: Diagonal Lines are extremely easy to both mark and quilt. They can be used in plain blocks, as background filler, in borders and in sashings, and over the whole quilt surface disregarding the pattern or design.

Double Diagonal Lines: also Double Parallel (Figure 4-3)

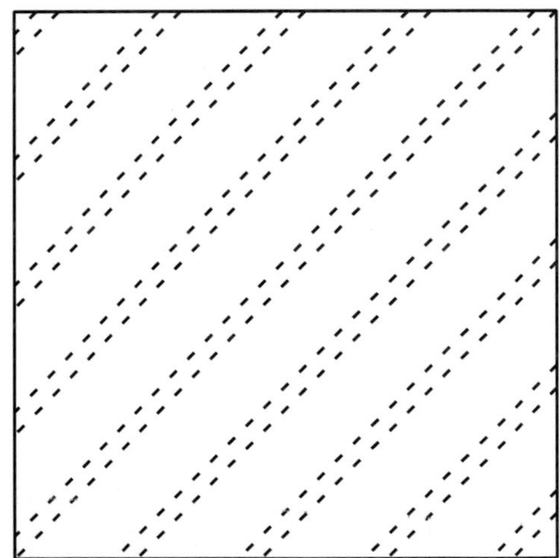

Figure 4-3.

RECOMMENDED MARKING: Mark on the quilt top as you go.

HOW TO MARK OR DRAW: The starting line for the Double Diagonal Lines is marked the same as for Diagonal Line (see Figure 4-2). The second line is marked ¼" from the first line (Figure 4-4). Mark the next line with spacing of 1" to 1½" and the fourth line spaced ¼" again (Figure 4-5). Continue

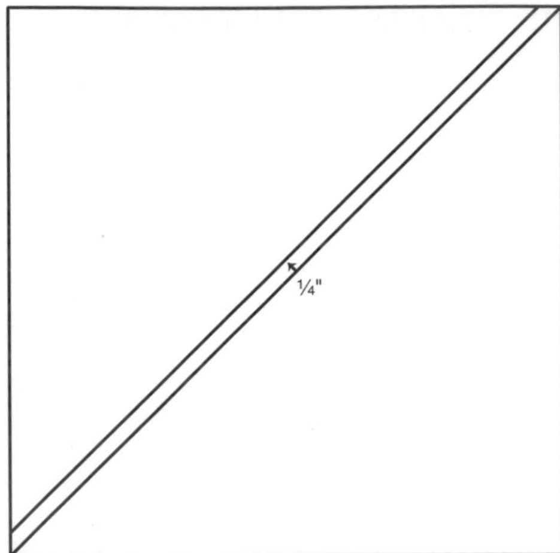

Figure 4-4.

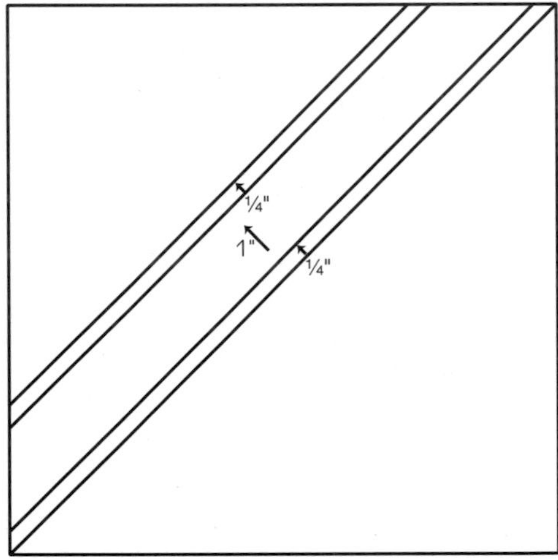

Figure 4-5.

marking with the same spacing until the area to be quilted is filled. Several lines can be marked and quilted and then more lines marked and quilted until finished.

HELPFUL NOTE: Check often to be sure that the lines are staying perfectly parallel with the starting line and on the bias or diagonal. The Double Diagonal Line design has been used since at least 1840 and is well worth the effort of quilting the extra lines. The double lines make it a beautiful quilting design.

TOOLS NEEDED: A long ruler with ¼" markings and a fabric marking pencil or pen.

WHERE TO USE: Double Diagonal Line quilting can be used in plain blocks, as background filler, in borders, in sashings, and over the whole quilt surface disregarding the pattern or design.

Triple Diagonal Lines: also Triple Rodding (Figure 4-6)

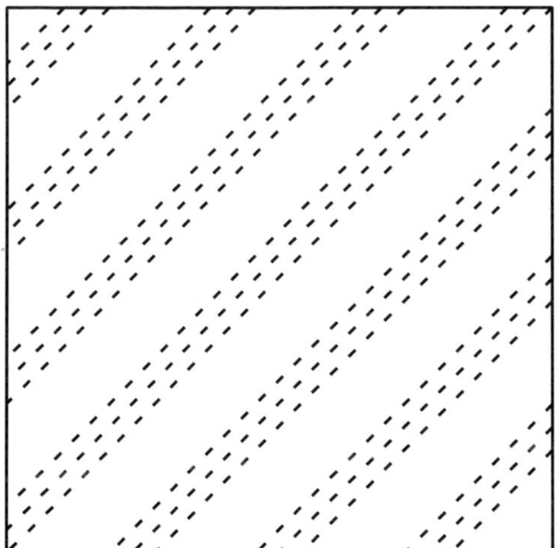

Figure 4-6.

Recommended Marking: Mark on the quilt top as you go.

How to Mark or Draw: The directions for marking the first line of Triple Diagonal Lines is the same as for Diagonal Lines (see page 51). After marking the first line, move the ruler ¼", mark a second line, move the ruler to space ¼", and mark the third line. The next spacing will be from 1" to 1½" from the third marked line. Mark this line, ¼" space, line, ¼" space and a third line (Figure 4-7). Continue marking and quilting until the area to be quilted is filled.

Another variation of multiple diagonal lines is to make the sets of lines in fives rather than three. The spacing between the five lines would be ¼". This is also a good design.

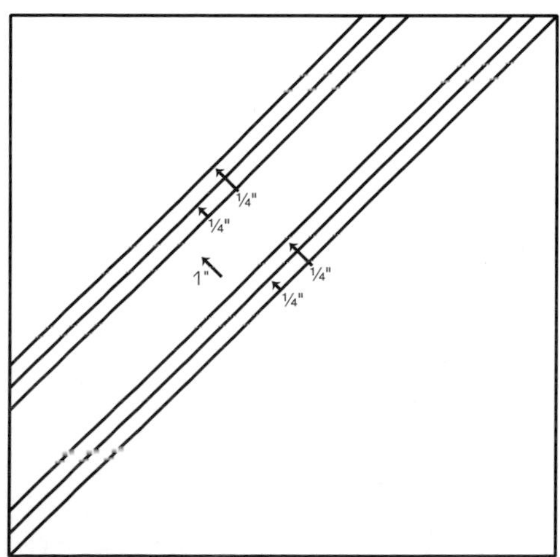

Figure 4-7.

Helpful Note: Always, the more quilting the better and Triple Diagonal Lines will prove that putting in that third line makes for a good quilting design.

Use the same ruler to mark the whole quilt. A carpenter's tape measure is a good device to use to mark the diagonal lines if the whole quilt surface is to be covered.

Tools Needed: A long ruler with ¼" markings and a fabric marking pencil or pen.

Where to Use: Use Triple Diagonal Lines in plain blocks, as background filler, in borders, in sashings, and over the whole quilt surface disregarding the pattern or design. This design is found on quilts dating around 1850 so was started a little later than Diagonal and Double Diagonal Lines.

Diamond: also Lozenge, Cross-Diamond Pattern, Diamond Cross-Hatching (Figure 4-8)

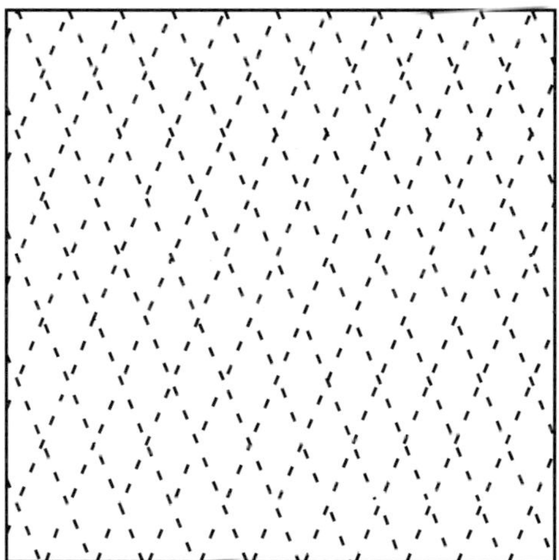

Figure 4-8.

Recommended Marking: Mark on the quilt top as you go.

How to Mark or Draw: This Diamond quilting design is based on the 45° diamond and dates from around 1830. This is actually a very easy design to mark and an easy way to start is to mark lines from corner to corner on a rectangle. This simple marking does not give a 45° diamond but is close enough and that is fine for quilting. Use the instructions given for Diamond Weave on page 60 to mark diamonds with this method (Figure 4-31).

To mark the starting lines for an accurate 45° diamond, mark a faint vertical guide line on the area to be marked. Place a ruler with the 45° marking on the right side of the ruler touching the guide line and the center area of the ruler between the edge and the 45° mark lined up with the guide line. On most rulers this will be the 1½" line on the ruler. Mark a line on the right edge of the ruler (Figure 4-9). Now, rotate the ruler so the 45° marking on the left side of the ruler is touching the guide line and the 45° marking on the right is lined up with the first line that was marked. The guide line should be crossing the center of this area or the 1½" line (Figure 4-10). What you have drawn should look like a teepee. Using these lines as the first marked lines, mark parallel lines that are spaced 1" to 2" apart to form diamonds across the area to be quilted (Figure 4-11).

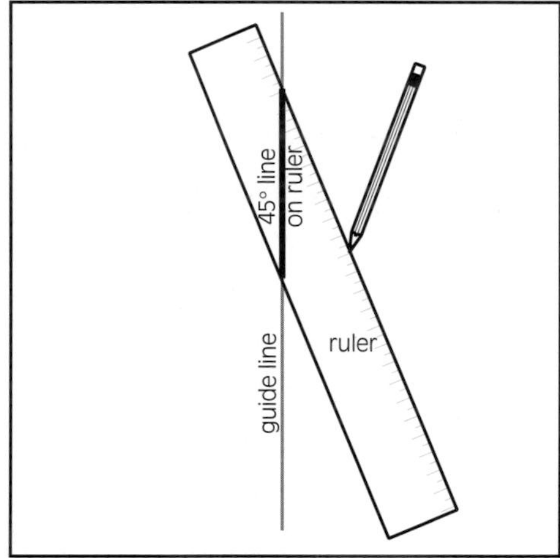

Figure 4-9.

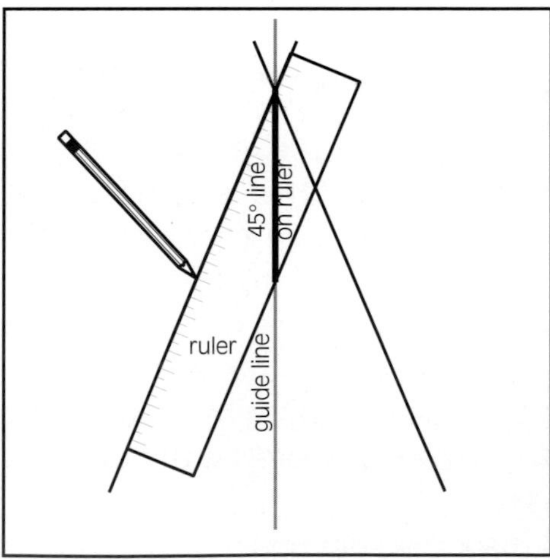

Figure 4-10.

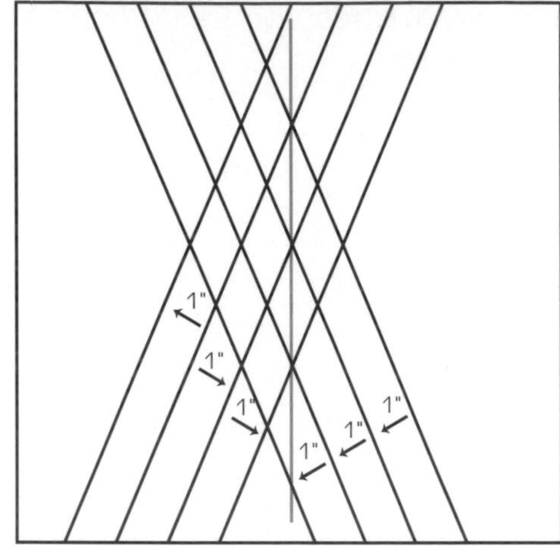

Figure 4-11.

Helpful Note: Practice drawing these beginning 45° lines and the parallel lines on paper before marking the quilt top. Check the markings often to see that the lines are still at 45° angles. An accurate 45° diamond template can be used to mark the starting lines.

Tools Needed: A long ruler with 45° markings and a fabric marking pencil or pen.

Where to Use: Diamond is a good design to use as background filler. It can also be used in plain setting blocks, in sashings, in borders, and as an allover quilting design disregarding the patchwork pattern or design.

Double Line Diamond: also Double Line Crosshatching (Figure 4-12)

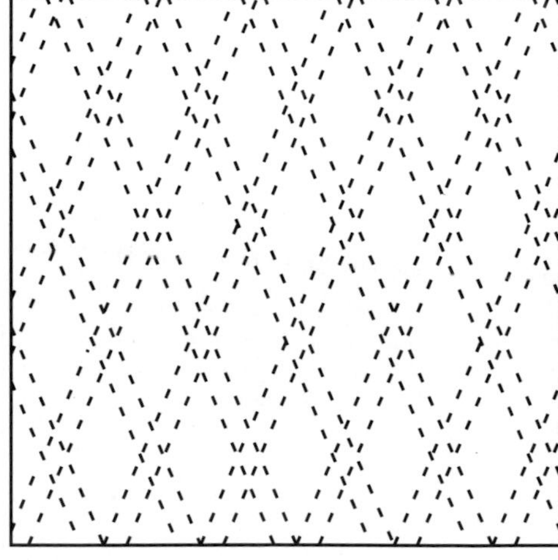

Figure 4-12.

Recommended Marking: Mark on the quilt top as you go.

How to Mark or Draw: Double Line Diamond is started the same as Diamonds. There are two ways, at least, to mark the starting lines. The easiest method uses a rectangle marked with an X from corner to corner. The instructions for Diamond Weave on page 60 are for this method.

For another method, read the instructions on page 54 to mark the first lines (Figure 4-9 and 4-10). This method gives an accurate 45° diamond marking which is not necessary in quilting. The parallel line spacing for the Double Line Diamond will be a line, ¼" space, a line, 1" to 2" space, a line, ¼" space, and a line (Figure 4-13). Mark parallel lines in the same sequence continuing across the surface until the area to be covered with the quilting design is filled.

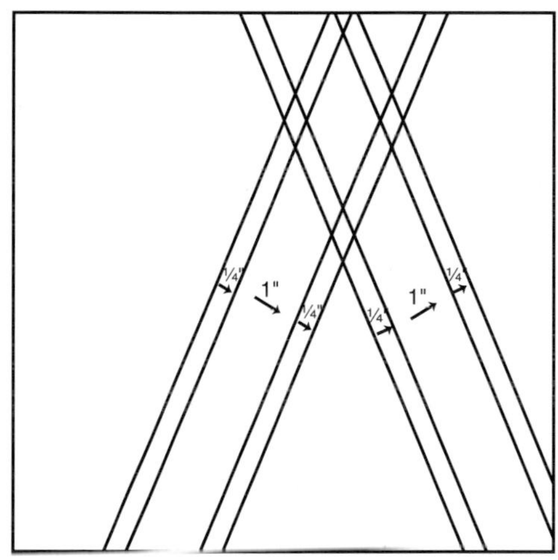

Figure 4-13.

The size of the diamonds can be determined by the amount of quilting desired in the area to be covered.

Helpful Note: The Double Line Diamond design has been used since the 1840's and is easy to mark and easy to quilt. It is worth the extra effort of quilting the second line.

Tools Needed: A long ruler with 45° markings and a fabric marking pencil or pen.

Where to Use: This design can be used in plain setting blocks, in plain setting blocks combined with Double Diagonal Lines in the patchwork blocks, in sashings, in borders, as background filler, and as an allover quilting design disregarding the patchwork pattern or design.

Hanging Diamonds (Figure 4-14)

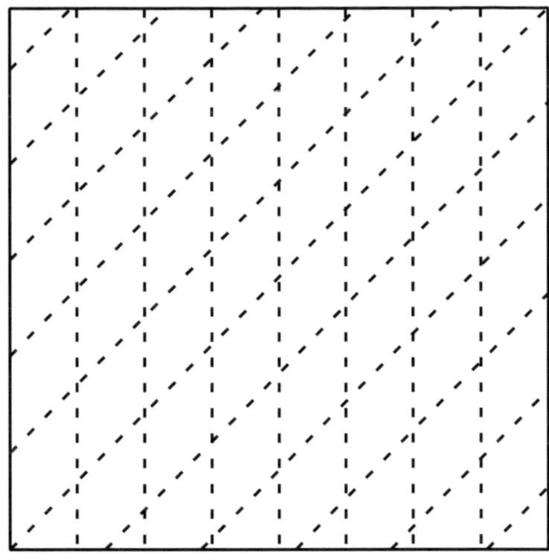

Figure 4-14.

Recommended Marking: Mark on the quilt top as you go.

How to Mark or Draw: Hanging Diamond is a quilting design that dates from around 1850. It is formed first by marking lines that run with the straight grain of the block or straight on the quilt and can be either vertical or horizontal. The crossing lines are marked on the diagonal or bias of the fabric. For this example, the straight line marking will be vertical (Figure 4-15). The space between the vertical parallel lines can be from 1" to 2".

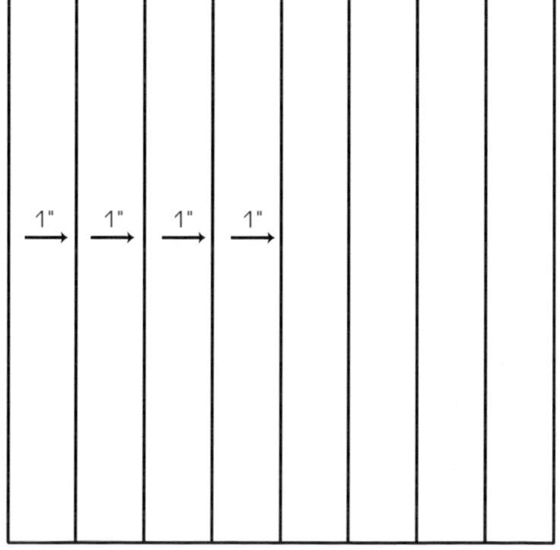

Figure 4-15.

After marking the straight vertical lines, place a ruler with a 45° mark so that the 45° marking is lined up on a straight line. That straight line can be the block or quilt edge or one of the vertical lines that were just drawn. Mark a diagonal line that crosses the vertical lines (Figure 4-16). Continue marking parallel diagonal lines that are spaced the same as the vertical parallel lines (1" to 2") until the surface to be quilted has been filled. Several lines can be marked and quilted and then more lines marked and quilted.

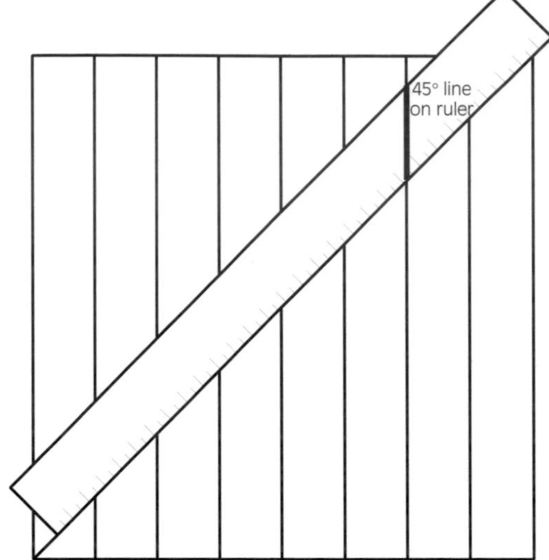

Figure 4-16.

Helpful Note: Hanging Diamonds is very easy to mark but not as easy to quilt as Diamond because of the lines that are marked on the straight grain of the fabric. It would work well for machine quilting.

Tools Needed: A long ruler with a 45° marking and a fabric marking pencil or pen.

Where to Use: This design can be used in plain blocks, as background filler, or over the whole quilt surface disregarding the patchwork pattern or design.

Double Hanging Diamond (Figure 4-17)

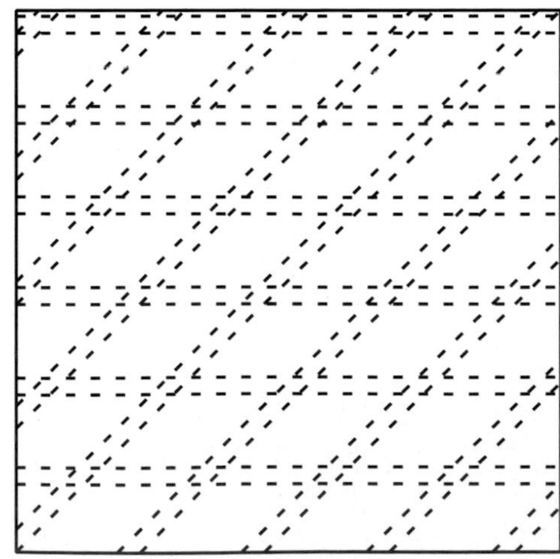

Figure 4-17.

Recommended Marking: Mark on the quilt top as you go.

How to Mark or Draw: Double Hanging Diamond is marked the same as Hanging Diamond (see page 55) except for the spacing between the quilting lines. The illustrations for marking the Double Hanging Diamond show the grid being marked with the straight lines on the horizontal of the block or quilt top.

Using a ruler along a straight line, either a block edge or the quilt edge, mark a straight line across the surface to be quilted. Next, move the ruler so that the next line to be marked will be spaced ¼" from the first line. Mark the second line. Now, move the ruler so that the next space will be from 1" to 2" and mark a third line. The fourth line will be spaced ¼" from this line (Figure 4-18).

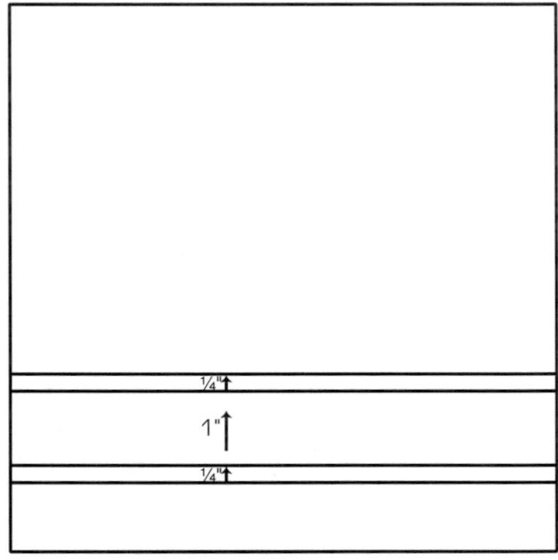

Figure 4-18.

The next step is to mark the diagonal lines to make the diamonds. With a long ruler lined up with the 45° marking along a straight line, mark the first line along the ruler edge. The spacing sequence for the diagonal parallel lines will be the same as for the horizontal or straight lines just marked. The spacing will be a line, ¼" space, a line, 1" to 2" space, a line, ¼" space, and a line (Figure 4-19). Continue marking in these sequences until the area to be covered is filled.

Helpful Note: This design is found on quilts dating around 1850. It is easy to mark and fairly easy to quilt. The Double Hanging Diamond looks better marked with the straight line vertically than horizontally (Figure 4-14). Horizontally, it looks more like Laying Diamond than Hanging Diamond.

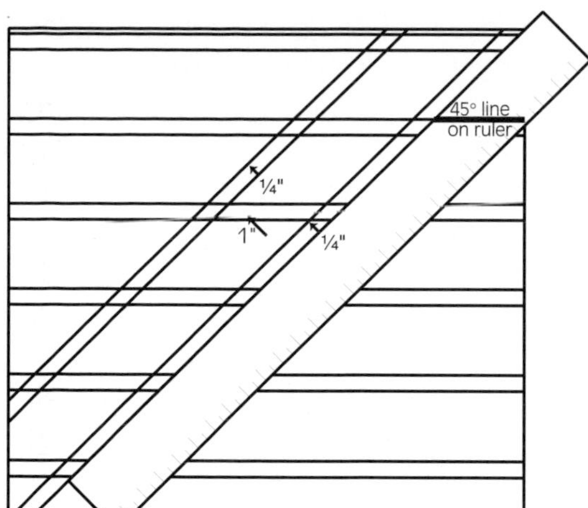

Figure 4-19.

TOOLS NEEDED: A long ruler with a 45° marking and a fabric marking pencil or pen.

WHERE TO USE: The Double Hanging Diamond design works well for an overall quilting design covering the whole quilt top and in blocks, both patchwork and plain setting blocks. It might be considered for a border design.

Triple Hanging Diamonds (Figure 4-20)

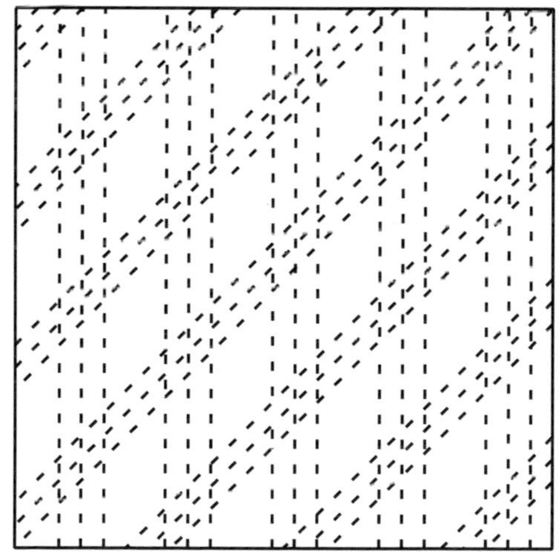
Figure 4-20.

RECOMMENDED MARKING: Mark on the quilt top as you go.

HOW TO MARK OR DRAW: Follow the directions for marking the Double Hanging Diamond design on page 56 except the straight lines will be marked vertically on the quilt top or block. The design can be marked either vertically or horizontally and by marking these two designs in different ways the two directions can be compared. The spacing for Triple Hanging Diamonds will be a line, ¼" space, a line, ¼" space, a line, space measuring from 1" to 2", a line, ¼" space, a line, ¼" space, a line. Use this sequence to mark both the vertical straight lines and the diagonal lines (Figure 4-21).

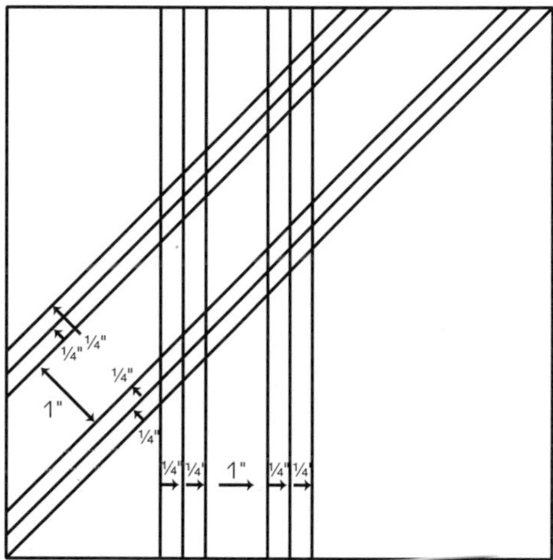

Figure 4-21.

HELPFUL NOTE: This design is about as old as the Double Hanging Diamond design. It is easy to mark and fairly easy to quilt. Be alert when marking that the spacing sequence stays the same. It is easy to miss a line in the triples and is messy to have to erase and correct.

TOOLS NEEDED: A long ruler with a 45° marking and a fabric marking pencil or pen.

WHERE TO USE: This design can be used in plain setting blocks, over patchwork blocks, or as an overall design that covers the entire quilt surface disregarding the surface design.

Diaper (Figure 4-22)

Figure 4-22.

RECOMMENDED MARKING: Mark on the quilt top using a template and long ruler as you go.

HOW TO MARK OR DRAW: This design surely got its name from the weave design in cloth diapers – back in the old days when cloth diapers were used.

The design is based on a 60° diamond or an equal-sided triangle. Make a template to use for a guide in marking the first lines. See page 26 in Chapter 2 and draw a large equal-sided triangle template. Place the template on the area to be marked and mark lines on two sides of the triangle by placing the ruler against the sides of the template (Figure 4-23). Continue by marking parallel lines spaced from 1" to 2" apart across the surface to be filled with the design (Figure 4-24).

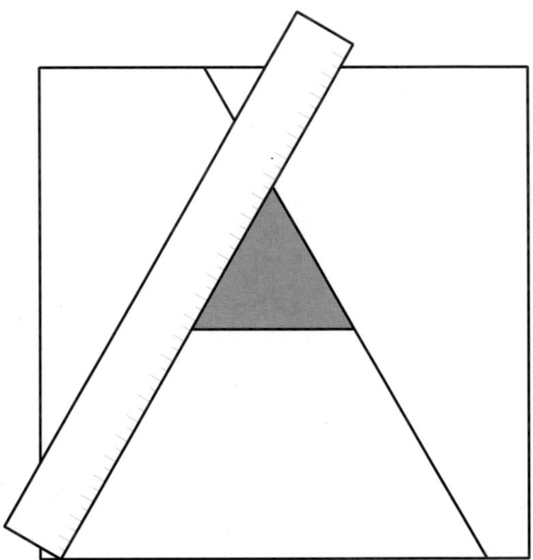

Figure 4-23.

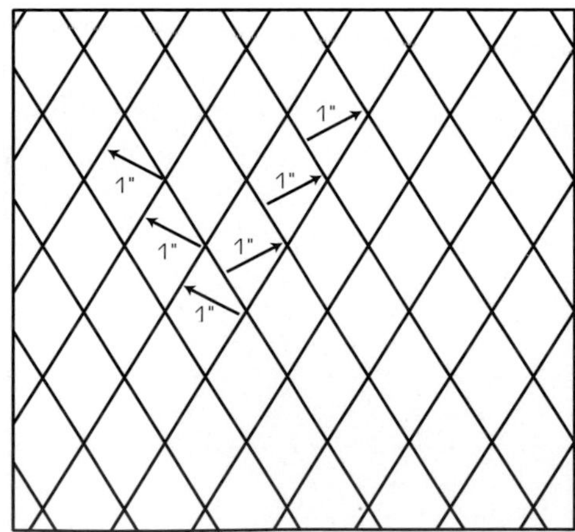

Figure 4-24.

After the lines for the diamond design have been marked, using a long ruler mark lines across the middle of the diamonds to form triangles (Figure 4-25).

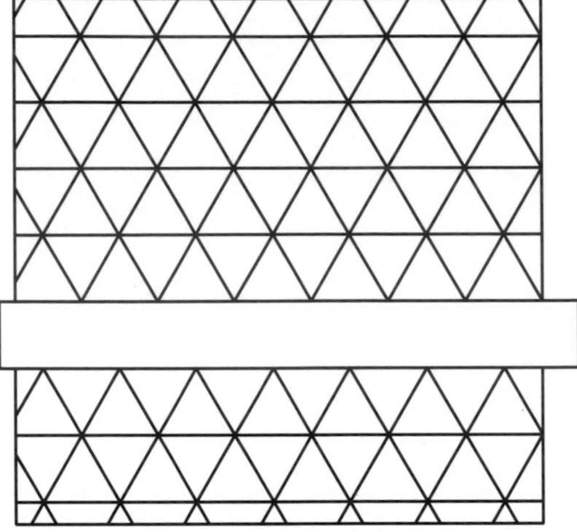

Figure 4-25.

HELPFUL NOTE: A purchased 60° diamond template or one of several rulers designed for marking 60° diamonds and triangles can also be used as a starting guide. Templates for the Baby Block pattern would also work for a starting guide. With a ruler and the template, check the alignment of the lines often, as you mark, to see that they are staying at 60°.

TOOLS NEEDED: A long ruler with 60° markings, template material, and a fabric marking pencil or pen.

WHERE TO USE: The Diaper design can be used as background filler, in plain setting block, over pieced blocks, or as an overall design that covers the entire quilt surface.

Concentric Diamonds (Figure 4-26)

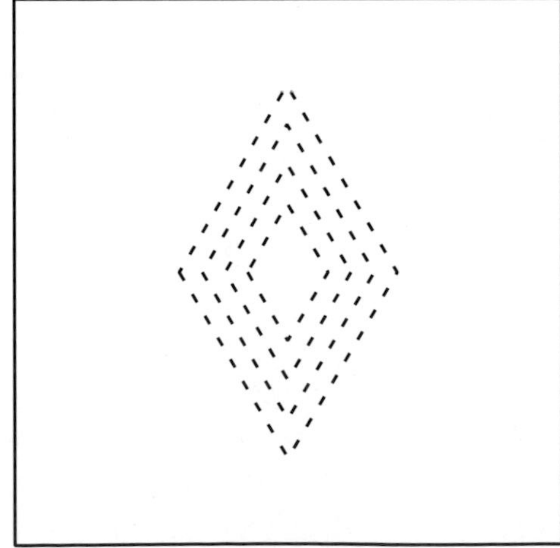

Figure 4-26.

RECOMMENDED MARKING: Use a diamond template and a ruler and mark as you go.

HOW TO MARK OR DRAW: A Concentric Diamond can be either a 45° diamond or a 60° diamond. For this illustration, a 60° diamond will be used. To make the template, draw a vertical line the length wanted for the diamond. Exactly across the middle of this line, draw a horizontal line. Using a ruler with a 60° marking, place the 60° mark along the horizontal line and the ruler edge touching the top of the vertical line. Draw a line from the top along the ruler edge to the center line (Figure 4-27). Draw lines on the other three sides to form the diamond template (Figure 4-28). Measure the inside horizontal center line and it should be the same as each of the four sides of the diamond. A 45° diamond template can be made in the same way by using the 45° marking on a ruler.

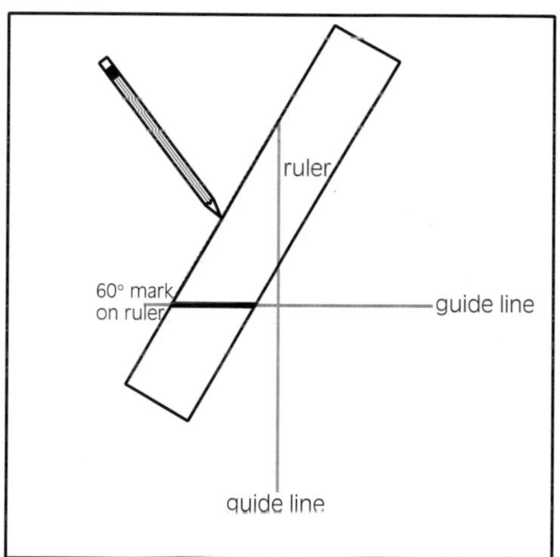

Figure 4-27.

To mark on the quilt top, place the diamond template on the quilt top where this design is wanted and mark around the template. With a ruler along the diamond markings, mark another diamond inside. The spacing between the lines should be determined by the size of the diamond. Mark the lines close together in a small diamond and more space in a larger diamond.

If this design is marked where the diamonds are end to end, mark a faint guide line to help in keeping the line of diamonds straight.

HELPFUL NOTE: Diamonds used in quilting designs do not have to be mathematically perfect as they do in piecing. To keep the diamonds inside the diamond marked so that the lines meet at the angles, it will help to mark a faint cross to use for a guide line (as used to make the template).

TOOLS NEEDED: A ruler with degree markings, template material, and a fabric marking pencil or pen.

WHERE TO USE: Concentric Diamonds can be used end to end for a border design. Figure 4-29 shows Concentric Diamonds with Diagonals and using this combination is a good way to fill an area to be quilted. The design can be used over the whole quilt surface by marking the diamonds diagonally across pieced blocks (example – Log Cabin blocks). It can be marked inside diamonds in pieced blocks such as in Eight-Pointed Stars. Use a Concentric Diamond in a plain block or the middle of the border and fill in with diagonal lines (Figure 4-29).

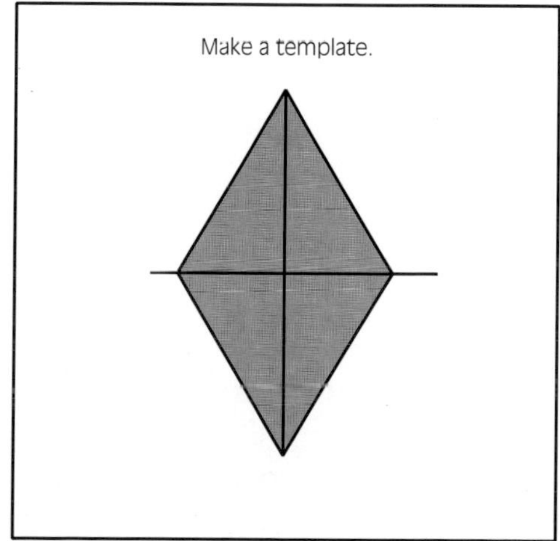

Figure 4-28.

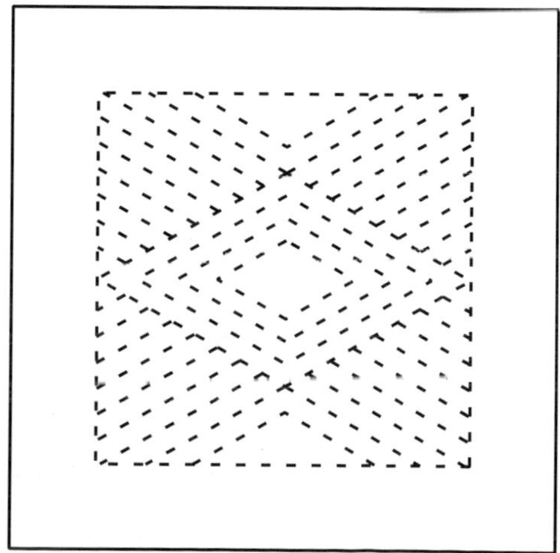

Figure 4-29.

Diamond Weave (Figure 4-30)

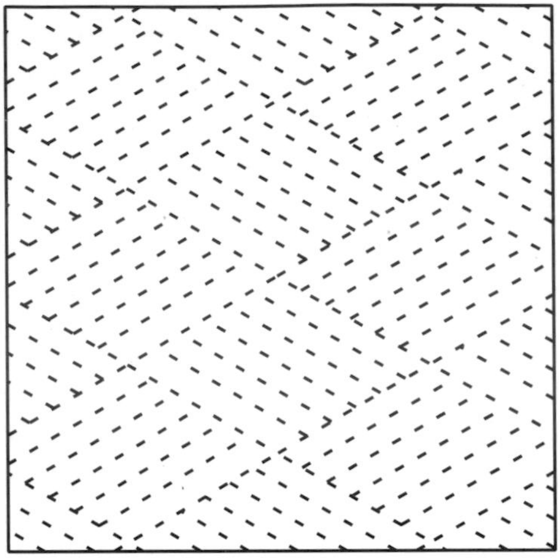
Figure 4-30.

RECOMMENDED MARKING: Mark with a ruler on the quilt top as you go.

HOW TO MARK OR DRAW: The Diamond Weave design looks best with the diamonds going end to end across the surface. To mark the first lines, use the ruler to mark faint guide lines that make a rectangle and mark quilting lines from corner to corner to form an X (Figure 4-31).

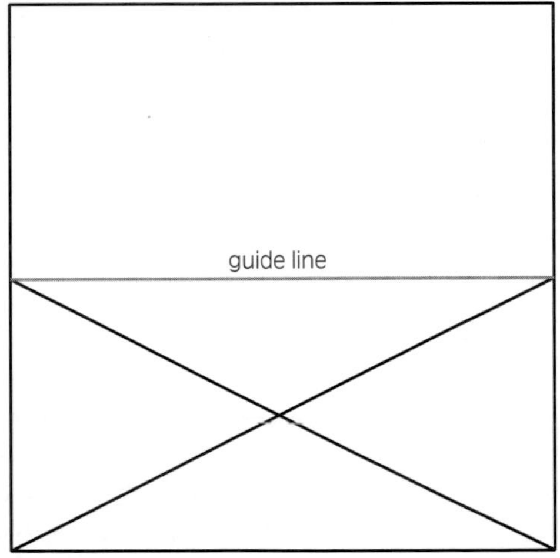

Figure 4-31.

Next, mark parallel lines from the X by moving the ruler so that the spacing between lines is 3" (Figure 4-32). The spacing can be more for larger diamonds but the 3" spacing makes a good design.

After the diamonds have been marked, mark lines inside the diamonds that are spaced either

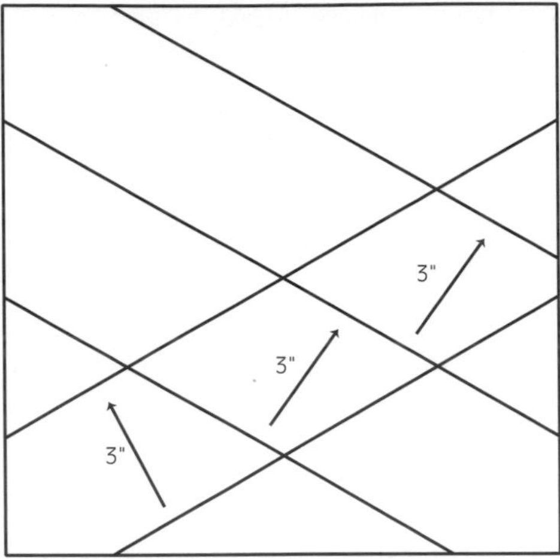

Figure 4-32.

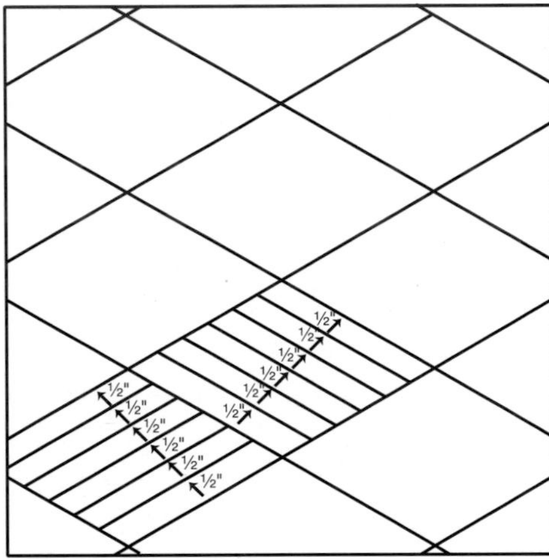

Figure 4-33.

½" or ¾" apart. Mark the lines in the diamonds by alternating the line direction in every other diamond (Figure 4-33). The illustration in Figure 4-33 was drawn with ½" spacing in the diamond.

The ¾" spacing will result in three lines inside the diamond instead of five.

HELPFUL NOTE: Be careful when marking the fill-in lines in the diamonds that the direction of the lines alternate from block to block. Erasing marked lines on fabric is messy. As with most quilting designs, practice on paper first before marking on the fabric helps.

TOOLS NEEDED: A long ruler and a fabric marking pencil or pen.

WHERE TO USE: Diamond Weave can be used as background filler, in plain setting blocks, and in borders.

Long Diamond (Figure 4-34)

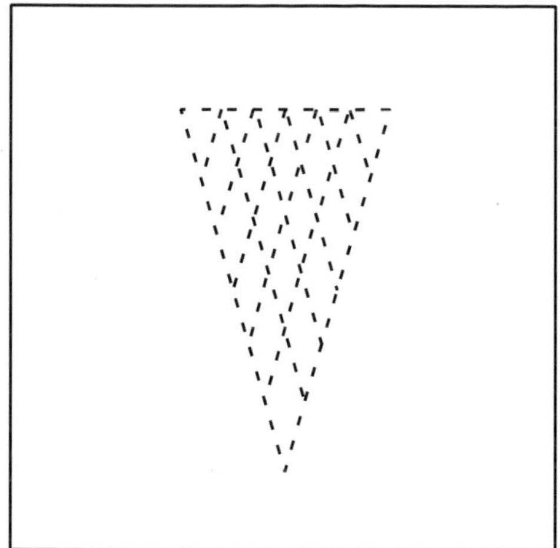

Figure 4-34.

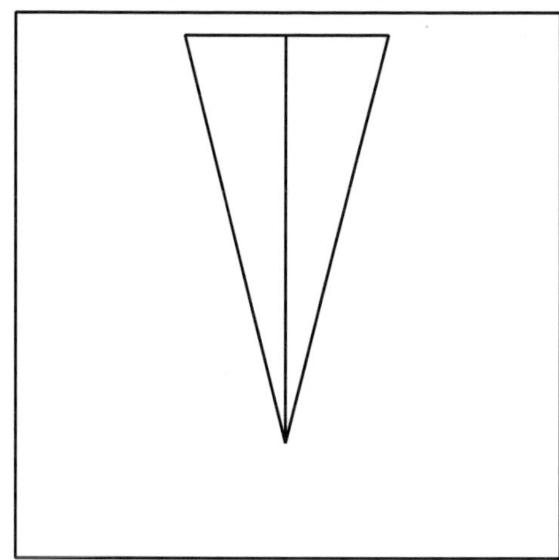

Figure 4-36.

Recommended Marking: Mark from a paper pattern on the quilt top before the quilt layers are assembled.

How to Mark or Draw: The size of the design found on traditional quilts is a width at the top of the design of 5" and the length on the Long Diamond of 9". This fits well in a 10" wide border. Before starting to draw the pattern, divide the border (not counting the corner square) by 5. If 5 does not divide into the length an equal number, see page 12 in Chapter 1 to determine how to make the design fit by paper folding.

Draw one Long Diamond on a sheet of paper to transfer to the paper pattern. At the top of the paper, draw a 5" long line across the paper. Next, draw a line starting from the exact center of this line (should be at the 2½" mark). Draw a line down the paper that measures 9" (Figure 4-35). This should make a large T. With a ruler, connect the ends of the top of the T with the base of the T to make a long triangle (Figure 4-36). Using a ruler, mark the outside lines of the triangle with a black felt tip pen.

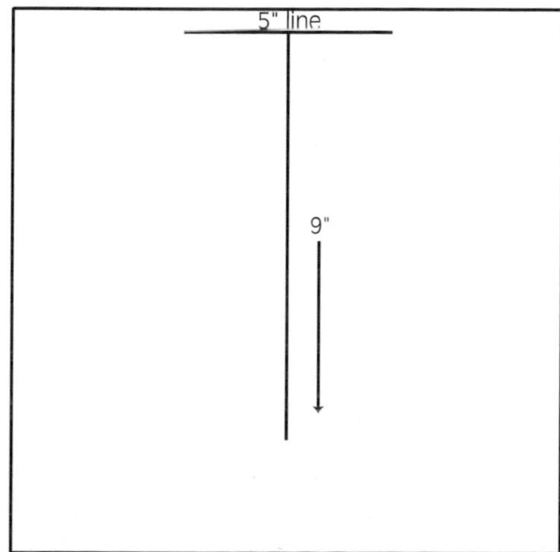

Figure 4-35.

Draw the pattern for transferring this design on a piece of paper that has been cut to fit the border. The paper should measure the width of the border and half the length of the border (minus the corners). Place the sheet of paper with the triangle that was just drawn under the paper pattern and, using a ruler and a black felt tip pen, trace triangles side by side until the pattern piece is filled (Figure 4-37). Inside the triangles, draw lines spaced ¾" apart parallel to the sides to fill the triangle with diamonds (Figure 4-38, page 62). These lines can be marked on the pattern or on the quilt top as you go.

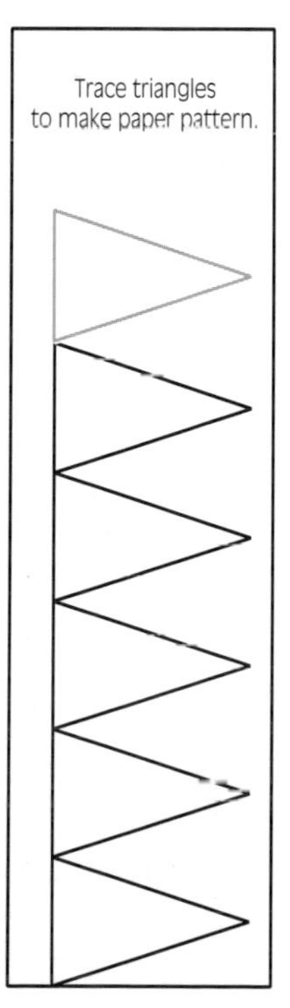

Figure 4-37.

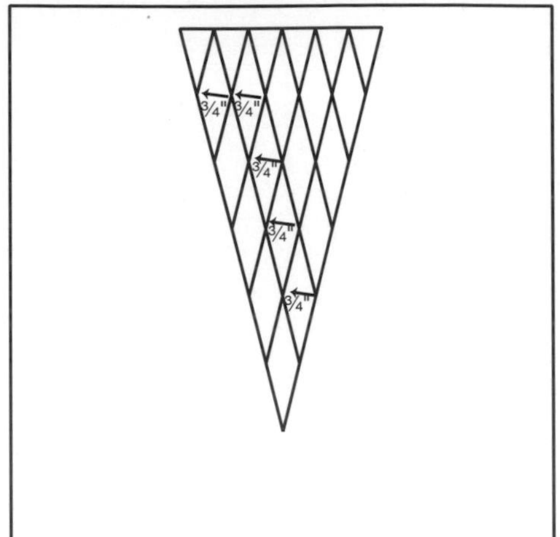

Figure 4-38.

Transfer the design to the quilt top by pinning the paper pattern face up to the back of the quilt top. Mark with a fabric marking pencil or pen.

Helpful Note: Long Diamond could probably be marked as you go but will be more accurate and easier to mark if done from a pattern before the quilt layers are assembled. Fill in the space between the long triangles with concentric triangles, scrolls, or another fancy design. A small Swag can be drawn at the top of the Long Diamond (Figure 4-39).

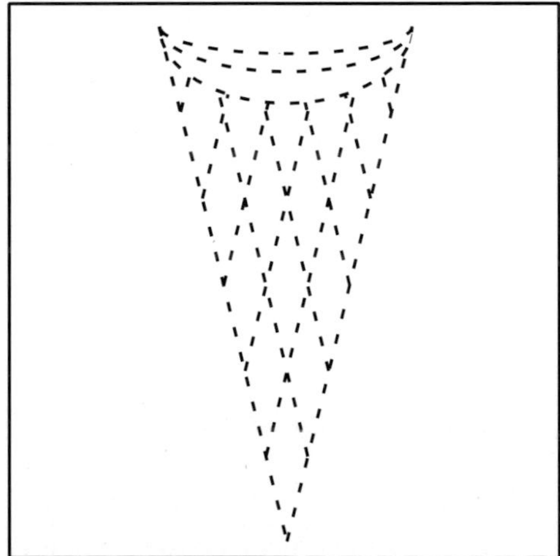

Figure 4-39.

Tools Needed: A ruler, pattern paper, black felt tip pen, and a fabric marking pencil or pen.

Where to Use: Long Diamond is a design for a wide border and can be marked with the sharp point to the center of the quilt or to the outside edge. It could also be used along the edge of a center medallion.

Running Diamond (Figure 4-40)

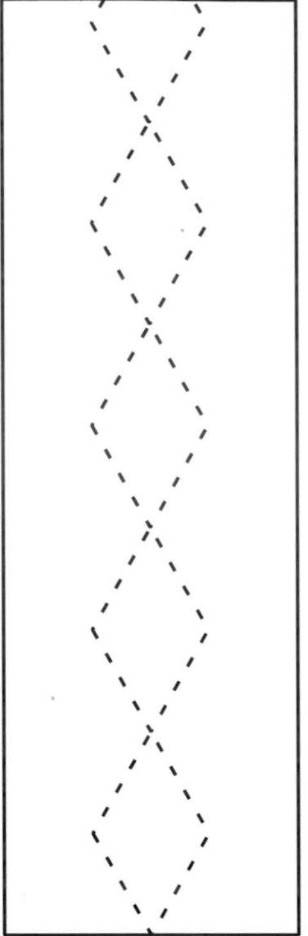

Figure 4-40.

Recommended Marking: Mark on the quilt top as you go using a diamond template.

How to Mark or Draw: This design dates from the early 1900's. To make the diamond template, determine the length on the diamond that is needed to fill the space to be quilted. Refer to the directions for making the design fit in Chapter 1 on page 12. For this example, the diamond will be 6" long. Draw a rectangle that is 6" long and half as wide (3" x 6"). Mark the center of all four sides of the rectangle and draw lines from center to center to form the diamond template (Figure 4-41).

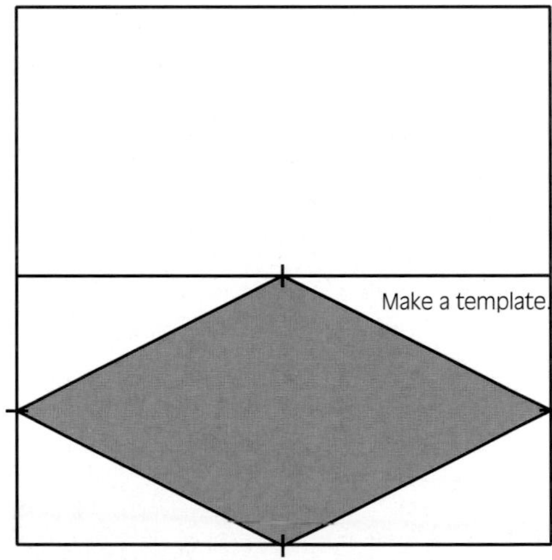

Figure 4-41.

To mark the quilt top, mark a faint guide line down the middle of the border or sashing where the Running Diamond will go. Line the diamond template up by placing the long ends of the diamond on the guide line. Mark around the template. Move the template with the diamond end touching the last drawn diamond and line it up again on the guide line and mark. Continue until the border is filled (Figure 4-42).

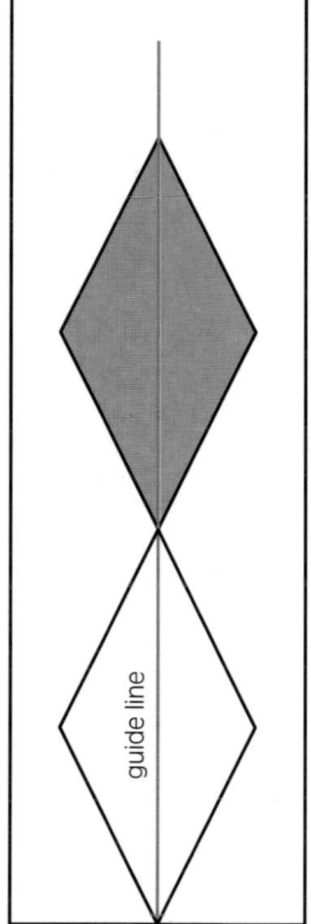

Figure 4-42.

Helpful Note: The width of the rectangle can be narrower or wider to make the diamonds fit the space better. Running Diamond is easy to mark and easy to quilt. Be sure that the ends of the diamonds touch each other so that the lines appear continuous. The 60° diamond can also be used to make this design. The diamonds can also be marked around a large circle or circular design such as the Mariner's Compass.

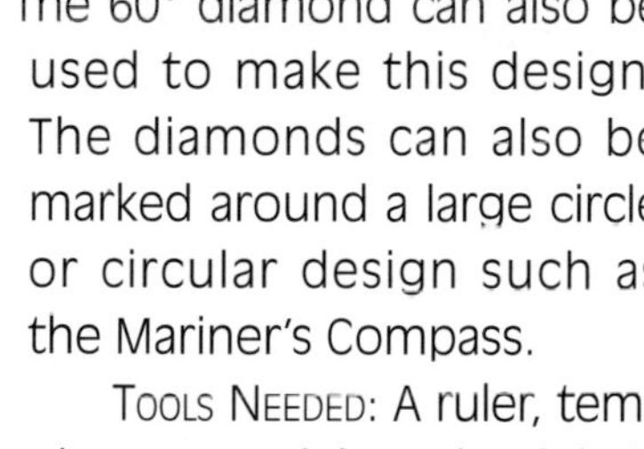

Tools Needed: A ruler, template material, and a fabric marking pencil or pen.

Where to Use: The Running Diamond design can be used in borders and in sashings.

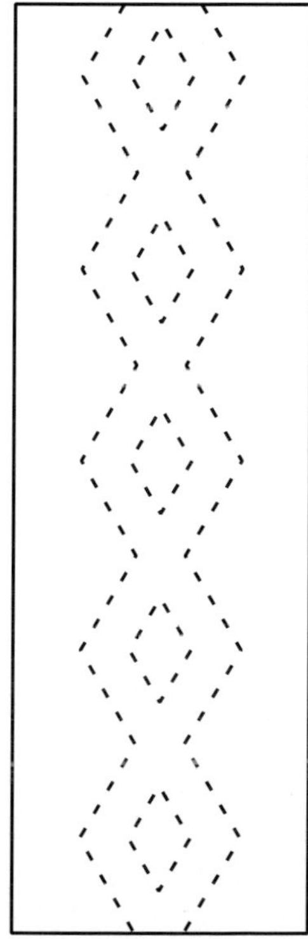

Figure 4-43.

Running Double Diamond

(Figure 4-43)

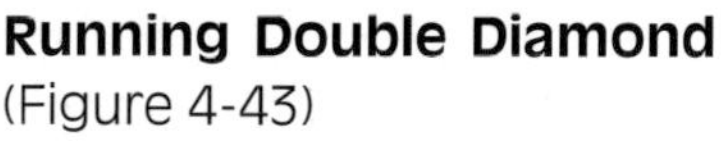

Recommended Marking: Mark using a template on the quilt top as you go.

How to Mark or Draw: Make a template by first drawing a string of at least five diamonds using the instructions for the Running Diamond on page 62. With a ruler mark a new outside line that is spaced ½" from the top and from the bottom of the Running Diamond (Figure 4-44). Next, mark a diamond inside the diamonds that is also spaced in ½" (Figure 4-45).

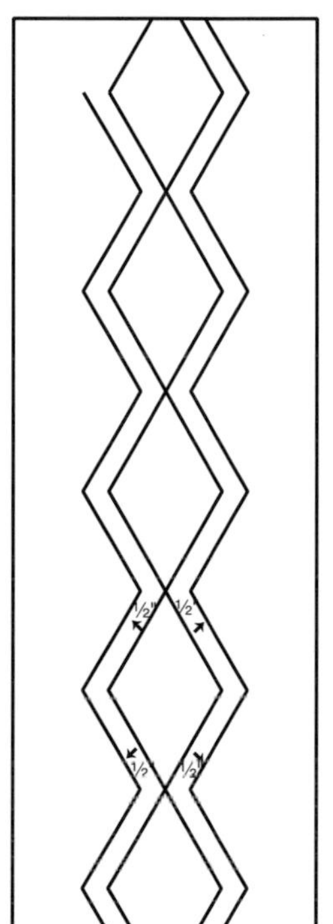

Figure 4-44.

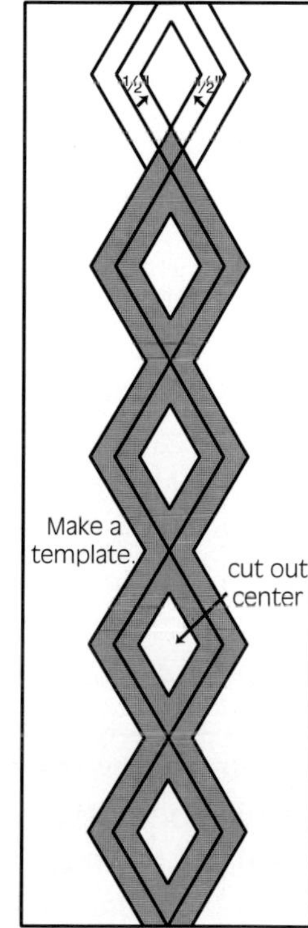

Figure 4-45.

The template is made by cutting out along the outside lines and the lines of the inside diamond.

To mark the quilt, mark a faint guide line along the center of the border or sashing and line the inside diamonds up along this line. Mark around the outside of the template and around the inside diamonds.

Helpful Note: This design is easy to mark and easy to quilt and looks much more complicated than it is. Be sure to use a guide line to keep the design straight.

Where to Use: This design can be used in sashings and in borders that are wider than one where the Running Diamond would be used.

Standing Diamonds (Figure 4-46)

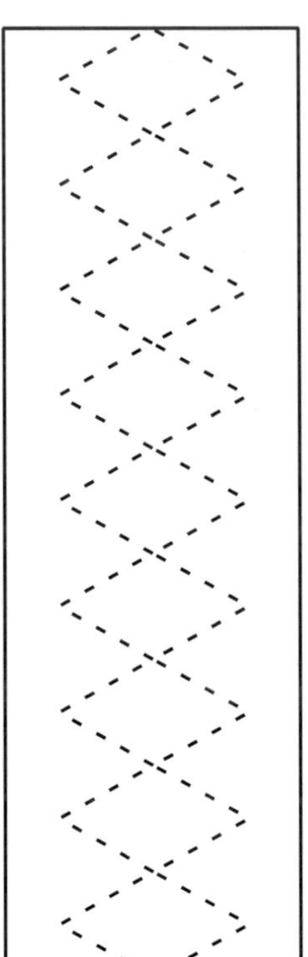

Figure 4-46.

Recommended Marking: Mark on the quilt top as you go using a diamond template.

How to Mark or Draw: To make a template for the Standing Diamonds, follow the same instructions for drawing the diamond as described for the Running Diamond on page 62. Read on page 12, Chapter 1, to determine how to make the design fit. Measure across the middle of the diamond for the space it will take.

For this design, the template will be used with the length of the diamond being placed vertically and the wide part of the diamond placed side to side.

Mark a faint guide line along the center of the border or sashing for placement of the template and for marking. Mark around the template for each diamond (Figure 4-47).

Helpful Note: The rectangle that is used to make the diamond template can be made longer and/or wider so that the diamonds exactly fit the space. This is an easy design to both mark and to quilt.

Tools Needed: A long ruler, template material, and a fabric marking pencil or pen.

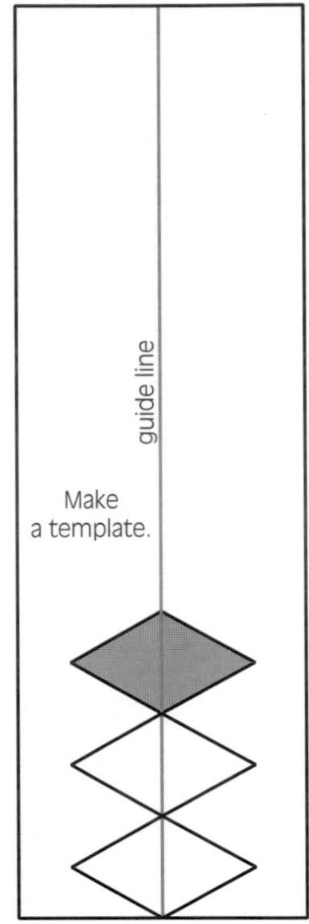

Figure 4-47.

Where to Use: This design, from around 1920, can be used in sashings. It will also work as a border design and, for both, would work well when the pieced blocks also contain diamonds.

Interlaced Diamonds: also; Interlocking Diamonds, Diamond Chain (Figure 4-48)

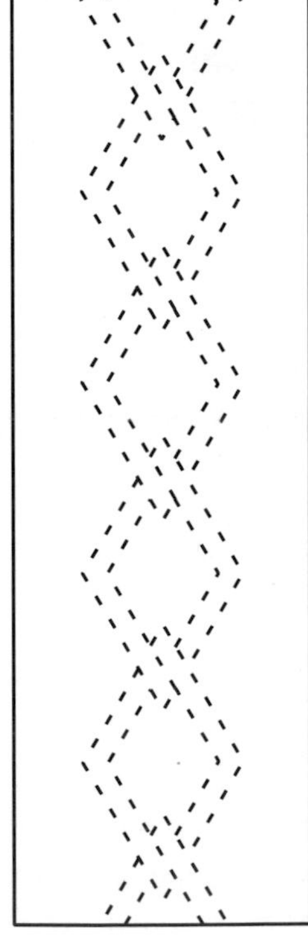

Figure 4-48.

Recommended Marking: Using a paper pattern, mark on the quilt top before the quilt layers are assembled.

How to Mark or Draw: Make a paper pattern by drawing a diamond on a piece of paper using the instructions for the Running Diamond on page 62. On a piece of paper, draw a string of four diamonds and with a ruler draw lines spaced ½" (or wider) around the outside of the diamonds (Figure 4-49).

The next step is tricky. Erase lines that cross

Figure 4-49.

where the diamonds overlap. Erase in the upper left and the lower right ends of each diamond (Figure 4-50). The top of the second diamond goes over the first diamond and the end of the first diamond goes under the top of the second diamond.

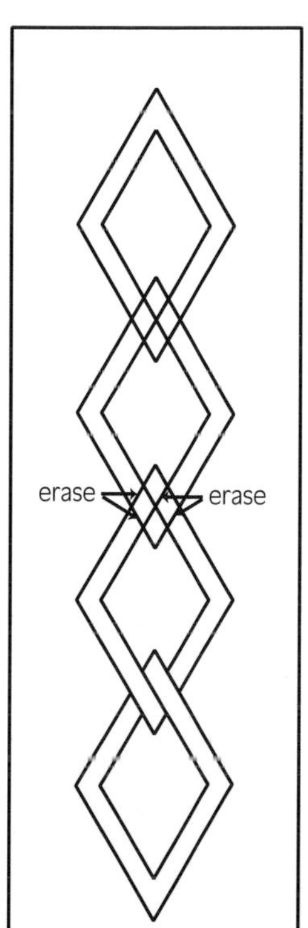

Figure 4-50.

Use this drawing to make a paper pattern to fit the border of the quilt. Place the string of diamonds drawing under the paper pattern piece that has been cut to fit the border. Draw the diamonds that have the interlace and then use the diamonds with plain ends to overlap as you move the drawing to continue filling the space of the whole border. Go over all the drawn lines with a black felt tip marker to make the lines easy to see through the fabric of the quilt top.

To mark the quilt top, pin the paper pattern with the pattern up and to the wrong side of the top and mark all the lines.

Helpful Note: Interlaced Diamonds can be drawn using a 60° diamond and this will make the design wider and appear fatter. This design is easy to quilt once the marking on the quilt top has been accomplished.

Tools Needed: A ruler, pattern paper, black felt tip pen, and a fabric marking pencil or pen.

Where to Use: Interlaced Diamonds is to be used as a border design.

Pyramidal Pattern (Figure 4-51)

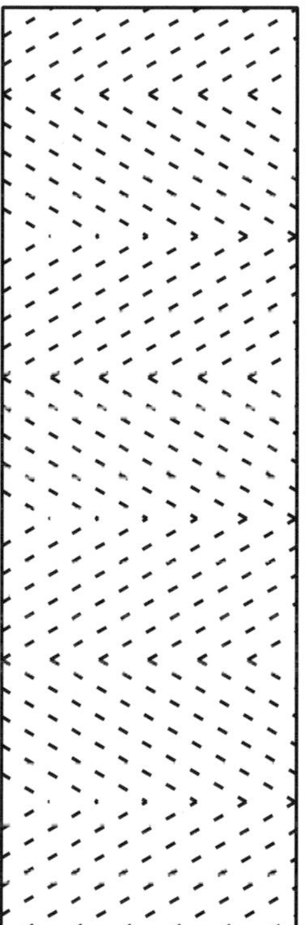
Figure 4-51.

Recommended Marking: Mark with a template and a ruler on the quilt top as you go.

How to Mark or Draw: Make a template by drawing a rectangle that is as long as the width of the border and will fit evenly into the length of the border. Follow the instructions on page 12, Chapter 1, on how to make a design fit. Mark the center of the short side of the rectangle and draw lines from the opposite corners to this center mark (Figure 4-52).

To mark the quilt top, place the wide part of the half-diamond template along the border seam, mark around the long

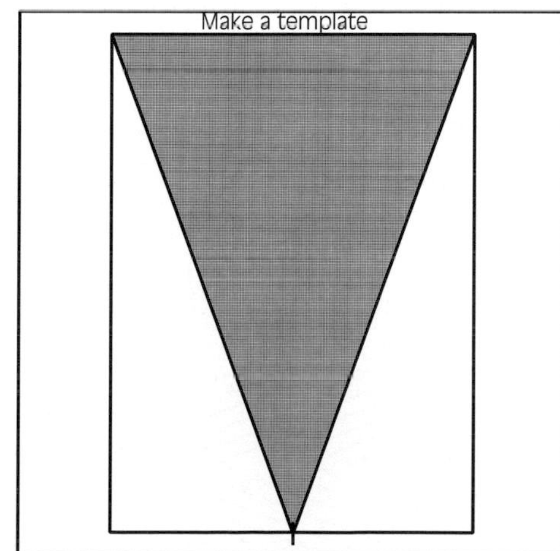

Figure 4-52.

points, move the template and continuing marking until the border area is filled with half-diamonds (Figure 4-53).

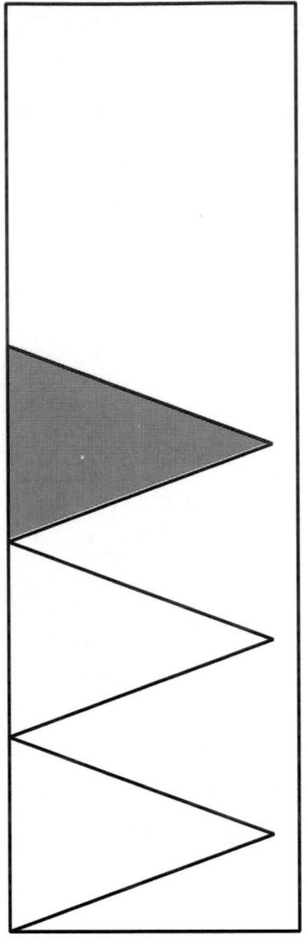

Figure 4-53.

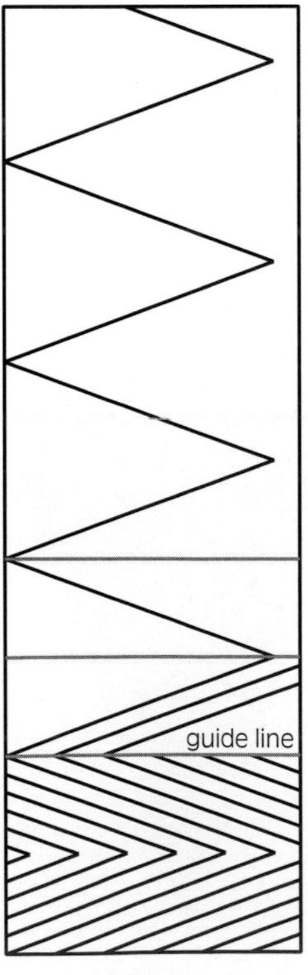

Figure 4-54.

To mark the fill-in lines, mark a faint guide line in the center of each half-diamond shape. Use a ruler to mark parallel lines that meet at the guide line (Figure 4-54). These lines can be marked and quilted one half-diamond at a time.

Helpful Note: Quilting the lines that were marked around the template first before marking the fill-in lines will keep the layers from shifting.

Be careful that the fill-in lines meet precisely at the guide line.

Tools Needed: A ruler, template material, and a fabric marking pencil or pen.

Where to Use: Pyramidal Pattern was found on a quilt dated 1840 and covered a three strip wide border and can be used on any quilt border.

Double Chevron: also Chevron, Herringbone (Figure 4-55)

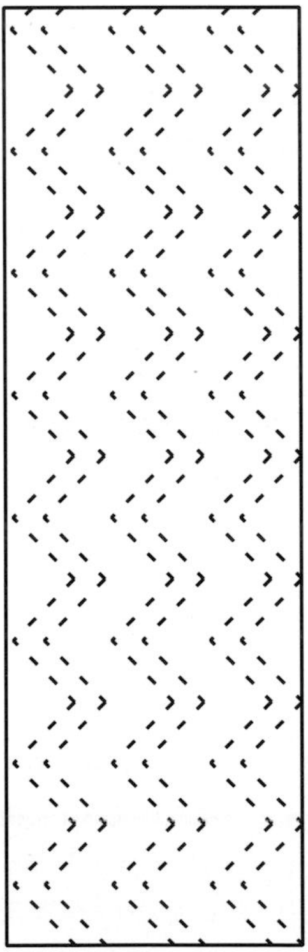

Figure 4-55.

Recommended Marking: Using a template, mark on the quilt top as you go.

How to Mark or Draw: Make a template by following the instructions for making a template for the Herringbone design on page 46.

Since there is space between the double chevron, to mark this design mark faint guide lines along the length that are evenly spaced. For this example, the border width was divided into thirds. The template will be placed with the points on the guide line or straight on the border. Mark both sides of the template, move and mark until the border is filled. The second row will be marked by placing the template on the next guideline and marking (Figure 4-56). Mark the third row.

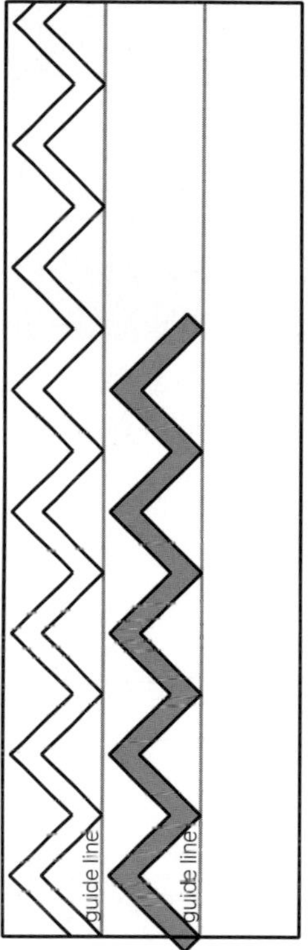

Figure 4-56.

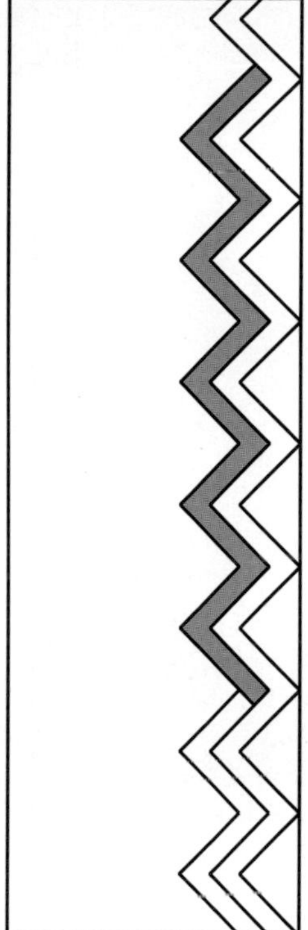
Figure 4-57.

Spacing can be done by lining the top of the template up with the bottom of the row above or by a guide line if more spacing is needed in the border.

Helpful Note: The design can also be drawn by placing the template next to an already drawn row which will give a pattern with no spacing (Figure 4-57) and is called just Chevron when marked this way. These are easy-to-mark and easy-to-quilt designs.

Tools Needed: A ruler, template material, and a fabric marking pencil or pen.

Where to Use: Double Chevron and Chevron can be used in borders, in plain setting blocks, or as an overall design disregarding the patchwork pattern or quilt design.

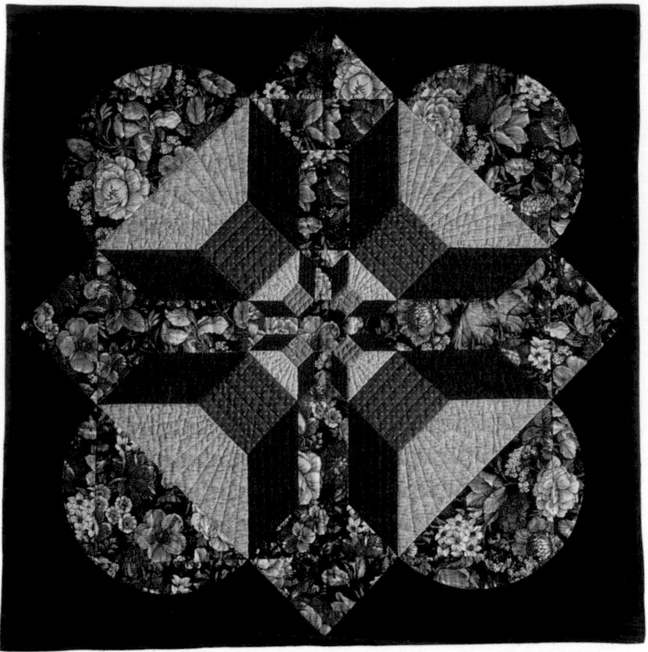

Plate 5-1. Radiating Lines (also Single Parallel Lines).
Prosperity by Starr C. Kaiser, 1991.

Plate 5-2. Echo (also Feathered Vine).
Love the Feel of Cotton by Mary Andra Holmes.

Plate 5-3. Concentric Design Lines (also Concentric Squares, Echo, By the Piece).
The Tangrams Step Out by Jenny Perry, 1994.

Plate 5-4. By the Piece (also Squares Crosshatch).
Amish Lilies by Lorraine Dickhaus.

Chapter Five
From the Quilt Pattern

The designs for quilting that have been included in this chapter are quilting lines that originate from the pieced or appliquéd design in the quilt or from another pattern for piecing or appliqué. Currently, the most used of these designs is probably By the Piece. This method of quilting seems to have been become popular after 1900. In the 1930's, it was popular on Flower Garden quilts.

A popular and effective design that has been found on quilts dating from the 1840's is Echo quilting. The quilting lines follow the pattern shapes to emphasize the pattern design and to fill in space. It is often associated with Hawaiian designs.

Stippling also dates from the 1840's and is gaining new popularity because the close quilting stitches of stippling are a good method of highlighting a design that requires the attention of the viewer.

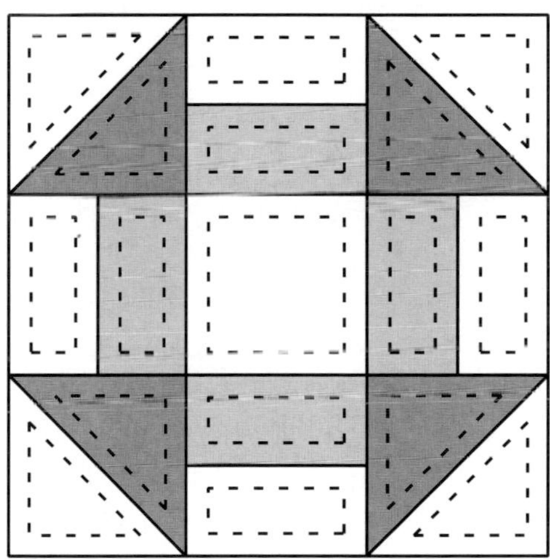

Figure 5-1.

By the Piece: also Outline Quilting, Outline the Piece, Self Quilting, Relief Quilting (Figure 5-1)

Recommended Marking: Mark each piece of a block or each piece as you go.

How to Mark or Draw: By the Piece is defined as quilting lines that are spaced ¼" from the seams of the pieces in a patchwork block. Quilting By the Piece is from as early as 1830 to the present. In the past, it was not used as much as it has been since the 1980's.

To mark the pieces in a block, use a ruler with ¼" marking, ¼" wide masking tape, or ¼" marker. Mark lightly with a pencil or chalk. Quilting can then be done piece by piece.

Helpful Note: Practiced quilters can quilt By the Piece by eye without marking which makes the quilting go faster. Quilting by this method has been popular because of the notion that it was easier to quilt if the quilting stitches did not cross the seam allowances of the pieced blocks. This is not necessarily true. Quilting By the Piece often involves more quilting than some other options.

Tools Needed: A ¼" marking device or masking tape and a fabric marking pencil or pen.

Where to Use: Use this design to quilt pieced blocks where emphasizing the pattern of the patchwork will enhance the quilt. Hexagon patterns such as Grandmother's Flower Garden are often quilted by the piece.

Figure 5-2.

Outline Quilting (Figure 5-2)

Recommended Marking: No marking required.

How to Mark or Draw: Outline Quilting

is quilting very close to the edge of the pieces in an appliquéd block. The quilting is done around the outside edge of the appliqué design. Quilting lines inside the appliqué piece, such as stems and vines in leaves, are considered detail quilting. These details should be marked with a fabric marking pencil or pen.

Helpful Note: Outline Quilting can be done around the pieces that are layered on top of other appliqué pieces. This enhances the look of the appliqué and gives it an almost stuffed appearance. The quilting lines around the appliqué pieces also make a stopping place for the background quilting design.

Tools Needed: No tools are needed as Outline Quilting is done by eye. Use a fabric marking pencil or pen to mark details inside the appliqué piece.

Where to Use: Use on all appliqué designs where an overall quilting design has not been used.

In the Ditch: also Ditch Quilting (Figure 5-3)

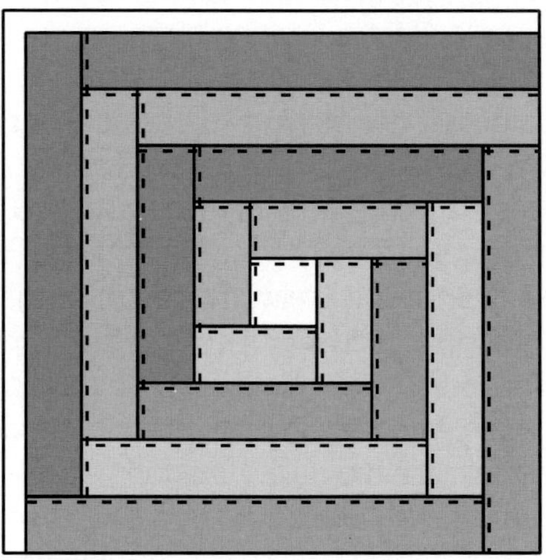

Figure 5-3.

Recommended Marking: No marking required.

How to Mark or Draw: The stitching for quilting In the Ditch is done very close to the seams of the pieces in the block. The stitching is easiest done on the piece away from the seam allowance.

Helpful Note: This is not one of the easier designs to quilt and can be boring.

Tools Needed: No tools needed.

Where to Use: In the Ditch Quilting is often used in Log Cabin blocks. It can be used when the design of the pieced block would show off better without quilting stitches interrupting the design. Mariner's Compass is a good example of a pattern where In the Ditch Quilting would be desirable. Use where it is preferrable not to have the quilting stitches make a secondary design.

Echo: also Concentric Ridges, Contour Quilting, Following Top Design, Freehand (Figure 5-4)

Figure 5-4.

Recommended Marking: Mark on the quilt top as you go.

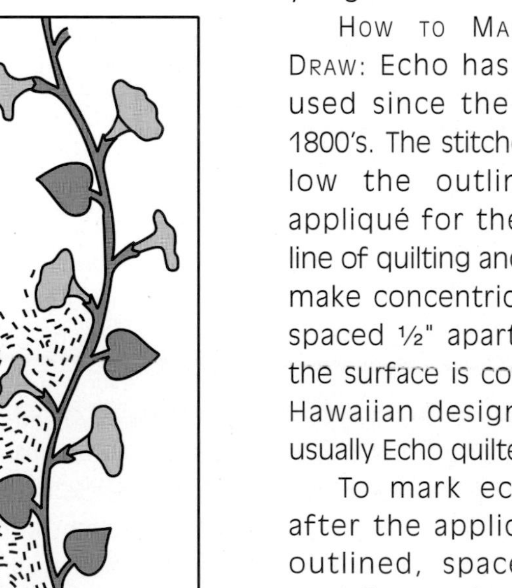

Figure 5-5.

How to Mark or Draw: Echo has been used since the early 1800's. The stitches follow the outline of appliqué for the first line of quilting and then make concentric rows spaced ½" apart until the surface is covered. Hawaiian designs are usually Echo quilted.

To mark echoes, after the appliqué is outlined, space the next line ½" from the outline stitches. A small ruler or seam gauge is good for marking.

The border for Morning Glory, a Mountain Mist pattern, shows Echo lines and how they look wiggly or wavy as they move out from the appliqué (Figure 5-5).

Helpful Note: Marks can be made at intervals of 1" or 2" with a seam gauge or ruler and quilted with out complete marking. Once marked, Echo lines are easy to quilt.

Tools Needed: A small ruler or seam gauge and a fabric marking pencil or pen.

Where to Use: Use as background filler with appliqué, especially in appliquéd borders. Use with Hawaiian designs. It can be used to echo pieces in pieced blocks such as Melon Patch and to follow the lines of a design in fabric.

Concentric Design Lines (Figure 5-6)

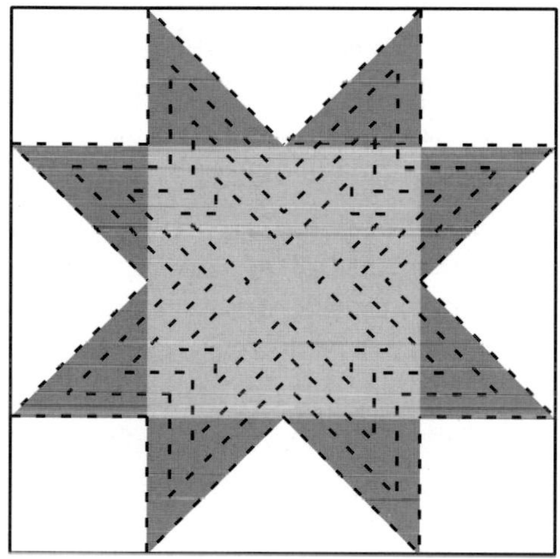

Figure 5-6.

Recommended Marking: Mark the design in each pieced block as you go.

How to Mark or Draw: This could also be considered as Echo Quilting since the quilting lines follow the patchwork pattern. Start by Outline Quilting in the ditch around the outside of the design (Sawtooth Star in this example). Using a ruler or masking tape, space the next lines to the inside of the design. The spacing should be from ¼" for a small (6") block up to ¾" for larger blocks. Four quilting lines including the Outline stitching should be sufficient to emphasize the design.

Helpful Note: Draw the pieced design on paper. Place tracing paper over this drawing and mark the lines that will be quilted to see how it will look and to get the feel for marking. The concentric design line quilting works best for large blocks.

Tools Needed: A ruler and a fabric marking pencil or pen or masking tape.

Where to Use: Use in any pieced block where the concentric lines will give new dimension to the design.

Radiating Lines: also Rays of Quilting (Figure 5-7)

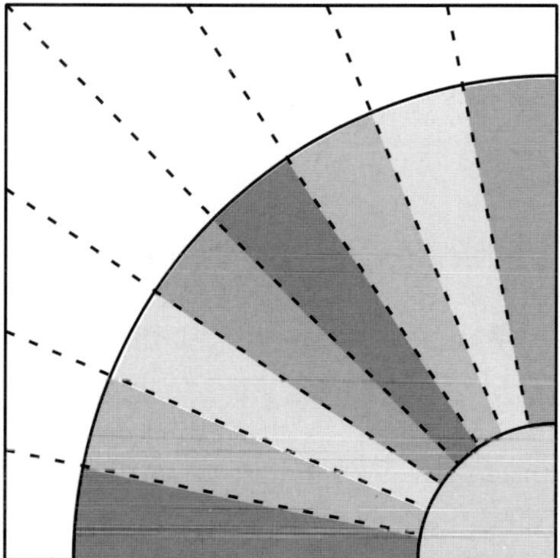

Figure 5-7.

Recommended Marking: Mark the design in each pieced block as you go.

How to Mark or Draw: The Radiating Lines shown here are used on a Fan block and for this pieced block, quilt In the Ditch along the pieces of the fan and extend the quilting lines out to the edges of the block. Use a ruler to mark the lines that extend across the background of the pieced block. Use the edge of the fan pieces as a guide.

Helpful Note: Masking tape could also be used for a guide therefore eliminating markings in the block's background.

Tools Needed: Masking tape or a ruler and a fabric marking pencil or pen.

Where to Use: Radiating Lines can be used in any patchwork design like the Fan that has a circular design. The lines can also radiate from a corner of either a block or a medallion and from a chosen point in an abstract design. Radiating Lines are often used in landscapes to indicate the rays of light from the sun or moon.

X's (Figure 5-8)

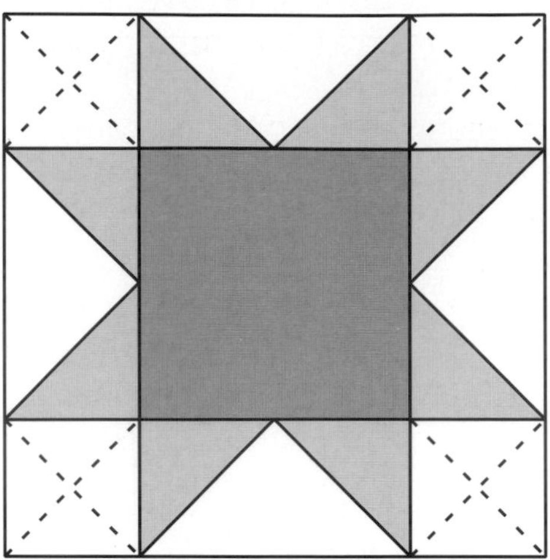

Figure 5-8.

Recommended Marking: Mark in the block as you go.

How to Mark or Draw: This is a very simple technique of marking from corner to corner in a piece of a patchwork block. Mark with a ruler diagonally from one upper corner to the opposite lower corner and another diagonal line from the other upper corner to the other lower corner. The quilting lines will form the X.

Helpful Note: The X can be quilted by eye on small squares or rectangles.

Use masking tape for a guide to eliminate marking lines.

Tools Needed: Masking tape or a ruler and a fabric marking pencil or pen.

Where to Use: Use X's in the squares, rectangles, or diamonds of a pieced block or in the connecting corner squares in sashings.

Stippling: also Meandering, Bunched, Pressed Quilting, Ripple, Vermicelli (Figure 5-9)

Figure 5-9.

Recommended Marking: No marking required.

How to Mark or Draw: Stippling is quilting lines that fill an area and are spaced approximately 1/16" apart. The lines of stitching are so close that it seems the quilting stitches almost touch each other. The quilting lines echo from a quilted design and are quilted by hand.

When close quilting is done by machine, it is referred to as meandering and is done free motion. The lines are usually wiggly, squiggly lines that do not cross.

Stippling around a design such as initials (Figure 5-9) or a pineapple or a feather gives the design much more prominence. It is definitely worth the time that it takes. Stippling has been found on quilts since the 1840's.

Quilt the main design first. By eye, quilt lines approximately 1/16" away from the outside line of the quilting of the main design. Keep quilting in echoes or waves, always spaced 1/16" or less, until the area to be stippled is filled with stitching.

Helpful Note: The area of Stippling should not be too large. It is time consuming and therefore best used as filler for a small area to emphasize a design.

Tools Needed: Only a needle, thimble, quilting thread, and plenty of time.

Where to Use: Stippling can be used as filler around another quilting design to highlight that design. It can be used in plain setting blocks, in a center medallion and on whole cloth quilts. A large piece in a patchwork block could have Stippling as filler for another quilting design in the piece.

From a Traditional Pieced or Appliqué Pattern

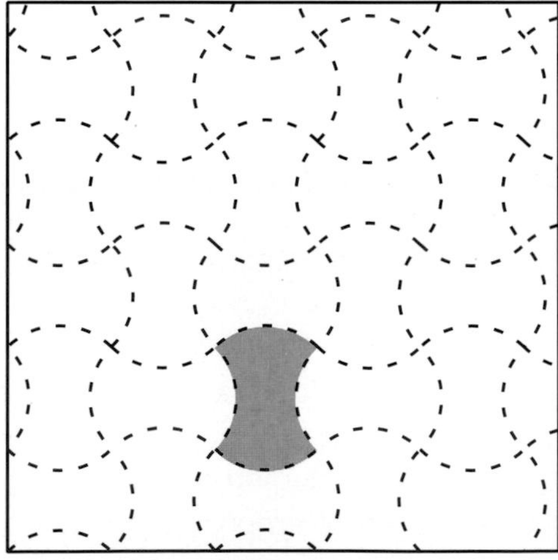

Figure 5-10.

Recommended Marking: The method of marking must be decided by the complexity of the pieced or appliqué pattern being used for a quilting design.

How to Mark or Draw: Most designs are easier marked using a paper pattern but the simpler designs can be marked using either a template or a ruler.

For a One-Patch Pieced design, use a template of the pattern piece and mark the quilt top as you go. The Spool pattern is a good example (Figure 5-10). The template needed is shown.

Marking for a simple traditional pieced pattern, such as a simple Nine-Patch Maple Leaf, can be done using a ruler and marking on the quilt top as you go. Mark the quilting lines by marking the seam lines that would be marked if you were drafting the pattern for piecing (Figure 5-11).

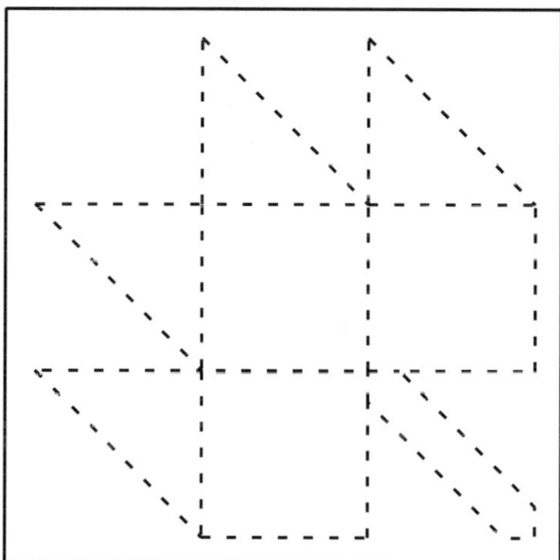

Figure 5-11.

When using a complicated pieced pattern such as the Mariner's Compass, draw the pattern on paper first (Figure 5-12). Darken the lines to be quilted with a black felt tip pen. Pin the pattern to the back of the quilt top and trace the pattern onto the fabric before assembling the quilt layers.

When using an appliqué pattern, make a paper pattern to use to mark the quilt top. Mark the quilt top by tracing the design from the paper pattern onto the quilt top before assembling the layers (Figure 5-13).

Tools Needed: The tools needed will have to be decided by whatever traditional pattern design has been chosen to be used as a design for quilting.

Where to Use: The One-Patch design can be used as an overall design disregarding the patchwork design. For example, use the Spool design on a Log Cabin quilt. Designs from pieced or appliqué patterns can be used in plain setting blocks to complement the other block pattern. For example, use the Mariner's Compass with a pieced pattern such as a Ship or with appliqué. A design from an appliqué pattern can duplicate the appliquéd block or be from another appliqué pattern that will complement a pieced block. The ways to use designs inspired from traditional patterns are endless.

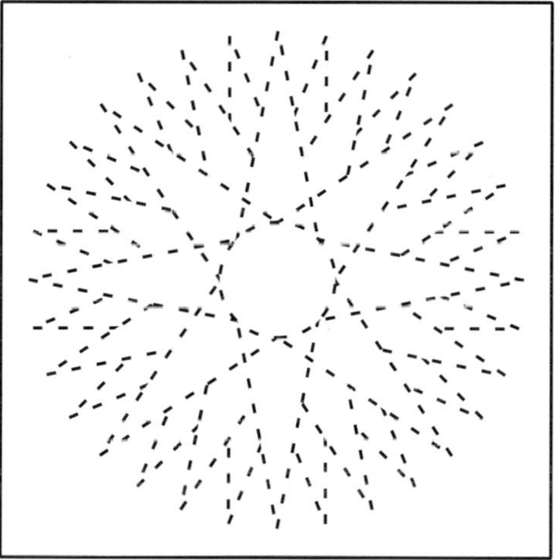

Figure 5-12.

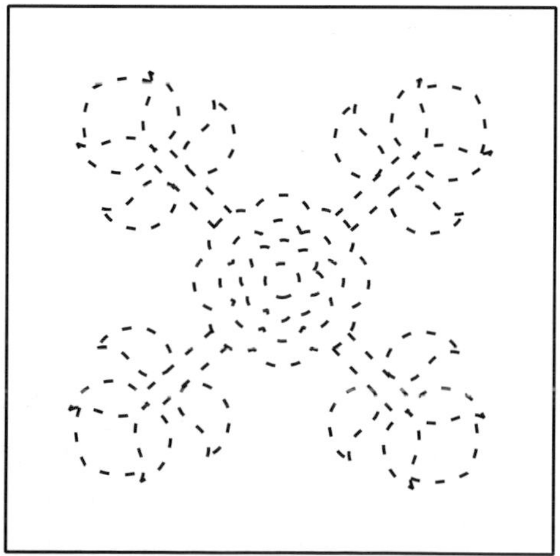

Figure 5-13.

Chapter Six
Circles

The largest number of designs for quilting are derived from circles or parts of a circle. The circle probably became a popular designing tool because quilters had many round objects from thimbles to cups and plates at their disposal to use in drawing and marking these designs. Most of the circular designs are also easy to quilt once they are marked.

The Clamshell has been used the longest of the circle designs. Single Line and Double Line Clamshells have been found on quilts dating from the early 1800's. It is obviously popular because it is easy to mark and easy to quilt.

One of the most familiar and also often used designs is the Fan. It is also an easy-to-mark design and was often used for quilts that were quilted by a group or at a quilting bee. This design was not found until after 1875. This is an aid in determining that a quilt with a fan design was not quilted before that time. One reason for the popularity of the Fan is that the marking can be done as you go.

Circular designs are a good complement to the geometric lines of pieced blocks.

Clamshell: also Shell, Overlapping Shells, Clam, Thimble Quilting. (Figure 6-1)

Figure 6-1.

Recommended Marking: For consistent size clamshells, mark using a template as you go.

How to Mark or Draw: The Clamshell design has been used since the mid-1800's. The design is made from circles in rows that appear to be placed one behind the other.

First, decide what size half circle will be best for the area that is to be filled with quilting. The size can vary from as small as a thimble to 3" (measurement across the center of the circle).

To make a template: on a straight line, draw a half circle using a compass, circle marking template, glass, cup, or spool. Draw a second half circle that is on the line and touching the other half circle. Draw one more half circle above these two that has the center sides of the circle touching the centers of the circles below (Figure 6-2).

Figure 6-2.

Another template can be made from a circle. Draw a circle the desired size and mark in four equal parts by drawing lines that cross the circle's center or at 90° with a protractor (Figure 6-3).

Figure 6-3.

To mark the quilt top, start on a straight line at the bottom of the area to be filled with quilting. This straight line can either be the quilt edge, a seam, or a faint guide line marked with a ruler. Mark half circles in a line horizontally across the quilt. Mark the second row by lining up the template or the lines on the circle template where the clamshells meet in the first row and the mid lines on the circle touching the center of two clamshells. Figure 6-4 shows marking the second row with both kinds of templates. Continue marking in rows until the surface is filled.

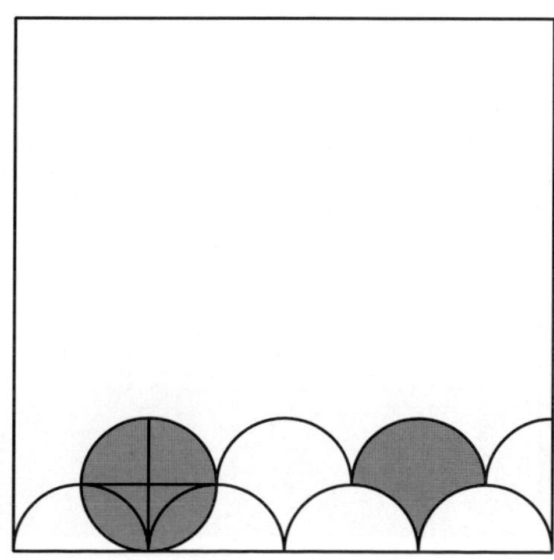

Figure 6-4.

Helpful Note: Clamshells are easy to quilt because the quilting lines are actually continuous across each row. A glass or cup can be used to do the marking. It does not take long to catch on to centering the circle as you mark. When the clamshell is very small, such as a thimble, the quilted area will look almost stippled. Purchasing a circle template is a good investment for marking all of the circular designs, especially the Clamshell.

Tools Needed: A round object or template and a fabric marking pencil or pen.

Where to Use: Clamshells can be used anywhere as background filler, in plain setting blocks, for background on appliqué blocks, in triangles where it is called Clouds in Triangle, in sashings and borders, or over the whole quilt surface disregarding the design of the patchwork.

Double Clamshell (Figure 6-5)

Figure 6-5.

Recommended Marking: Mark using templates as you go.

How to Mark or Draw: Double Clamshell is marked in the same way as the single line Clamshell using either one of the templates seen in (Figure 6-4). After a row or several rows of clamshells have been marked, a second line is marked inside each Clamshell. Space this second line ¼" inside the first Clamshell. Marking this second echo line is easier when using a second template but can be quilted by eye or freehand.

To make this second template, follow the directions and make a template like the one in

Plate 6-1. Teacup (also By the Piece).
Morisco by Jane Blair, 1984. Collection of the Museum of the American Quilter's Society.

Plate 6-2. Fan.
Stary, Stary Night by Cheryl F. Slaughter, 1991.

Plate 6-3. Concentric Circles (also Squares Crosshatch, Rose, By the Piece, Diagonal Lines).
Roses by Starlight by Arleen Boyd, 1985. Collection of the Museum of the American Quilter's Society.

Plate 6-4. Clamshell (also In the Ditch, Parallel Lines).
Kentucky Bouquet by Starr C Kaiser, 1990.

Figure 6-2. Mark off another line ¼" inside the round part of the template and make a new template this size (Figure 6-6).

Mark the inside line of the Double Clamshell by placing the second template inside the already marked Clamshells. Place the long point of the template inside the Clamshell and mark around the rounded top (Figure 6-7).

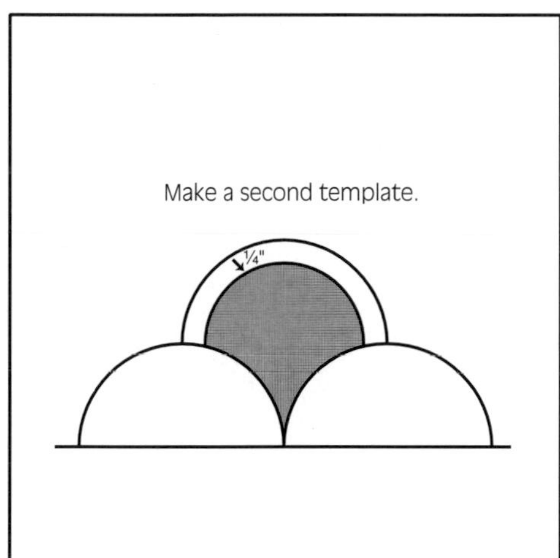

Figure 6-6.

Figure 6-7.

Helpful Note: The double lines can be used on any size Clamshell, except perhaps one marked with a thimble, but are especially effective on the larger Clamshells. Quilting this second line is a little harder since the needle has to travel through the batting to the next line rather than being continuous quilting stitches. The look of the quilted design is well worth the effort, however.

Tools Needed: Template material and a fabric marking pencil or pen.

Where to Use: The Double Clamshell (from early 1800's) can be used as background filler, in plain setting blocks, in borders and sashings, and as an overall quilting design disregarding the quilt pattern.

Scallops: also Shells (Figure 6-8)

Recommended Marking: Mark with a template as you go.

How to Mark or Draw: Make a template following the directions on page 74 (Figure 6-2). Since this is a design used in borders, decide what size Scallop or Shell will best fill the space to be quilted.

Using the template, mark one row of Scallops along the edge of the border. This can be the border seam or the outside edge. Next, mark single Scallops above every set of two Scallops or what would be in the second row (Figure 6-9).

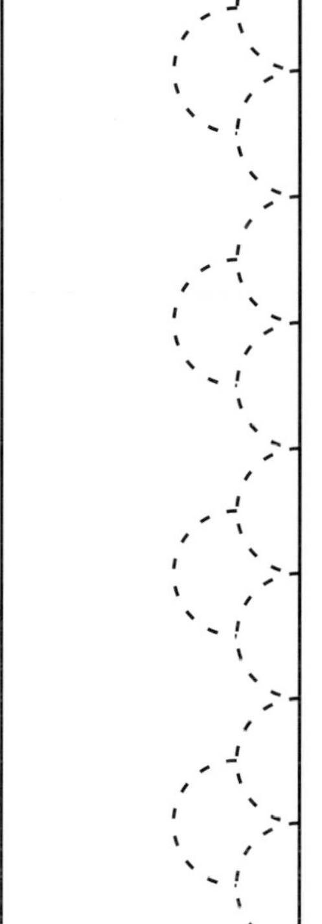
Figure 6-8.

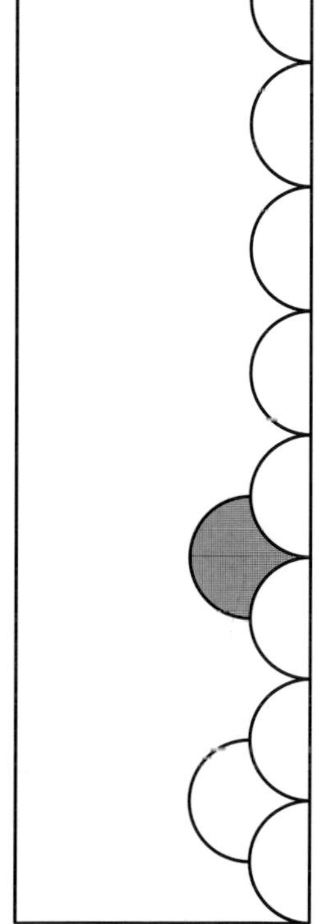
Figure 6-9.

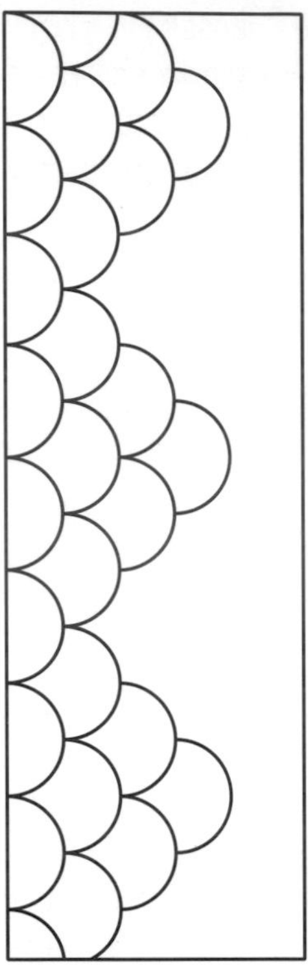

Figure 6-10.

The Scallop can be marked with more rows when the border is wider. In Figure 6-10, the Scallop is marked for a wider space and from the border seam so the scallop appears to be hanging down.

Helpful Note: Marking the Scallops on paper first will aid in determining when and how to best space the groups or sets. This design could be double lined, if desired.

Tools Needed: Template material and a fabric marking pencil or pen.

Where to Use: Scallops are to be used as a border design and could also be used in a whole cloth quilt to define a border or design division. If used in a whole cloth quilt, quilt a straight line from which to build the Scallop.

Half Moons: also Demilunes (Figure 6-11)

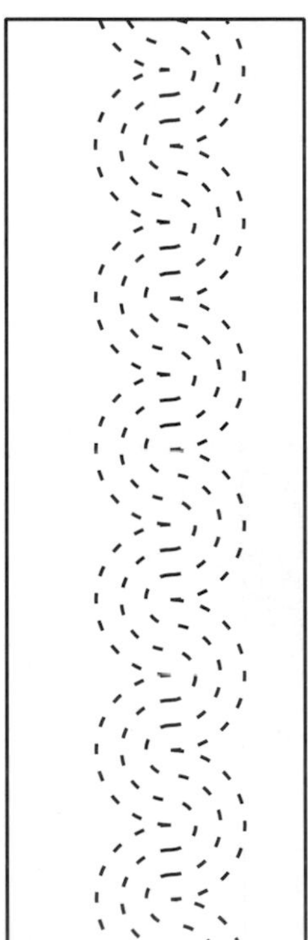

Figure 6-11.

Recommended Marking: Mark the quilt top from a paper pattern before the quilt layers are assembled.

How to Mark or Draw: To draw the design on the paper pattern, decide what size circle is needed to fill the length of the border. See page 12 in Chapter 1 on how to make a design fit. With a compass or pencil and string, draw a circle this size on graph paper. For an example, use a 6" circle. Inside this circle, draw two more concentric circles that are equally spaced. The example is a 6" circle and so the next one will be a 4" circle and the third circle will be a 2" circle. Mark lines across the circles to divide them into four parts (Figure 6-12). Go over the circle lines with a black felt tip marker.

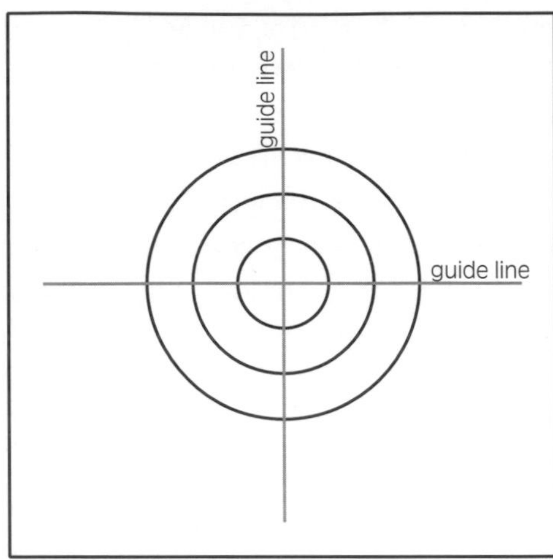

Figure 6-12.

On the pattern paper that has been cut to fit the border, mark a center guide line down the length of the paper. Place the piece of graph paper under the pattern paper with the center marks of the circles lined up with the guide line. Mark the upper halves of the circles, move the graph paper design so that the center line of the circle is lined up with the edge of the largest half circle (Figure 6-13). Mark the lower halves of the circles, move the underneath paper, mark the

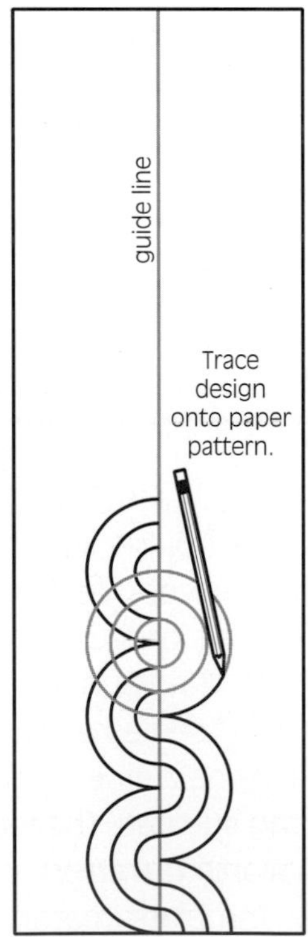

Figure 6-13.

upper halves, and continue marking upper and lower half circles until the border is filled. Go over the design on the paper pattern with a black felt tip pen.

To mark the design on the quilt top, pin the paper pattern to the wrong side of the quilt top and trace the design.

HELPFUL NOTE: When moving the circles and lining up from lower markings to the upper markings, the small circle should always be matching the lines of the middle circle. This will make a smooth flow of the design. Drawing the concentric circles on graph paper makes drawing the center lines across the circles easier.

TOOLS NEEDED: A long ruler, pattern paper, compass or circle drawing device, black felt tip pen, and a fabric marking pencil or pen.

WHERE TO USE: The Half Moons or Demilunes are to be used in borders. The center of the design could follow the seam of a double border.

Church Window (Figure 6-14)

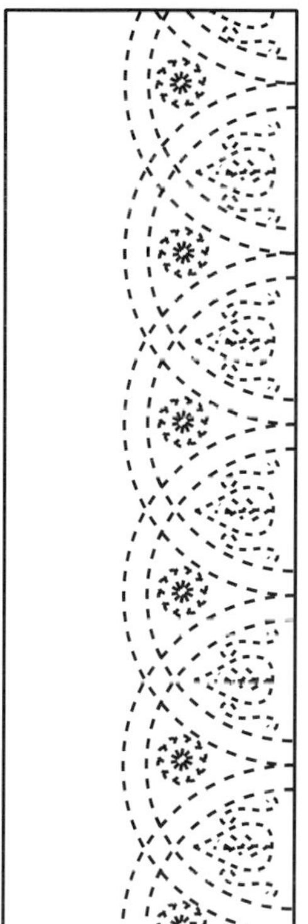

Figure 6-14.

RECOMMENDED MARKING: Mark using templates on the quilt top as you go or can be marked from a paper pattern.

HOW TO MARK OR DRAW: The Church Window design is large semicircles that overlap. Find a large round circular object (dinner plate, salad plate, pan) that half of the circle will fill the width of the border. On poster board, draw around the plate, or circular object and mark the circle in four equal parts (Figure 6-15). Cut the circle in half to make the template.

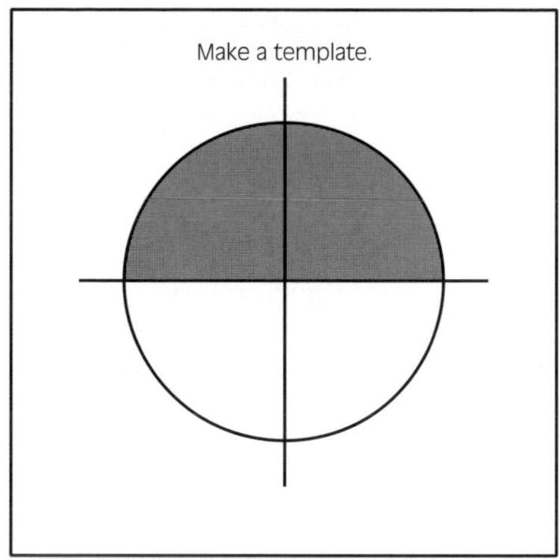

Figure 6-15.

To mark the border of the quilt top, use the template to mark several of the half circles following the edge of the quilt. These are marked the same as one row of the Clamshell design (see Figure 6-4).

Next, line up the center marking on the half circle template with the place where two of the large half circles meet. Mark another half circle that will overlap two of the first drawn circles (Figure 6-16). Continue by marking overlapping half circles.

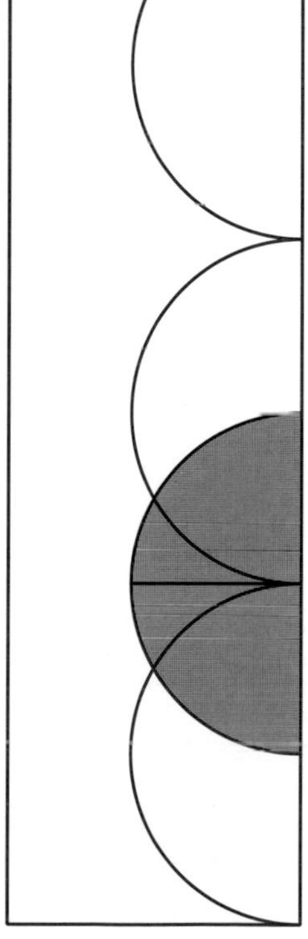

Figure 6-16.

Figure 6-17.

These overlapping half circles are double lined. Space the double line inside ½" by measuring with a seam gauge or small ruler. Mark this second line as you go (Figure 6-17).

Fillers such as Crosshatch, Roses, Spirals, Leaves, or Hearts can be placed in the windows.

Helpful Note: Ovals can also be used to mark the Church Windows. Choose fillers that fit the theme of the other quilting designs used in the quilt.

Marking the designs in the Church Windows will be easier from a paper pattern.

Tools Needed: A large circle, template material, and a fabric marking pencil or pen.

Where to Use: Use the Church Window designs for wide borders.

Teacup: also Wine Glass, Lemon Peel, Orange Peel, Interlocking Circles, Chain Quilting (Figure 6-18)

Figure 6-18.

Recommended Marking: Using a template, mark on the quilt top as you go.

How to Mark or Draw: The Teacup quilting design has been used since the mid 1800's. It was named for the household items used to mark the circles. The circles can be as small as a thimble or spool to the size of a tea cup. The size depends on the amount of quilting desired.

To make a template, choose a circle size. A 2" or 2½" circle is a good size. Mark lines across the center of the circle to form a cross or lines marked at 90° with a protractor (Figure 6-19).

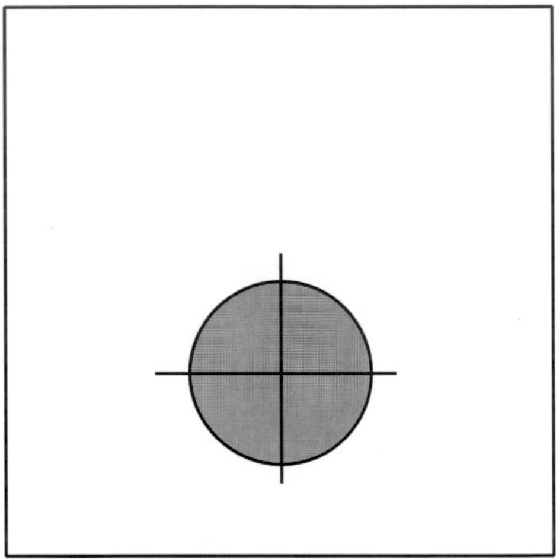

Figure 6-19.

There are two ways to start marking the Teacup design. To mark by the first method, mark a row of half circles along a straight line (the edge of a block or the quilt edge). These will look like Clamshells (page 74). Place the template with the cross lines touching two of the half circles and one touching where the two half circles meet (Figure 6-20). Mark a complete circle, move the

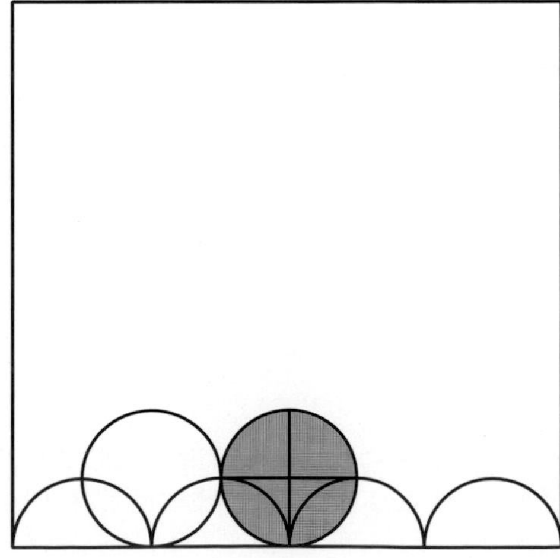

Figure 6-20.

template to the next two half circles and mark. Continue until the area to be quilted with this design is filled.

Marking with the second method can be done by marking a faint guide line across the middle of the block or quilt top. Line up one of the cross marks on the circle template with the guide line and mark around the entire circle. Move the template, still using the guide line, and continue marking a row of circles. Move the template up so that the bottom of the circle touches the guide line and the cross marks are lined up with the top of two circles and the point where two circles meet at the guide line (Figure 6-21). Continue overlapping the circles and marking to fill the area to be quilted.

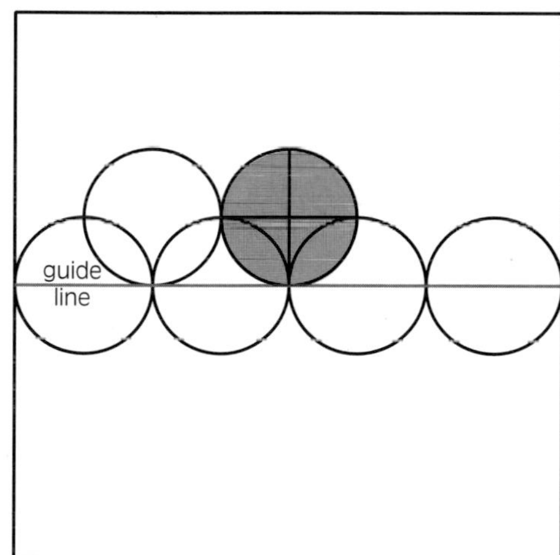

Figure 6-21.

Helpful Note: The design can stop at a block edge or seam and does not have to always make a complete circle. A circle template can be used for marking.

This design is easy to mark and fairly easy to quilt. Practice marking on paper before starting to mark the quilt top.

Tools Needed: A circle, template material, a ruler, and a fabric marking pencil or pen.

Where to Use: Teacup can be used as background filler, in plain setting blocks, in a center medallion, in borders and sashings, and as an overall design disregarding the patchwork design of the quilt top. The design is called Lemon Peel or Orange Peel when the circles are very small.

Overlapping Circles (Figure 6-22)

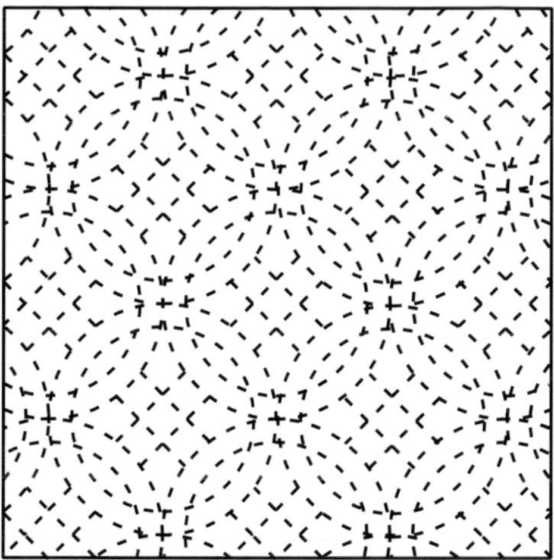

Figure 6-22.

Recommended Marking: Mark with a template on the quilt top as you go.

How to Mark or Draw: Using a large circle, make a template following the directions for the Teacup template on page 80. Draw a second smaller circle inside the first circle. The space between the two circles should be from ¼" to ¾" depending on the size of the first circle (Figure 6-23). Cut out the center of the template to make a ring.

To mark, draw double half circles along a straight line such as the quilt edge or a marked guide line. Mark a row of the double half circles. Move the template up and line up the marks (90°) on the template with the tops of two of the half circles and with the center where the two half cir-

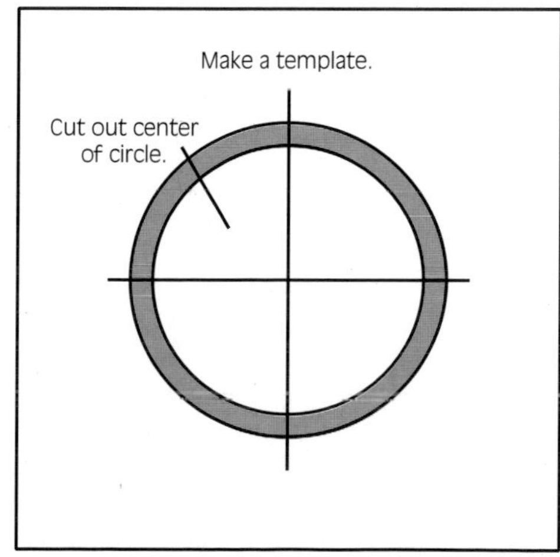

Figure 6-23.

Figure 6-24.

cles meet. This time mark around the entire circle template inside and out (Figure 6-24). Continue marking double circles until the area to be quilted is filled.

After the Double Circles have been quilted, mark and quilt the large space in the circles with Squares Crosshatching.

Helpful Note: This design was used in a large border area but could be marked with smaller circles and used as a filler design. If the design is small, the Crosshatch would not be marked in the large space. Practice marking the design on paper first.

Tools Needed: A circle, template material, ruler, and a fabric marking pencil or pen.

Where to Use: Use the design in a large border area and the smaller version in setting blocks and as background filler.

Fan: also Baptist Fan, Methodist Fan, Shell, Rainbow, Elbow, Wave, Concentric Arcs, Clamshell, Peacock Fan, Wall Sweep (Figure 6-25)

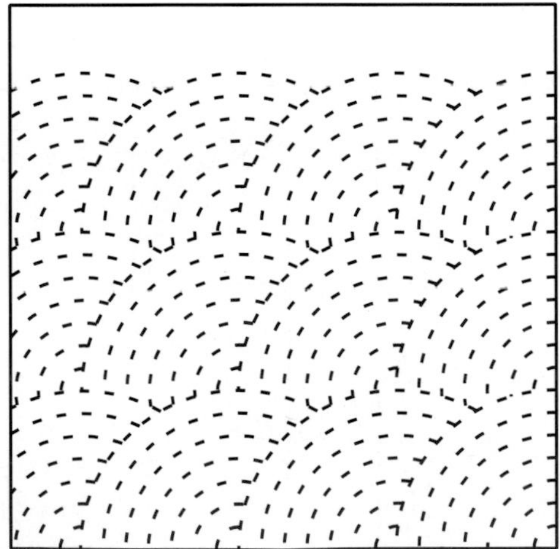
Figure 6-25.

Recommended Marking: Mark using a circle marking template or pencil and string on the quilt top as you go.

How to Mark or Draw: The best method of marking the Fan is a template. To make the template, cut a 1" wide, 12" long piece from template material. Use either cardboard or template plastic. On one end, punch a small hole for a pin hole. From this small hole, mark the template off in 1" spacings. Use a hole punch to punch a hole on each of these inch markings (Figure 6-26). Number the holes starting with 1 at the pin hole end.

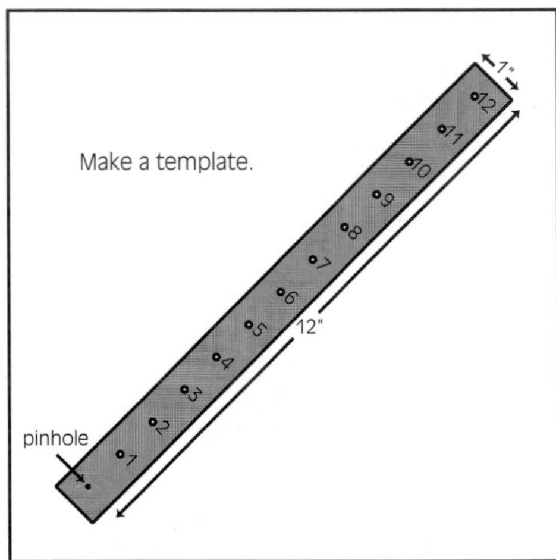

Figure 6-26.

To mark with this template, place the end with the small pin hole at the lower right corner of the quilt top. Stick a pin through this hole and all the layers of the quilt. Place a pencil in the next (or #1) hole and mark from the quilt edge to the other edge. Move the pencil to the next hole (#2) and mark. Continue until the fan has from 5 to 9 concentric arcs. Move the pin and the template to the left and place the pin next to the last line of the fan and the edge of the quilt. Start with the pencil in the first hole and mark the same as the first fan (Figure 6-27). Mark fans all the way across the quilt top. The second row is marked by placing the pin in the corner where two fans meet (Figure 6-28).

For another method of marking, tie a string around a pencil. Use the string for a compass by holding it in the corner and placing the pencil where the line is to be and marking with the string tight. Measure the space desired and move the pencil and mark. The string can be marked

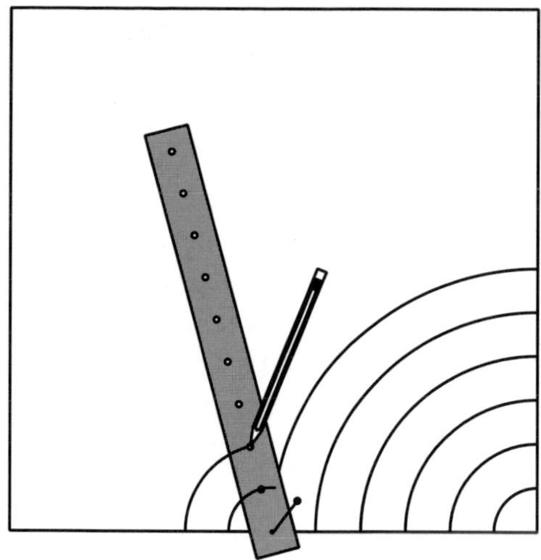
Figure 6-27.

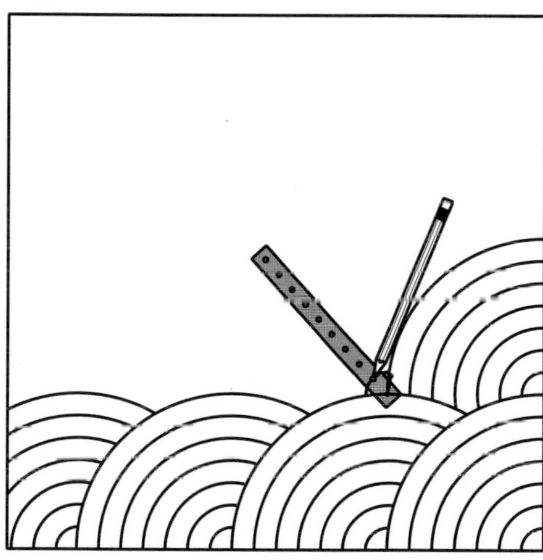
Figure 6-28.

with a permanent marker at 1" intervals or whatever spacing is desired and the string moved to the next marking rather than measuring the space on the quilt top.

Helpful Note: Even though this design is very easy to mark, practice a few fans on paper before marking the quilt. Quilting must be started from a corner of the quilt and not from the center. It can be quilted in a hoop.

Tools Needed: A ruler, hole punch, template material, and a fabric marking pencil or pen.

Where to Use: Use Fans on any pieced quilt. It is an overall design that complements most any pieced quilt, especially scrap quilts. It is a good design often used for group quilting. The names of Baptist Fan and Methodist Fan for this design probably came from quilting bees done in these churches.

Circles (Figure 6-29)

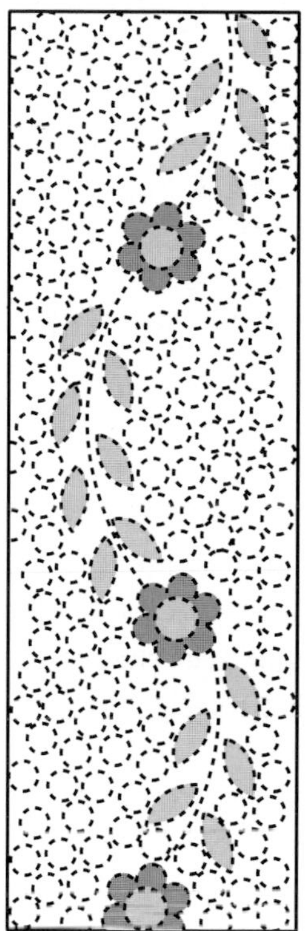
Figure 6-29.

Recommended Marking: Mark on the quilt top as you go.

How to Mark or Draw: Choose a circle size suitable for the area that is to be filled with quilting. The circle to be marked can be from a thimble, spool, button, or larger circle-shaped object or a circle template. Place the circle on the quilt top and mark around it. The Circles can be very close together or with some space between. Small Circles give the best effect and can be placed touching to give a cross-hatch look.

Helpful Note: The peel-off stick-um circles that can be purchased in office supply stores can be used as a template, quilted around and removed leaving no marking on the quilt top. They can be used several times before they loose their stickiness.

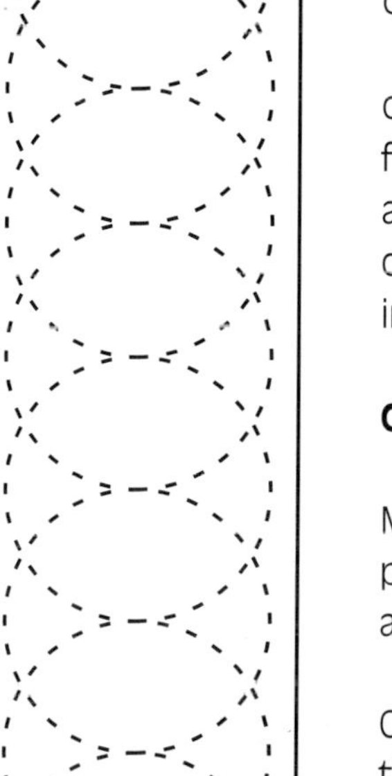
Figure 6-30.

Tools Needed: A circle shape and a marking pencil or pen.

Where to Use: Circles can be used as background filler, especially with appliqué, and as an allover quilting design disregarding the patchwork pattern.

Circles Chain (Figure 6-30)

Recommended Marking: Mark, using a circle template, on the quilt border as you go.

How to Mark or Draw: Choose a circle that will fit the width of the border.

If the placement of the circles will be, for example, 1" from the bor-

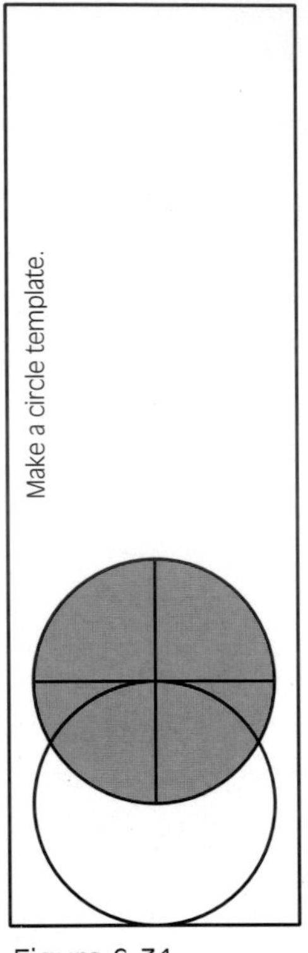

Figure 6-31.

der seam, marking a faint guide line for the top of the circles to hit will help in keeping the chain straight. Any round object can be used or make a template following the instructions on page 75, Figure 6-3.

The circles are marked one at a time with each circle touching the previous circle. To mark the second circle, when starting it is necessary to line up the center of the circle with the side of the first circle (Figure 6-31).

Helpful Note: This design is easy to mark and fairly easy to quilt. It is found on Amish quilts.

Tools Needed: A circle template and a fabric marking pencil or pen.

Where to Use: The Circles Chain can be used in borders and sashings.

Concentric Circles: also Concentric Rings (Figure 6-32)

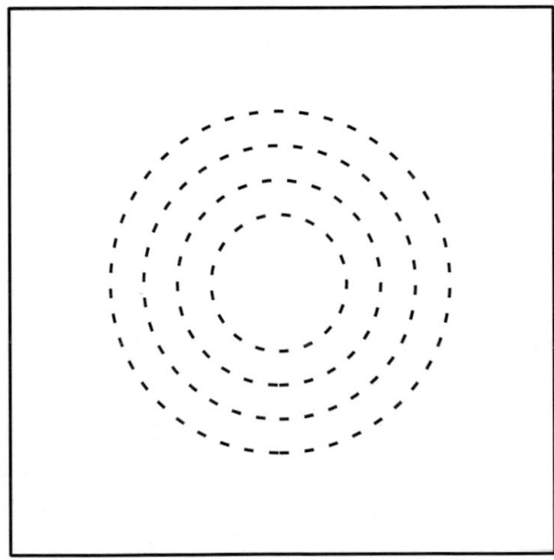

Figure 6-32.

Recommended Marking: Use a template to mark on the quilt top as you go.

How to Mark or Draw: Concentric circles are simply circles in circles. They can be marked with equal spacing between circles or with the amount of space decreasing like the ripples of water from a pebble thrown in water. The example shows evenly spaced circles.

Make a Fans marking template as described on page 82, Figure 6-26, or use a pencil and string as a compass.

To mark Concentric Circles, place the small hole with a straight pin in the center of the area to be marked. This area could be the center of a pieced or plain setting block. With a pencil in a marking hole, draw a complete circle. Move the pencil to the next marking hole that will space the next circle as desired and mark another circle (Figure 6-33). Continue until the number of circles needed to fill the area is reached.

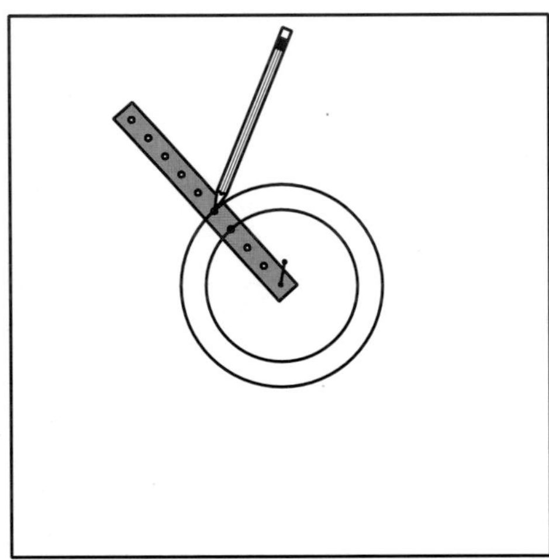

Figure 6-33.

Helpful Note: The number of Concentric Circles and the spacing between can vary depending on the amount of space to be filled and the look wanted.

Tools Needed: Template material and a fabric marking pencil or pen.

Where to Use: Concentric Circles can be used over pieced blocks such as the Mariner's Compass, Drunkard's Path, or the Square in a Square where the circles will soften the edge of the pieced design. Use them as fillers in spaces between pieced designs or in plain setting blocks. It can be used as an overall design by starting in the quilt center and marking circles all the way to the quilt's edges. When used to outline the rows of hexagons in the flowers in Grandmother's Flower Garden, it is called Concentric Rings.

Concentric Fans (Figure 6-34)

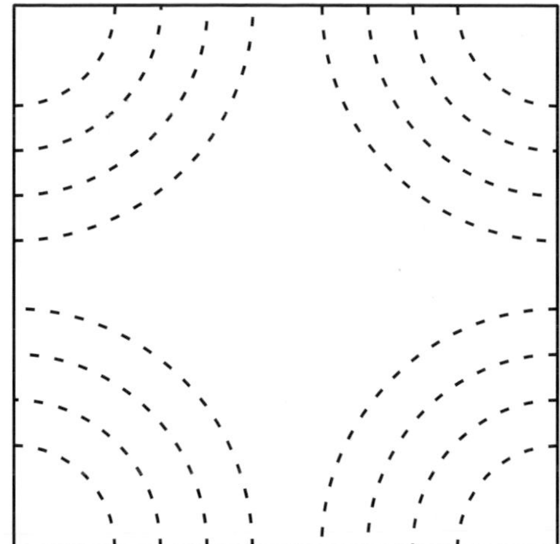

Figure 6-34.

Recommended Marking: Mark the block as you go using a template.

How to Mark or Draw: Use a fan marking template as described on page 82, Figure 6-26. The design is marked in all four corners of a block and is marked the same as Fans.

Start marking by placing the straight pin in a corner and marking quarter circles with spacing as desired to fill the corner (Figure 6-35). Usually, four lines are good but the lines should come close to meeting in the centers of the block.

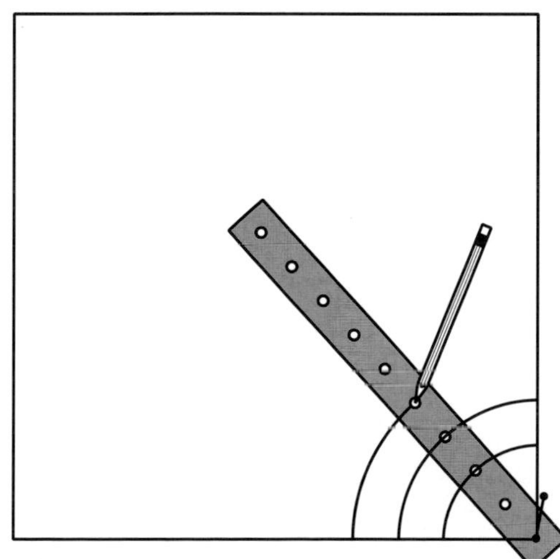

Figure 6-35.

Mark each corner in the same manner.

Helpful Note: A pencil and string can also be used as a compass for marking.

Tools Needed: Template material and a fabric marking pencil or pen.

Where to Use: Concentric Fans can be used in appliqué or embroidery blocks as a framing for the design. It could also be used to frame a quilting design in the center of a plain setting block. The plain space could be crosshatched.

Circle in a Circle (Figure 6-36)

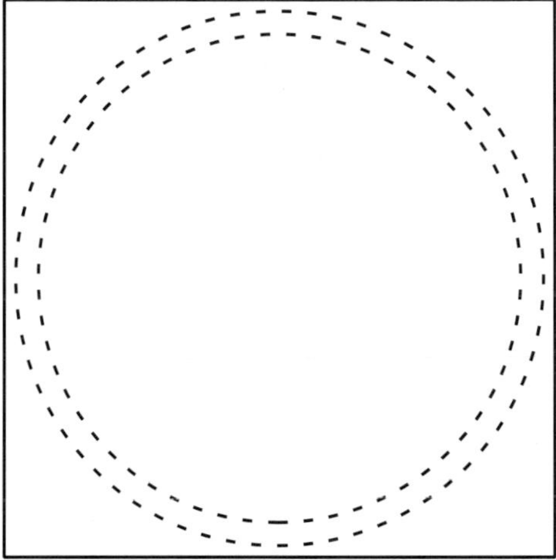

Figure 6-36.

Recommended Marking: Mark using a template as you go.

How to Mark or Draw: To mark, a circle is needed that is big enough to fill the area. Since the Circle in a Circle is usually in a large space, a plate, pan, fan marking template (page 82), or a pencil and string can be used to mark the first circle. The second circle should be spaced either ½" or 1" inside the first circle. If using a plate for the first circle, the second circle can be spaced by marking with a small ruler. Mark with small lines and go back and fill in a solid line.

Helpful Note: The Circle in a Circle Variation can be used as framing for another quilting design or can be Crosshatched (Figure 6-37).

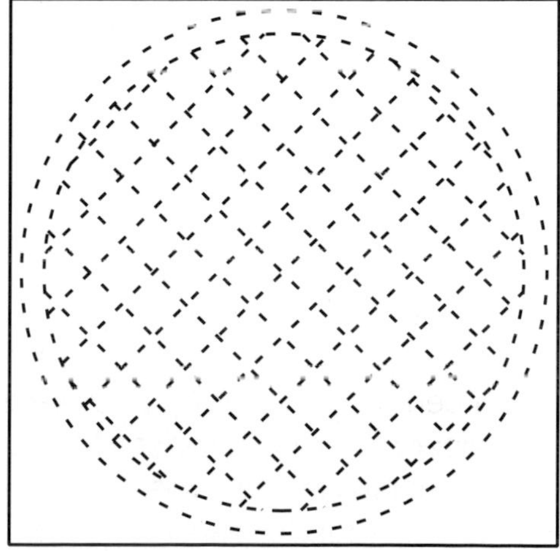

Figure 6-37.

Tools Needed: A large circle or template material and a fabric marking pencil or pen.

Where to Use: Use in plain setting blocks, in the plain space of a pieced pattern such as the Double Wedding Ring design, or use a half Circle in a Circle in a plain triangle.

Spiral: also Snail-Creep, Concentric Circles (Figure 6-38)

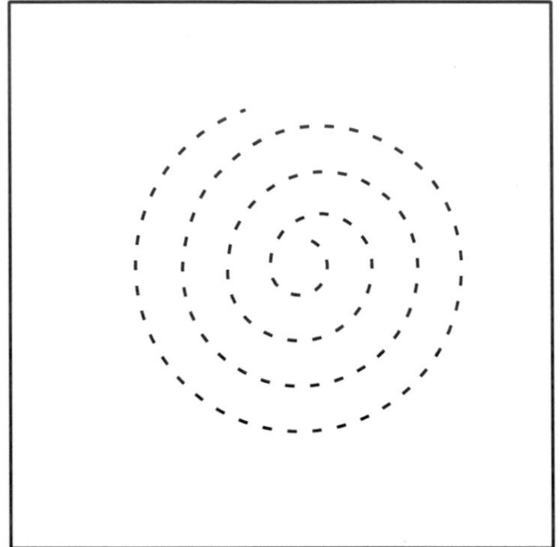

Figure 6-38.

Recommended Marking: Mark freehand on the quilt top as you go or mark from a paper pattern before the quilt is assembled.

How to Mark or Draw: Draw a Spiral by starting at a center point and draw part of a small circle and by eye continue drawing around this starting point and expanding the spacing between lines until the Spiral is the size desired. It is easier than it sounds and, by practicing, the ability to draw Spirals freehand improves. When a Spiral has been drawn that looks good, mark the lines with a black felt tip pen and use this Spiral for a paper pattern.

If you must have a more perfect design, draw four Concentric Circles with a pencil (Figure 6-32). Connect one circle to the next with a curving slanting line. Erase the lines where the slanted lines cross the original circle lines (Figure 6-39).

Helpful Note: The freehand Spiral is easy to draw and actually looks better than the one drawn from perfect circles. It may be preferrable to make a paper pattern for marking the quilt top so that all the Spirals are the same.

Tools Needed: A fabric marking pencil or pen and paper for a pattern, if used.

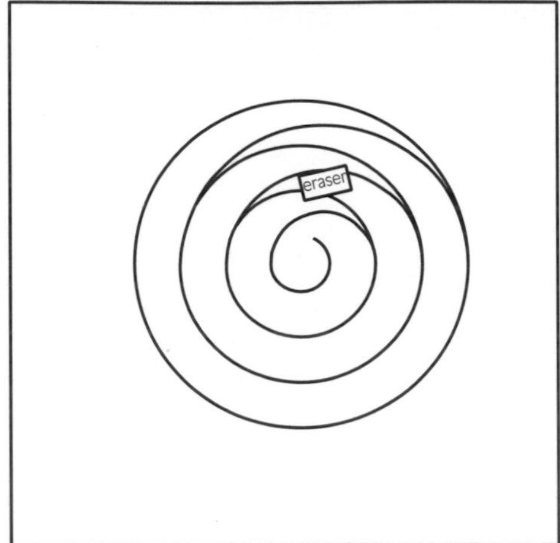

Figure 6-39.

Where to Use: Spirals can be used on the stems of feathers, in scallops of a border, as filler in plain setting blocks, in borders, and in sashings. They add a look of elegance anywhere they are used.

Interlocking Swirl (Figure 6-40)

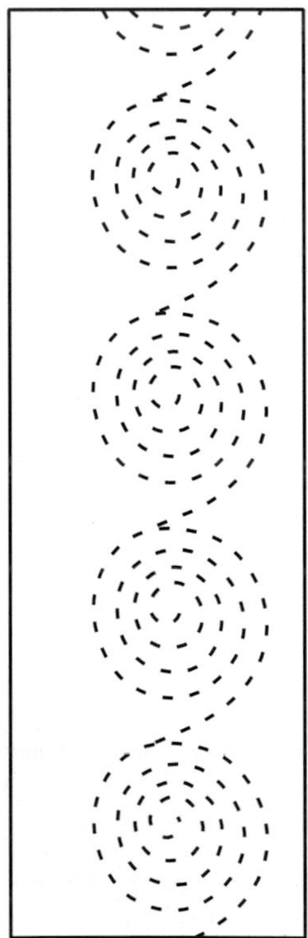

Figure 6-40.

Recommended Marking: Mark from a paper pattern before the quilt is assembled.

How to Mark or Draw: On a piece of paper, draw a Spiral in the size that is suitable for the width of the space to be filled. Follow the instructions on page 87 to draw a Spiral (Figure 6-41).

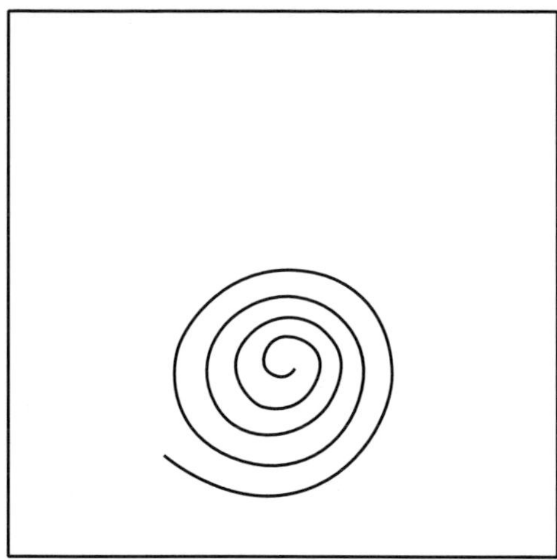

Figure 6-41.

Make a paper pattern by cutting a piece of paper to fit the border or area to be filled with the design. Draw a straight guide line on the pattern paper in order to keep the Spirals spaced evenly from the edge. Place the drawing of the Spiral under the paper for the pattern and trace the Spiral. Space the Spirals close together (½" to 1") in a row to make the Interlocking Swirl (Figure 6-42). After the Spirals have been traced, connect one Spiral to the next by drawing a line from the bottom or open end of the Spiral up to the upper side of the one beside it. Draw around the design

Figure 6-42.

with a black felt tip pen to make tracing onto the fabric easier.

To mark the quilt top, pin the paper pattern, with the design up, to the wrong side of the quilt top and trace the design onto the surface of the quilt top.

Helpful Note: Drawing the Spirals freehand makes for a better design. Since drawing a small Spiral is easiest, the design can be enlarged to the needed size on a photocopy machine. After a Spiral has been drawn that you like, the lines can be cleaned up by erasing and redrawing lines to make them smooth.

Tools Needed: Pattern paper, black felt tip marker, and a fabric marking pencil or pen.

Where to Use: Interlocking Swirl is a good border design and can be used in sashings or to frame a center medallion.

Ocean Wave Quilting (Figure 6-43)

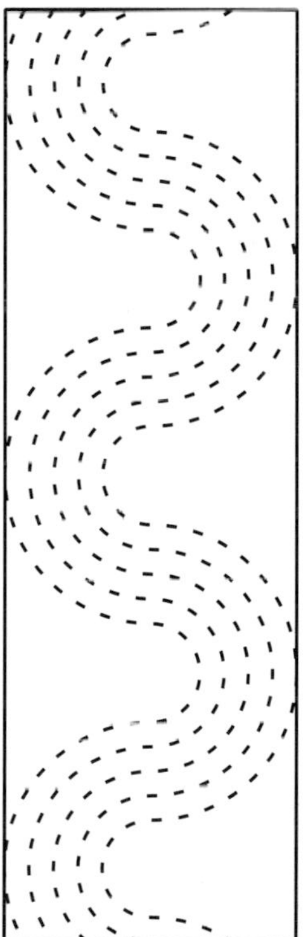

Figure 6-43.

Recommended Marking: Mark, using a circle template, as you go.

How to Mark or Draw: Ocean Wave quilting is a border design from the late 1800's. Make a circle template following the directions on page 75, Figure 6-3). The size of the circle template must be decided by the width of the border to be quilted.

To mark the quilt top, draw a faint guide line the length of the border and centered. Place the template with the center mark on the guide line and mark a half circle above the guide line. Move the template and, with it touching the last half circle, draw a half circle below the guide line (Figure 6-44). Continue drawing half circles above and below the guide line until the border area is filled. Use a seam gauge or small ruler and mark the next line with dash marks (Figure 6-45). This line can then be completed by connecting the dash lines or connected when quilting.

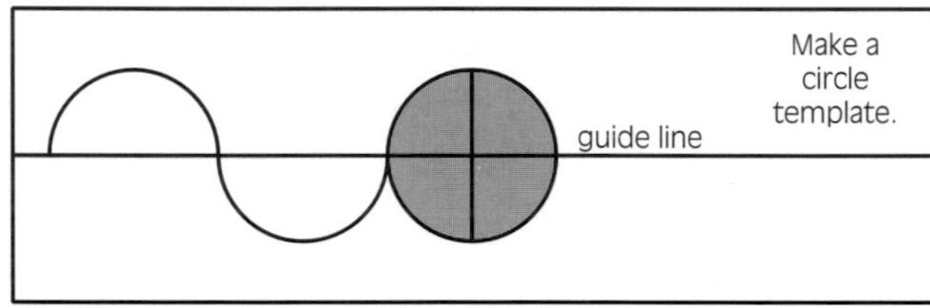

Figure 6-44.

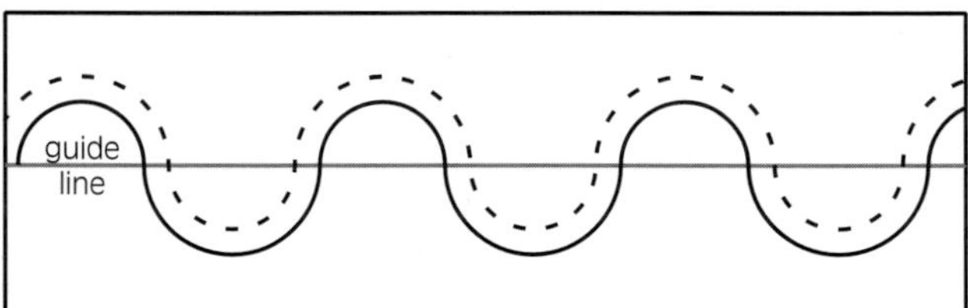

Figure 6-45.

The lines of the wave can be spaced very close (¼") to as much as 1" apart. Decide the spacing by how much quilting is desired or the amount of space to be filled. Mark on each side of the original line until the Ocean Wave is as wide as needed.

Helpful Note: Draw a few of the waves on paper first to practice before actual marking on the quilt. This design is fairly easy to mark and is easy to quilt.

Tools Needed: A ruler, template material, a seam gauge or small ruler, and a marking pencil or pen.

Where to Use: This design works well on a quilt border that has a nautical theme (Sailboat or Mariner's Compass) and for multiple borders with the design overlapping all the borders.

Floral Circles (Figure 6-46)

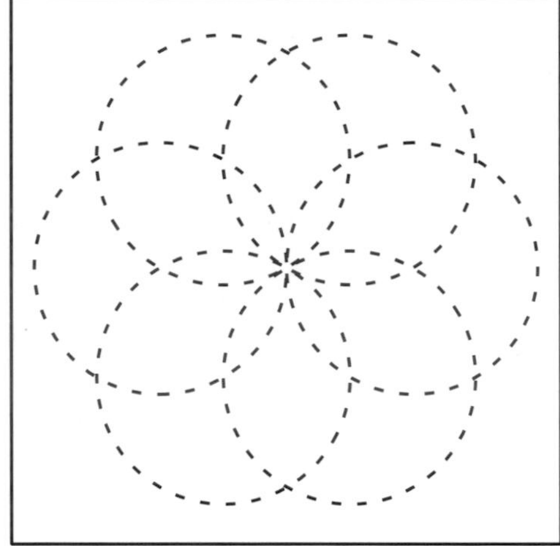

Figure 6-46.

Recommended Marking: Mark the quilt top from a paper pattern before the layers are assembled.

How to Mark or Draw: This design is formed by overlapping six circles to form a circular design. To make the pattern, cut a piece of paper the size of the block or area to be filled with the design. Using a ruler with the 60° marking, draw a straight line across the center of the paper. Mark the center of this line. Next, with the bottom of the ruler slanted to the right, place the 60° marking of the ruler on the guide line and the ruler edge on the center mark and mark along the edge of the ruler. Move the ruler, with the bottom slanting to the left, and line up the 60° mark on the center line. Have the ruler edge touching where the lines cross. Mark along the ruler edge to form crossing lines (Figure 6-47).

A circle template is needed for the next step of drawing the design. Make a circle template by following the instructions on page 75, Figure 6-3, or by using a circle marking template. The size of the circle will be decided by dividing the size wanted in half. For example, if the design will fill a 12" square (leaving a little space between the design and the seam), a 5" circle would be a good size.

Place the circle template with the center marking lined up with one of the 60° lines and the circle edge touching the center and draw around the circle. Move the template to the next 60° line and draw around the template

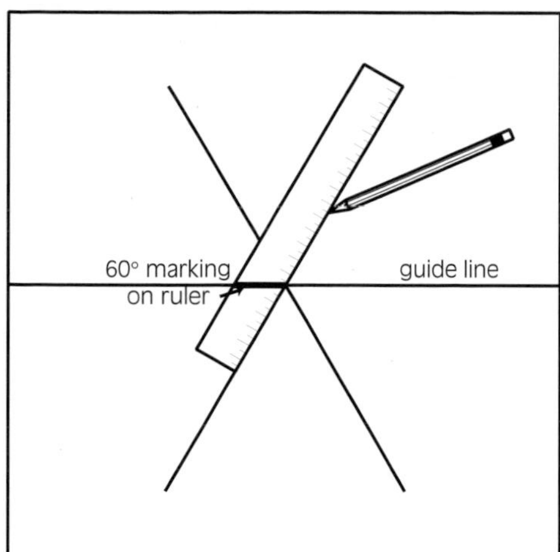

Figure 6-47.

(Figure 6-48). Continue until a circle has been drawn on each 60° mark. Outline this design with a black felt tip marker. Pin the design to the wrong side of the quilt top and trace onto the quilt top.

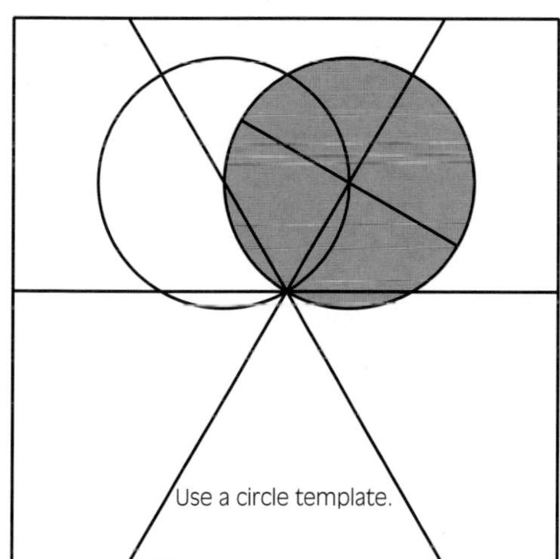

Figure 6-48.

Helpful Note: The circles can be double lined to give another look to this design. Floral Circles are actually easier to draw than they look.

Tools Needed: Template material, pattern paper, a 60° ruler, black felt tip pen, and a fabric marking pencil or pen.

Where to Use: Floral Circles is a good design for a plain setting block. It would be appropriate for corner squares in a border.

Star Flower (Figure 6-49)

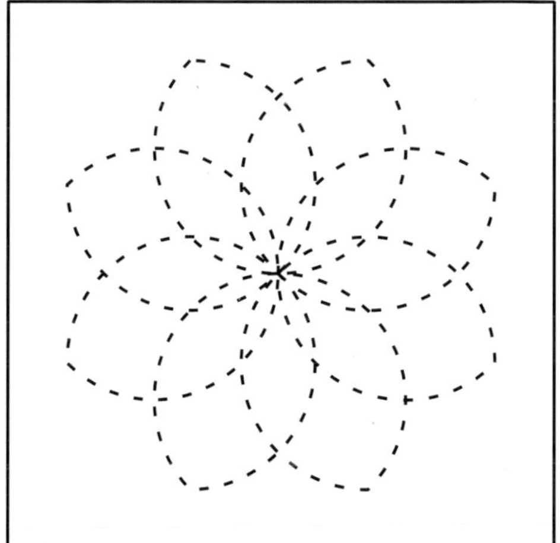

Figure 6-49.

Recommended Marking: Mark from a paper pattern before the quilt layers are assembled.

How to Mark or Draw: Cut a piece of paper the size of the area to be filled with the design. With a ruler, mark lines from center to center both vertically and horizontally, and diagonally from the corner to corner (Figure 6-50).

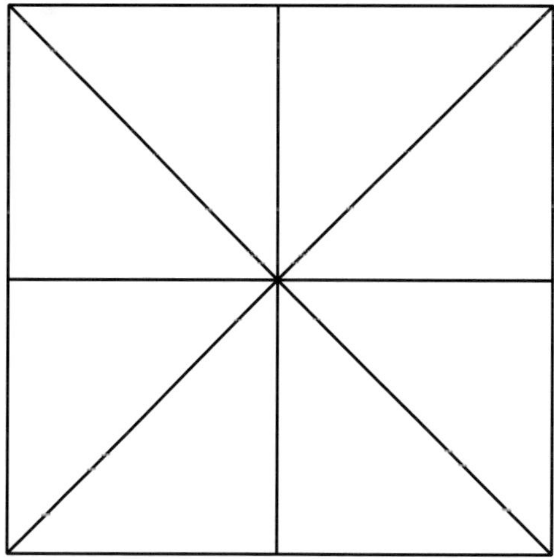

Figure 6-50.

Make a circle template following the instructions on page 75, Figure 6-3.

Determine the size circle needed for the template by taking half of the width of the block. Place the circle template on the pattern paper with the circle centered on one of the lines and the edge of the template touching the center of the paper. Draw around the template and move the template to the next line. Draw another circle that overlaps the first one. Continue until eight circles have been drawn or one circle is drawn on each of the lines. Erase the outermost lines between interacting circles (Figure 6-51). Go over the lines that are left with a black felt tip marker to make a useable pattern.

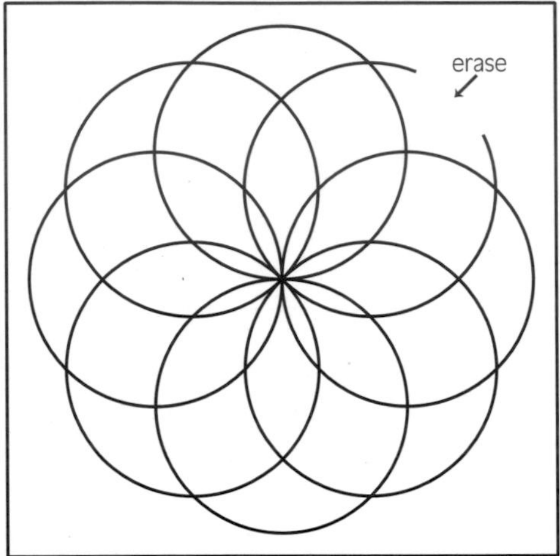

Figure 6-51.

Trace the design onto the quilt top by pinning the pattern to the wrong side of the quilt top.

Helpful Note: The Star Flower can be varied by outlining some sections of the design (Figure 6-52). Mark lines spaced ¼" inside the design lines. This can be done on the pattern or on the quilt as you go.

Tools Needed: Template material, pattern paper, ruler, black felt tip marker, and a fabric marking pencil or pen.

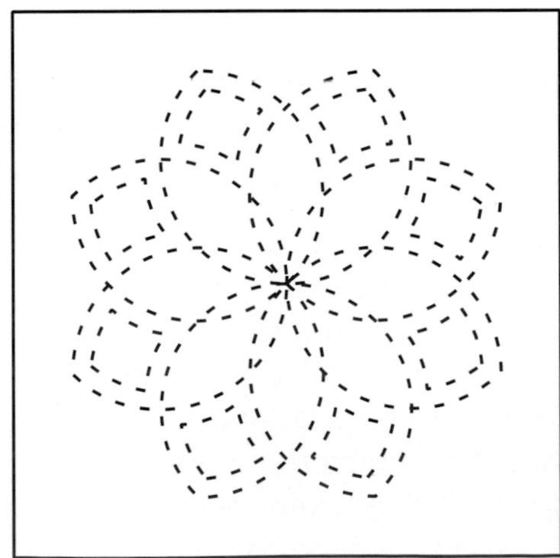

Figure 6-52.

Where to Use: This Amish design is a good choice for plain setting blocks.

Cross-in-a-Circle (Figure 6-53)

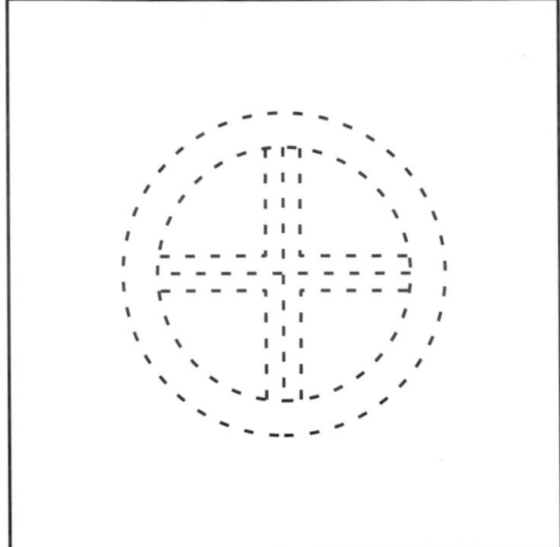

Figure 6-53.

Recommended Marking: Mark using a template and a ruler as you go.

How to Mark or Draw: The Cross-in-a-Circle dates from around 1850 and is a large design that will cover a patchwork pattern or fill a plain setting block.

Draw a Circle in a Circle following the directions on page 85, Figure 6-36. Make the spacing between the outside circle and the inside circle 1". With a ruler, mark a cross bar in the center of the inside circle (Figure 6-54). The spacing of the lines in the pie shape is ½" from the center lines.

Helpful Note: The cross bar and the lines in the pie shape could be marked with masking tape, thereby avoiding pencil marks.

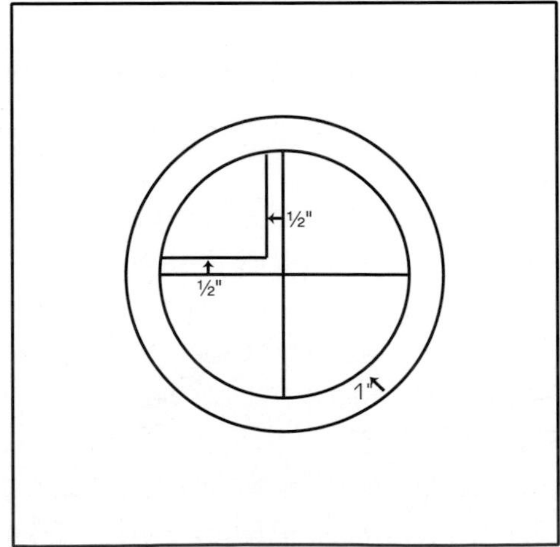

Figure 6-54.

Tools Needed: A large circle, ruler, and a fabric marking pencil or pen.

Where to Use: This design could be used in a plain setting block or over a pieced block.

Arcs (Figure 6-55)

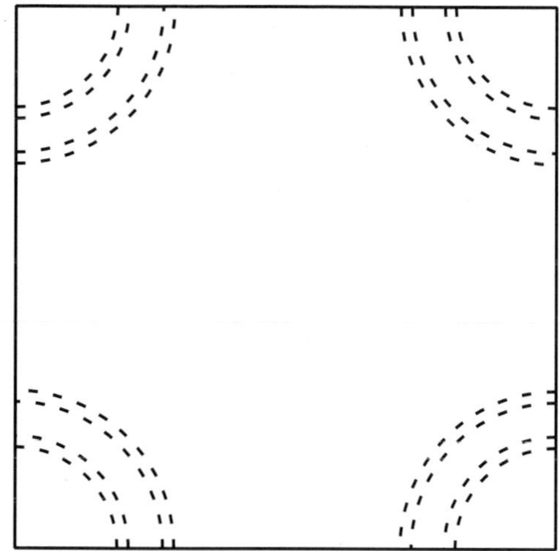

Figure 6-55.

Recommended Marking: Mark on the quilt top as you go.

How to Mark or Draw: Arcs are quarter circles and can be marked freehand using the elbow as a compass point. They can also be marked using a fan marking device as described on page 82, Figure 6-26.

This design is used in the corners of a block as a filler. To mark, place the anchoring pin in the corner of the block and mark the quarter circle from seam to seam. Move the pencil to the next desired spacing and mark another quarter circle (Figure 6-56). The spacing between lines can be varied. Mark each of the corners the same.

Figure 6-56.

Figure 6-57 shows Simple Arcs used as a single quilting line. The open spaces could be filled with leaves, flowers, teardrops, hearts, etc.

Helpful Note: This design should be kept in mind when there is open space that would benefit from being broken into smaller areas. The arc lines can be single, double, or triple, or any variation of these. If the quarter circles are fairly small, a circle template could be used to mark the arcs.

Tools Needed: Template material for fan marking tool and a fabric marking pencil or pen.

Where to Use: Arcs have been used since the mid 1800's. Use them in corners of plain setting blocks (with another quilting design, such as a Feather Circle) and in the corners of pieced blocks such as a Sunburst or Mariner's Compass blocks. They could be used in the joining blocks of sashings and borders.

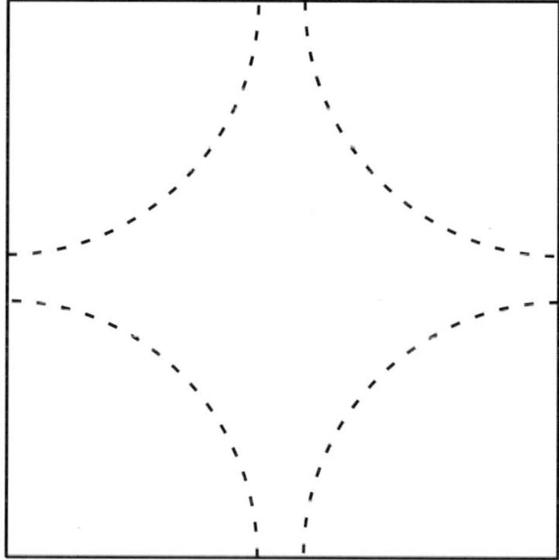

Figure 6-57.

Plate 7-1. Scrolling Vine (also Single Parallel Lines, In the Ditch).
Oriental Poppy by Leureta Thieme, 1996. Collection of the Museum of the American Quilter's Society.

Plate 7-2. Simple Scroll (also In the Ditch, Rope).
Downtown America by Phyllis Miller, 1989.

Plate 7-3. Four Petaled Flower (also Triangles, By the Piece, Feathered Circle, Straight Feather).
Tribute to Hallmark® by Jane Culvey, 1982.

Plate 7-4. Swag (also Long Diamond, Squares Cross-hatch, Princess Feather, Outline Quilting).
Spring Beauties by Phyllis Miller, 1994.

Chapter Seven
Ovals, Crescents, and Curves

Many of the designs in this chapter have a relationship with the Circle. Of the designs in this chapter, the most often used and the most familiar design is the Pumpkin Seed. The Amish used this shape often in their designs. It is popular because it can be used as a basis for floral and border designs. The Pumpkin Seed shape is also found in appliqué designs as petals and leaves.

The Scrolling Vine is a curving design that can be used in a variety of ways. The vine can be used to create borders of flowers and leaves. When repeated it becomes Waves. Follow the instructions for drawing this vine to use not only in designs for quilting but also when a vine is needed for appliqué.

Swags is a good design for a border. It is most effective when used in designing a whole cloth quilt to define the borders.

Ovals: also Shell Variation (Figure 7-1)

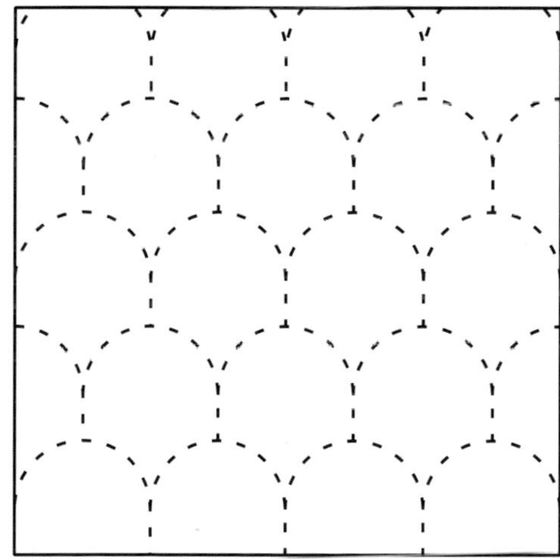

Figure 7-1.

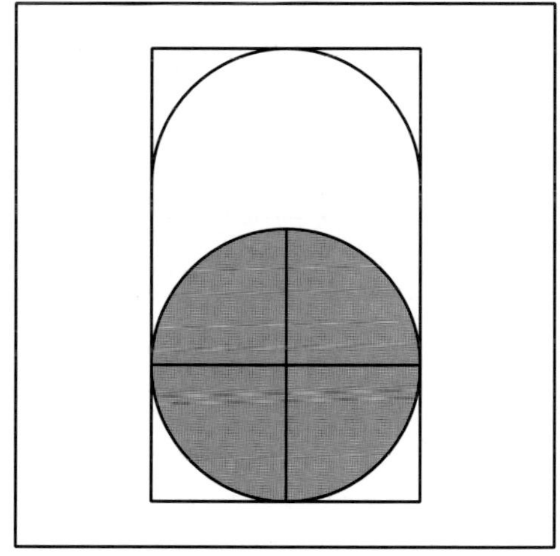

Figure 7-2.

Recommended Marking: Mark the quilt top as you go using a template or from a paper pattern marked before the quilt is assembled.

How to Mark or Draw: First, an oval shape is needed. An oval is a rectangle with the corners rounded off. Draw a rectangle determined by the height and width needed to fill the area where the design will be used. For an example, the rectangle will be 3" by 5". Use a 3" circle (or width of the rectangle) and mark the curve of the circle at both ends of the rectangles. (Figure 7-2).

To finish the template, mark lines on the oval that are centered vertically and horizontally (Figure 7-3, page 94). Cut out the oval template.

The oval shape can be used to mark an overall design like the Clamshell (Figure 6-1) and is marked in the same way. Figure 7-4, page 94, shows the placement of the template when marking the second row of ovals.

Helpful Note: The oval template can also be made by cutting out a paper rectangle, folding the paper in fourths, and cutting the curve on

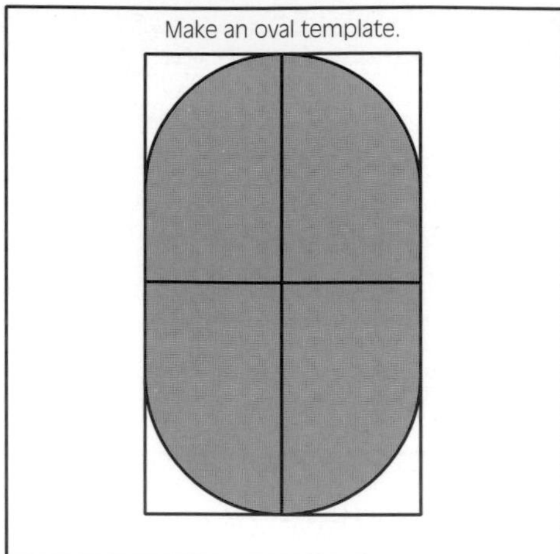

Figure 7-3.

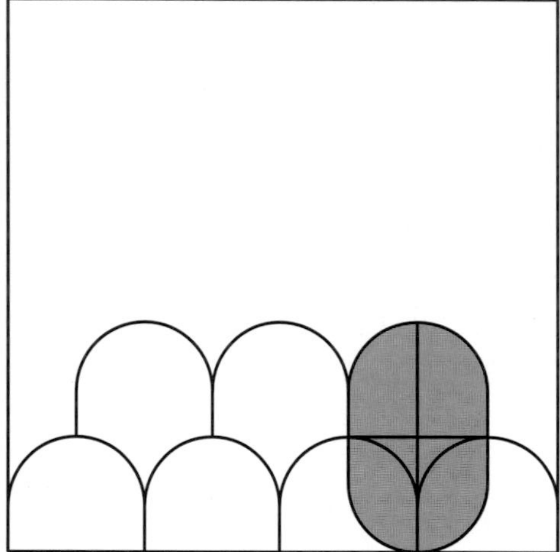

Figure 7-4.

the corners by eye. This makes a very acceptable oval and is much easier when a large oval is desired. A roasting pan or oval platter can be used when a large oval is needed for a central framing in a whole cloth design or a center medallion. Longer ovals make good designs.

Tools Needed: Template material or an oval object and a fabric marking pencil or pen.

Where to Use: Ovals can be substituted for circles in many of the circular designs. Try Ovals for Double Clamshell (Figure 6-5), Scallops (Figure 6-8), Church Window (Figure 6-14), and Teacup (Figure 6-18). The Ovals can be double lined, especially when used for framing. The Ovals can be used to mark fans for a border and are called Gothic Fans (Figure 7-5). Fans made from Ovals can be varied by the size of the rectangle and/or the way they are overlapped. Make a paper pattern for the oval fans. Experiment with Ovals for many new design discoveries.

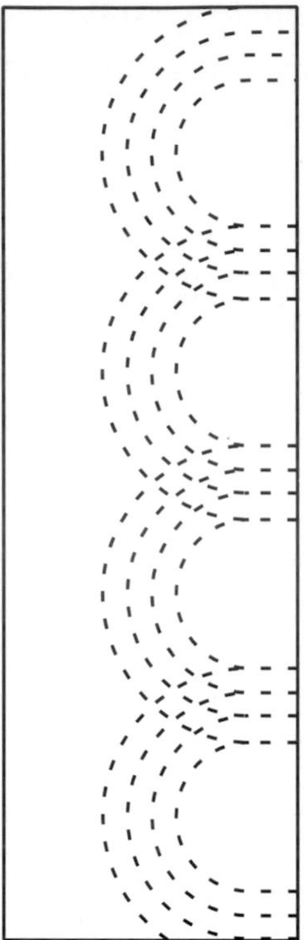

Figure 7-5.

Overlapping Ovals (Figure 7-6)

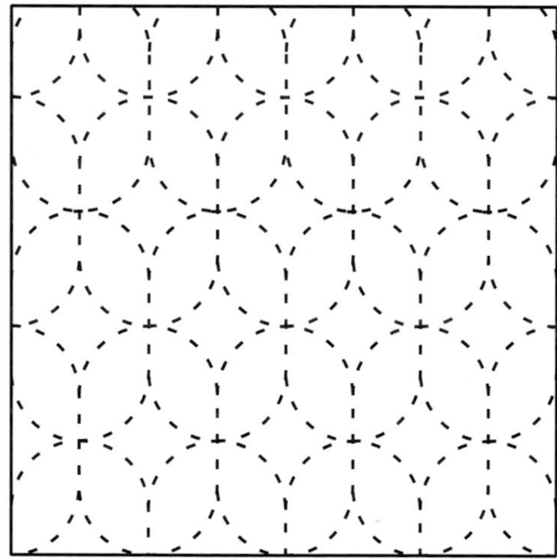

Figure 7-6.

Recommended Marking: Using a template, mark on the quilt top as you go.

How to Mark or Draw: Overlapping Ovals are marked in the same way as the Teacup design. First, an oval template is needed. One method of making an oval is described on page 93. Another way to make an oval is by paper folding. Cut a piece of paper into a rectangle. For example, use a 3" x 5" rectangle. Fold the rectangle in half down the length and then half of the width. Draw the curve for the oval in one corner (Figure 7-7). This gives a softer curve than the oval made using a circle although it is surprisingly close in shape. Refold the paper and cut along the drawn curve line. Mark the oval with lines across the middle both vertically and horizontally (see Figure 7-3). Use this oval for a template.

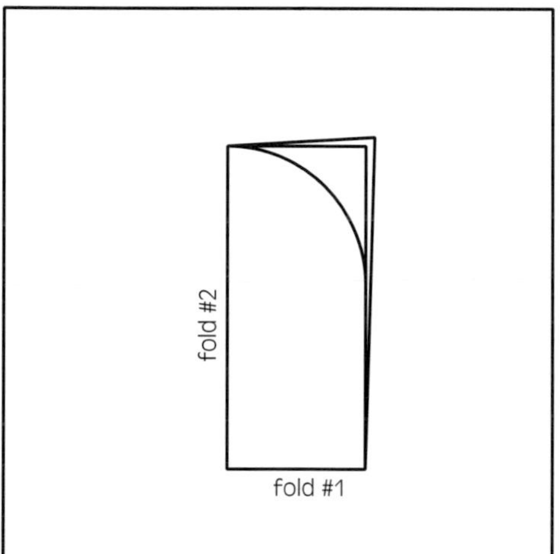

Figure 7-7.

Begin marking the quilt top by placing the center line of the oval template on a straight line which can be the edge of the quilt or block seam or a drawn faint guide line. Draw a line of half ovals. Move the oval template so that the horizonal center lines up with the top of the already drawn half ovals and the vertical center line touches where two half ovals meet. Draw around the oval template (Figure 7-8). Continue moving and overlapping the template and marking until the area to be quilted is filled.

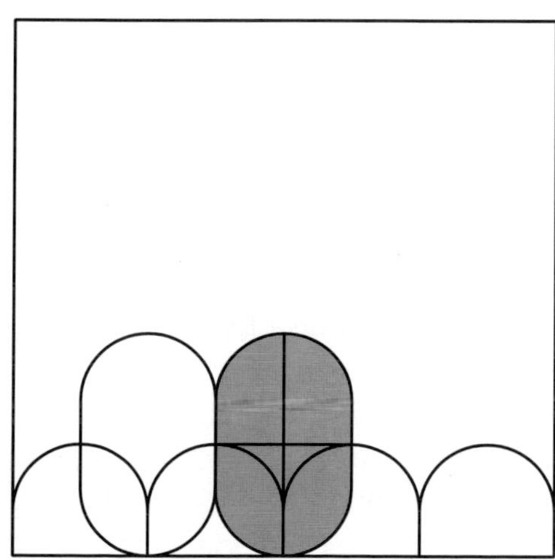

Figure 7-8.

Helpful Note: Overlapping Ovals are easy to mark and easy to quilt. Be careful when overlapping to keep the rows as straight as possible. Marking can begin in the middle of the area to be quilted and marked from there. Marking a faint guide line will be necessary for a starting point. Mark all the way around the template when starting in the center of the area.

Tools Needed: Template material and a fabric marking pencil or pen.

Where to Use: This design can be used as an overall design disregarding the patchwork pattern. It can be used as a filler in plain setting blocks, as background filler for appliqué, and in borders and sashings.

Oval Chain: also Interlocking Ovals, Lozenge (Figure 7-9)

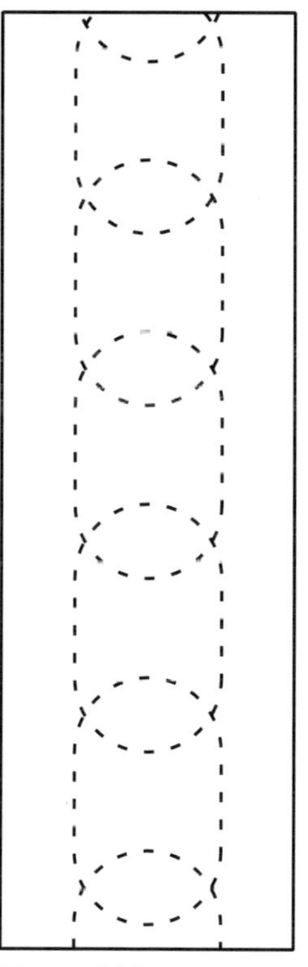

Figure 7-9.

Recommended Marking: Use a template to mark the quilt as you go.

How to Mark or Draw: Make an Oval template following the directions in Figure 7-2 and 7-3. Determine the size of the oval by the width of the sashing or border. The ovals overlap in the chain approximately ⅓ of the length of the oval. Punch holes in the Oval template to use as an aide in overlapping (Figure 7-10, page 96).

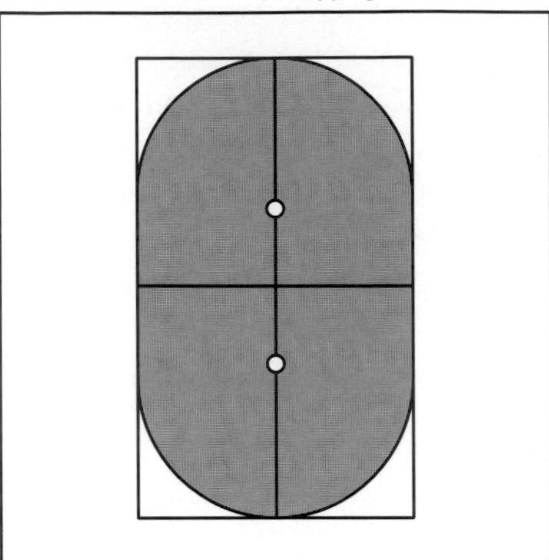

Figure 7-10.

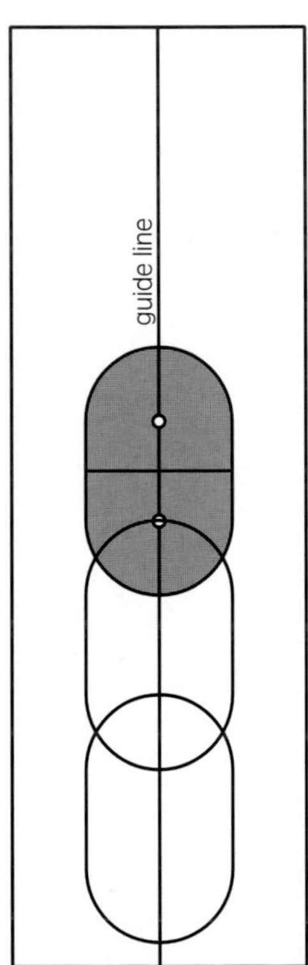

Figure 7-11.

To mark the quilt top, place the template in the strip to be quilted, mark all the way around the template. Move the template so that the hole in the template is over the end of the already drawn oval (Figure 7-11). Continue marking and quilting until the border or sashing is filled.

HELPFUL NOTE: Marking a faint guide line in the center of the border or sashing helps to keep the chain straight. Making an oval template that is shaped like a football also makes a good design. This design is easy to mark and easy to quilt.

TOOLS NEEDED: Template material and a fabric marking pencil or pen.

WHERE TO USE: Use the Oval Chain in sashings and borders. This is a frequently used Amish design. The look of the chain can be varied by overlapping the ovals so that the ends of the ovals touch.

Crescent (Figure 7-12)

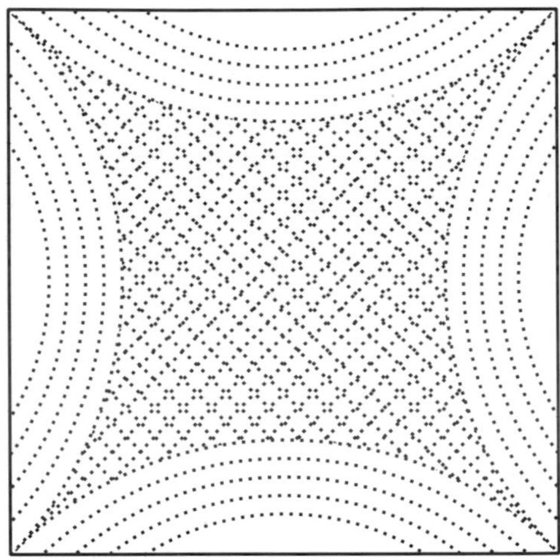

Figure 7-12.

RECOMMENDED MARKING: Using a template, mark on the quilt top as you go.

HOW TO MARK OR DRAW: The Crescent is the shape of the moon between the new moon and the first quarter. The easiest way to draw a Crescent is freehand. Decide on the length of the crescent first. For this example, the block size will be 10" and the length of the crescent will be 10". Cut a piece of paper the length (10") and half as wide (5"). Mark the paper in the center. Fold the paper lengthwise into three equal parts. Starting at the center mark on one of the fold lines, draw a curving line to the upper right corner of the paper (Figure 7-13). Fold the paper in half and trace the curving line on the other side; unfold paper. Make a template from this crescent shape.

A second method that can be used to make a

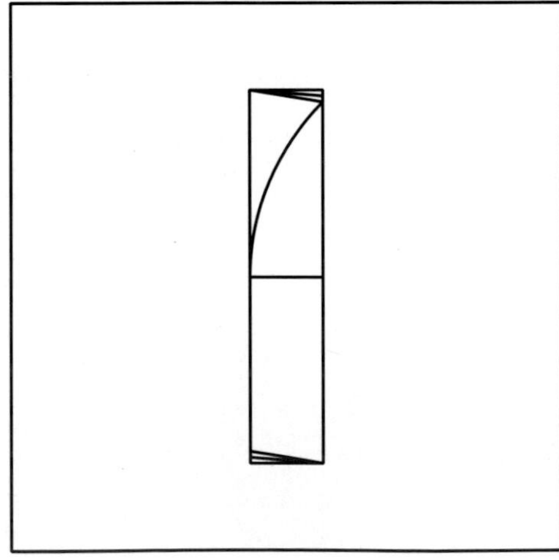

Figure 7-13.

Crescent is to draw on paper a square the size of the block where the Crescent will be used. Use a pencil and string for a compass and place the pencil on the corner of the block and the string in the center of the block. Draw a circle around the block (Figure 7-14). The Crescent appearing outside the square can be used to make a template.

To mark the quilt top, place the straight edge of the template along the seam line with the arc inside the square and mark around the curve of the template (Figure 7-15).

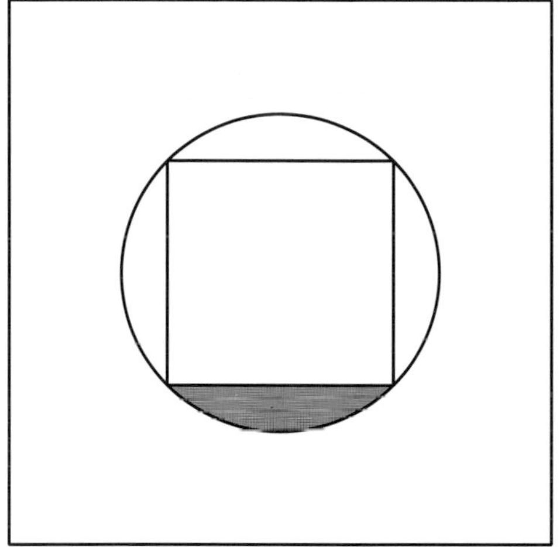

Figure 7-14.

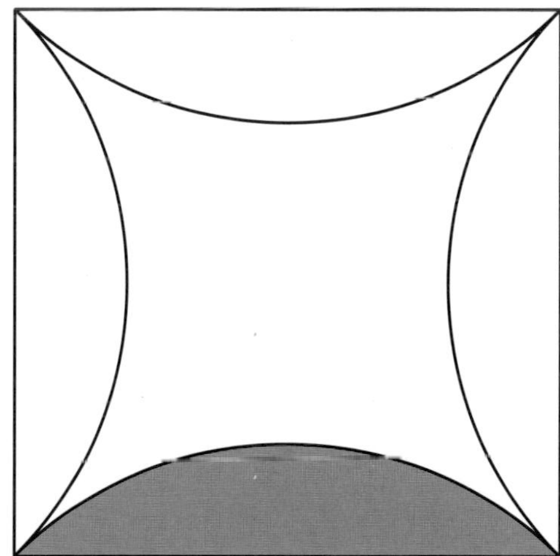

Figure 7-15.

Helpful Note: The width of the Crescent can vary from very skinny to plump. This is truly a design where there are no rules.

Tools Needed: Template material, a pencil and string, and a fabric marking pencil or pen.

Where to Use: Use the Crescent in a plain setting block. Fill the center with Squares Crosshatching and Echo the lines of the Crescent as did the quilter in the 1830's quilt where this design was found (Figure 7-12).

The Crescent can also be used as framing for other motifs and designs and invites creativity.

Radiating Curves (Figure 7-16)

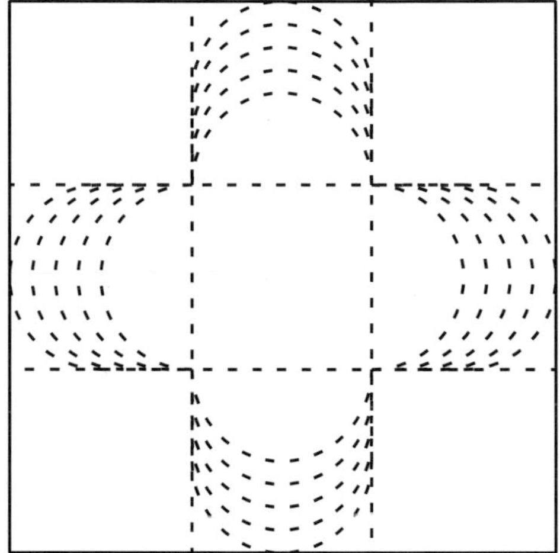

Figure 7-16.

Recommended Marking: Mark with a template as you go.

How to Mark or Draw: Although this design looks like Crescents, it is actually a semi-circle. To determine the size circle needed to make a template, measure the width of the sashing or area to be filled. Draw a circle this size using a fan/circles marking template (page 82, Figure 6-26). Since the design is formed from marking a half circle, mark the circle in half and use one side for a template (Figure 7-17).

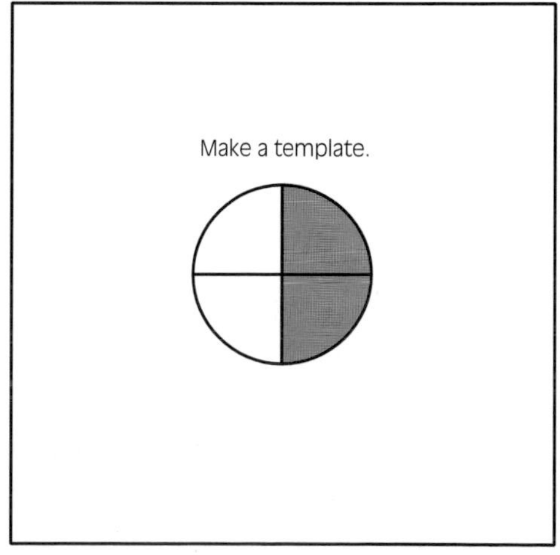

Figure 7-17.

Figure 7-18.

To mark the quilt top, place the template with corners of the template at the junction of the sashing and mark along the curve. Move the template 1" (can be ½" and mark along the curve only (Figure 7-18). Continue to move and mark until the sashing is filled.

The curves can radiate from the center of the quilt or can radiate from top to bottom and left to right in the sashings.

Helpful Note: The connecting area between blocks in the sashing creates a good place for either Concentric Circles or another quilting design. This 1870's design is an easy-to-mark and easy-to-quilt design. Think about the way the curves will radiate before beginning marking.

Tools Needed: Template material, a circle, and a fabric marking pencil or pen.

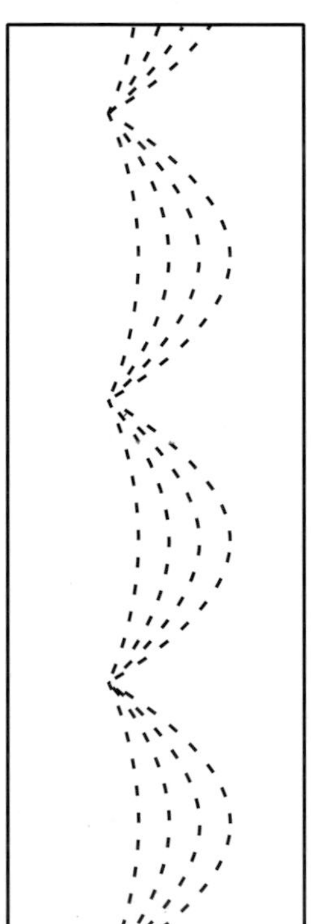

Figure 7-19.

Where to Use: Radiating Curves is a good design for sashings and could also be used in a border, particularly one that frames a center medallion.

Swag: also Lined Hammock (Figure 7-19)

Recommended Marking: Use a paper pattern to mark the quilt top before the layers are assembled.

How to Mark or Draw: First, determine the length of the swag needed to fit the border. Do this by cutting a piece of paper the width desired and half of the length of the border. Fold this paper in equal amounts (in half and then in half again and in half again, if needed). One of these divisions will be the length that each Swag will need to be, so cut off one of these parts to use in drawing the Swag pattern. The length of the paper for one Swag should be more than double the width.

Mark the center of this piece of paper and then fold it lengthwise in half and then in half again. Draw a gently curving line from one corner on the edge of the paper to the center mark on the first fold line. Draw a second curving line from the same corner to the lower center mark of the paper (Figure 7-20). This second line can be drawn to the third fold if a slimmer Swag is desired. If interior Echo lines are wanted in the Swag, mark those lines now. To avoid peaks at the bottom of the Swag, curve your line so it follows a fold line when it reaches the center fold. Fold the paper in half and trace the half of the drawn swag onto the other half of the paper (Figure 7-21). Outline the Swag with a black felt tip marker and the design is now ready to transfer to the pattern paper.

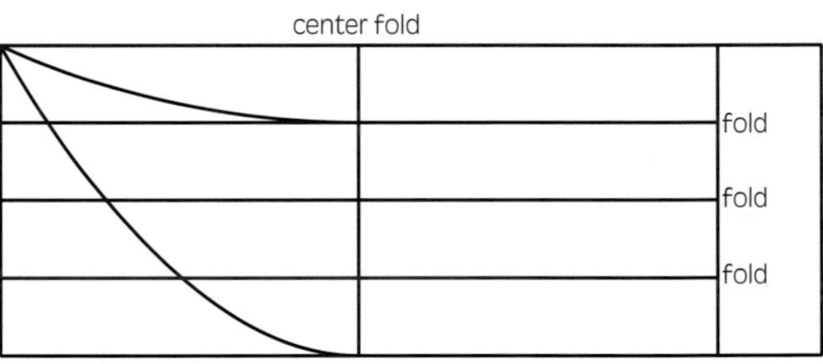

Figure 7-20.

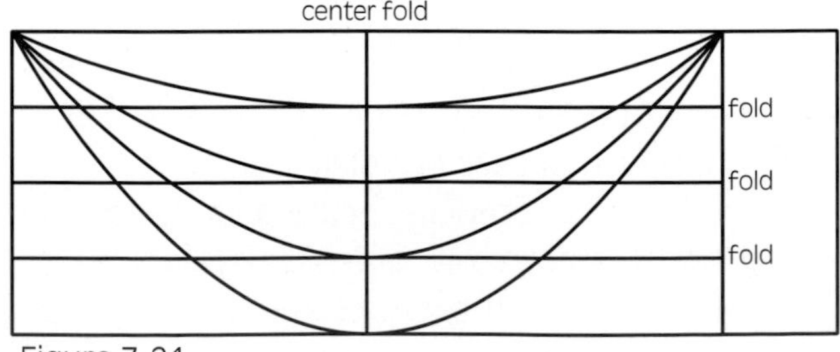

Figure 7-21.

To make the paper pattern, cut another piece of paper half of the length of the border. Mark the corner square on the paper so that the Swags will end at the corner square and the design can be changed to fit the corner.

Begin at the end of the paper that will be the middle of the quilt and trace the Swags by moving the design paper to the next position (Figure 7-22). When the pattern is drawn, outline the lines with a black felt tip marker. Pin the paper pattern to the wrong side of the quilt top and trace the design onto the quilt.

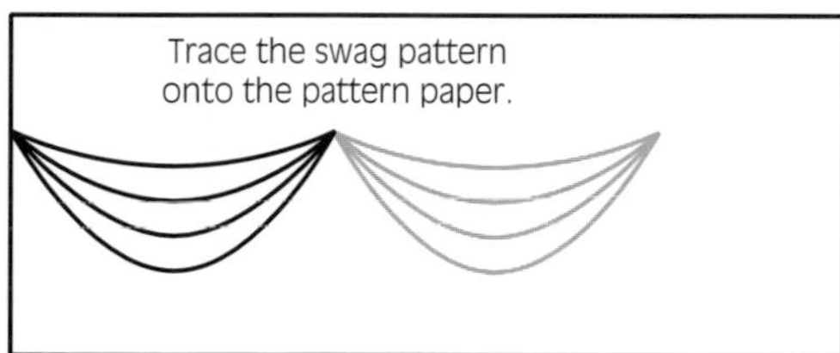

Figure 7-22.

Helpful Note: Drawing Swags is much easier than it sounds. They are also easy to quilt and add an elegant touch to a quilt. Tassels, flowers, or other designs can be added to the Swags. If the quilt is not square, it will be necessary to make a paper pattern for both the side and the end borders.

Tools Needed: Pattern paper, black felt tip marker, and a fabric marking pencil or pen.

Where to Use: Use as a border design when the border is plain fabric (not pieced) and in a whole cloth quilt to define the border edge.

Swag Variation with Tassels (Figure 7-23)

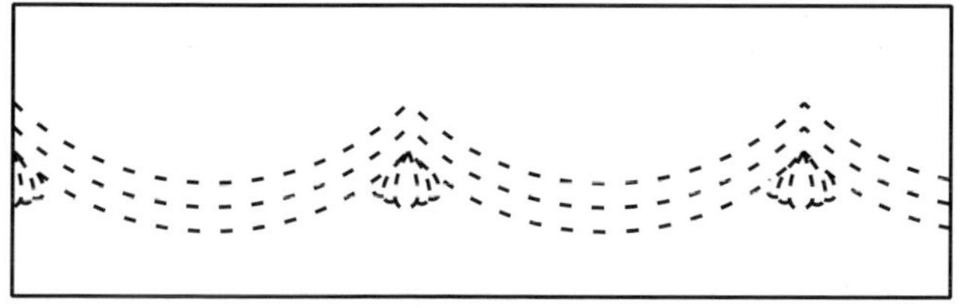

Figure 7-23.

Recommended Marking: Mark from a paper pattern before the quilt layers are assembled.

How to Mark or Draw: Follow the instructions on page 98 for making a paper pattern for the Swag. After the paper has been folded to determine the size of the Swag, cut the paper leaving two divisions attached. This is necessary to be able to draw in the tassels. Fold this cut paper lengthwise in half and in half again.

Mark the first curving line from the corner to the second fold line and then draw a second line by echoing the first line. The spacing between the quilting lines can be from ½" to 1" depending on the space to be filled. Draw a third Echo line with the same spacing (Figure 7-24). Trace the design onto the second swag section of the paper so that there are two echoing Swags. Draw the tassel between the two Swags (Figure 7-25).

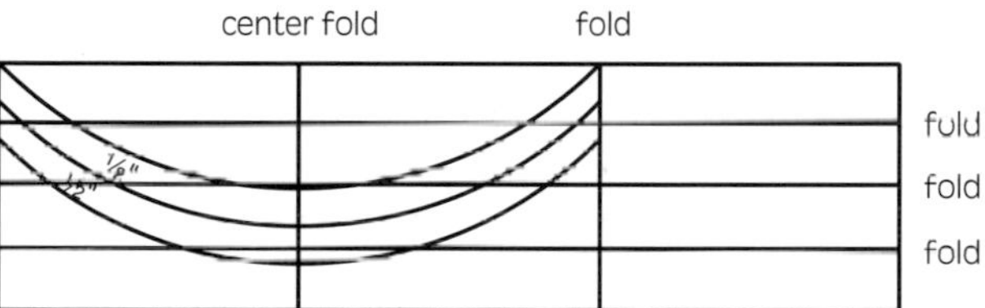

Figure 7-24.

Figure 7-25.

The tassels between the Swags are drawn like Feathers. The outline for the tassels can be drawn using a circle. See Chapter 9 for how to draw Feathers.

Go over the drawing with a black felt tip marker. The drawing is now ready to be traced onto the pattern paper that is cut to fit the border. Start at the end of the paper that will be the center of the quilt. Outline the drawing with a black felt tip marker so that the design is easy to trace onto the quilt top.

To mark the quilt top, pin the paper pattern to the wrong side of the top and trace the design onto the quilt top.

Helpful Note: The depth of the curve can be varied. The Swag can also be echoed several more times, if desired.

Tools Needed: Pattern paper, black felt tip pen, and a fabric marking pencil or pen.

Where to Use: Use this design for borders and for whole cloth quilts to define the border edge.

Overlapping Swags (Figure 7-26)

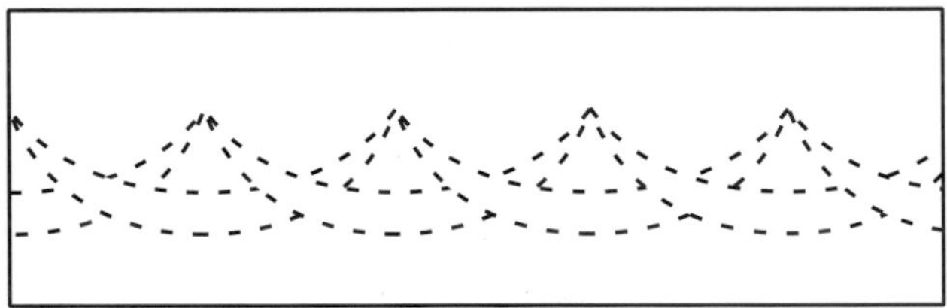

Figure 7-26.

Recommended Marking: Mark from a paper pattern before the quilt layers are assembled.

How to Mark or Draw: A crescent shaped template is needed to make the paper pattern. Follow the directions for drawing a Swag on page 98. On the folded paper, draw the first curving line from the corner to the center of the second fold and the second curving line from the corner to the center of the third fold (Figure 7-27). Make a template from this shape.

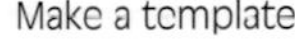

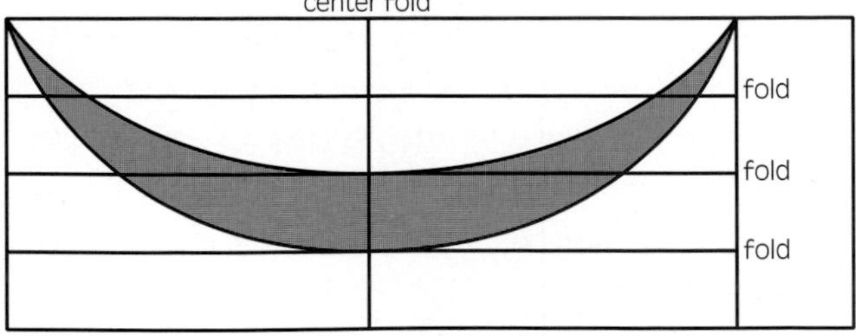

Figure 7-27.

To make the paper pattern, cut a piece of paper to fit the border. Draw a guide line, if needed. Place the template with the ends on the guide line and draw around the shape. Move the template with the end touching the one just drawn and draw another Crescent or Swag. Continue until the pattern paper is filled. Go back to the first swag and mark the center between the points. Place the template with the end touching this center mark (Figure 7-28) and draw around the design. Move the template and continue drawing Crescents on top of Crescents. Erase lines so that one Swag appears to go over one and under the next one (Figure 7-29). Go over the design lines with a black felt tip pen to finish the paper pattern.

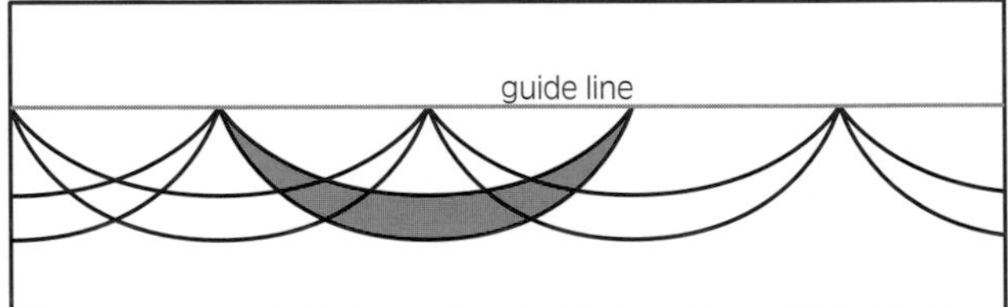

Figure 7-28.

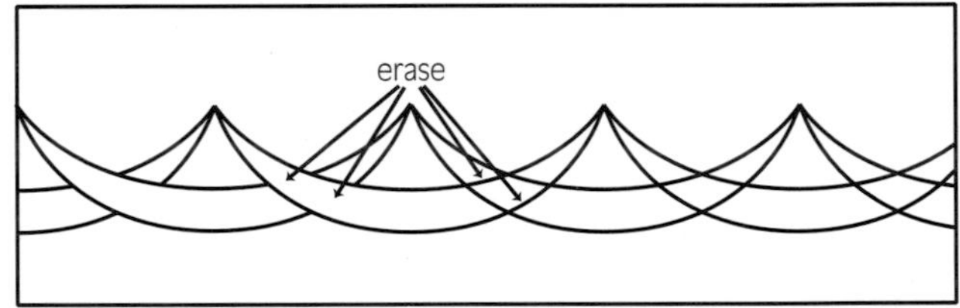

Figure 7-29.

Pin the paper pattern to the wrong side of the quilt top and trace the design onto the fabric of the quilt top.

Helpful Note: A finial can be added at the points where the swags meet to add elegance to the design.

Tools Needed: Template material, pattern paper, black felt tip pen, and a fabric marking pencil or pen.

Where to Use: Overlapping Swags can be used in plain borders or on a whole cloth quilt as a border division from the central design.

Scrolling Vine (Figure 7-30)

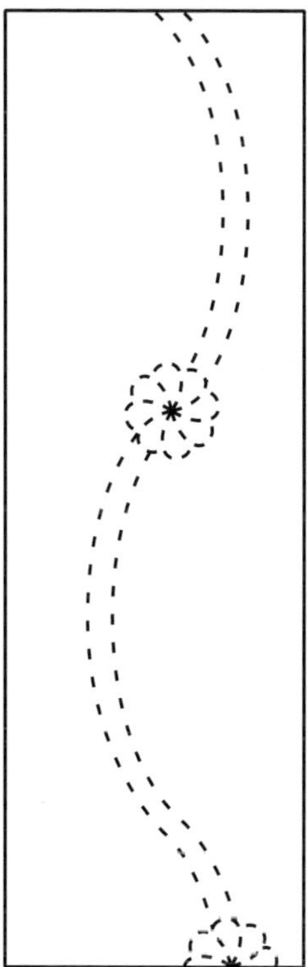

Figure 7-30.

Recommended Marking: Mark from a paper pattern before the quilt layers are assembled.

How to Mark or Draw: This is the same curving vine that is found in appliqué patterns in border designs. Follow the directions on page 98, Figure 7-20, to determine the length of the vine sections. Two sections will be needed to draw the vine. Fold the sections in half and in half again lengthwise. On the first section, draw a gentle curve from the corner of the middle fold (or second fold) to the center of the bottom edge. Fold this one section in half and trace the curve onto the other side of the section (Figure 7-31).

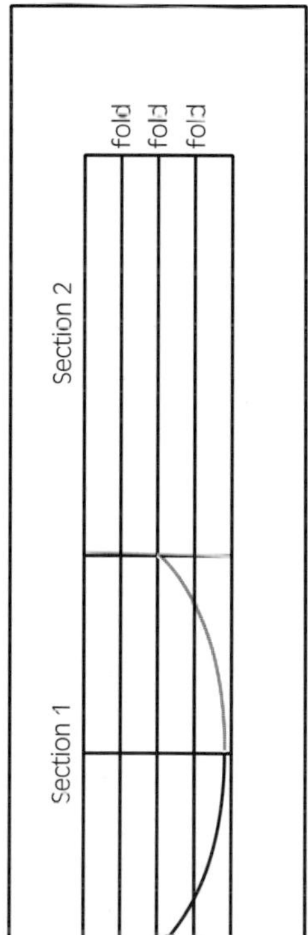

Figure 7-31.

Unfold the paper and refold in half the whole length of the two sections. Fold again on the fold line that divides the two sections. Trace the curved line which should be on the upper half of the second section (Figure 7-32).

Unfold the paper and the lines should look like those in Figure 7-33.

With a seam gauge or ruler, mark and draw a second line spaced ¼" or ½" from the original line. Go over the lines with a black felt tip marker and the vine is complete and ready to trace onto a paper pattern that fits the quilt top.

Helpful Note: The Scrolling Vine can be used to

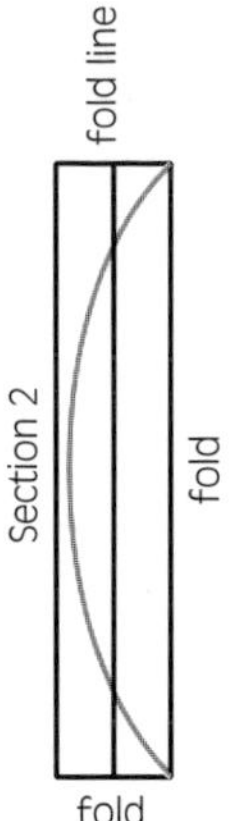

Figure 7-32.

connect other designs such as a rose or a bow. It can also be used for the stem for a Feather Vine.

Tools Needed: Pattern paper, black felt tip pen, and a fabric marking pencil or pen.

Where to Use: Use the Scrolling Vine in sashings and in borders.

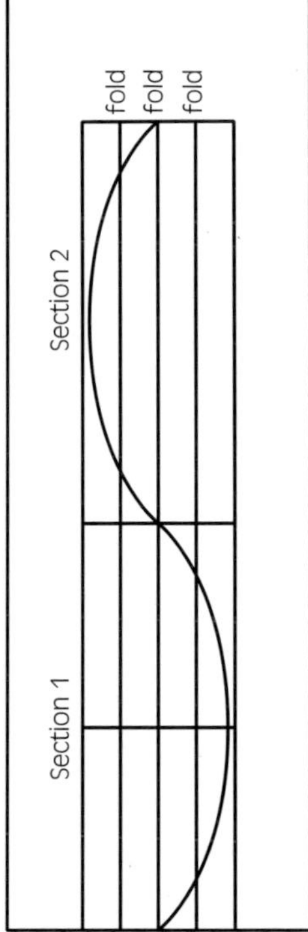

Figure 7-33.

Simple Scroll: also Wave Quilting (Figure 7-34)

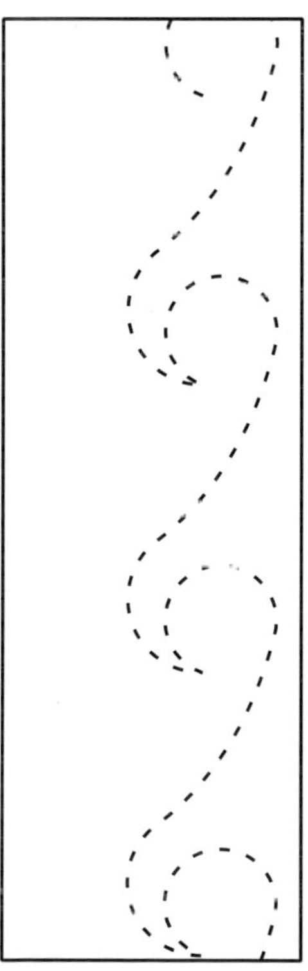

Figure 7-34.

Recommended Marking: Mark by drawing freehand as you go or mark from a paper pattern before assembling the quilt layers.

How to Mark or Draw: Draw the Simple Scroll freehand by starting a curving line at the left top of the area and continuing the curving line down to the bottom left ending with a partial circle that curves back and about half way up in the space (Figure 7-35, page 102). Continue drawing these wave looking lines across the surface. The idea is to have an informal line of waves.

To draw a more structured scroll where all of

Figure 7-35.

the scrolls are the same, first cut a piece of paper the desired width and length of one scroll. Fold this paper in half and then in half again. Unfold the paper and refold lengthwise in half and in half again (Figure 7-36).

fold fold fold
fold
fold
fold

Figure 7-36.

Two circles will be needed with one circle the size of the width of the border and another that is ¾ of that size. For this example, the size of the Scroll will be 3" wide by 8" long. Determine the circle size by measuring the folds on the paper. Place the large (3") circle on the left end of the paper and draw around the circle. Draw around the smaller circle (2¼") by placing it on the lower right hand side of the paper. Start the Scroll by drawing around the top of the left circle and extending the line at an angle to the lower right circle and around that circle to the same fold line that the large circle started on (Figure 7-37). Use a black felt tip pen to go over the lines for the Simple Scroll.

Make a paper pattern by cutting a length of paper to fit the border. Trace the Scroll onto the paper by moving the drawing underneath the pattern paper. Go over the Simple Scrolls or Waves with a black felt tip pen. Pin the paper pattern to the back of the quilt top and trace the design onto the top.

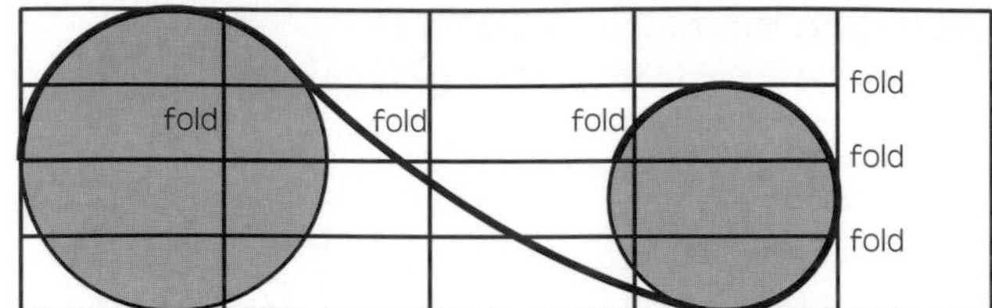

Figure 7-37.

Helpful Note: Drawing the Scroll freehand is the best method. The Scrolls do not have to be identical and, with practice it becomes easy to draw them where they look very much alike. If used on a quilt with a nautical theme, they actually look better drawn freehand so that the look is like real waves.

Tools Needed: Circle templates, pattern paper, black felt tip pen, and a fabric marking pencil or pen.

Where to Use: The Simple Scroll is a good border design. The design can be used as an overall design and as background filler for pieced or appliquéd blocks that have a nautical theme.

Scroll: also Scrolled Frame (Figure 7-38)

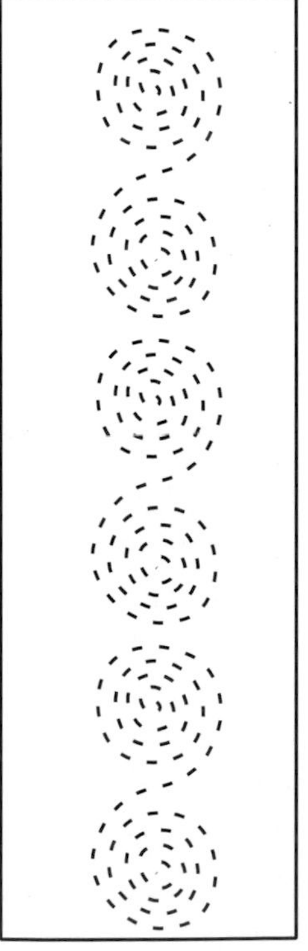

Figure 7-38.

Recommended Marking: Using a paper pattern, mark the quilt top before the layers are assembled.

How to Mark or Draw: Determine the size Scroll needed for the space to be filled. See Chapter 1, page 12, for instructions on making a pattern fit.

On a piece of paper, draw one spiral the size needed (see page 86). Use this spiral for the left side of the design. The tail of the spiral should be at the top of the paper. The spiral on the right side is drawn by rotating the first spiral so the tail of the spiral is at the bottom of the paper and tracing (Figure 7-39). Connect the two spirals by drawing a slanting line from the top of the left spiral to the bottom of the right spiral (Figure 7-40).

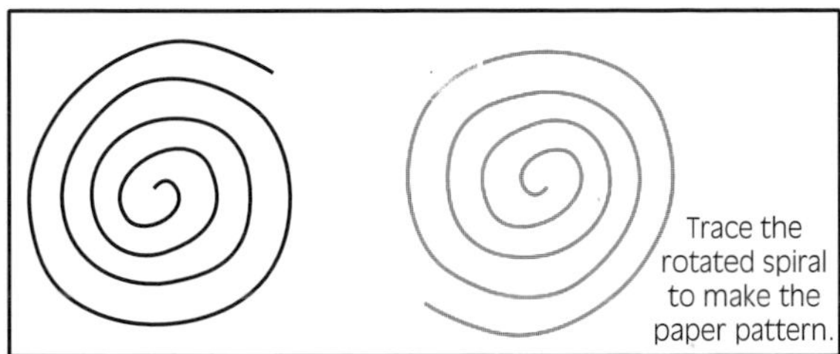

Figure 7-39.

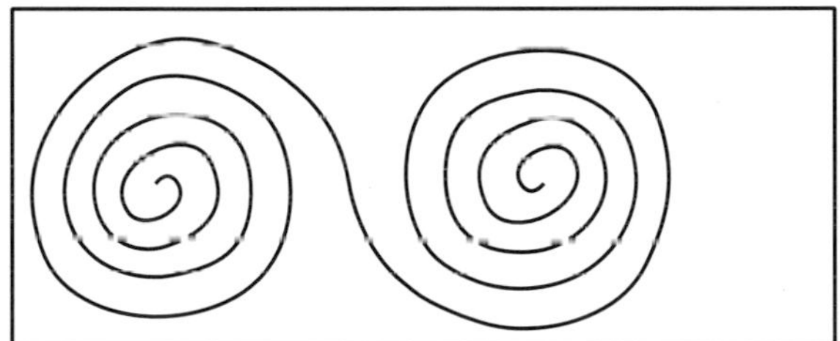

Figure 7-40.

Make a paper pattern by drawing the Scroll in a continuous line on paper cut to fit the border or sashing of the quilt. Space can be left between each Scroll in the amount needed to make the design fit the border. Go over the design with a black felt tip pen.

Mark the design on the quilt top by pinning the paper pattern to the wrong side of the quilt top and tracing the design onto the fabric.

HELPFUL NOTE: The two Spirals are placed close together to make the Scroll. The Spirals do not have to be identical. Variety in this design is pleasing.

The Scroll Variation changes some of the parts of the design (Figure 7-41).

TOOLS NEEDED: Pattern paper, black felt tip pen, and a fabric marking pencil or pen.

WHERE TO USE: Use the Scroll design in borders and sashings. It can also be used as a frame around a central design in a medallion quilt.

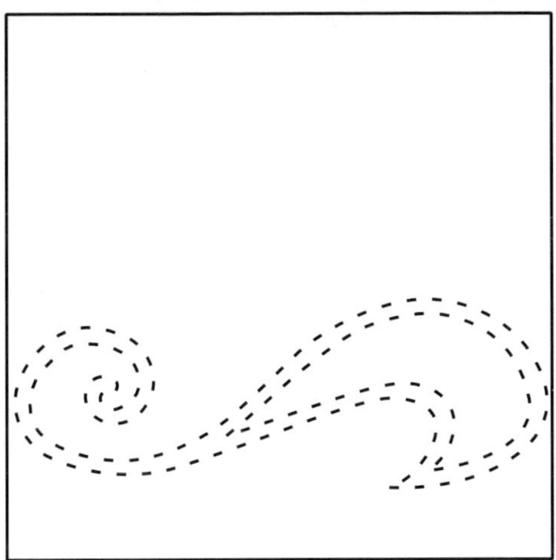

Figure 7-41.

Pumpkin Seed: also; Melon, Orange Peel, Ellipse (Figure 7-42)

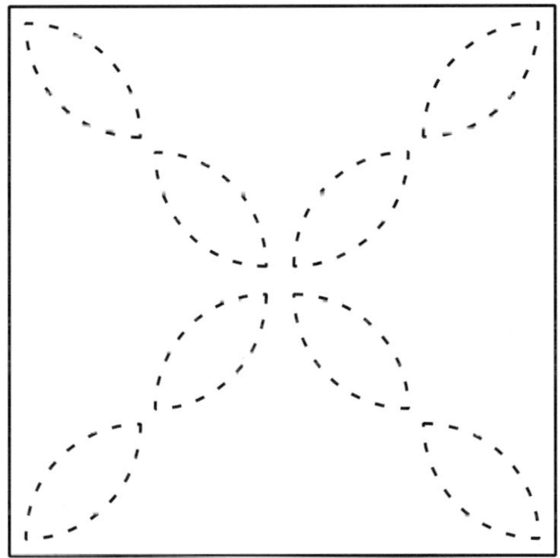

Figure 7-42.

RECOMMENDED MARKING: Mark with a template as you go or with a paper pattern. Determine the method of marking by the complexity of the design.

HOW TO MARK OR DRAW: The Pumpkin Seed has many uses and was used frequently in Amish quilts. To draw a Pumpkin Seed template, read the instructions on page 80 for drawing the Teacup design. The Pumpkin Seed template is a section of a circle or of the Teacup design (Figure 7-43, page 104).

The size of the Pumpkin Seed can vary from rather small to quite large depending on the desired design and the space to be filled.

HELPFUL NOTE: The Pumpkin Seed shape can be

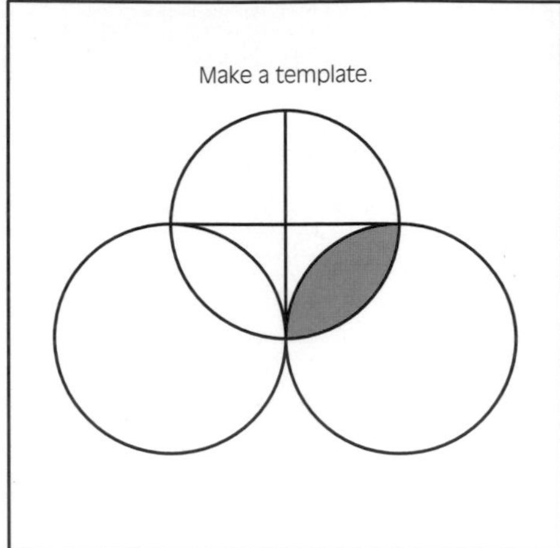

Figure 7-43.

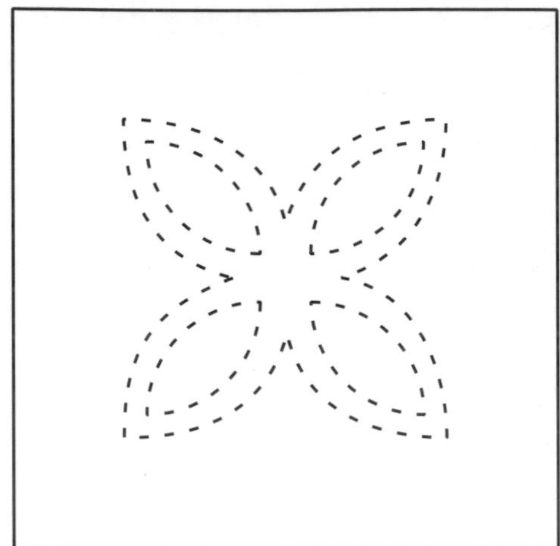

Figure 7-45.

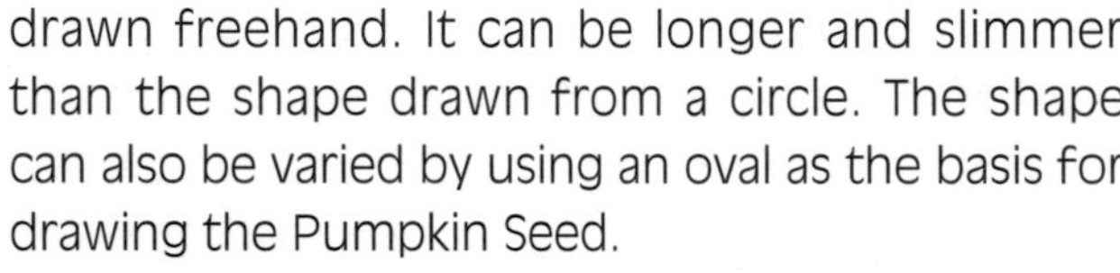

drawn freehand. It can be longer and slimmer than the shape drawn from a circle. The shape can also be varied by using an oval as the basis for drawing the Pumpkin Seed.

Tools Needed: Template material and a fabric marking pencil or pen.

Where to Use: The uses for the Pumpkin Seed are limited only by the imagination. It can be used to make a Simple Floral (Figure 7-44), Four Petaled Flower (Figure 7-45), Border I (Figure 7-46), Border II (Figure 7-47), and in other designs to make leaves, buds, and flower petals.

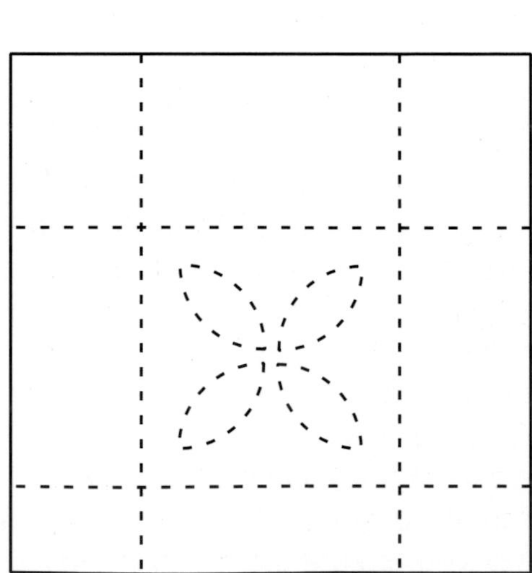

Figure 7-44.

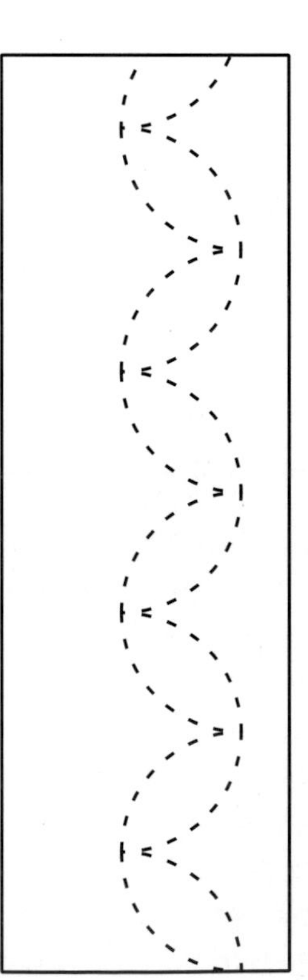

Figure 7-46.

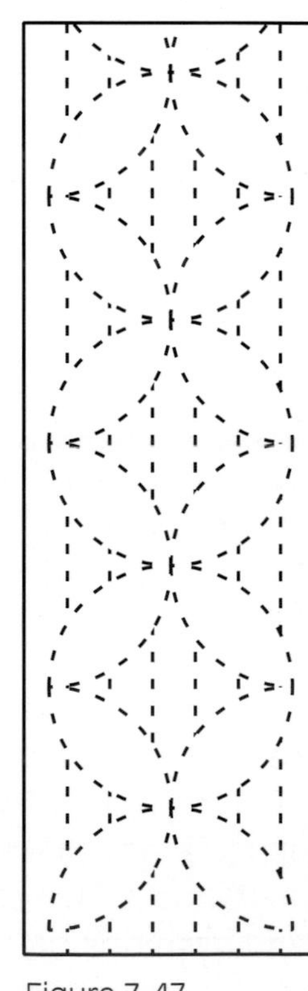

Figure 7-47.

Chapter Eight
Ropes and Cables

The designs in this chapter were designed for borders and/or sashings. They are admired because they look complicated. These designs are often the touch that makes a quilt look finished and contained. Even though they look complicated, they are really not hard to draw, mark, or quilt.

The oldest design for quilting for borders that has been given a rope name is the Running Rope Pattern. It was found on a quilt dated 1800 – 1825. It is another design that is derived from the circle. The concentric half circles overlap to form a continuous design.

The Double Cable is the most often used design of the cables. It varies from very narrow to wide. It probably became a popular design in the late 1800's and was a popular and often-used design for Amish quilts. The Amish used cables frequently in the borders and in the strips of bar quilts. As more lines were added to the cable, it was given new names.

The Twist Cable is composed of five lines on each side for a total of ten lines weaving over and under. It can be dated back to the 1860's so it can be assumed that the Double Cable was also being used at about the same time or before. As is true with most designs for quilting, the most impressive cable designs are the ones where there are more quilting lines close together.

Clamshell Rope (Figure 8-1)

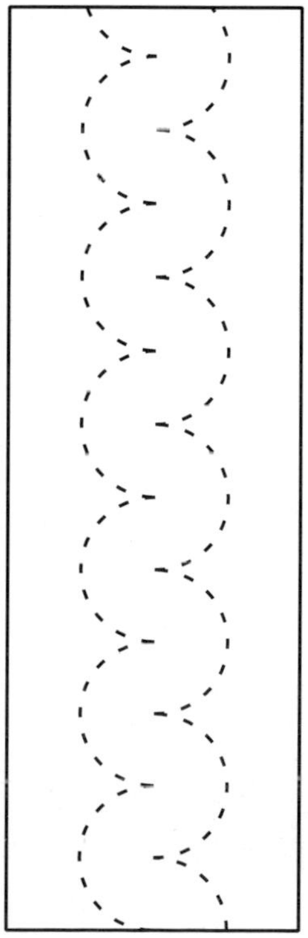

Figure 8-1.

Recommended Marking: Using a template, mark as you go.

How to Mark or Draw: A circle template is needed to mark this design. Make a circle template following the instructions for the Clamshell template on page 75, Figure 6-3. The circle needed for the Clamshell Rope is determined by the width of the border or sashing.

To mark the Clamshell Rope, draw a faint guide line along the middle of the border. Using the circle template, mark a row of half circles above the guide line. Move the circle template so that the center of the template is lined up with the place where two of the half circles meet. Mark a half circle below the guide line (Figure 8-2). Continue marking above and below the guide line until the border or sashing is filled.

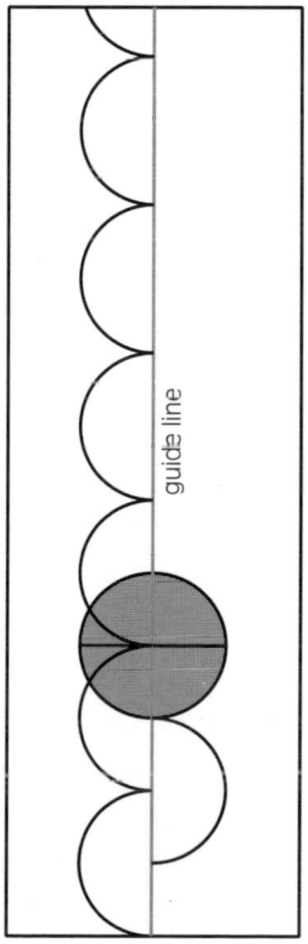

Figure 8-2.

Helpful Note: This design is easy to vary to fit a narrow or wide sashing or border and is easy to mark and quilt.

Tools Needed: A circle template and a fabric marking pencil or pen.

Where to Use: Use the Clamshell Rope in sashings and in borders.

Plate 8-1. Double Cable (also By the Piece, Feathered Garland).
Friendship Quilt by Penny Gilmore, 1991.

Plate 8-2. Triple Cable (also Triple Plaid, By the Piece, Plain Church Windows, Outline Quilting).
Thanksgiving Star by Anita Shackelford, 1984.

Plate 8-3. Triple Cable (also Teacup).
Churn Dash, Collection of Anita Shackelford, ca. 1930.

Plate 8-4. Double Cable Variation (also Diagonal Lines, Butterfly, Fan Pattern, Traditional Rose).
Amish Diamond by Karen Riggins, 1984.

Diamond and Rope (Figure 8-3)

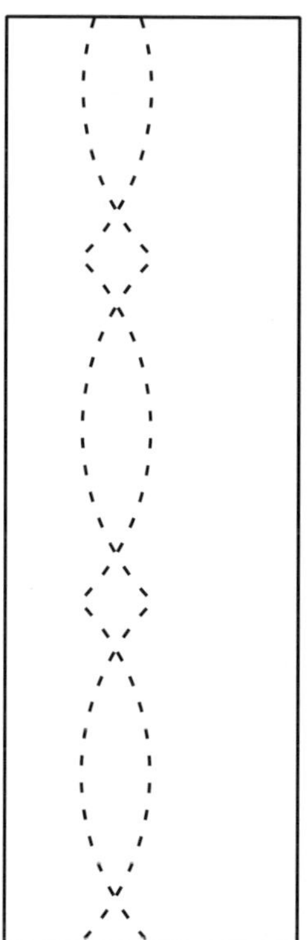

Figure 8-3.

RECOMMENDED MARKING: Mark as you go using a template.

HOW TO MARK OR DRAW: This design is derived from overlapping the lines of half a Melon shape (large Pumpkin Seed). To make a template, decide the length that one section of the design needs to be (see Chapter 1, page 12). Draw a square this size. With a pencil and string or a circle marking tool, draw a circle around the square (Figure 8-4). Make a template by overlapping this circle in the same way that the template was made for the Pumpkin Seed (Figure 7-43). Draw lines across the center of the melon shape from end to end and across the middle (Figure 8-5).

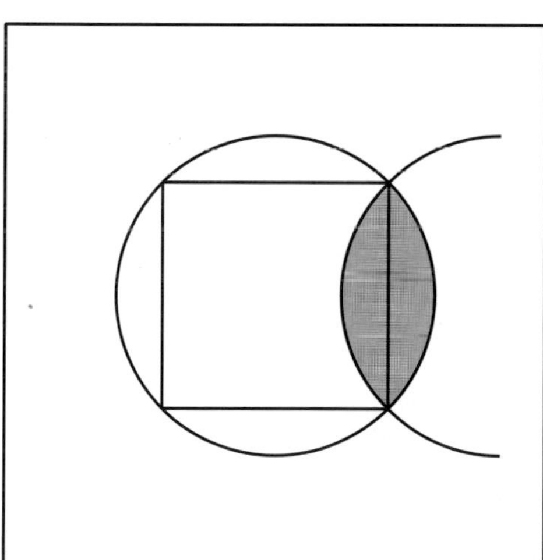

Figure 8-4.

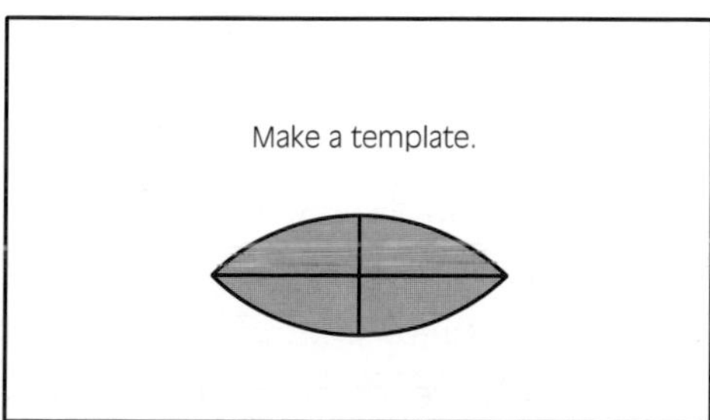

Figure 8-5.

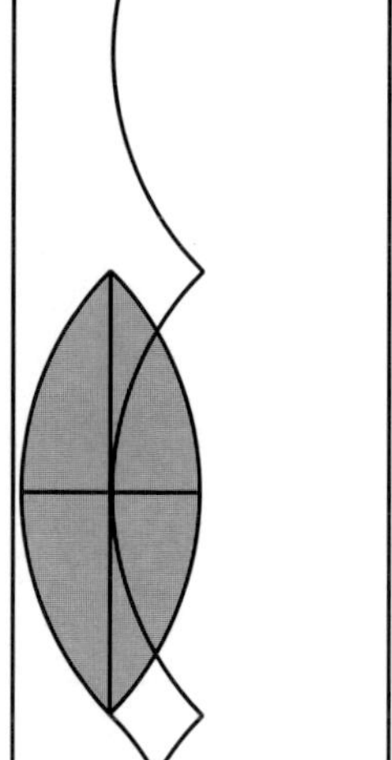

Figure 8-6.

To mark the Diamond and Rope design, place the edge of the template on the outside edge of the border or sashing and mark around one side of the template. Move the template, mark around the same half of the template, and continue moving and marking to make a string of these half melons. Next, place the edge of the template on the other edge of the border and mark around half the template (Figure 8-6). Continue marking and overlapping the half melons.

If the design does not fill the entire width of the border or sashing, mark faint guide lines the width of the design and use the guide lines to line up the template.

HELPFUL NOTE: Drawing the Diamond and Rope on paper first will help in lining the design up where it is straight and even from the edges and seams. It is actually fairly easy to draw and quilt. A plate can be used for drawing large circles when making the template.

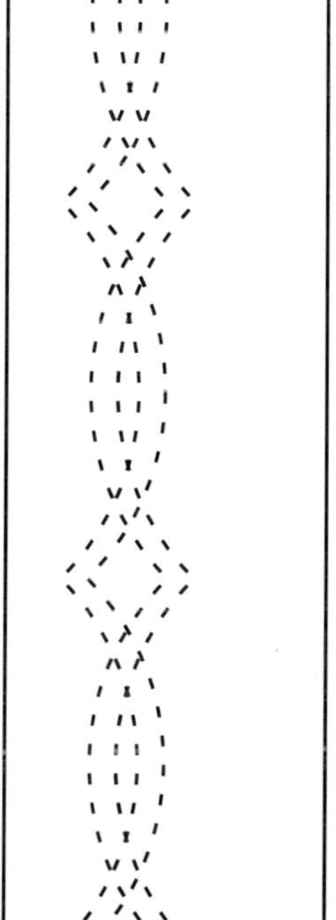

Figure 8-7.

TOOLS NEEDED: Template material, a circle drawing device, and a fabric marking pencil or pen.

WHERE TO USE: This design can be used in sashings and in borders, especially in Amish designs.

Double Diamond and Rope (Figure 8-7)

RECOMMENDED MARKING: Using a paper pattern, mark the quilt top before assembling the quilt layers.

HOW TO MARK OR DRAW: Cut paper for the pattern

to fit the border where the design will be used. On the pattern paper, draw the Diamond and Rope design exactly as described on page 107, Figure 8-3.

The double lines can now be drawn by moving the template up ¼" from the lower curved line and drawing a second line (Figure 8-8). After the double lines have been drawn for the bottom of the design, place the template ¼" below the upper curve of the design and draw the second line (Figure 8-9). Continue until all the lines of the design are doubled. Go over all the design lines with a black felt tip pen.

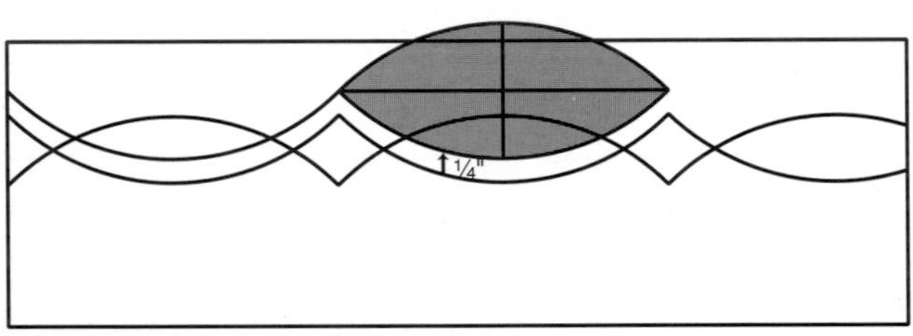

Figure 8-8.

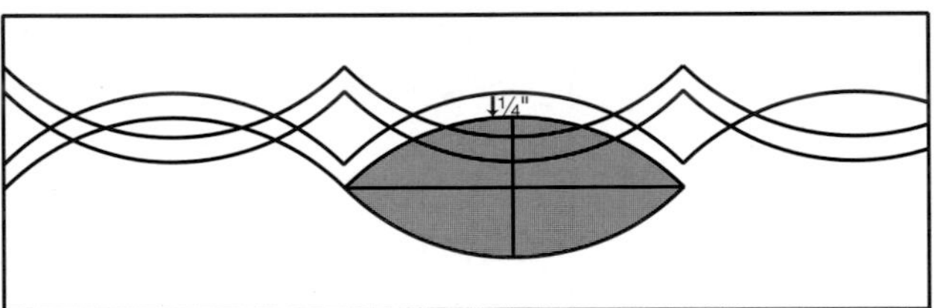

Figure 8-9.

To mark the design on the quilt top, pin the pattern to the wrong side of the quilt top and trace the design onto the fabric.

HELPFUL NOTE: This design is easy to quilt and looks good with the double lines. For a wider design, the double line spacing can be more than ¼".

TOOLS NEEDED: Template material, pattern paper, a black felt tip pen, and a fabric marking pencil or pen.

WHERE TO USE: This design is good for narrow sashings or narrow borders.

Diamond and Rope Cable (Figure 8-10)

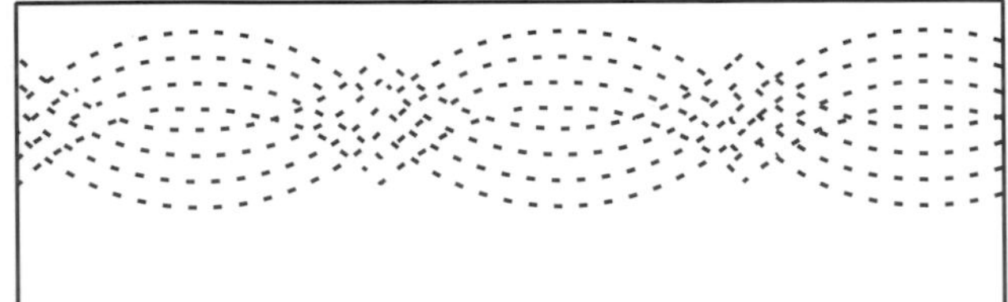

Figure 8-10.

RECOMMENDED MARKING: Mark the quilt top using a paper pattern before the quilt layers are assembled.

HOW TO MARK OR DRAW: On a piece of pattern paper cut to fit the size of the border, draw the Double Diamond and Rope as described on page 107. To draw the cable that intertwines the Diamond and Rope, place the melon template with the end of the template centered in the diamond and the upper edge of the template spaced ¼" from the rope line (Figure 8-11). Draw around the entire template and continue drawing around the template for each section of the Diamond and Rope.

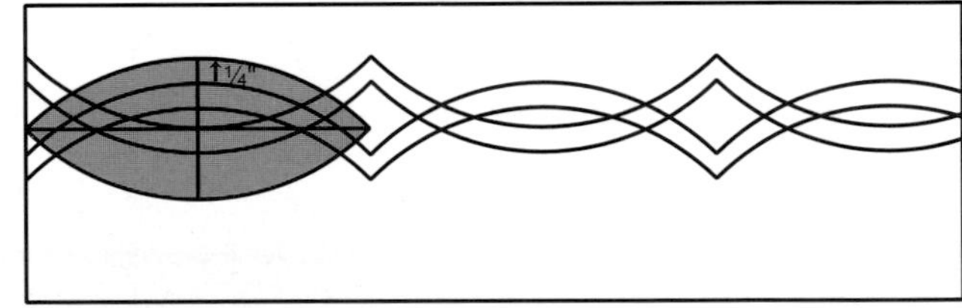

Figure 8-11.

Draw the next lines of the cable by moving the template to the top of the design with the end in the center of the diamond and the upper edge of the template spaced ¼" from the last drawn line (Figure 8-12). Draw around the entire template and repeat in the same manner for each section of the design. When the design is

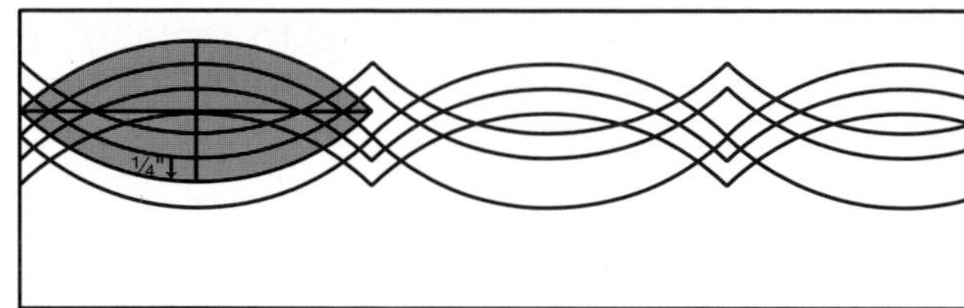

Figure 8-12.

complete, go over the lines with a black felt tip marker.

To mark the design on the quilt top, pin the paper pattern to the wrong side of the quilt top and trace the design onto the fabric.

Helpful Note: The spacing between the lines can be wider. A spacing of ½" is good but could be 1" for a design as wide as 8".

Tools Needed: Template material, pattern paper, a black felt tip marker, and a fabric marking pencil or pen.

Where to Use: The Diamond and Rope Cable is designed to use in borders but could be successfully used in a bar or strippie quilt.

Rope (Figure 8-13)

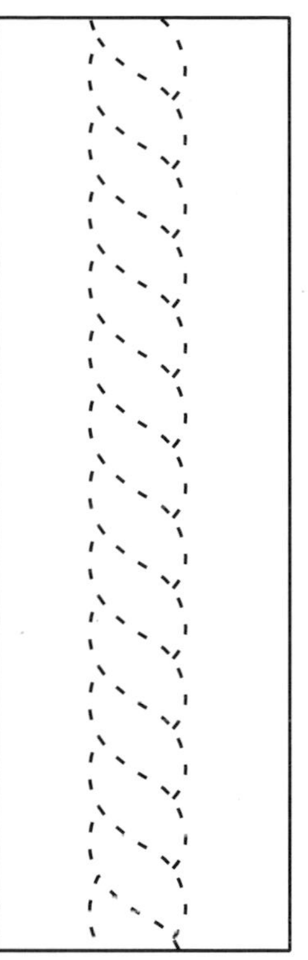

Figure 8-13.

Recommended Marking: Mark using a template as you go.

How to Mark or Draw: The lines in the Rope design resemble very lazy S's.

Use the full-size drawing (Figure 8-14) to make a template to use to mark the Rope directly onto the quilt top.

The marks on each side of the template are used to match up the pieces of the Rope as you move the template. Use a seam for a guide to keep the Rope straight or mark a faint guide line.

Helpful Note: The template for the Rope can be enlarged or reduced on a

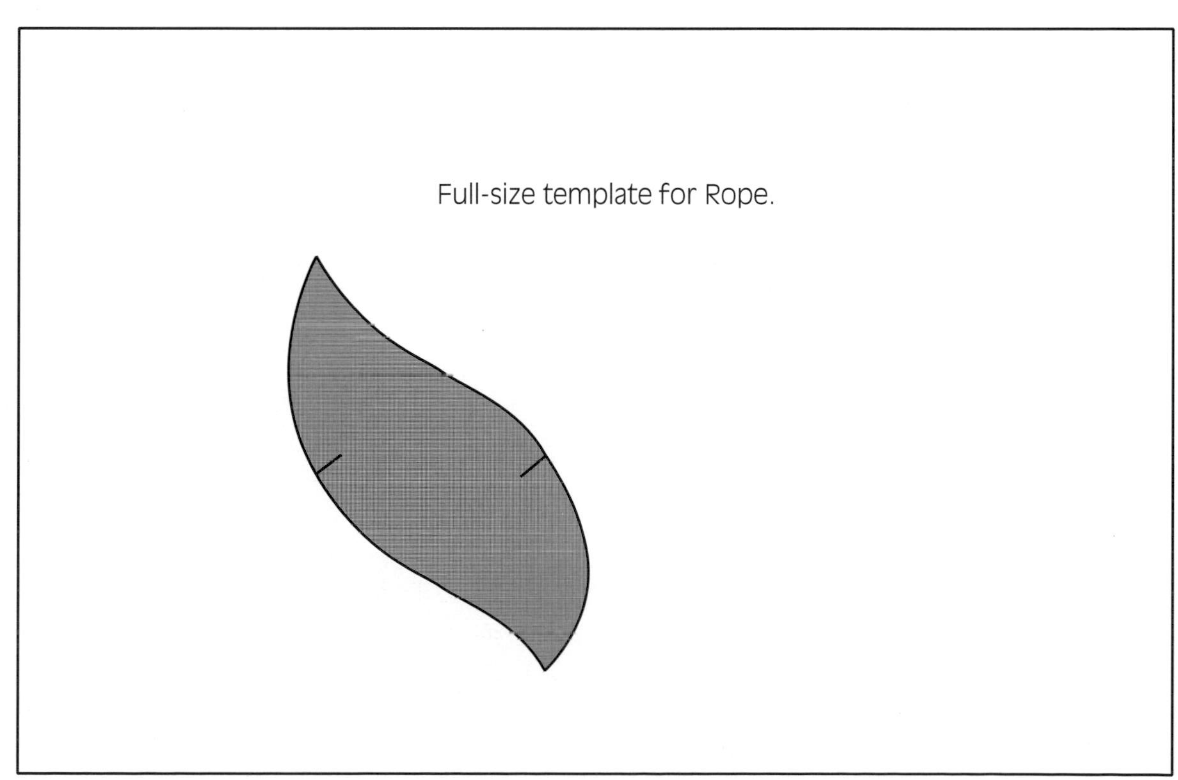

Full-size template for Rope.

photocopy machine. Practice marking a few sections of the Rope on paper before beginning marking on the quilt.

Tools Needed: Template material and a fabric marking pencil or pen.

Where to Use: The Rope is a good design for narrow sashing or a narrow border.

Twisted Braid: also Twisted Rope, Braid (Figure 8-15)

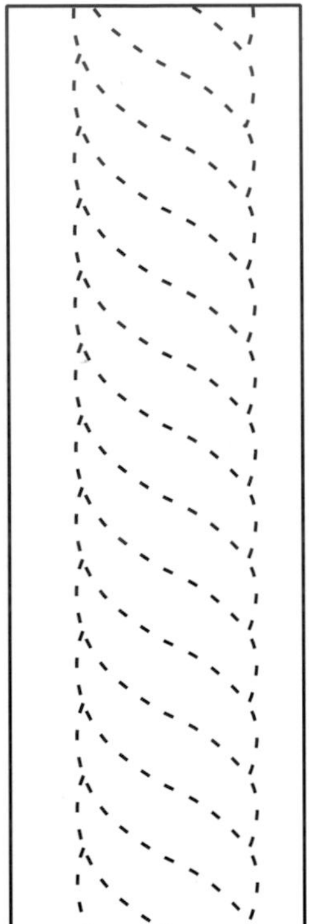

Figure 8-15.

Recommended Marking: Mark using a template as you go.

How to Mark or Draw: The two full-size drawings can be used to make the templates for drawing a small and a large Twisted Braid (Figure 8-16). The marks on the templates are used to match the design as you draw. The arrow in the large template is a directional arrow to aide in lining up the template so the design will be straight up and down. The sections of the design can be enlarged or reduced on a photocopy machine.

Draw a faint guide line on the quilt top or use a seam as a guide to keep the Twisted Braid straight.

Helpful Note: Practice drawing the design on paper before beginning to mark on the actual quilt. This design can be drawn on pattern paper and marked before the quilt layers are assembled. This is especially helpful when figuring out how to turn the corner of a border.

Tools Needed: Template material and a fabric marking pencil or pen.

Where to Use: Use this design in the borders or sashings.

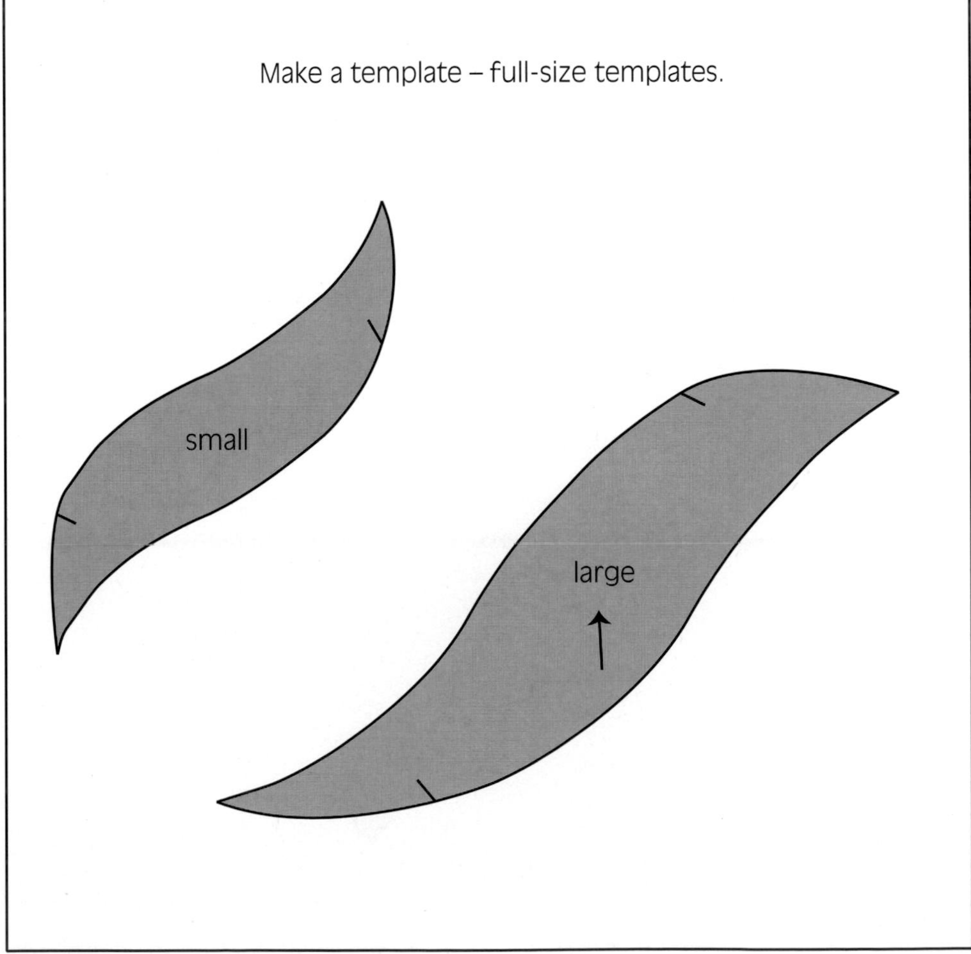

Figure 8-16.

Running Rope Pattern (Figure 8-17)

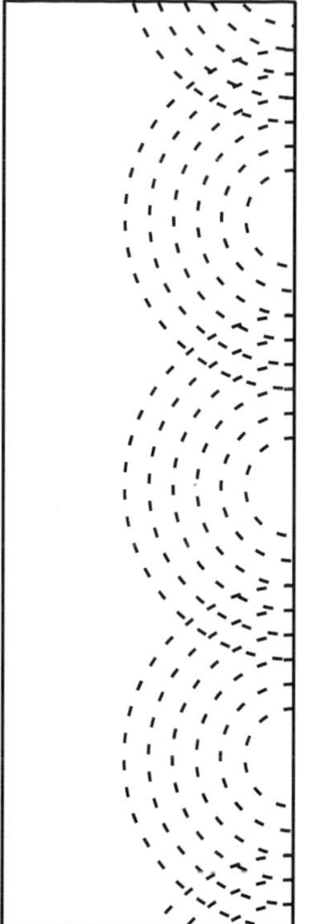

Figure 8-17.

RECOMMENDED MARKING: This design can be marked as you go or use a paper pattern to mark the design on the quilt top before the layers are assembled.

HOW TO MARK OR DRAW: The Running Rope Pattern was found on quilts dating from the very early 1800's. The design is overlapping concentric half circles and is used as a border design.

First, determine the size of the largest half circle needed to fill the border width. Using a Circle/Fan marking tool as described on page 82. Figure 6-26, or a pencil and string for a compass, start by drawing the largest half circle first. Use the edge of the quilt or the border seam for a straight guide. Draw decreasing half circles (at least six) that are spaced from ¼" to 1" apart (Figure 8-18). The spacing will depend on the size of the half circles. Choose the spacing that looks best to you.

Figure 8-18.

Start the second section of the Running Rope by drawing the largest half circle first and starting on the end of the half circle that is third from the center. Repeat the drawing, decreasing half circles always being careful that the beginning of the line touches the next half circle (Figure 8-19).

If using a paper

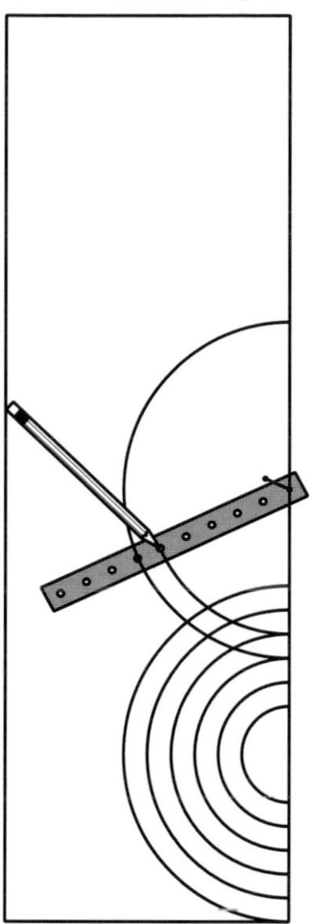

Figure 8-19.

pattern, pin the pattern to the back of the quilt top and trace the design on the fabric.

HELPFUL NOTE: If marking directly on the quilt, practice drawing a few sections of the design before beginning to mark on the actual quilt.

TOOLS NEEDED: A Circle/Fan marking template or tool and a fabric marking pencil or pen.

WHERE TO USE: Use the Running Rope Pattern for quilt borders. It could also be used in a bar or strippie quilt.

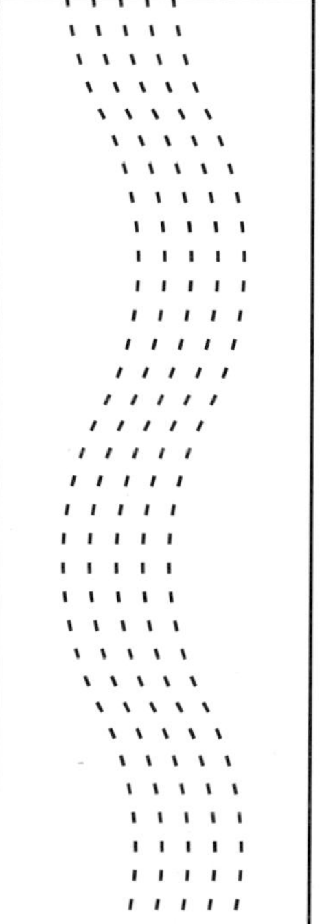

Figure 8-20.

Running Rope II (Figure 8-20)

RECOMMENDED MARKING: Using a template, mark on the quilt top as you go.

HOW TO MARK OR DRAW: This design is derived from a very gently curving line that is echoed to fill the sashing or border area.

To make a template, cut a piece of paper

that is 1½" wide and 8" long. Draw lines on the paper to make a 1" wide drawing with ¼" spacing along the outside edge. Mark a center line the length of the paper. Fold the paper in half and in half again (Figure 8-21). Draw a gentle curving line starting at the drawn center line and drawing down to the first fold and up to the middle fold. At the middle fold, continue drawing another curving line that goes up to the third fold and down to the drawn center line (Figure 8-22). Use the bottom of the design, including the ¼" below the 1" line to make a template.

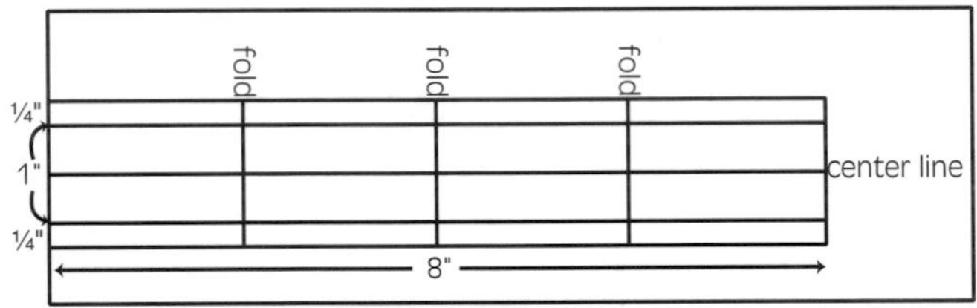

Figure 8-21.

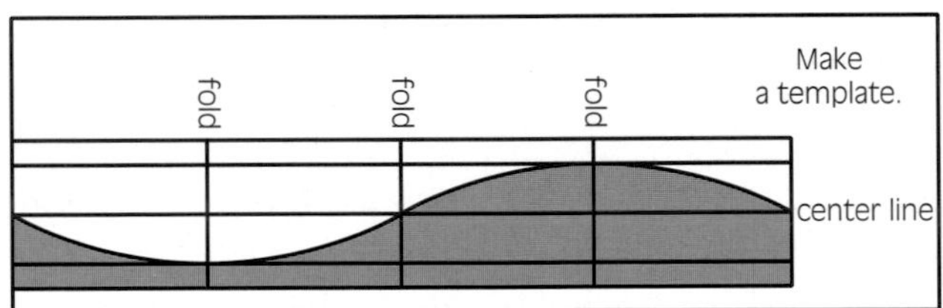

Figure 8-22.

To mark the quilt, draw a faint guide line down the center of the border or sashing. Place the template with the left top end and the drawn center line on the left section of the template on the guide line. Mark along the template edge, move the template and after lining up again, mark another section. Echo this first line by moving the template from both sides of the first marking and spacing the lines ¼" or ½" from the previous line (Figure 8-23). Use a seam gauge or ruler to keep the spacing even. Mark and quilt until the border or sashing is filled.

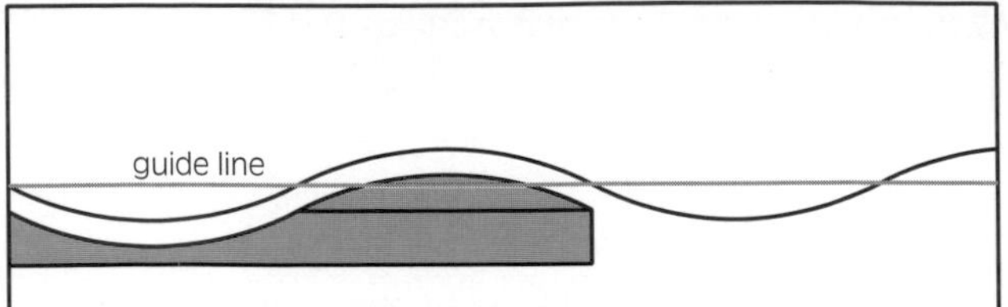

Figure 8-23.

Helpful Note: The Running Rope can be made wider by echoing more lines as desired. Seven or nine lines make a good design. This design is easy to draw and quilt.

Tools Needed: Template material, small ruler or seam gauge, and a fabric marking pencil or pen.

Where to Use: Running Rope II is designed for use in both borders and sashings. With wider spacing between lines, it could be used as an overall design disregarding the surface design of the quilt.

Braided Rope (Figure 8-24)

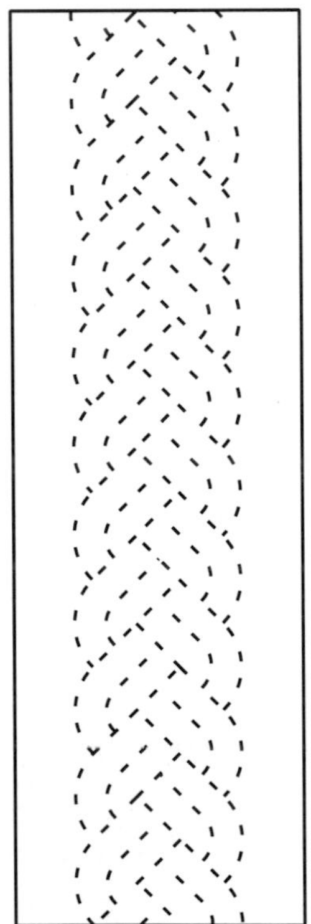

Figure 8-24.

Recommended Marking: Use a paper pattern to mark the quilt top before the layers of the quilt are assembled.

How to Mark or Draw: On a piece of paper, draw an oval that is twice as long as it is wide (example: 3" by 6") following the instructions on page 93, (Figure 7-2). Divide the oval in half across and down the center. Using a ruler, mark an inside line that is half way to the center and parallel to the outside of the upper part of the oval or a second smaller oval. Mark a guide line on this drawing by marking a 45° diagonal line from the inside oval up to the center line. Do this on both sides of the half oval drawing (Figure 8-25). This horseshoe-type drawing is now ready to be used to draw the Twisted Rope onto the pattern paper.

To draw the design for the pattern, draw a

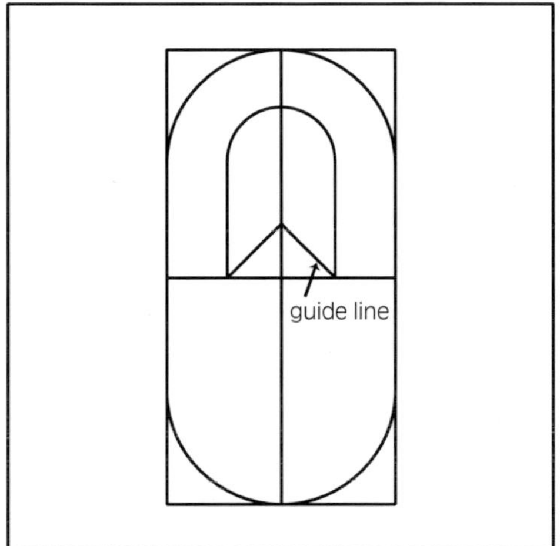

Figure 8-25.

guide line down the center of the paper that has been cut to fit the border. Place the paper drawing under the pattern paper with the guide line on the drawing lined up with the guide line on the pattern paper. Trace the right half of the design (looks like a candy cane) that is above the guide line. Move the paper, keeping the guide line on the center line, and with the top of the cane touching the one before, and trace around half of the design again. Continue until several have been drawn (Figure 8-26).

Next, place the drawing back at the beginning and with the other guide line of the drawing lined up with the pattern guide line. The section to be traced will now be below the guide line. The corners of the quarter design on the drawing should fit into the corner of the sections already drawn above the guide line (Figure 8-27). Trace the design, move the drawing paper, trace, and continue fitting and tracing these sections until the pattern paper is filled. Go over the design lines with a black felt tip pen.

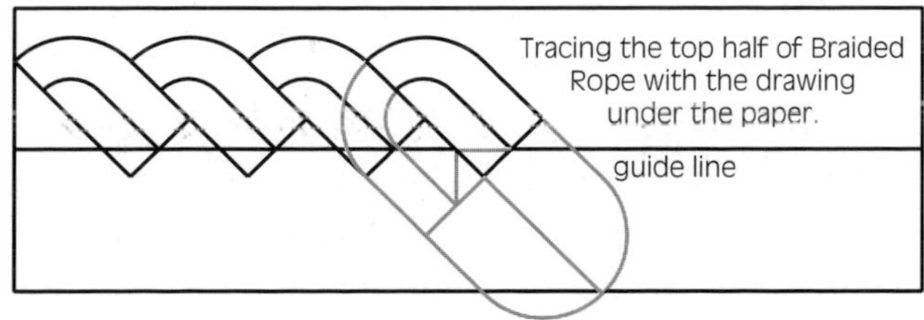

Figure 8-26.

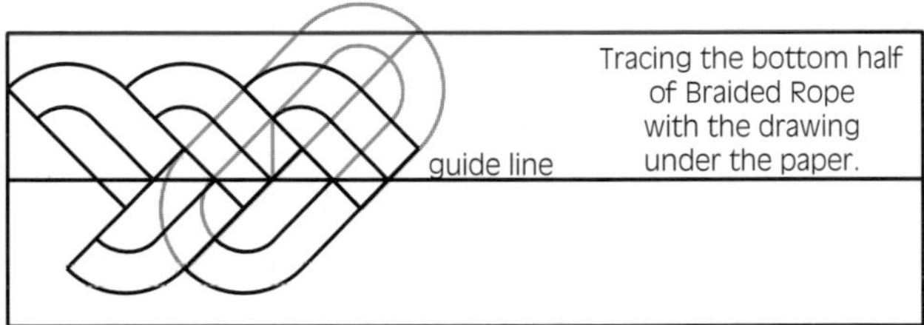

Figure 8-27.

To mark on the quilt top, pin the paper pattern to the wrong side of the quilt top and trace the design onto the fabric.

Helpful Note: A template can be made for this design and marked as you go although it is not any faster and not as neat as marking from a paper pattern.

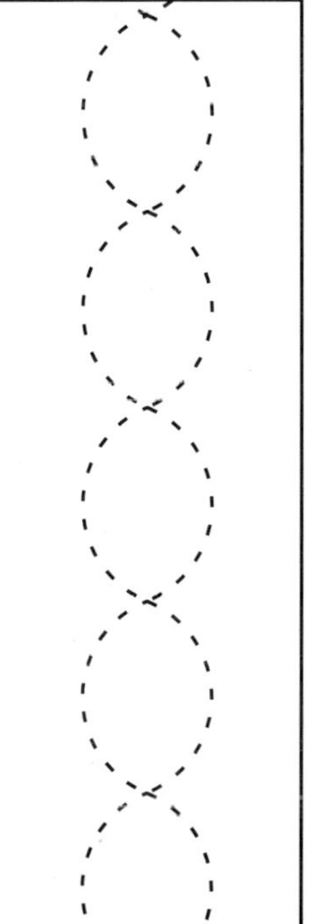

Figure 8-28.

Tools Needed: Pattern paper, a black felt tip marker, and a fabric marking pencil or pen.

Where to Use: Use this design in borders.

Single Cable: also Lozenge (Figure 8-28)

Recommended Marking: Mark, using a template, as you go.

How to Mark or Draw: The width and the length of the Single Cable can be varied from slender to plump. The most used shape is an ellipse or melon shape. When looking at the moon in the third quarter, the light part of the moon is the shape. An ellipse can be drawn using a Circle template or a Circle/Fan marking template. A 2" circle makes a good size ellipse.

Draw a 4" square. Draw lines across the center of the square and diagonally from corner to corner. Draw two circles (2") with the first circle centered on a diagonal line and the second circle centered on the next center line (Figure 8-29). Draw a center guide line down the center of the part where the circles overlap to make a template.

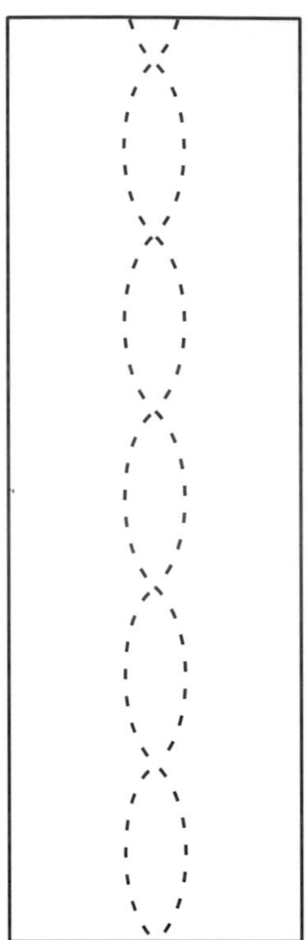

Figure 8-31.

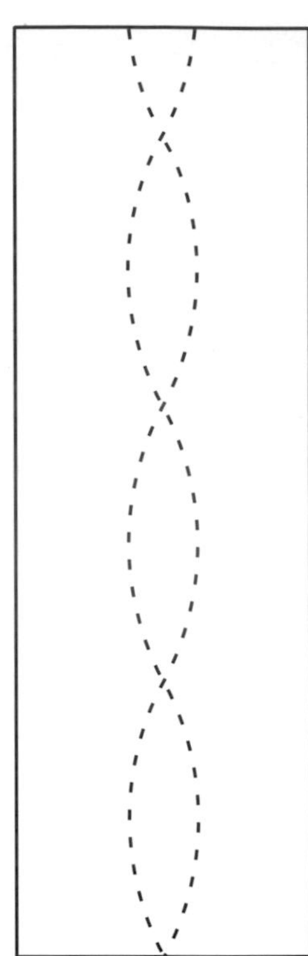

Figure 8-32.

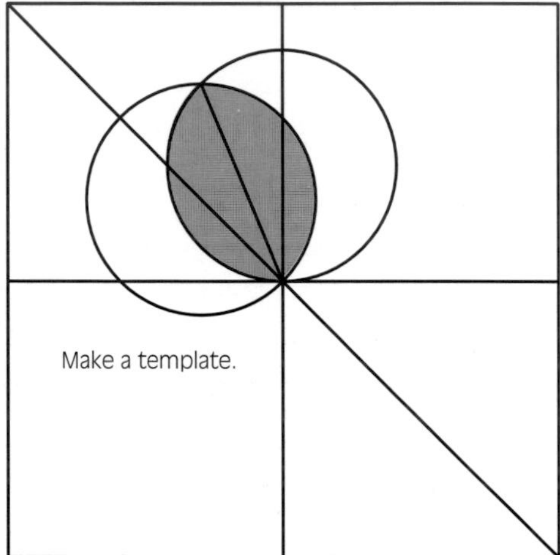

Figure 8-29.

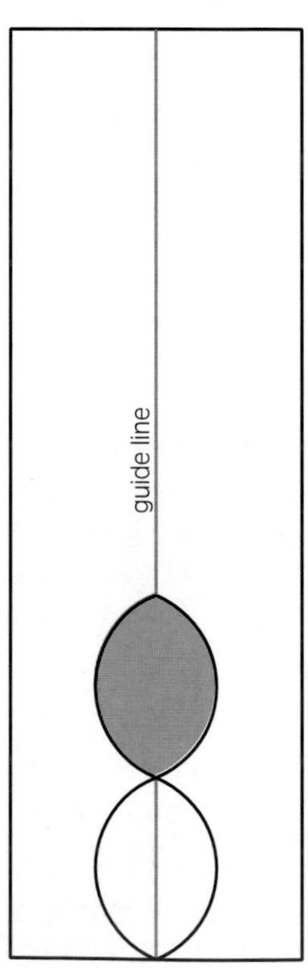

Figure 8-30.

On the area to be marked on the quilt top, mark a faint center guide line. Line up the center line on the template with the guide line and mark around the entire template. Move the template with the end touching the just drawn ellipse and mark (Figure 8-30). Continue marking and quilting until the area is filled.

If a narrow design is desired (Figure 8-31), use the Pumpkin Seed shape for a template. See the directions for drawing the Pumpkin Seed on page 104 (Figure 7-43). Follow the same method of marking as when using the ellipse.

The Single Cable can also be drawn by using the template (Figure 8-22) for Running Rope II. Mark all of the fold lines to use as guides. Draw one continuous curving line by marking along the template the length of the border. To draw the second line of the cable, move the template so the end of the template lines up with the mid-mark of the curve of the first drawn line. The two lines weave over and under to form a graceful narrow Running Single Cable (Figure 8-32).

Helpful Note: All three of these Single Cables are easy to draw and easy to quilt. Decide which template to use by the width of the design and the look that is desired.

Tools Needed: Template material and a fabric marking pencil or pen.

Where to Use: The Single Cable is a good design for narrow borders and sashings. The templates can be placed around circles, ovals, diamonds, or squares to make a framing device for another quilting design.

Lozenge: also single cable (Figure 8-33)

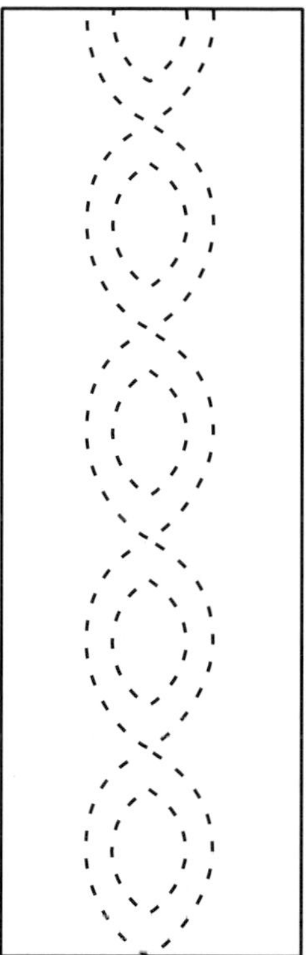

Figure 8-33.

RECOMMENDED MARKING: Use a template to mark the quilt as you go.

HOW TO MARK OR DRAW: To make the template, draw an ellipse following the instructions on page 114, Figure 8-29. Using a ruler, draw dashed lines spaced ½" from the ellipse to make a second larger ellipse (Figure 8-34). Fill in the dashed lines to make the template (Figure 8-35). Cut out the center area of the template.

To mark the design on the quilt, mark a faint guide line down the center of the border or sash-

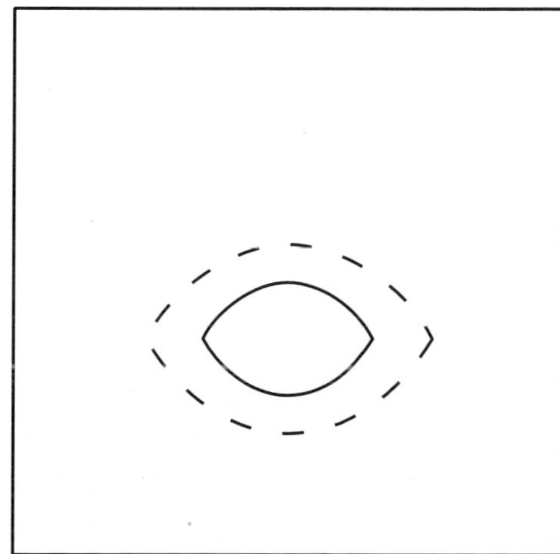

Figure 8-34.

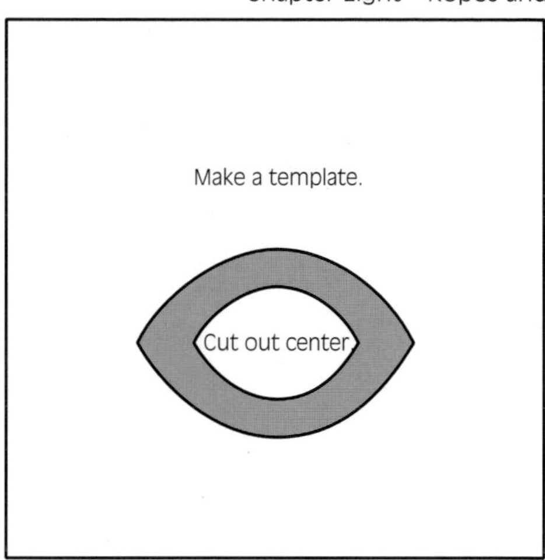

Figure 8-35.

ing. Place the template with the center on the guide line and mark around the inside and outside of the template. Move the template so that it touches the previous marking and mark again. Continue until the border is filled.

HELPFUL NOTE: The design can be enlarged but is usually found on narrow borders or sashings. The design is easy to mark and easy to quilt.

TOOLS NEEDED: Template material and a fabric marking pencil or pen.

WHERE TO USE: Use the Lozenge in narrow sashings and borders.

Double Cable: also Cable, Chain, Rope, Braid, Twist, Single Cable, Worm, Scalloped Chain (Figure 8-36)

RECOMMENDED MARKING: Mark, using a template, on the quilt top as you go or using a paper pattern to mark before the layers of the quilt are assembled.

HOW TO MARK OR DRAW: Make a template using the instructions for the Lozenge cable (Figure 8-35). Mark a faint guide line down the length of the center of the border. Mark the design on the quilt by placing the template on the guide line and marking around the inside and the outside of the template.

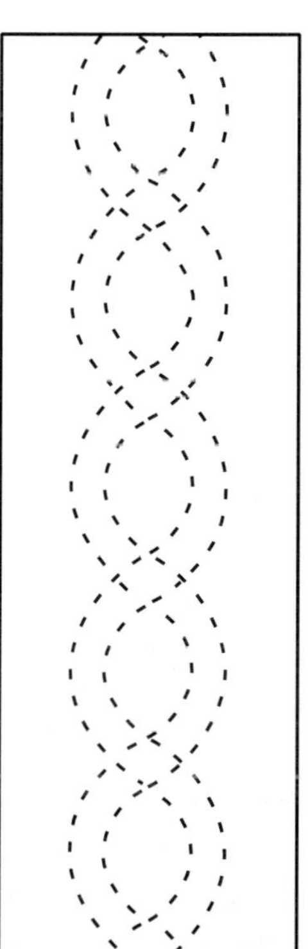

Figure 8-36.

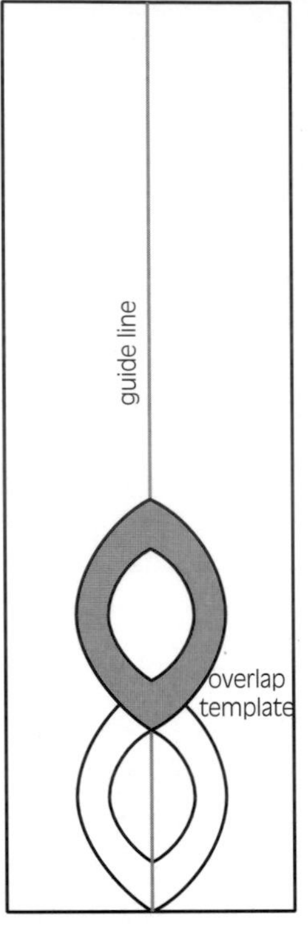

Figure 8-37.

The second section of the cable is marked by overlapping the template with the previously drawn section so that the end of the template touches the end of the inside ellipse (Figure 8-37). Continue overlapping the template and marking until the border is filled.

A Double Cable Variation (Figure 8-38) is drawn in the same way except this time erase the lines drawn on the left side of the template where the ellipses overlap (Figure 8-39).

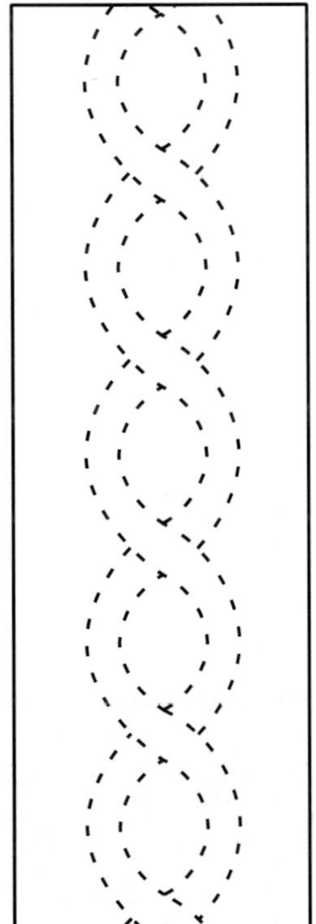

Figure 8-38.

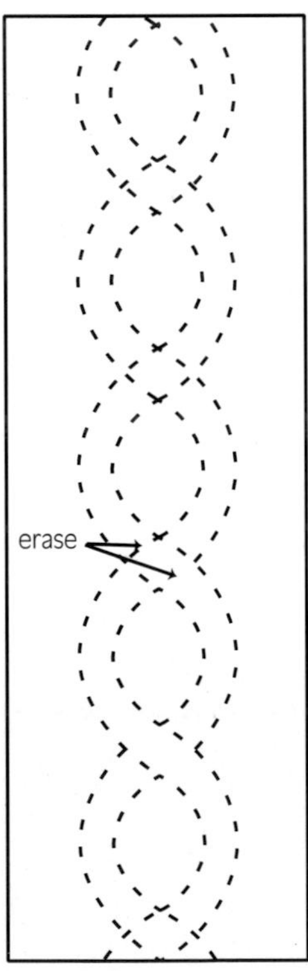

Figure 8-39.

Another kind of template can be made for drawing this interweaving cable by drawing several of the ellipses, erasing the lines, and using a section for a template. Mark the template so that it is easy to connect the sections when marking the quilt (Figure 8-40). Using this template requires marking two guide lines for the outsides of the design in order to keep it straight.

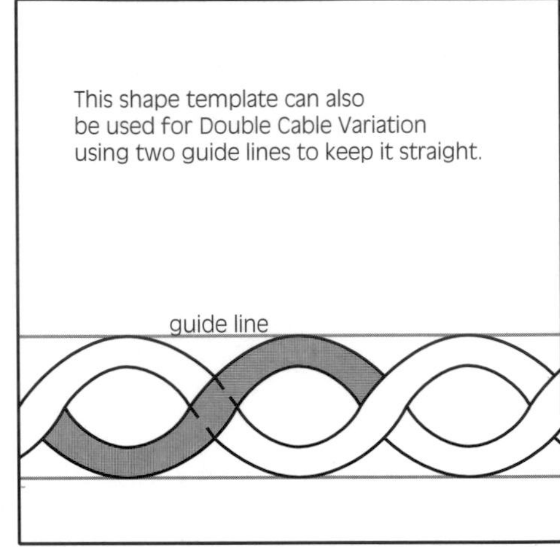

Figure 8-40.

Helpful Note: The Double Cable is fairly easy to mark and is easy to quilt. It can be varied by using the Pumpkin Seed shape or the Running Rope template in place of the Lozenge template.

Tools Needed: Template material and a fabric marking pencil or pen.

Where to Use: The Double Cable is used primarily in borders but could also be used in sashings.

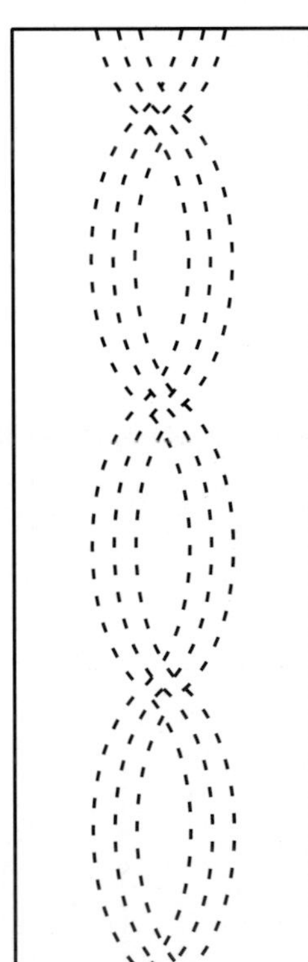

Figure 8-41.

Twisted Rope: also Double Cable (Figure 8-41)

Recommended Marking: Mark from a paper pattern before the quilt layers are assembled.

How to Mark or Draw: On a piece of paper, draw the Scrolling Vine following the instructions on page 101, Figure 7-33.

For the paper pattern, cut a piece of paper to fit the border. Mark a center guide line down the length of the paper. Place the vine drawing with the lengthwise center line on the guide line and trace the vine line. Continue tracing the vine the length of the pattern paper. Move the drawing up ½", trace the second line, move the drawing up again ½" and trace the third line (Figure 8-42).

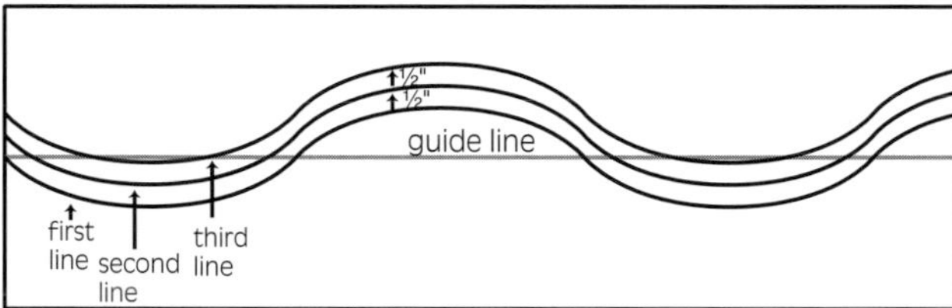

Figure 8-42.

To draw the lower part of the cable, place the drawing so that the left end of the vine is lined up with the fold line between the two units and the lengthwise center on the guide line. Trace the vine line continuing until the paper is filled. Move the drawing up ½", trace the vine line and again to make the third line (Figure 8-43). The cable could be used as is but to make the sections of the cable or rope appear to weave over and under, erase lines as shown (Figure 8-44). Go over the design lines with a black felt tip marker.

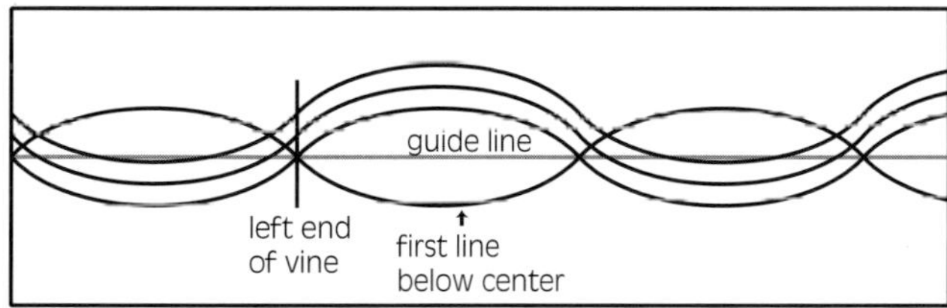

Figure 8-43.

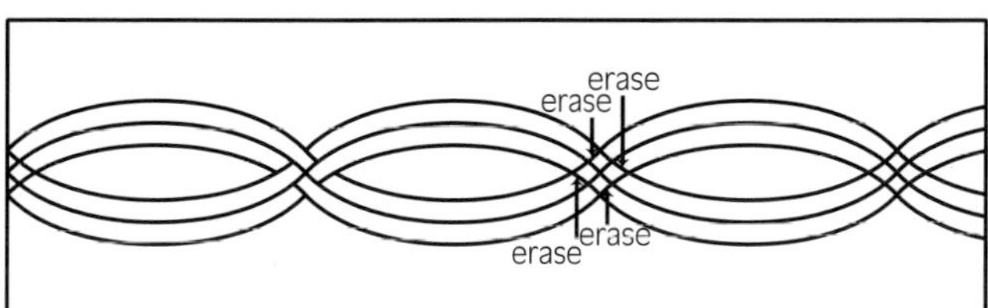

Figure 8-44.

To mark the quilt top, pin the pattern paper to the wrong side of the quilt top and trace the design onto the fabric.

Helpful Note: The Twisted Rope is easier to draw than it looks. It is easy to quilt. The spacing between the lines can be varied depending on the length and the width of the area to be filled.

Tools Needed: Pattern paper, a black felt tip marker, and a fabric marking pencil or pen.

Where to Use: This is a good border design.

Triple Cable: also Braided Cable, Multiple Line Cable, Worm, Chain (Figure 8-45)

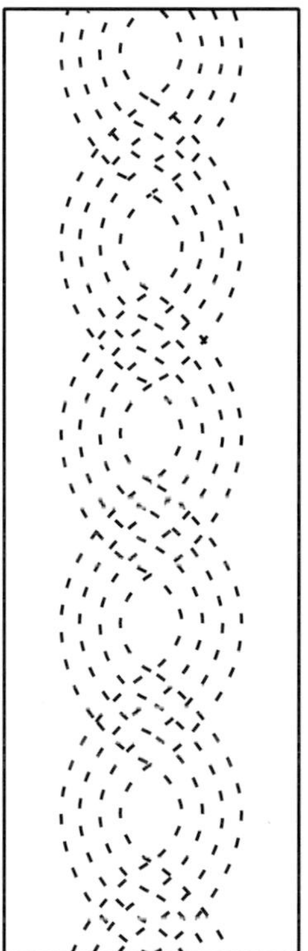

Figure 8-45.

Recommended Marking: Use a paper pattern to mark the quilt top before the quilt layers are assembled.

How to Mark or Draw: Cables seem to be named for the number of spaces or strands on each side of the cable rather than the number of quilted lines. For the Triple Cable, draw on a piece of paper an ellipse following the directions on page 114, (Figure 8-29). Drawing the cable unit for the Triple Cable follows the same procedure as described for the Double Cable except there are more concentric ellipses in this cable. Using a ruler, make dash lines spaced ½" apart to make four increasingly larger ellipses. Connect the dash lines with a black felt tip pen (Figure 8-46). This drawing is now ready to use to transfer the Triple Cable sections to the pattern paper.

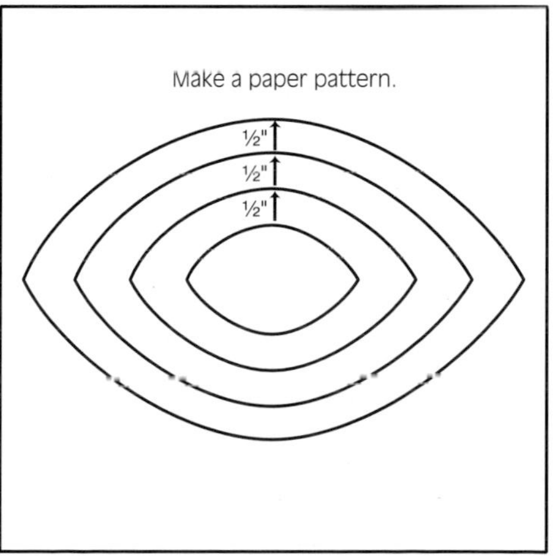

Figure 8-46.

Place the drawing paper under the pattern paper that has been cut to fit the border of the quilt. Start at the end of the pattern paper that will be the center of the quilt border. Trace one cable section and move the drawing so the end of the cable section overlaps and touches the center ellipse of the already drawn unit (Figure 8-37). Continue moving the paper and tracing until the border is filled.

To draw Braided Triple Cable (Figure 8-47), a variation of the Triple Cable, erase lines so that where the sections overlap or join the cable appears to be woven.

The Chain Triple Cable (Figure 8-48) is made by erasing the juncture lines so that the cable strands go over and under by sections.

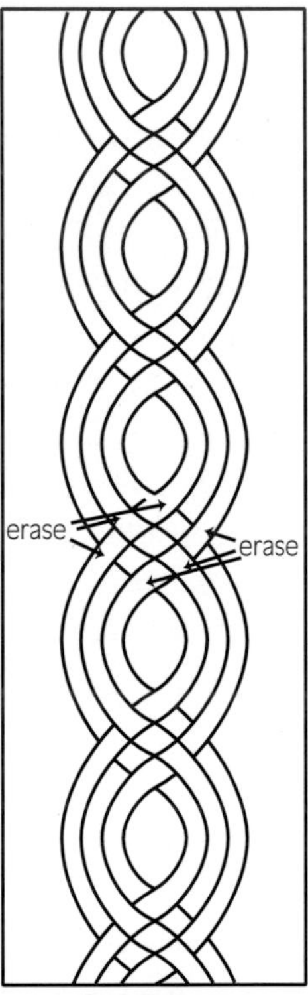

Figure 8-47.

Figure 8-48.

When satisfied with the pencil drawing, go over the lines with a black felt tip pen. Pin the paper pattern to the wrong side of the quilt top and trace the cable design onto the fabric.

Helpful Note: The shape for the start of the cable section can be the Pumpkin Seed or the shape of the Running Single Cable. These two shapes make slimmer cables.

Tools Needed: Pattern paper, circle template, a black felt tip marker, and a fabric marking pencil or pen.

Where to Use: Use Triple Cables in borders. It can be used in the bar or strippie quilts and is often found in Amish quilts.

Twist Cable: also Five-Strand Cable, Cable, Rope, Chain, Worm, Plait (Figure 8-49)

Figure 8-49.

Recommended Marking: Use a paper pattern to mark the quilt top before the quilt layers are assembled.

How to Mark or Draw: Follow the instructions for drawing the cable unit as described for the Triple Cable adding two more concentric ellipses for a total of six (Figure 8-50).

Trace the cable unit onto pattern paper by overlapping the units in the same manner as for the Triple Cable.

To make the design called Chain Twist (Figure 8-51), erase the pencil lines in the intersections so that one set of five strands goes up and over the lower strands.

Go over the design lines on the paper pattern with a black felt tip marker.

To mark the design on the quilt top, pin the

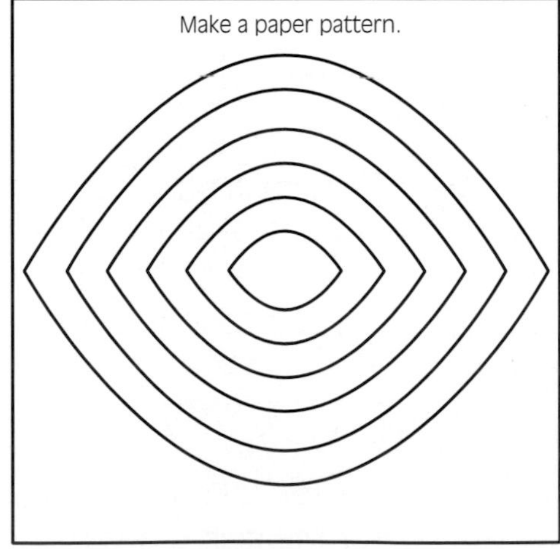

Figure 8-50.

Figure 8-51.

pattern to the wrong side of the quilt top and trace the design onto the fabric.

Helpful Note: Cables are actually fairly easy to draw after doing the first one. They are easy to quilt and the more strands in the cable the more elegant the design.

Tools Needed: Pattern paper, a circle template, a black felt tip marker, and a fabric marking pencil or pen.

Where to Use: Cables are designed for borders but can also be used in bar or strippie quilts and, of course, in whole cloth quilt designs.

Twisted Rope Cable: also Eight Row Cable (Figure 8-52)

Figure 8-52.

Recommended Marking: Use a paper pattern to mark the quilt top before the quilt layers are assembled.

How to Mark or Draw: Follow the instructions for drawing the cable unit as described for the Triple Cable adding four more concentric ellipses for a total of eight.

Trace the eight line cable unit onto the pattern paper by overlapping the units in the same manner as for the Triple Cable and the Twist Cable. When the pattern paper is filled, go over the lines with a black felt tip pen.

Erase the lines in the intersections of the units so that one set of eight lines goes up and over the lower lines for a Twisted Rope Cable Variation (Figure 8-53).

Figure 8-53.

Go over the desired design lines with a black felt tip pen.

To mark the quilt top, pin the paper pattern to the wrong side of the quilt top and trace the design onto the fabric.

Helpful Note: It is easier to draw the variation if the lines that go over and under are first outlined with a black felt tip marker and then erase the remaining lines.

Tools Needed: Pattern paper, a circle template, a black felt tip pen, and a fabric marking pencil or pen.

Where to Use: Use this design in wide borders where a lot of quilting is desired.

Classical Cable (Figure 8-54)

Figure 8-54.

RECOMMENDED MARKING: Use a paper pattern to mark the quilt top before the quilt layers are assembled.

HOW TO MARK OR DRAW: The Classical Cable is based on the Fan design. To determine the size fan needed to draw this design, divide the width of the border in half. For a 6" wide border, the fan size would be 3".

On a piece of paper, draw a center guide line. Using a Circle/Fan marker or a compass, draw the outside arc (3") of a fan. See Figure 6-27, page 83, for directions on drawing the Fan. Next, using the guide line and the point where the first arc meets the guide line, draw a complete Fan with spacing between the arcs of ½" (Figure 8-55). The outside line of the Fan should be at 3".

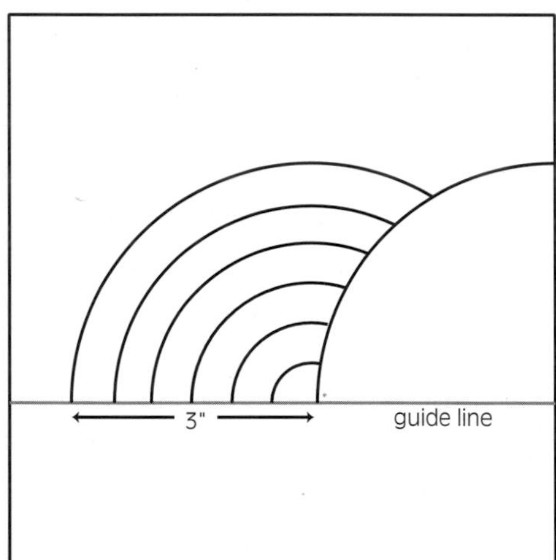

Figure 8-55.

On a new piece of paper, draw a center guide line. Place the paper with the Fan that was just drawn under the new paper and trace the Fan above the guide line. Flip the Fan drawing upside down, line up the guide lines, and trace the upside down Fan below the guide line. The first or short line of the lower Fan should touch the large or outside line of the upper Fan (Figure 8-56).

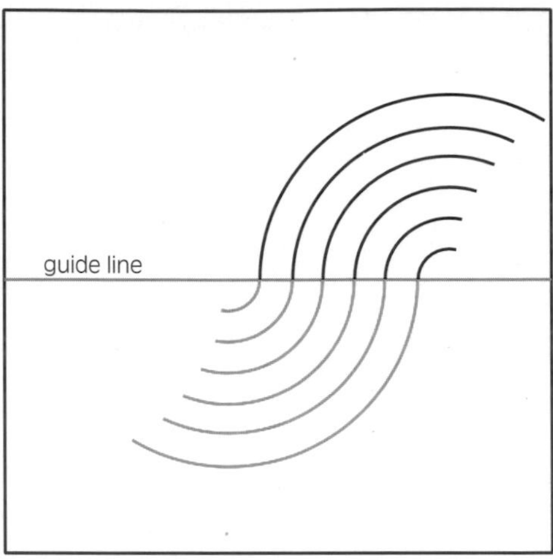

Figure 8-56.

On the pattern paper (cut to fit the border), draw a center guide line the length of the border. Start at the center end of the pattern paper and trace the Cable from the drawing paper. Move the drawing to the left with the center guide lines matching and the Cable touching the one that was just drawn (Figure 8-57). Continue until the border pattern paper is filled. Go over the design lines with a black felt tip pen.

To mark the quilt top, pin the paper pattern to the wrong side of the quilt top and trace the design onto the fabric.

HELPFUL NOTE: This design is easy to draw to fill the entire width of a border. It takes less thinking than some of the other Cable designs.

TOOLS NEEDED: Pattern paper, a Circle/Fan mark-

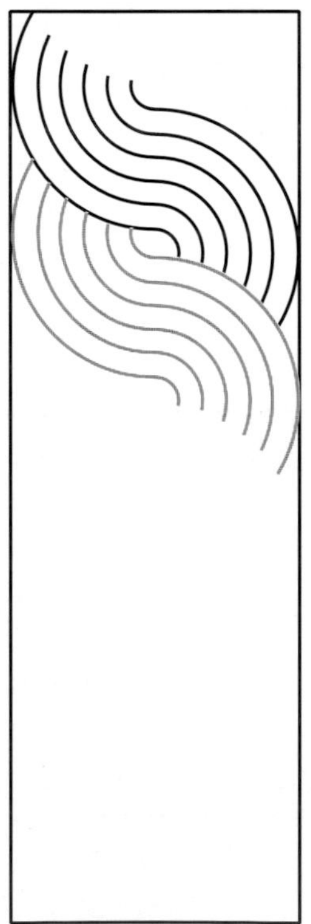

Figure 8-57.

er or a compass, a black felt tip pen, and a fabric marking pencil or pen.

WHERE TO USE: Use in borders especially Amish designs. It could also be used in bar or strippie quilts and in whole cloth quilts.

Chain Links (Figure 8-58)

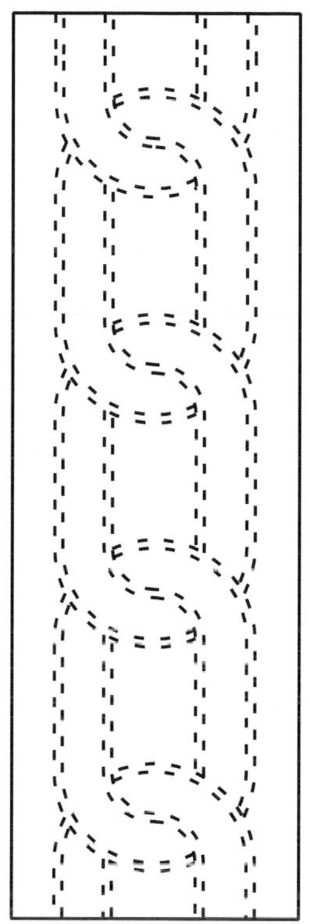

Figure 8-58.

RECOMMENDED MARKING: Mark the quilt top, using a paper pattern, before the layers of the quilt are assembled.

HOW TO MARK OR DRAW: On a piece of paper, draw an oval following the instructions on page 94, Figure 7-3. An oval that is 4" wide and 6" long makes a good design. Inside the oval, draw a second line spaced ⅛", from the original oval. Draw this line by using a ruler and making dash marks and then filling in the line. The next step is to draw a smaller oval in the center. Draw this line by making dash marks 1" from the original oval lines. Outline this small oval by drawing a line spaced ⅛", inside the oval (Figure 8-59).

Mark a guide line down the center of the pattern paper. Place the drawing of the oval under the pattern paper and trace around all the lines.

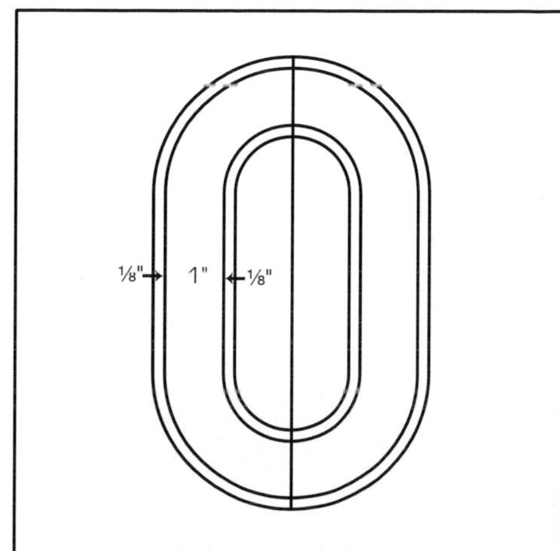

Figure 8-59.

Move the drawing so the double lines of the small center oval overlap and trace around all the lines again (Figure 8-60). Continue until the pattern paper is filled.

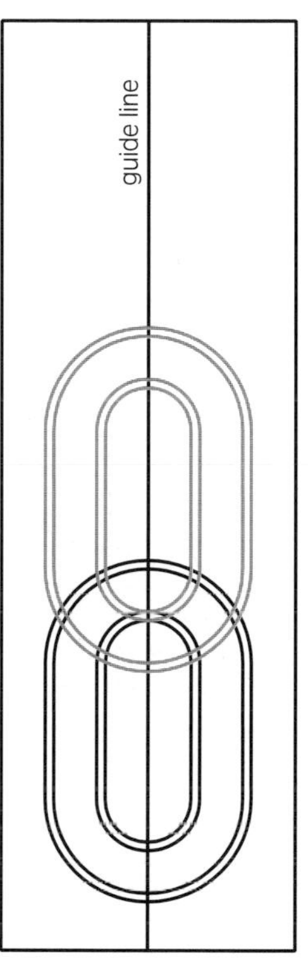

Figure 8-60.

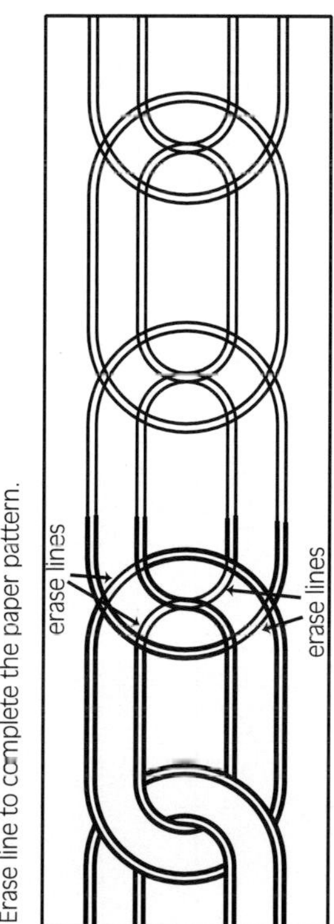

Figure 8-61.

With a black felt tip marker, go over the lines in the design that will make the links and erase the unnecessary lines (Figure 8-61). The pattern is now ready to be transferred to the quilt top.

Pin the paper pattern to the wrong side of the quilt top and trace the design onto the fabric.

HELPFUL NOTE: The Chain Links can be done without double lining the outside and inside of the oval.

TOOLS NEEDED: Pattern paper, a circle template,

a small ruler, a black felt tip marker and a fabric marking pencil or pen.

WHERE TO USE: Chain Links is a good design to use in borders and in sashings. It was frequently used on Amish quilts.

Diamond Cable (Figure 8-62)

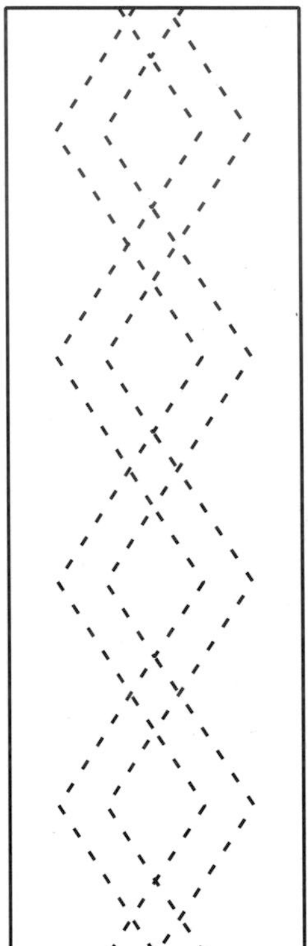

Figure 8-62.

RECOMMENDED MARKING: Use a template to mark the design on the quilt as you go.

HOW TO MARK OR DRAW: Determine the size diamond needed. See page 12 on how to make a design fit. To draw the diamond, first draw or cut out a rectangle the size needed. For an example, use a 4" wide by 6" long rectangle. Mark the rectangle in the center vertically and horizontally. Using a ruler, draw a diagonal line from the outside center to the top center on all sides (Figure 8-63).

Next, a smaller diamond is needed in the center and the space between the two can vary from slim to fat. For the 4" x 6" diamond, a ¾" spacing is good. Lay the ruler along the diamond lines and draw a smaller diamond inside. Cut out the diamonds to make a template (Figure 8-64).

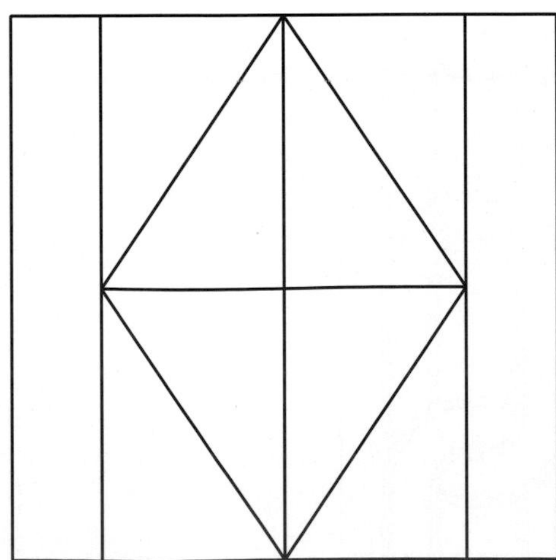

Figure 8-63.

Make a template.

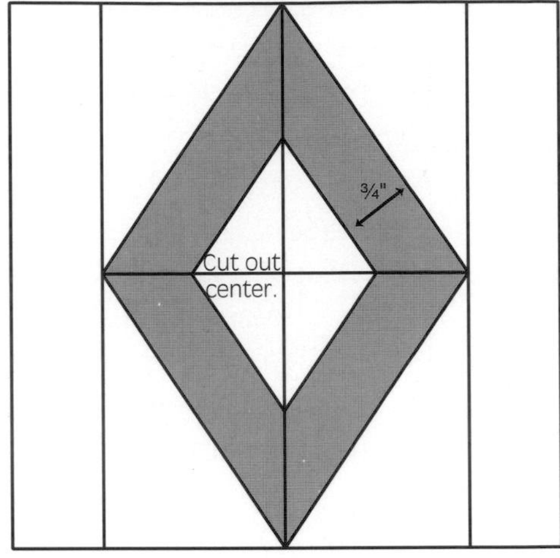

Figure 8-64.

To mark the quilt, mark a faint guide line down the center of the area where the design will go. Place the diamond template with the points on the long end of the diamond in line with the guide line and draw around the inside and outside of the template. Drawing the diamonds where they touch end to end is called Diamond String (Figure 8-65).

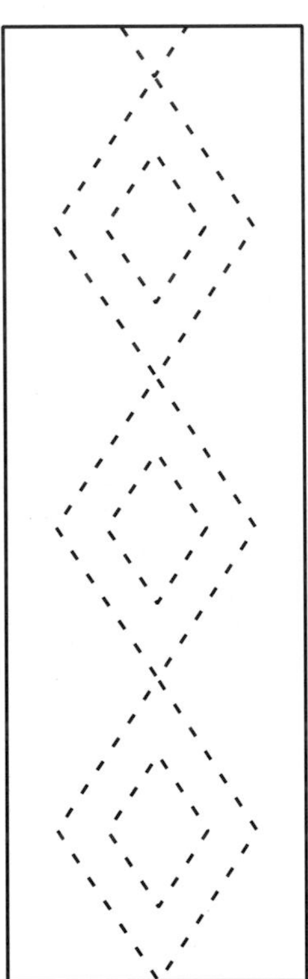

Figure 8-65.

Diamond Cable (Figure 8-62) is formed when the template overlaps the previously drawn diamond. The end of the diamond template should touch the end of the inside diamond each time it is moved and marked.

Weaving Diamond Cable (Figure 8-66) is the same as the Diamond Cable with the crossing lines erased to give the appearance of the lines going over and under.

HELPFUL NOTE: The Diamond Cables are easy to mark and easy to quilt. The lines can be doubled and tripled as is found in other cable designs.

TOOLS NEEDED: Template material and a fabric marking pencil or pen.

WHERE TO USE: Use these designs in borders and in sashings and to frame another design.

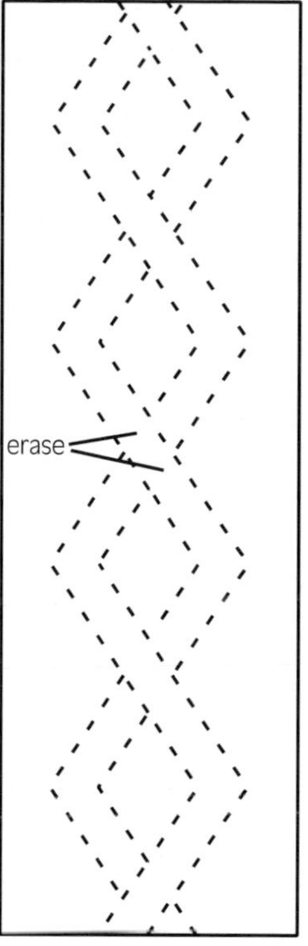

Figure 8-66.

Diamond Rope (Figure 8-67)

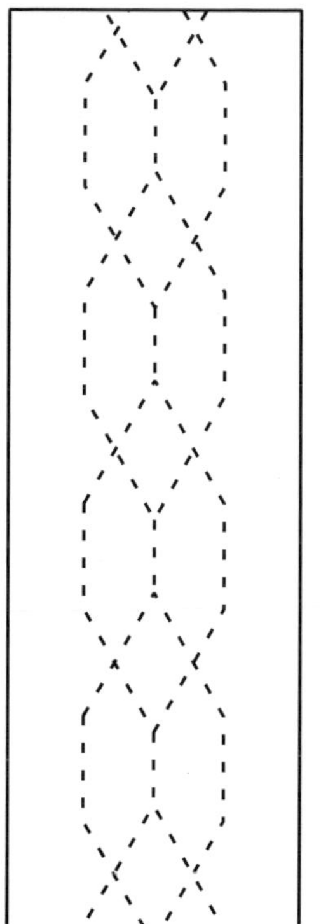

Figure 8-67.

RECOMMENDED MARKING: Use a paper pattern to mark the quilt top before the quilt layers are assembled.

HOW TO MARK OR DRAW: This Amish design is so lovely and is nearly impossible to describe how to draw it. Therefore, Figure 8-68 is a full-size pattern to use to make a paper pattern of the Diamond Rope.

To make a paper pattern, draw one unit. The next unit is drawn by overlapping the end small diamond to make the rope. Go over the design lines with a black felt tip pen.

To mark the quilt top, pin the pattern paper to the wrong side of the quilt top and trace the design onto the fabric.

HELPFUL NOTE: The design unit can be reduced or enlarged using a copy machine.

TOOLS NEEDED: Pattern paper, a black felt tip pen, and a fabric marking pencil or pen.

WHERE TO USE: Use in small borders or sashings.

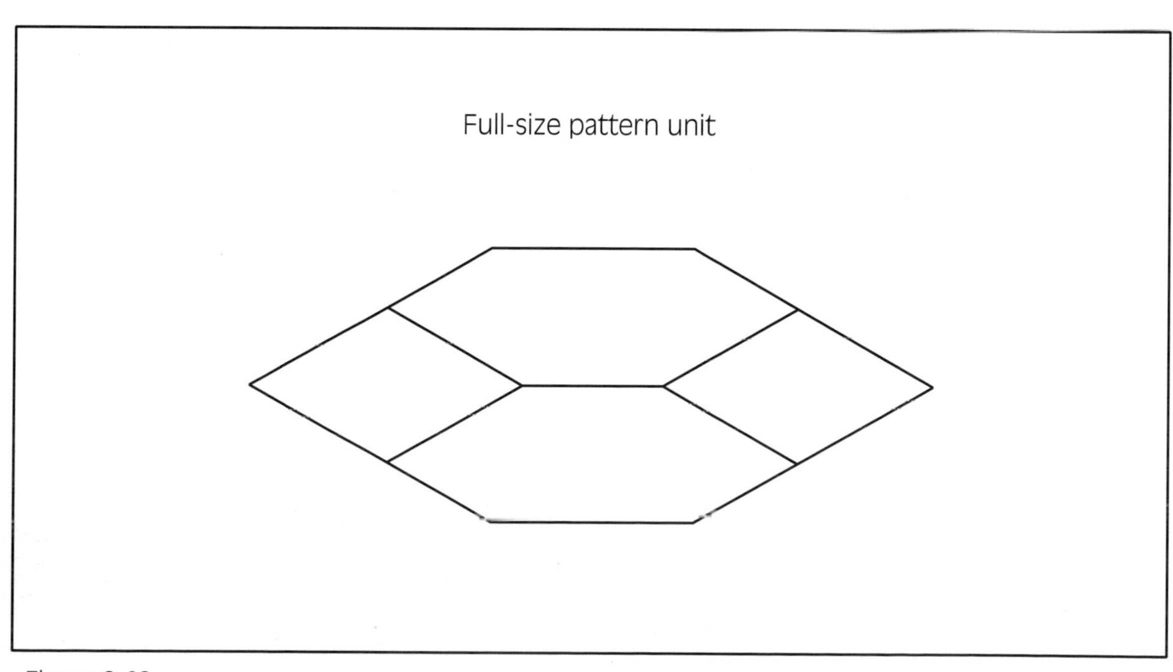

Figure 8-68.

Plate 9-1. Hearts (also Butterfly, Tulip, Bow).
Peace and Love by Frances Stone, 1985. Collection of the Museum of the American Quilter's Society.

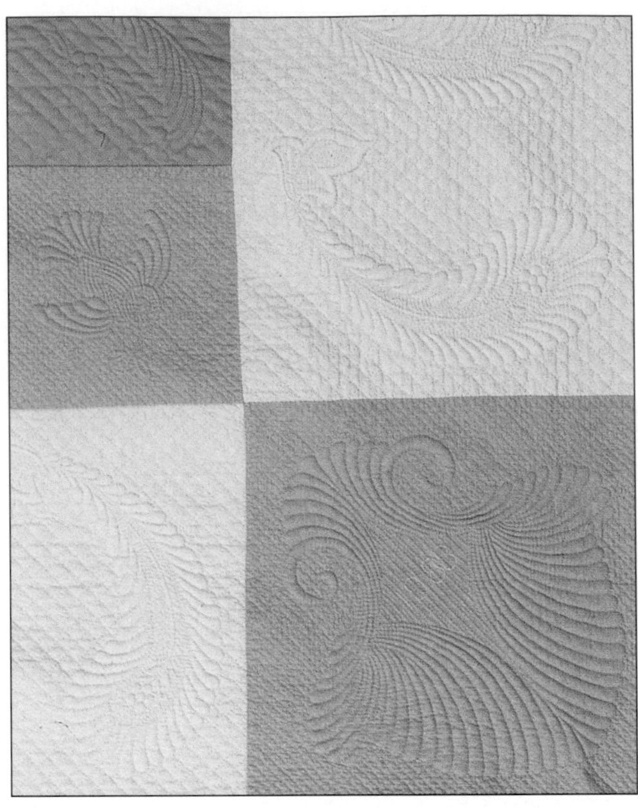

Plate 9-2. Ostrich Plume (Fiddlehead, Diagonal Lines, Other Feather Variations).
Amish Spring with Feathers and Lace by Beverly M. Williams, 1989. Collection of the Museum of the American Quilter's Society.

Plate 9-3. Feathered Garland (also Meandering, Paisley, Ostrich Plume).
Ohio Bride's Quilt by Debra Wagner, 1989. Collection of the Museum of the American Quilter's Society.

Plate 9-4. Feathered Pineapple (also Diamond, Echo).
Nature's Walk by Hazel B. Reed Ferrell, 1984. Collection of the Museum of the American Quilter's Society.

Chapter Nine
Hearts and Feathers

In the mid-1800's, the Heart was a symbol of love and was reserved for bridal quilts. Engaged girls used Hearts in the quilt being made for their wedding bed. Heart designs add a nostalgic note to a quilt, and today they are used in quilts other than wedding quilts.

Of all the designs for quilting, the Feathered designs are the ones that quilters use to add elegance to their quilts and to show off their quilting abilities. Any shape can have Feathers added to the design to take it from common to beautiful. Feathered designs have been used since at least the early 1800's.

The Feathered Circle is the number one Feathered design. Quilters over the years have used from very small Feathered Circles to very large ones for the central medallion design in whole cloth quilts. The design has had many variations of fillers for the center of the Feathered Circle. It is one of the designs for quilting that always seems to be a good choice.

Although the Feathered Pineapple is not found as often today as it was in the nineteenth century, it is a good choice for fancy quilting. The pineapple is a symbol of hospitality and symbolic designs were popular during the 1800's.

The Feathered designs for borders and sashings are the grand finales for a quilt. The Feathered Vine, Feathered Cable, and Feather Twist are three of the traditional Feathered border designs that have been often used and admired. The Amish use Feather Borders often, but their ne plus ultra *design is the Feathered Garland.*

Feathering designs is not difficult. Being able to draw your own Feathered designs will liberate you forever.

Heart (Figure 9-1)

Figure 9-1.

RECOMMENDED MARKING: Use a template to mark on the quilt top as you go.

HOW TO MARK OR DRAW: Hearts have been found as quilting and as appliqué designs since the early 1800's. In the 1800's, Hearts were reserved for bridal quilts. Today, there is the freedom to put Hearts anywhere and everywhere.

First, decide what size Heart will be needed for the design. Generally, drawing the Heart requires a square the size of the space that is to be filled. For this example, cut a 4" square from paper. Fold the square in half.

To get curved perfection, a circle is needed that is the size of half of the square (2"). The circle can be any round object such as a spool, a circle template, a small glass, etc. Place the circle at the top of the folded paper and draw around the top only (Figure 9-2, page 126). Now, draw a line along a ruler with the edge touching the bottom of the fold and angling up to the place where the circle ended (Figure 9-3, page 126). Trace the half Heart onto the other side of the folded paper (Figure 9-4, page 126).

If the bottom part of the Heart looks too sharp,

redraw by placing the angling line a little lower (Figure 9-5). Remember each heart can be different. So, when the Heart drawing suits you, make a template.

Helpful Note: Usually, the lower part of the Heart looks better drawn freehand to the fold line. Draw the half Heart completely freehand without the use

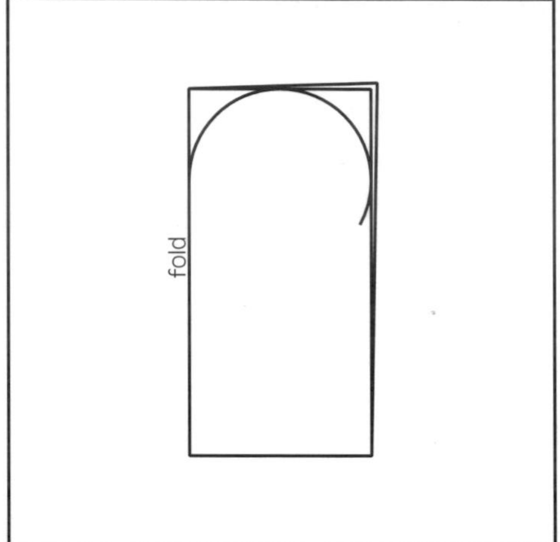

Figure 9-2.

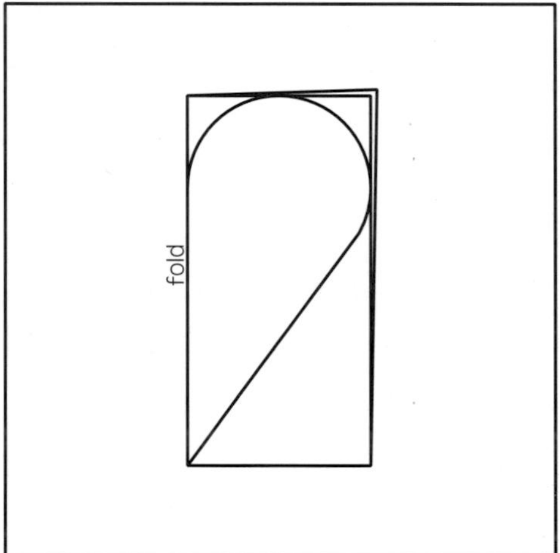

Figure 9-3.

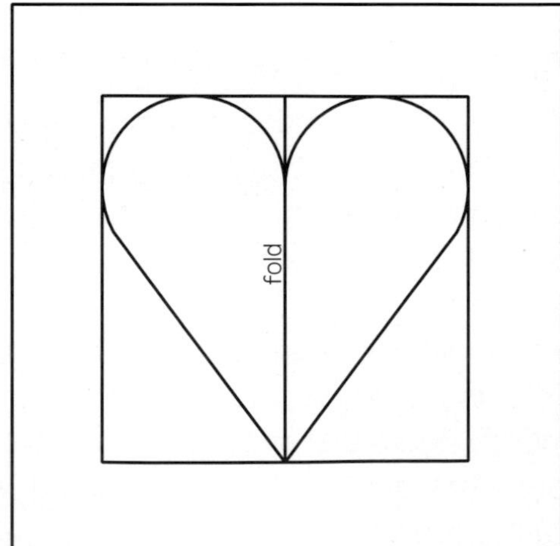

Figure 9-4.

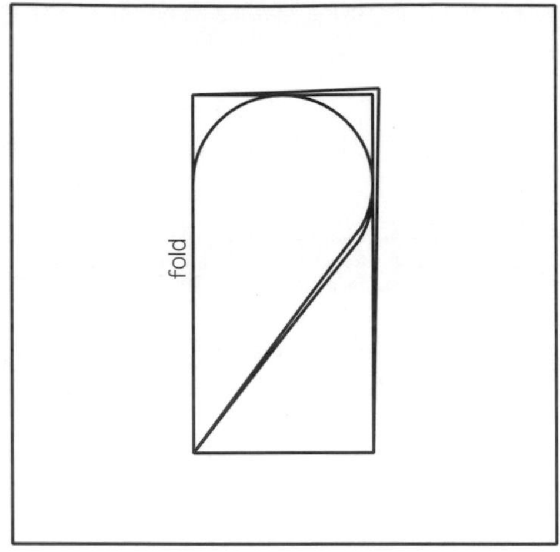

Figure 9-5.

of the circle or a ruler or cut the shape out freehand with scissors. It is amazing how good Hearts done in this manner look. The Heart can be single lined or double lined as shown in Figure 9-1. Hearts can be long and slim or short and plump depending on the space to be filled. Folk art Hearts are good.

Tools Needed: A round object, template material, and a fabric marking pencil or pen.

Where to Use: The Heart can be used as the basis for a Feathered Heart. It could be used in the plain blocks of a pieced block, in connecting blocks in sashing, placed randomly on the background, and in the corners of plain setting blocks. The Double Lined Heart can be used as a framing for names, initials, dates, or another quilting design. The Heart is an appropriate design for a wedding quilt, album quilt, and a baby quilt.

Heart Corner Design (Figure 9-6)

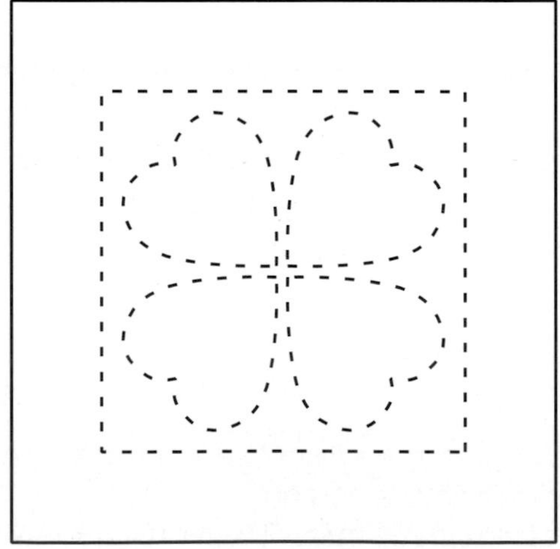

Figure 9-6.

Recommended Marking: Mark with a template as you go.

How to Mark or Draw: Draw the size Heart needed following the instructions on page 125 for drawing a Heart. On a piece of paper, draw a square the size needed for a corner square. Draw diagonal lines on the square from corner to corner. Trace the Heart drawing by placing the center line of the Heart on a diagonal line. When a Heart has been drawn on each diagonal line, cut out the Hearts to make the template (Figure 9-7).

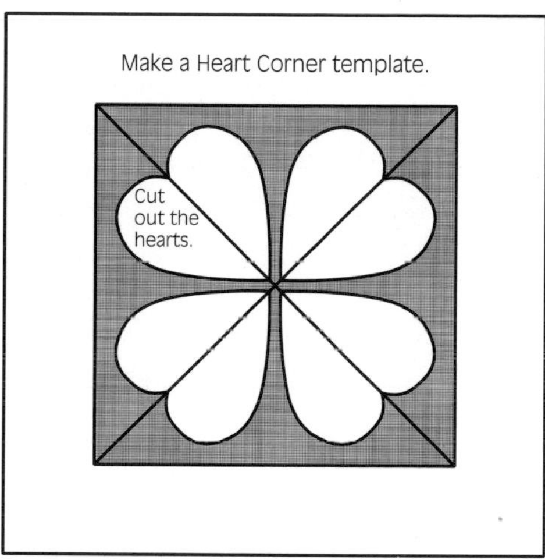

Figure 9-7.

To mark the quilt, place the template on the corner square and draw around the Heart shapes.

This design could also be marked from a Heart-shaped template by marking faint guide lines diagonally from corner to corner and lining the template up on the guide lines.

Helpful Note: This template is easily made by drawing the design on freezer paper and ironing the paper onto poster board or cardboard. It is easier to cut the Hearts out of the heavy paper than it is to cut template plastic.

Tools Needed: Template material and a fabric marking pencil or pen.

Where to Use: This arrangement of Hearts is intended for corner designs in connecting squares of sashing or borders. The design could also be used in squares that are formed by quilting lines.

Heart String (Figure 9-8)

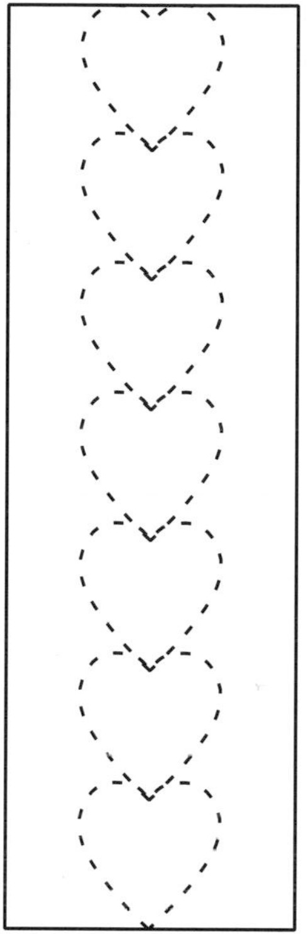

Figure 9-8.

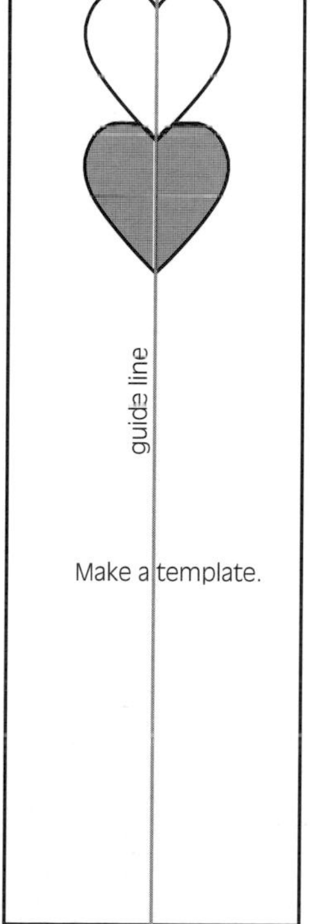

Figure 9-9.

Recommended Marking: Mark using a template as you go.

How to Mark or Draw: Draw the size Heart needed following the instructions on page 125 for drawing a Heart. Make a Heart template.

To mark the design on the quilt, mark a faint guide line down the length of the sashing or border. Mark the sashing or border by placing the heart center on the guide line. Mark around a Heart and move the Heart so the long point of the Heart is touching the indented top of the Heart (Figure 9-9).

Helpful Note: Draw several of the Hearts in the string and then these can be quilted before marking more.

Tools Needed: Template material and a fabric marking pencil or pen.

Where to Use: Use the Heart String in narrow sashings and narrow borders.

Line of Hearts (Figure 9-10)

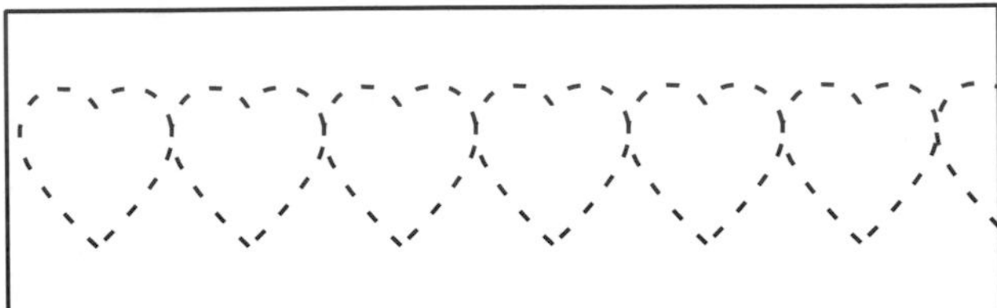

Figure 9-10.

Recommended Marking: Mark using a template as you go.

How to Mark or Draw: Draw the size Heart needed following the instructions on page 125 for drawing a Heart. Make a Heart template.

To mark the design on the quilt, place the Heart template straight up and down. Use a seam, straight edge, or a faint marked guide line as a guide to placing the top of the heart. Mark around the template and move the template so that the side of the Heart touches the side of the one drawn before (Figure 9-11). Continue marking Hearts side by side until the border or sashing is filled.

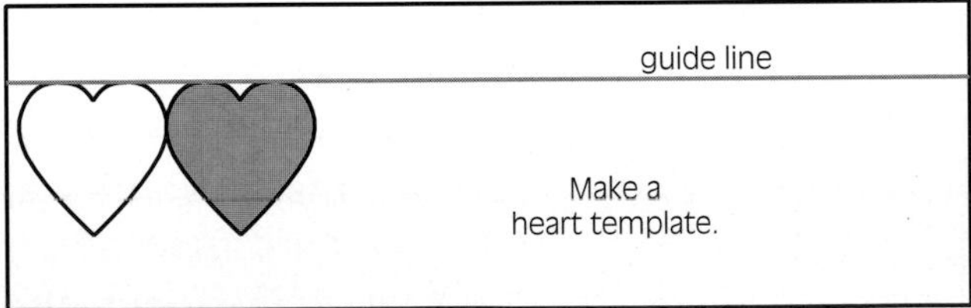

Figure 9-11.

Vary the design by drawing a smaller Heart inside the original Heart. Decide the amount of spacing between the two Hearts by their size. The spacing can be from ¼" to ½". Cut out the center to make a template (Figure 9-12) for this Line of Hearts Variation (Figure 9-13). Mark the quilt top in the same way as when marking the Line of Hearts.

Helpful Note: Be careful that the Heart template is straight up and down before marking. Several Hearts can be marked and then quilted before marking more Hearts.

Figure 9-12.

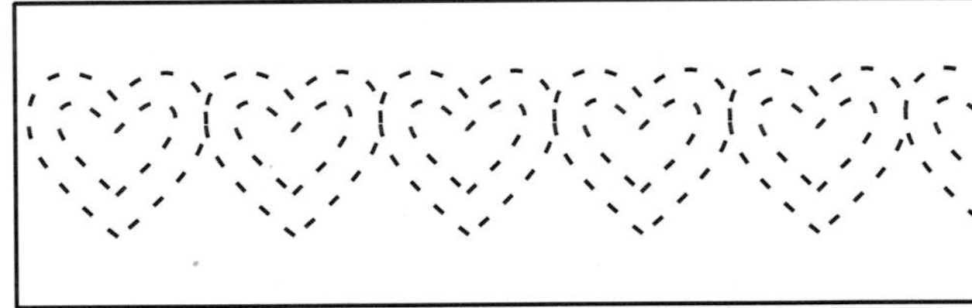

Figure 9-13.

Tools Needed: Template material and a fabric marking pencil or pen.

Where to Use: Use the Line of Hearts in narrow sashings and narrow borders.

Circle of Hearts (Figure 9-14)

Recommended Marking: Using a paper pattern, mark the design on the quilt top before assembling the quilt layers.

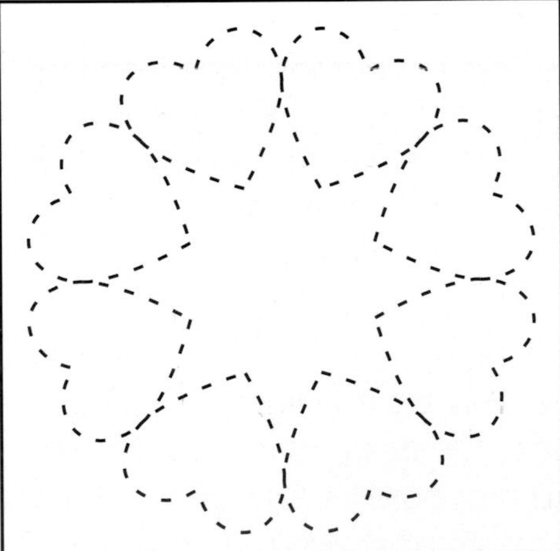

Figure 9-14.

How to Mark or Draw: On pattern paper, draw a square the size of the block or area where the Circle of Hearts will go. Mark off the square in the centers and diagonally from corner to corner. Using a Circle/Fan marking template, a pencil and string compass or a round object (plate), draw a circle that is approximately ⅔ the size of the square. Now, measure the distance between two of the division lines on the circle to determine the size heart that is needed (Figure 9-15). Read the instructions for drawing a Heart on page 125.

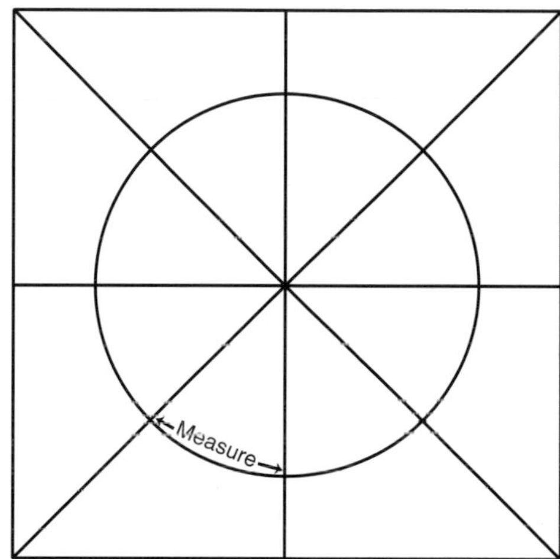

Figure 9-15.

On another piece of paper, draw a Heart in the size required. Go around the Heart with a black felt tip marker. To draw the Hearts in the circle, place the Heart drawing under the pattern paper with the circle. Place the Heart with the widest part on the circle line and trace (Figure 9-16). Draw Hearts in all the sections of the circle in the same manner. Go around all the Hearts with a black felt tip marker.

To mark the design on the quilt top, pin the paper pattern to the wrong side of the quilt top and trace the design onto the fabric.

Helpful Note: The size of the circle can be decided by a circle or by the size of a square. The Circle of Hearts should fill nearly the whole area where the design will be quilted.

Tools Needed: Pattern paper, a black felt tip pen, a circle, a ruler, and a fabric marking pencil or pen.

Where to Use: The Circle of Hearts can be used in plain setting blocks or as a part of a design for a whole cloth quilt.

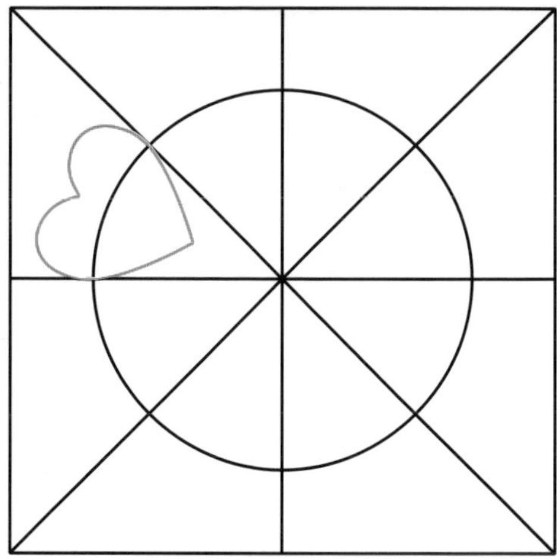
Figure 9-16.

Heart Wreath (Figure 9-17)

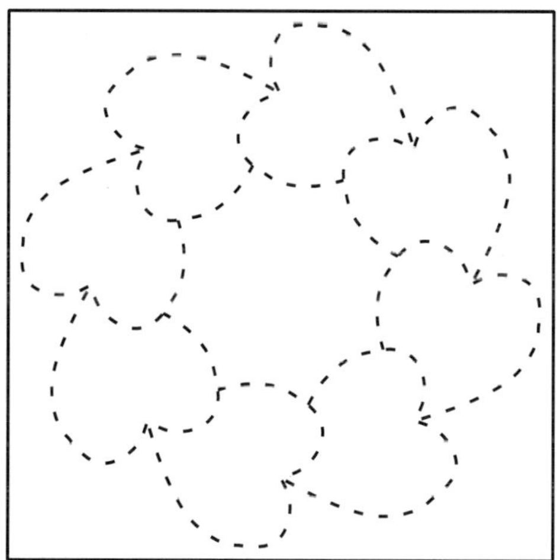
Figure 9-17.

Recommended Marking: Using a paper pattern, mark the design on the quilt top before assembling the quilt layers.

How to Mark or Draw: Follow all the instructions on page 128 for making the Circle of Hearts up to the placement of the Hearts on the pattern paper.

For the Heart Wreath, the Heart will be placed between two of the lines with the indentation of the Heart and the point of the Heart on the circle. The inside of the Hearts will overlap slightly (Figure 9-18, page 130).

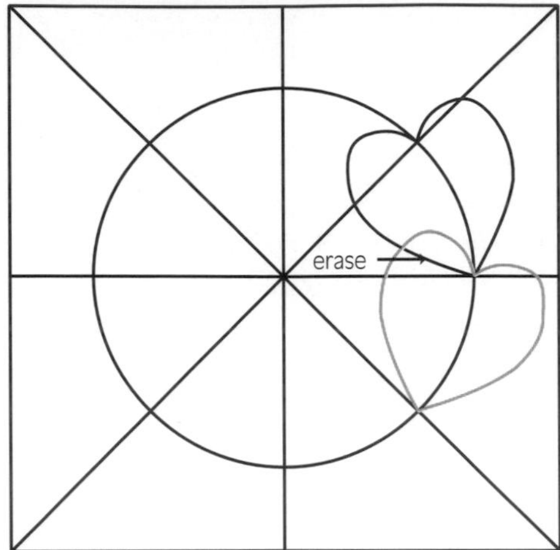

Figure 9-18.

Draw Hearts around the entire circle. Erase the unwanted inside lines where the Hearts overlap. Go around the lines of the design with a black felt tip pen.

To mark the design on the quilt top, pin the paper pattern to the wrong side of the quilt top and trace the design onto the fabric.

HELPFUL NOTE: Make the Hearts in the wreath smaller by dividing the measurement between the two division lines in half so that two Hearts fit into the space instead of one Heart. A template can be made of the design, if wanted. Add a background filler to the center of the design.

TOOLS NEEDED: Pattern paper, a black felt tip pen, a circle, a ruler, and a fabric marking pencil or pen.

WHERE TO USE: The Heart Wreath can be used in plain setting blocks or as part of the design for a whole cloth quilt.

Feathers, called plumes in the early 1800's, are the most popular way to add elegance and interest to a quilt. Because they are so popular and the space where they are used varies so much, it is advantageous to be able to draw the Feathers to suit the quilt. Once you learn to draw your own Feathers, you will see that it is possible to draw Feathers in any shape that would enhance your quilt.

For a design that looks complicated, Feathers are actually not hard to draw. Playing or doodling on paper will give you the confidence to draw your own Feathers and, therefore, be assured that the Feather will perfectly fit the place where you wish to use it.

Since there is no end to the different shapes that can be feathered and the sizes that those Feathers can be, the examples of Feathers included here are the traditional Feather designs that have been used during the last two centuries.

Feathers are like individual signatures. There is no standard "right" Feather and they reflect the individual quilter. By following the basic instructions for drawing Feathers, the hope is that you will draw and quilt Feathers that are uniquely your own.

The following instructions are very basic and, hopefully, will get you started drawing Feathers. **Fine Feathers** *by Marianne Fons and* **Quilting with Style** *by Gwen Marson and Joe Cunningham are two recommended books on drawing Feathers.*

Feather Band: also Straight Feather, Straight Plume (Figure 9-19)

Figure 9-19.

RECOMMENDED MARKING: Make a paper pattern to use to mark the quilt top before the quilt layers are assembled. With practice, Feathers can be marked directly onto the quilt top using an outline template.

HOW TO MARK OR DRAW: The Feather Band is an easy Feather design to draw and will be used to illustrate the basics of drawing Feathers. To start, on a piece of paper draw a center line or stem (the feathers are attached to the stem). Draw guide lines on each side of the stem that are spaced 1½" from the stem. The two outside guide lines should be 3" apart (Figure 9-20).

For practice purposes, do not draw on this

guide line
1½" stem
1½" guide line

Figure 9-20.

paper but instead use tracing paper over this sheet for practice drawing. The guide lines can then be used over and over.

The individual pieces that make up a feathered design are formed from a partial circle with a tail or are half of a traditional heart (Figure 9-21). Sometimes the design will require that you draw the right half of a heart and other times it will be necessary to draw the left side of the heart. By drawing many of the half hearts, you will get a feel for the flow of the lines needed to draw Feathers. So, place a piece of tracing paper over the heart on this page and with a pencil trace half (right) hearts and more half hearts. When the pencil begins to almost automatically draw the heart, practice on the other half (left) heart. Draw a lot of these, also.

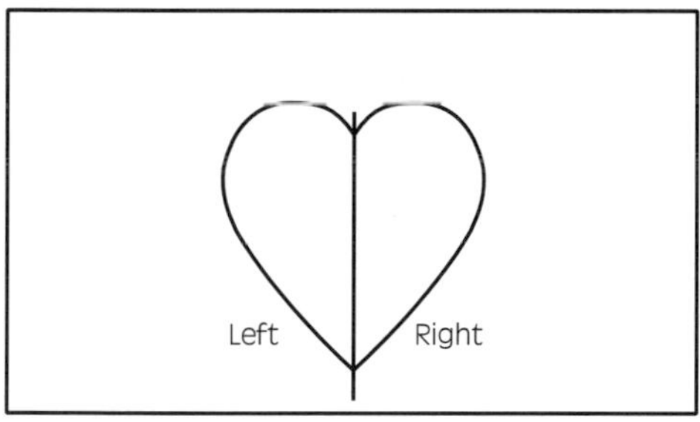

Figure 9-21.

Now, you are ready to draw an actual Feather and practice will be on the Feather Band. An arc or half circle is needed to form the curve at the top of each Feather in the Feather Band. When looking at Feathers on quilts, notice that some of the Feathers have small curves and are slim and other Feathers have plumper curves and make larger Feathers. Buttons (come in many sizes), coins (pennies, dimes, nickels, quarters), a circle template, spools, thimble, or any small round object can be used for a guide to draw the curves. I particularly like buttons since they are always available, come in a multitude of sizes, and are easy to move on the paper.

Place a piece of tracing paper over the paper with the stem and guide lines.

Using a ruler, draw in the stem line. Next, place the round object (button) with the top of the button on the top guide line and draw around the upper half of the button or round object (Figure 9-22).

Figure 9-22.

Move the button so that it touches the half circle that you just drew and mark around half of it again. Continue until the entire top guide line is filled with curves (Figure 9-23).

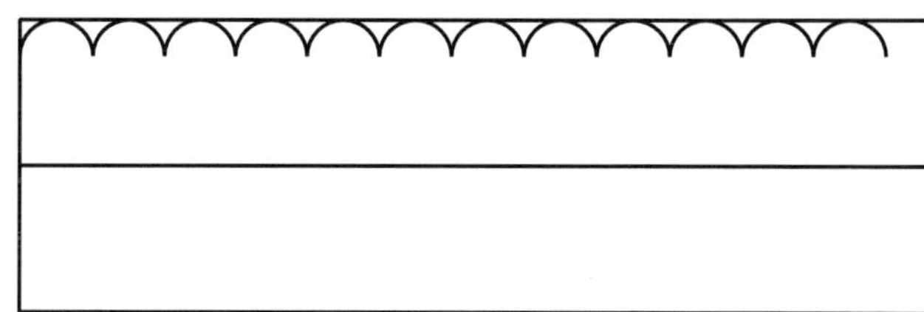

Figure 9-23.

You are ready to draw Feathers! Still drawing on the tracing paper, place the pencil lead on the left side of the first curve and draw over the curved guide and make a curving tail or a half heart down to the stem line. Drawing quickly usually makes for smoother lines. The problem with this step in the drawing can be that the tail will come down too straight and not curve back like a heart. The bottom of the Feather should end approximately in line with the start of the curve (Figure 9-24, page 132). Repeat this same exercise several times until you feel comfortable drawing this half of the heart.

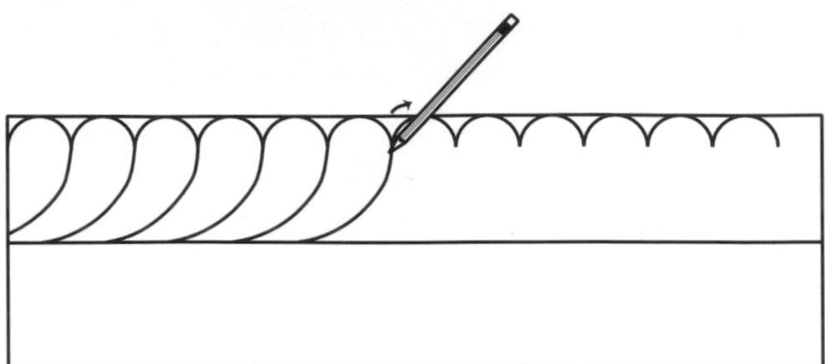

Figure 9-24.

The lower part of the Feather Band requires drawing the left side of the heart and this time the curve guides will be along the bottom guide line. Draw curved guides, on the tracing paper, with the button for the bottom of the Feather Band. Practice drawing the Feathers from this direction by starting at the left of the curve, following the curve and bringing the tail up to the center stem (Figure 9-25). The tails of the Feathers do not have to meet at the stem. Actually, the Feathers look better if they do not meet. Practice drawing Feathers on the bottom of the stem several times.

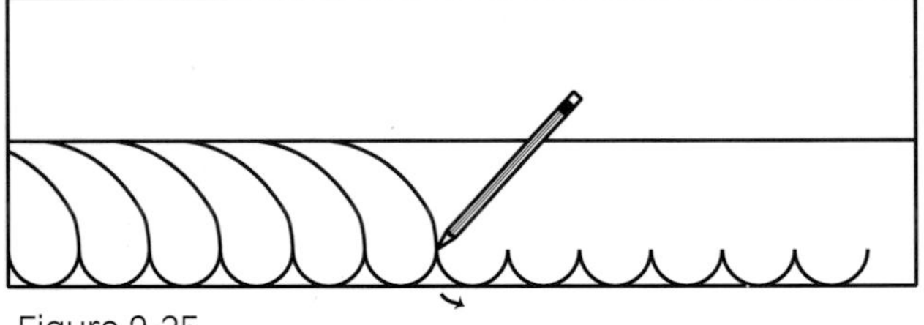

Figure 9-25.

For the next exercise and to complete the whole design, use another sheet of tracing paper, draw the stem, and mark curves using a button on both the top and bottom guide lines. Draw around the curves and to the stem from both the top and the bottom. Look at your Feather Band from a distance. Looks pretty good, doesn't it?

On another sheet of tracing paper, do another exercise by marking the curves and starting on the right side of the paper and drawing the Feathers to the left. This time you will be drawing the left side of the heart on the top of the stem

Figure 9-26.

and the right side of the heart on the bottom (Figure 9-26).

Do the same exercises using different size buttons and different spacing from the stem to see what a variety of Feather Bands is possible.

Drawing Feathers along curving lines, around circles, around a heart, and other shapes follows the same methods as drawing on a straight line. Feathers drawn on curving lines and circles will mean that the feather tails on the inside curves of the stem will be farther apart than the ones on the outside of a curve. This is true for the inside of a circle and for the outside. Remember the tails should not meet and, in fact, this would be impossible to accomplish on curves and circles. Stem lines can be double, tripled, or more, if desired.

To make a paper pattern for the Feather design that you have drawn, go over the Feather lines with a black felt tip marker. Using a black felt tip pen, trace the Feather design onto pattern paper that has been cut to fit the area of the quilt where the Feather will be.

Mark the quilt top by pinning the paper pattern to the wrong side of the quilt top and trace the design onto the fabric.

To make a template for a Feather design, draw the desired Feather design on paper first. If using template plastic, transfer the outside curved lines and the stem to the plastic or draw the Feather design on freezer paper and iron to poster board or cardboard. Cut around the outside lines and along the stem line. The dotted lines on the template show lines that will be marked directly onto the quilt top. It is not necessary to mark these on the template (Figure 9-27).

To use the template, place it on the assembled quilt layers and mark around the outside and along the stem line. Follow the curves, just as you

Feather Band Template (Figure 9-27)

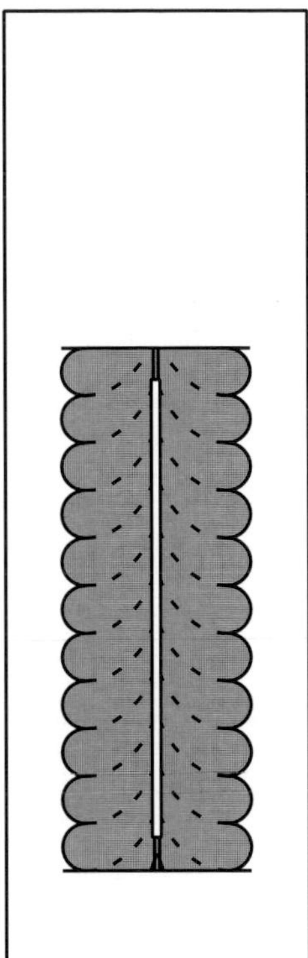

Figure 9-27.

did on paper, to mark the tails of the Feathers freehand directly onto the fabric of the quilt.

Helpful Note: Feathers are fun to draw and drawing your own will liberate you from searching for a pattern that is the perfect fit or the perfect feather.

Tools Needed: Tracing paper, pencil, ruler, pattern paper, black felt tip pen, small round objects (buttons or coins), and a fabric marking pencil or pen.

Where to Use: Use the Feather Band for borders and sashings or for framing in a medallion or whole cloth quilt design.

The following traditonal Feather designs have been used frequently on quilts over the last two centuries. Even though there have been many variations of each of these designs, each different variation of a particular Feather shape was similiar enough that the designs shown here are historically representative of each Feather design.

Follow the instructions for drawing the Feather Band to draw the Feathers in each of these designs. The outside guide lines and the stem line will change for each design. The design would be transferred to the quilt top in the same way and the same tools will be needed for drawing and marking the Feathered designs.

For each of these traditional designs, a template will be shown which can also be used to give you ideas for drawing the guide lines. Suggestions will also be given for where to use each of these different Feather designs.

Straight Feather: also Straight Plume (Figure 9-28)

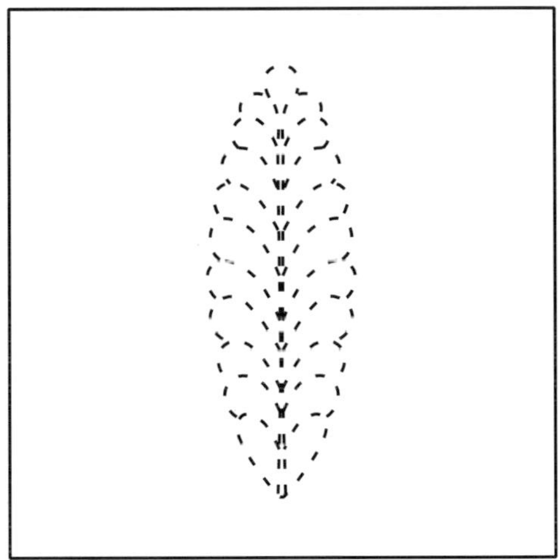

Figure 9-28.

Straight Feather Template (Figure 9-29)

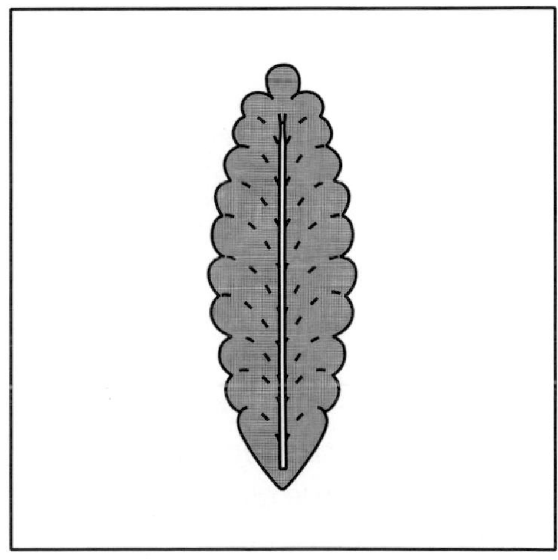

Figure 9-29.

WHERE TO USE: Place the Straight Feather end to end and use in the border. Place around a circle or star with six or eight of the Straight Feathers radiating out to form a large circular design. It can be placed in the center with Princess Feathers on each side to form a corner design.

Ostrich Plume: also Ostrich Feather (Figure 9-30)

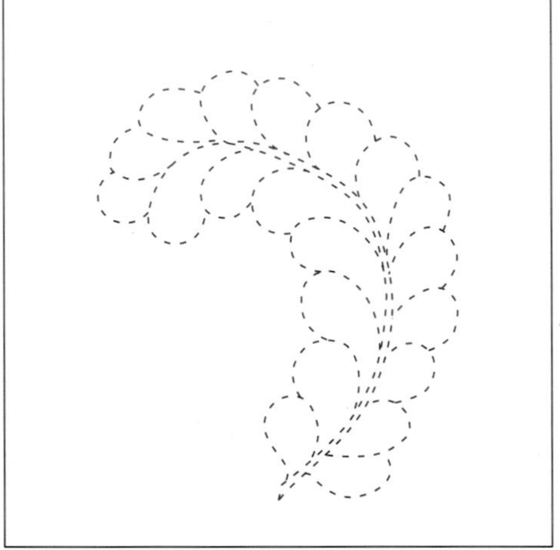

Figure 9-30.

Ostrich Plume Template (Figure 9-31)

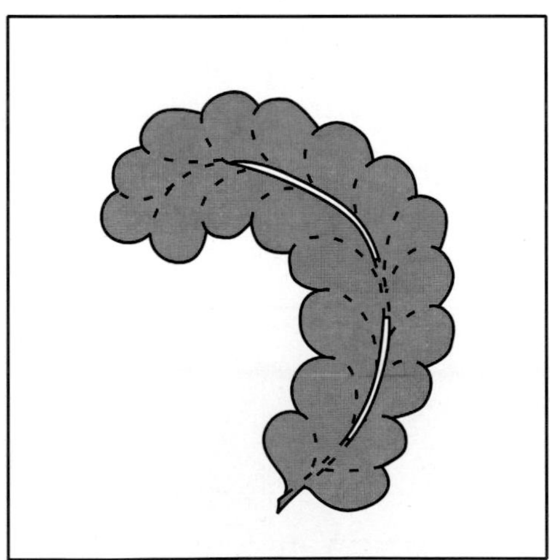

Figure 9-31.

WHERE TO USE: The Ostrich Plume shown is a small one. A larger one would have many more individual feathers in the plume. It can be used end to end in border areas, in plain setting triangles, and with the Straight Plume to form a grouping.

Feather Scroll (Figure 9-32)

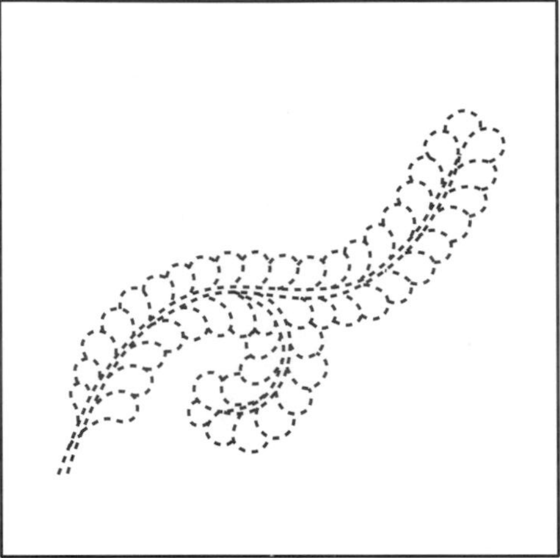

Figure 9-32.

Feather Scroll Template (Figure 9-33)

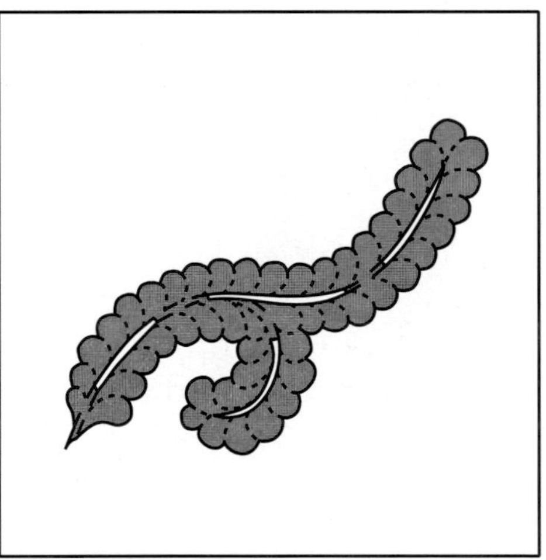

Figure 9-33.

Because of the intricacies of this design, marking from a paper pattern rather than a template is recommended.

WHERE TO USE: Use in a grouping for a corner design for a whole cloth quilt or for a center medallion appliqué type quilt. These could be used in plain setting blocks. Rose Kretsinger of Kansas made these famous by using them on her appliqué quilts.

Princess Feather: also Feather Tendrils, Curved Feathers, Prince's Feather, Princess Feather Plume (Figure 9-34)

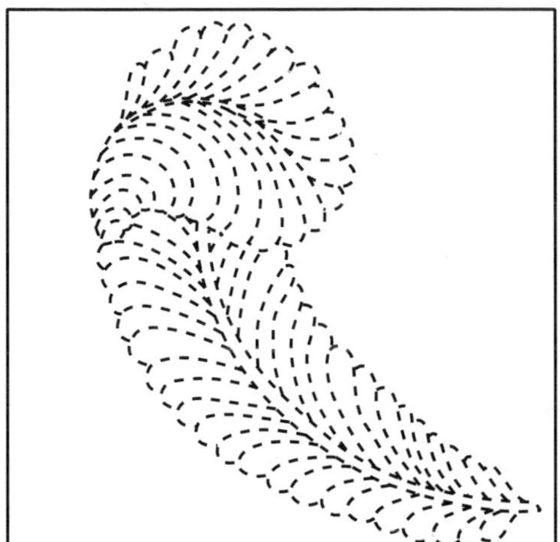

Figure 9-34.

Princess Feather Template (Figure 9-35)

Figure 9-35.

Because of the intricacies of this feather design, marking from a paper pattern rather than a template is recommended. Placement guide lines for drawing would be around the places where the feather curves occur. As you can see, this design has varying size curves for the feathers and they are very long and slender.

WHERE TO USE: Use the Princess Feather end to end for a border design. Two of them placed together make a good design to use in plain setting blocks or in open areas in an appliqué quilt. They can be used placed end to end around a circle or oval to make a framing for a central design in a whole cloth quilt. From a circle or star, radiate six to eight of the Princess Feather designs out to form a large circular design. The Princess Feather is so elegant and so lovely that it could be used anywhere with success.

Plumed Swastika (Figure 9-36)

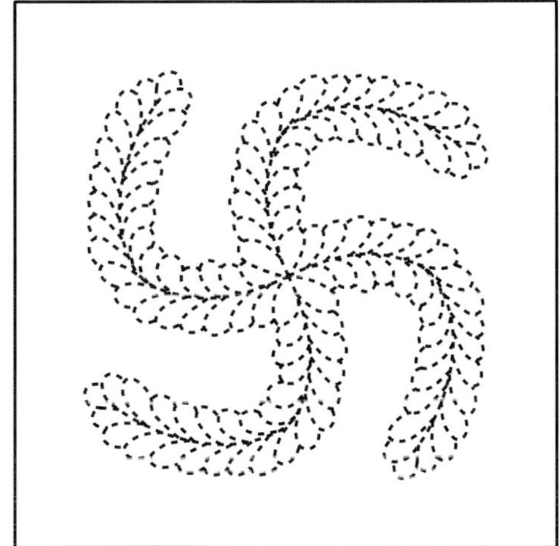

Figure 9-36.

Plumed Swastika Template (Figure 9-37)

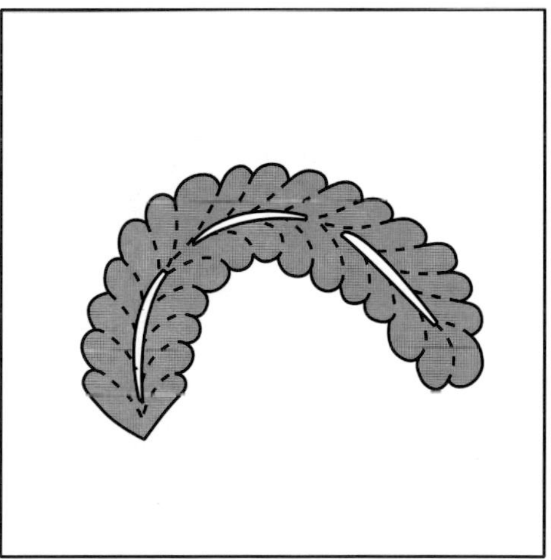

Figure 9-37.

Mark a faint T guide line on the center of the area where the design will go and place the template on a guide line and mark the one section. Move the template to the next guide line to mark the second one. Continue until four sections have been marked to make the Plumed Swastika.

WHERE TO USE: This design can be used for a center design in a whole cloth quilt. It could also be used in large plain setting blocks. The name is not appealing but the design certainly is.

Fiddlehead (Figure 9-38)

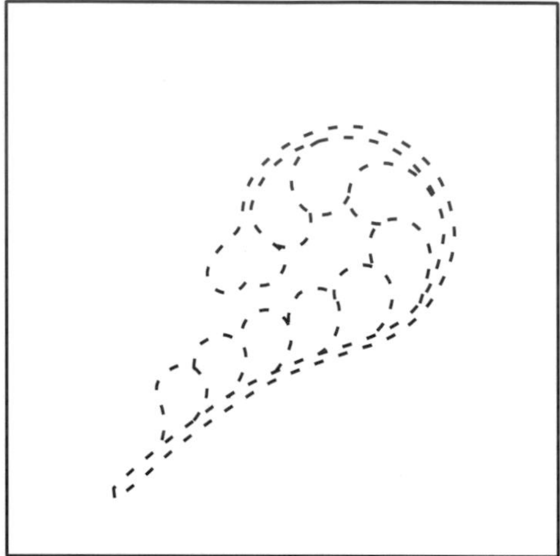

Figure 9-38.

Fiddlehead Template (Figure 9-39)

Figure 9-39.

WHERE TO USE: Fiddlehead is a design often used on Amish quilts. It is a good design for triangles. Two of them could be used on each side of a straight feather for a grouping to use in a corner or a plain setting block. In a grouping, have one Fiddlehead lean to the left, reverse the design and lean the other to the right. The Fiddlehead could be placed end to end in a narrow border or sashing.

Feather Rosette (Figure 9-40)

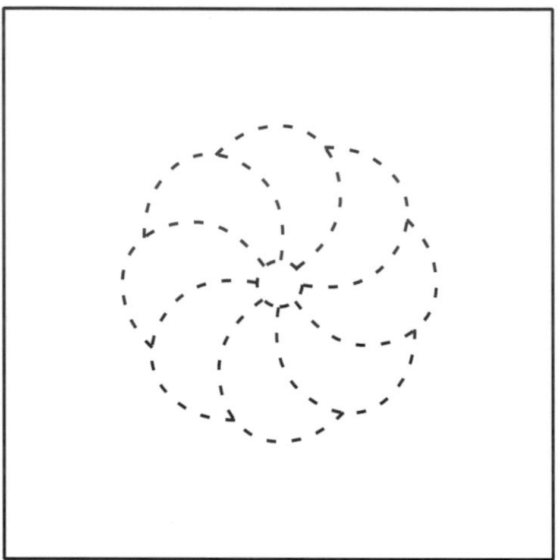

Figure 9-40.

Feather Rosette Template (Figure 9-41)

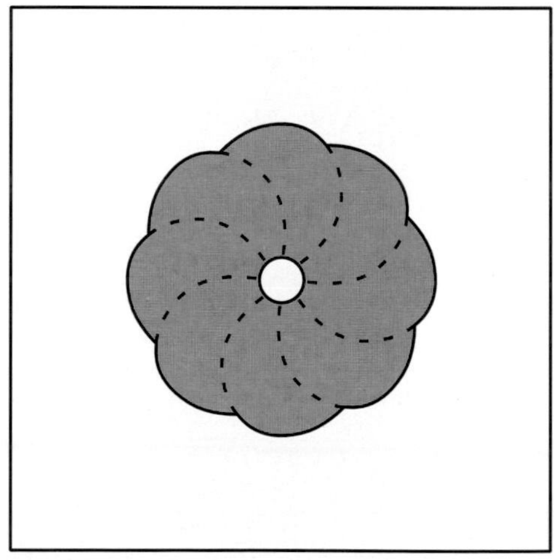

Figure 9-41.

WHERE TO USE: Use the Feather Rosette as a finial with swags, in corner setting blocks of sashing, or combined with a leaf for a small filler design.

This design will work any place a flower design is wanted.

Feathered Circle: also Feather Circle, Feathered Wreath, Crown, Circle of Feathered Swirls (Figure 9-42)

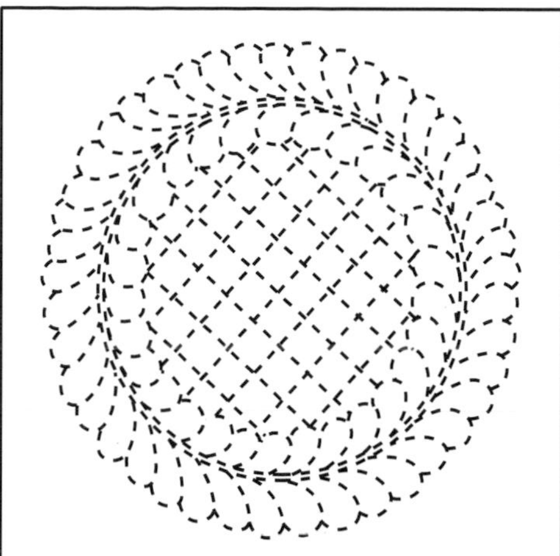

Figure 9-42.

Feathered Circle Template (Figure 9-43)

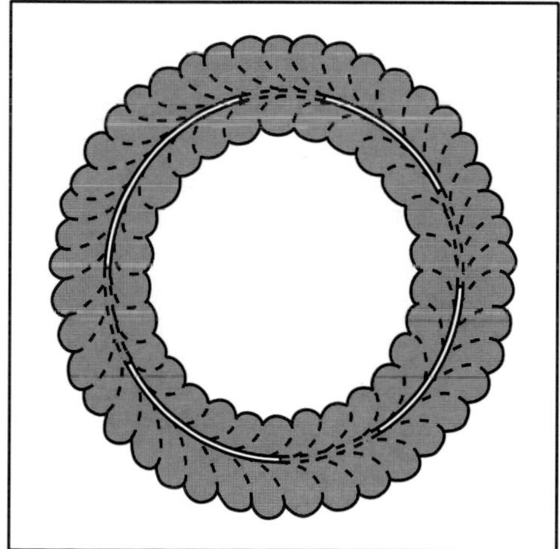

Figure 9-43.

The Feathered Circles design is one of the most often used of the feathered designs. See Chapter 6, page 85, for directions for drawing a circle. For the Feathered Circle, draw the outside circle first and use that for the outside guide. Determine the spacing between this guide line and the stem by how large the first circle is and how wide you want the feathered part to be. A double line stem is preferred for the Feathered Circle. The circle can be feathered both outside and inside the circle stem or just on the outside. Fill the center of the Feathered Circle with any of the designs used for background fillers.

Where to Use: The Feathered Circle is a perfect design for plain setting blocks. The size of the Feathered Circle can vary from 6" to a very large circle to use in the center of a whole cloth quilt design. Use the small ones in the small blocks in sashing. A half feathered circle can be used for the triangles used in a blocks-on-point setting.

Paisley (Figure 9-44)

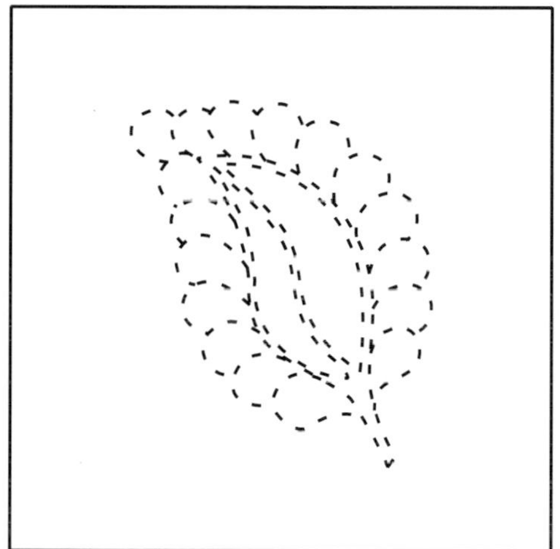

Figure 9-44.

Paisley Template (Figure 9-45)

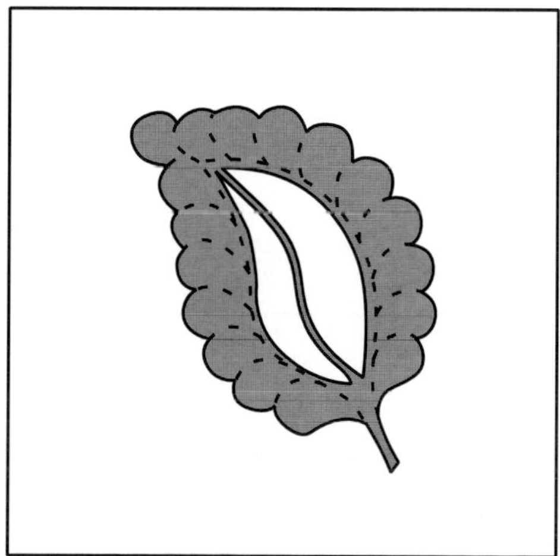

Figure 9-45.

Where to Use: Draw four of the Paisley designs with the stems pointing to the center of an X.

Use this design in plain setting blocks. Placed end to end they could be used as a border design. They can also be used in plain triangles and placed at random as fillers in the background, especially whole cloth quilt designs.

Lace Vein Feather (Figure (9-46)

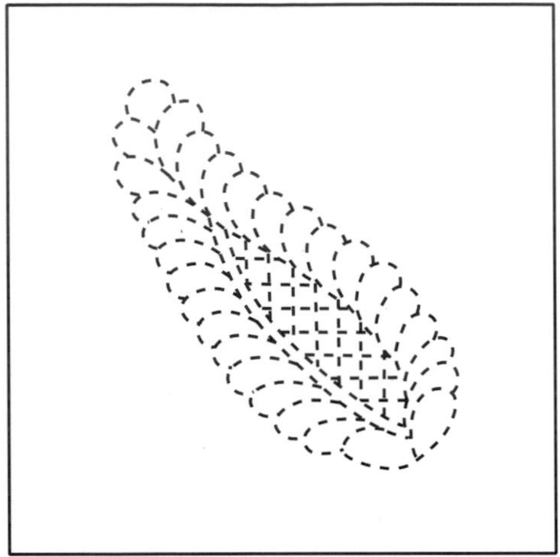

Figure 9-46.

Lace Vein Feather Template (Figure 9-47)

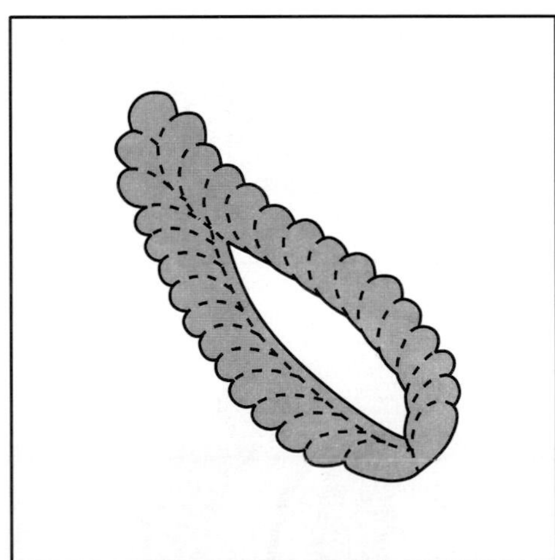

Figure 9-47.

This design would probably be easier to mark from a paper pattern.

WHERE TO USE: This design makes a good border design when placed end to end or by alternating the direction of the feathers by having every other one reversed. Four of them together would make a good design for a plain setting block. Mark the center crosshatch using a ruler after the Lace Vein Feather design has been quilted.

Feather Swag: also Feather Hammock (Figure 9-48)

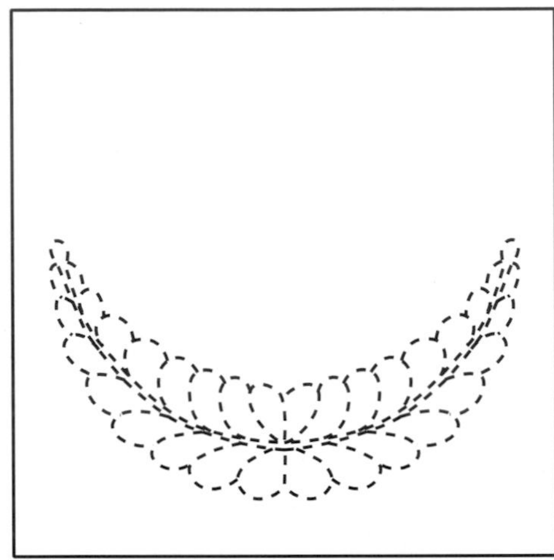

Figure 9-48.

Feather Swag Template (Figure 9-49)

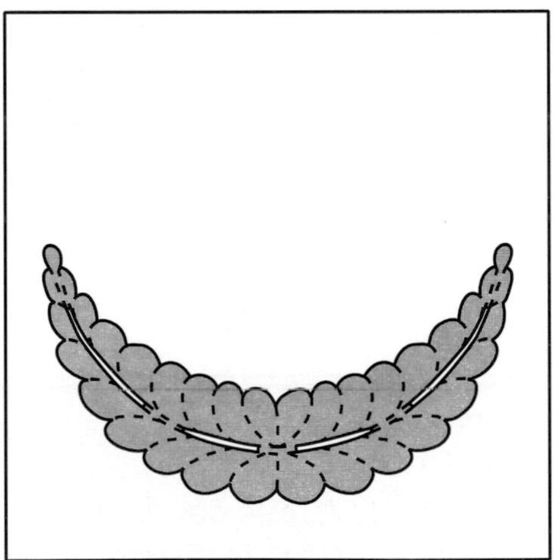

Figure 9-49.

Follow the directions in Chapter 7, page 98, to draw a swag to use for a guide in drawing this design so that it will fit.

WHERE TO USE: The Feather Swag is a good border design.

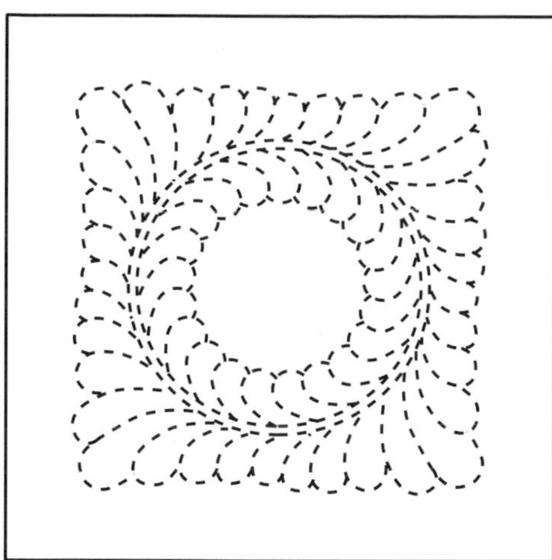
Figure 9-50.

Feathered Circle-in-a-Square (Figure 9-50)

Feathered Circle-in-a-Square Template (Figure 9-51)

Figure 9-51.

First, draw the square to fit the place where the design will go and then draw the circle inside the square. Fill the area in the center of the circle with a filler design. This is a design that is probably best marked using a paper pattern.

WHERE TO USE: The Feathered Circle-in-a-Square is, of course, designed for a plain setting square but can be used side by side for a border design or for the corner blocks of a border.

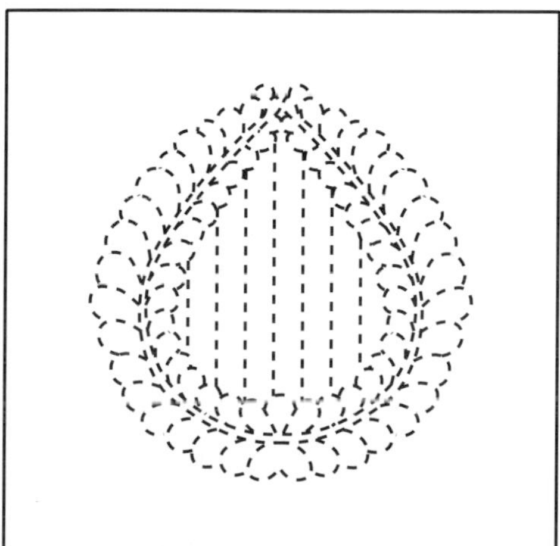
Figure 9-52.

Feathered Harp: also Feathered Lyre (Figure 9-52)

Feathered Harp Template (Figure 9-53)

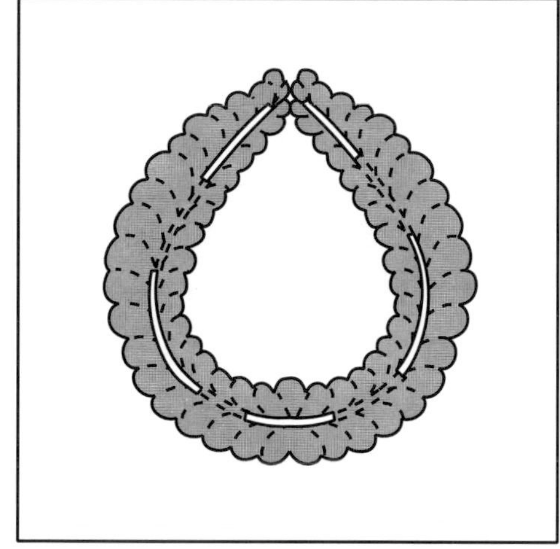
Figure 9-53.

Mark the harp strings with a ruler after quilting the feathered part of the harp.

WHERE TO USE: Use the Feathered Harp in plain setting blocks and in designs for whole cloth quilts. It could be used in the corners of the border.

Feathered Heart (Figure 9-54)

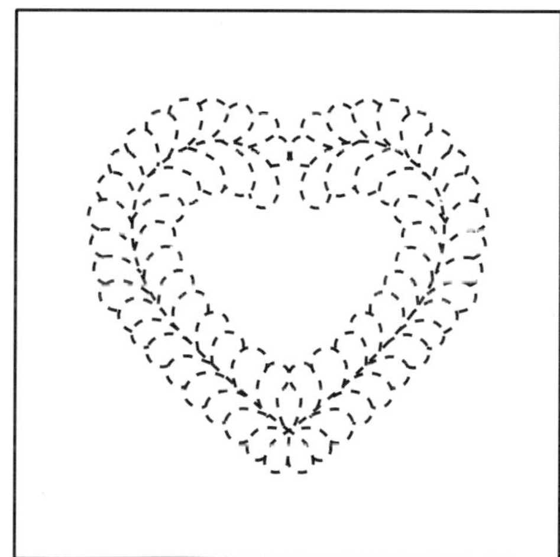
Figure 9-54.

Figure 9-55.

Feathered Heart Template (Figure 9-55)

See page 125, Figure 9-1, for directions on drawing a heart. The heart looks good double lined. For a variation, draw feathers around the outside of the heart shape only. The center of the heart can be filled with any one of the variety of filler designs.

WHERE TO USE: The Feathered Heart is a good design for plain setting blocks and in whole cloth quilt designs or medallion appliqué designs where there is ample space for quilting designs. This design is especially suited for quilts made to commemorate a wedding or anniversary.

Feathered Pineapple: also Pineapple (Figure 9-56)

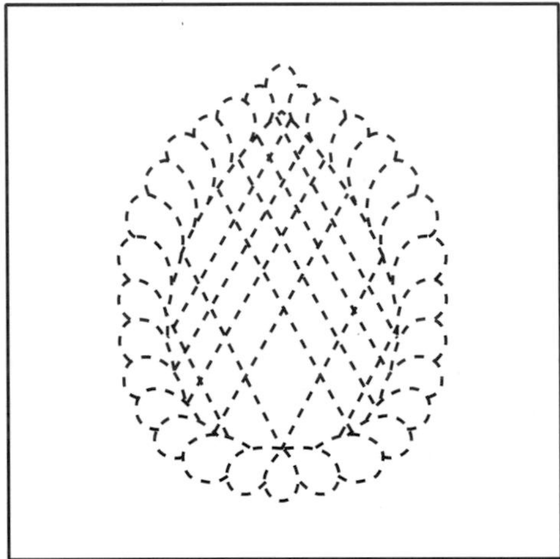

Figure 9-56.

Feathered Pineapple Template (Figure 9-57)

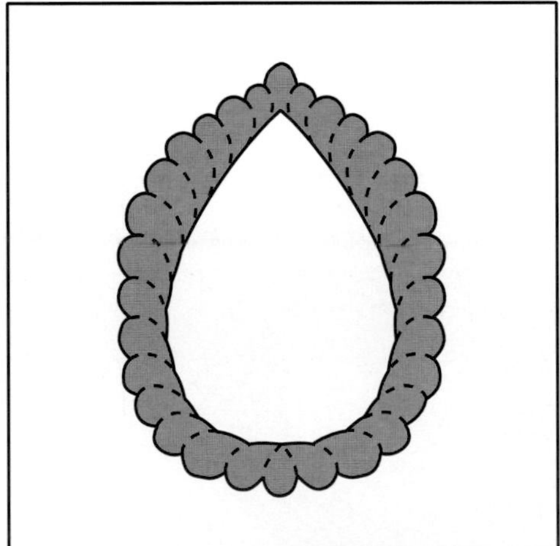

Figure 9-57.

Mark the Pineapple lines in the center, using a ruler, after the Pineapple is quilted. Note that the inside of the feathers also are curved.

WHERE TO USE: The Feathered Pineapple is a good design for plain setting blocks and to use in the corners of the border. The Pineapple is a symbol of hospitality and would be a good design for a friendship quilt.

Feathered Vine: also Feather Vines, Continuous Vine Feathers (Figure 9-58)

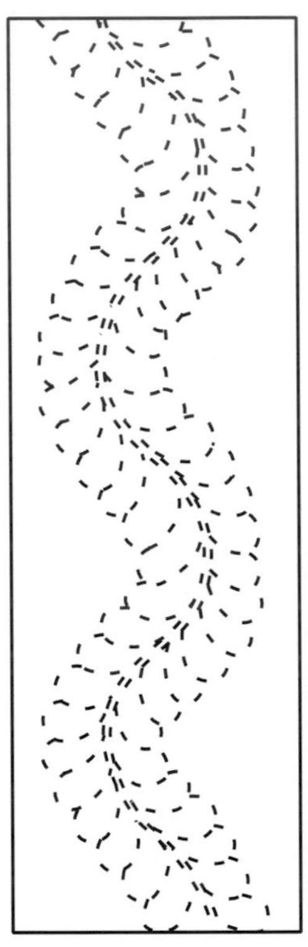

Figure 9-58.

Feathered Vine Template (Figure 9-59)

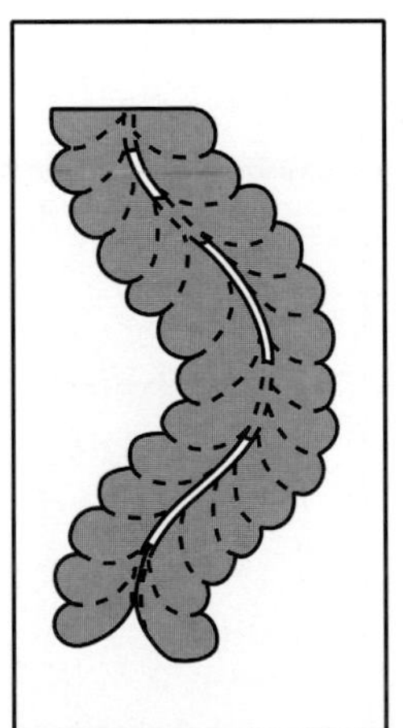

Figure 9-59.

To make the guide lines for drawing the Feathered Vine, follow the directions in Chapter 7, page 101, for drawing a Scrolling Vine. Note that the template must be a section long enough for the feathers to overlap when the template is moved to the next position.

WHERE TO USE: The Feathered Vine is a border design. It can be used in a whole cloth quilt design to define a section of the design or to act as a framing device.

Feathered Cable: also Running Feather, Undulating Feather (Figure 9-60)

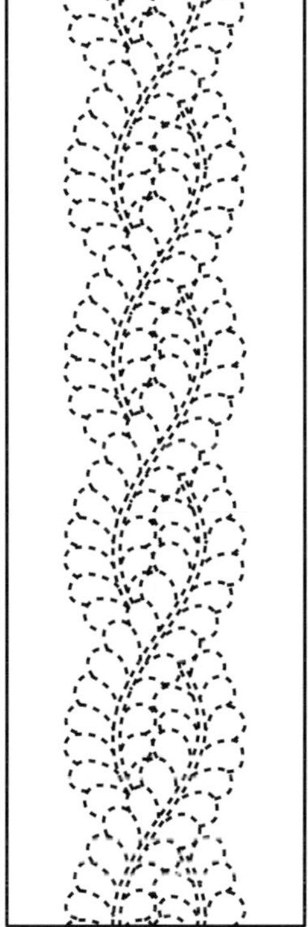

Figure 9-60.

Feathered Cable Template (Figure 9-61)

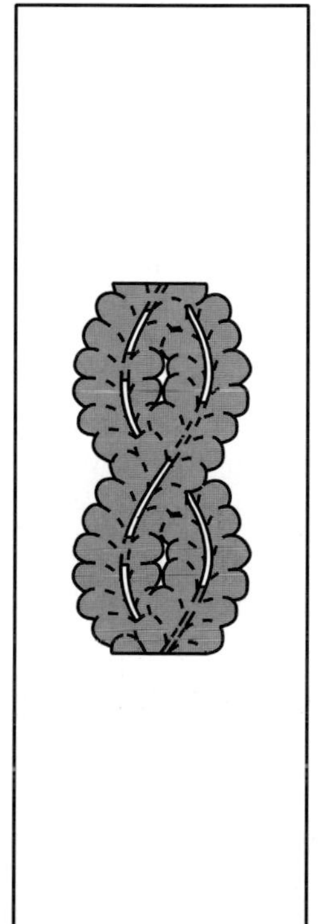

Figure 9-61.

For a guide to draw this design, draw a Chain Triple Cable following the instructions for drawing a cable on page 118, Figure 8-48). The preferred marking on the quilt top is from a paper pattern. If using a template, two sections of the cable are needed and be sure that the feathers will overlap when moving the template to the next marking place.

WHERE TO USE: Use the Feathered Cable in borders and in whole cloth quilt designs.

Feather Twist (Figure 9-62)

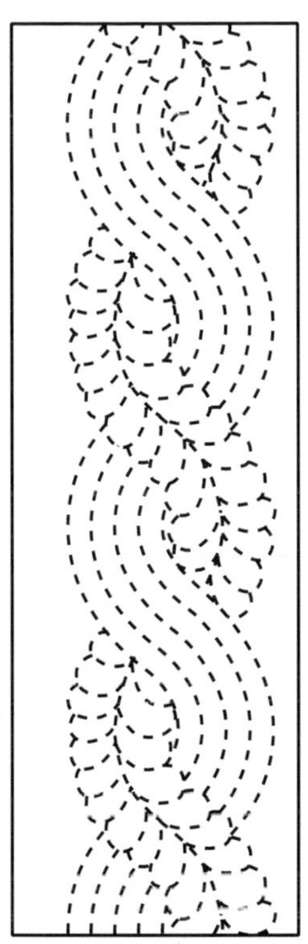

Figure 9-62.

Feather Twist Template (Figure 9-63)

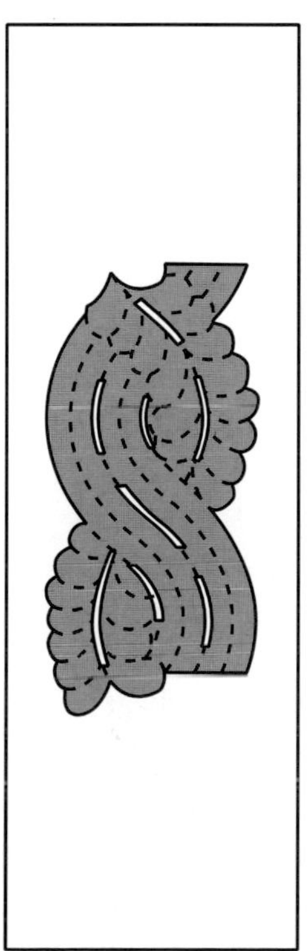

Figure 9-63.

Follow the directions for drawing any one of the multiple line cables described in Chapter 8 and use the cable for a guide to draw in the feathers. In this design, only one twist of the cable is feathered and the other is left with the cable lines. Although this design is easier marked using a paper pattern, experienced template makers should be able to make and mark from a template. The template should include both the upper and lower curve of the feathers so the feathers will overlap when moving the template to the next positon.

WHERE TO USE: Feather Twist is a border design.

Finger Feather (Figure 9-64)

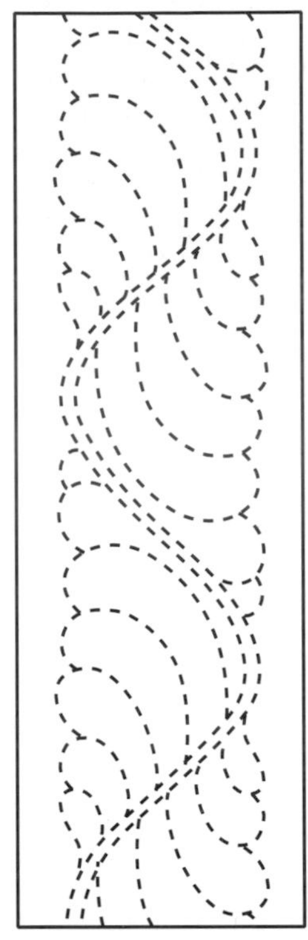

Figure 9-64.

Feathered Garland: also Feather Scroll, Continuous Scroll, Amish Feathers (Figure 9-66)

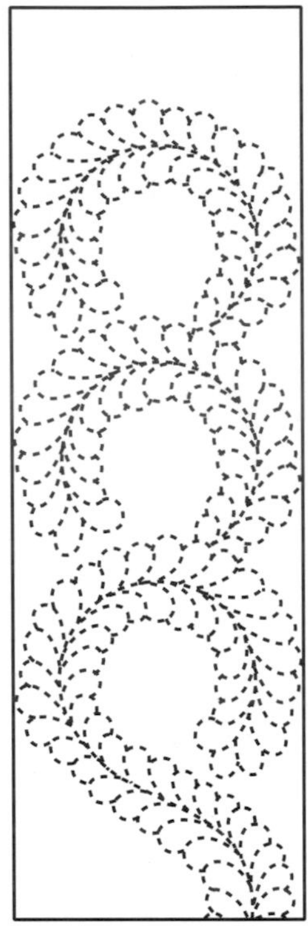

Figure 9-66

Finger Feather Template (Figure 9-65)

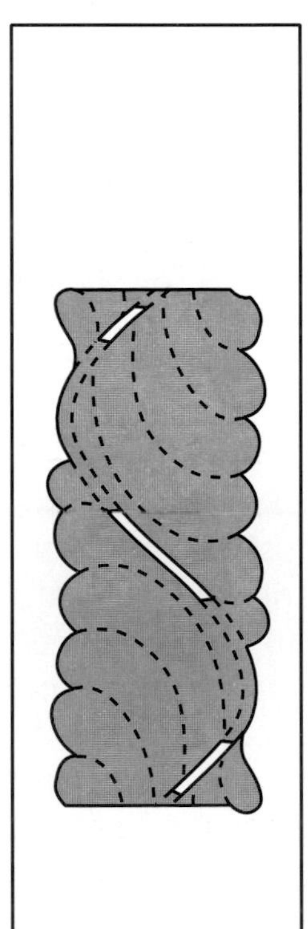

Figure 9-65.

The stem of the Finger Feather is deeply curving. Use a half circle to draw the curves for the stem. The outside guides of the design are straight lines. Note that the upper feathers in the design flow in one direction and the lower feathers in the opposite direction. Be sure that the feathers will overlap when moving the template to the next position.

WHERE TO USE: This design, from the Amish, is used in borders, in sashings, and in the strips of a bar-quilt.

Feathered Garland Template (Figure 9-67)

Figure 9-67.

This design is derived from circles that aren't completely closed circles. A plate makes a good circle to use in drawing the guides for this design. The circular sections of the design are the same, only some are flipped or reversed to make the number or the desired design needed to fill the border space. Experienced quilters can mark the Feathered Garland using a template although the preferred marking method would be from a paper pattern.

Two of the templates as shown could be used with a Princess Feather to make a good corner design.

WHERE TO USE: The Feathered Garland is one of the most elegant and beautiful border designs. Use the design in borders and especially in the designing of whole cloth quilts.

Peacock Fan (Figure 9-68)

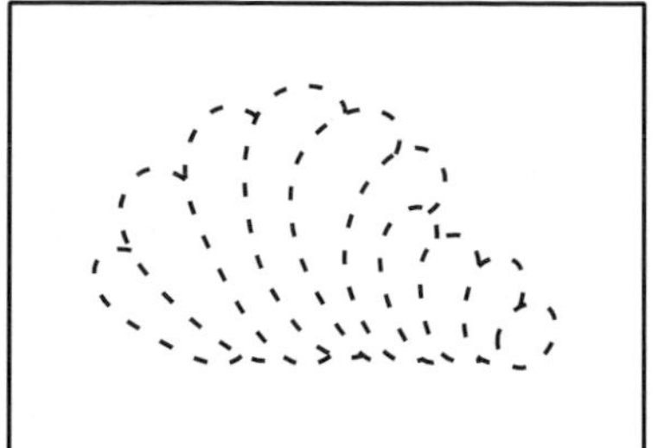

Figure 9-68.

Peacock Fan Template (Figure 9-69)

Figure 9-69.

Where to Use: Place the Peacock Fans side by side to create a border design. It could be used in plain setting blocks, in corners as a filler design, and in the bar or strippie quilt.

Feathered Triangle (Figure 9-70)

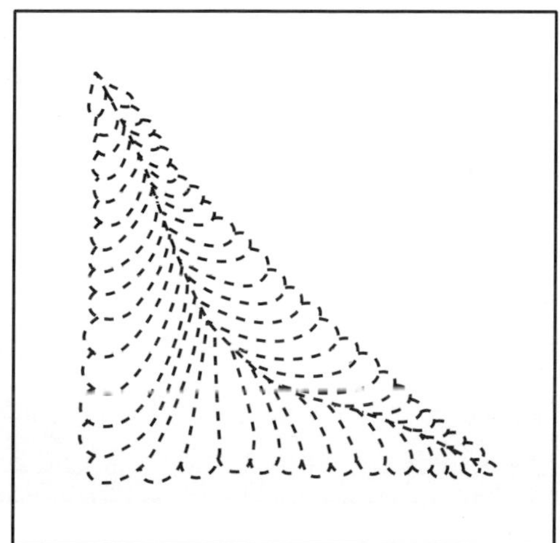

Figure 9-70.

Feathered Triangle Template (Figure 9-71)

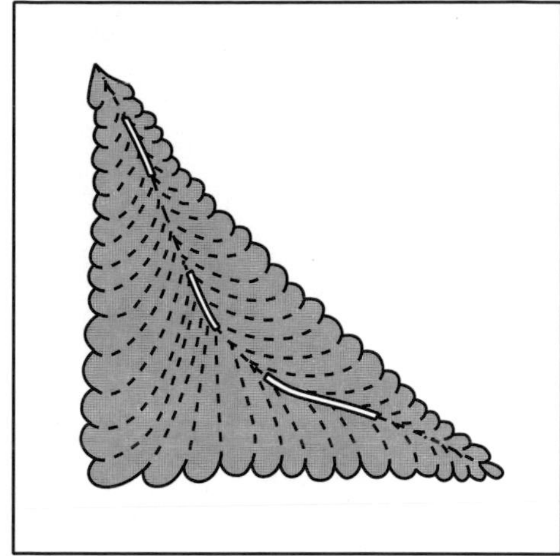

Figure 9-71.

Where to Use: The Feathered Triangle is perfect for triangular set blocks in a quilt where the blocks are set on point. Place two of the feathers in a square plain block. The design could be used in a border design by placing the corner of the triangle toward the outside edge of the quilt to form a scalloped look.

Plate 10-1. Urns, Leaves, Florals (also Meandering, Zig-Zag, Squares Crosshatch).
Floral Urns by Debra Wagner, 1992. Collection of the Museum of the American Quilter's Society.

Plate 10-2. Waves (also Single Parallel Lines, In the Ditch).
Rabbit Boxes by Phyllis Miller, 1990.

Plate 10-3. Acanthus (also Swag).
Splendor of the Rajahs by Joyce Stewart, 1985. Collection of the Museum of the American Quilter's Society.

Plate 10-4. Dog Rose, Bird (also Basketweave, Leaves).
Judy, Doris, and the Devil by Phyllis Miller, 1995.

Chapter Ten
Representational, Naturalistic, and Combinations

Representational defines designs that are derived from images of people, places, and objects. These designs may be realistic, such as an eagle, or symbolic, such as a heart for love. Designs that are representational include such designs as hands, baskets, anchors, bows, and horseshoes.

Naturalistic defines designs that are derived from forms found in nature such as leaves, flowers, birds, fruit, and animals. Often a design may be both naturalistic and representational. A good example is the pineapple which is a form found in nature but it is also symbolic of hospitality.

The designs included in this chapter are only traditional designs that have been referred to in previously printed material. These designs are considered traditional because they have been used often and have been passed on from one generation to another. The designs included here are representative and have many variations as each quilt artist has intrepreted them a little differently.

Combinations are designs that have two or more traditional quilting designs put together to form another design. Only a few design combinations have been included although quilters of the past were both creative and prolific in mixing designs to suit a particular quilt. The possibilities for new design combinations are endless. Hopefully, the ones shown here will fuel your imagination to experiment by using the many designs in this book in new or different combinations.

The designs for quilting included in this chapter are the intrepretations of many different quilt artists. They were originally drawn by a quilter and have been admired, handed down, and used until today many of them are considered standard designs for quilting. Many of these designs can only be duplicated by copying or by drawing an original intrepretation. The ones that can be drawn by using instructions in the preceding chapters will usually be a combination of designs and can be drawn by following the instructions for each individual design.

Cross (Figure 10-1)

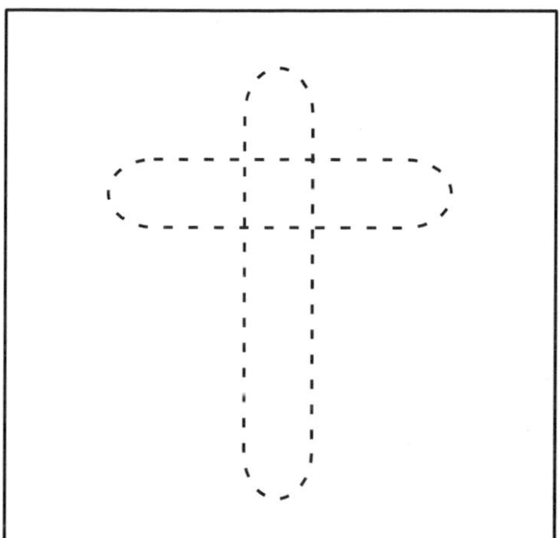

Figure 10-1.

Draw the Cross by using Straight Parallel Lines and rounding off in the same way as for an Oval. This design was found on quilts in the 1930's. It is a religious symbol.

Horseshoe (Figure 10-2)

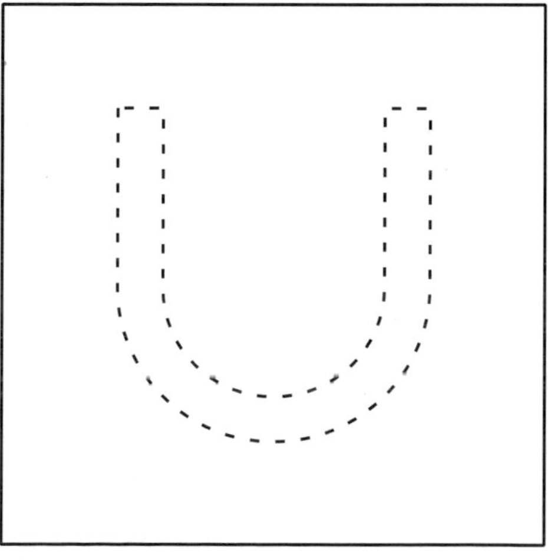

Figure 10-2.

Follow the instructions for drawing an Oval (see p. 93.). The Horseshoe is a symbol of good luck and was used as a quilting design in the 1930's.

Wheel (Figure 10-3)

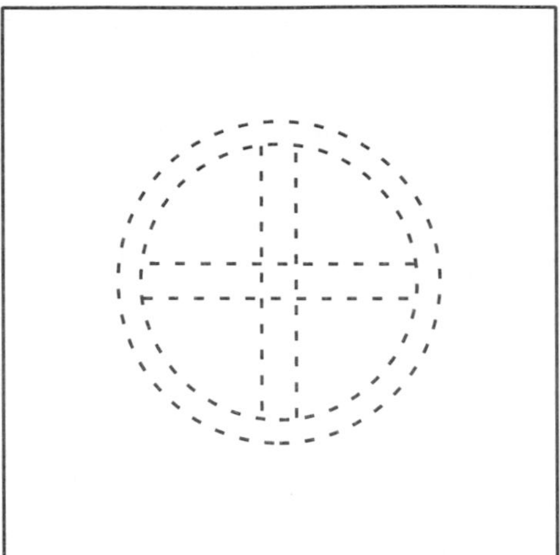

Figure 10-3.

Draw two Concentric Circles and draw the cross in the center of the circles using straight parallel lines. The Wheel design dates from around 1850 and represented divine guidance. It is thought to be symbolically used in quilts by women who migrated to the west. The Wheel was used in plain setting blocks.

Hex Wheel (Figure 10-4)

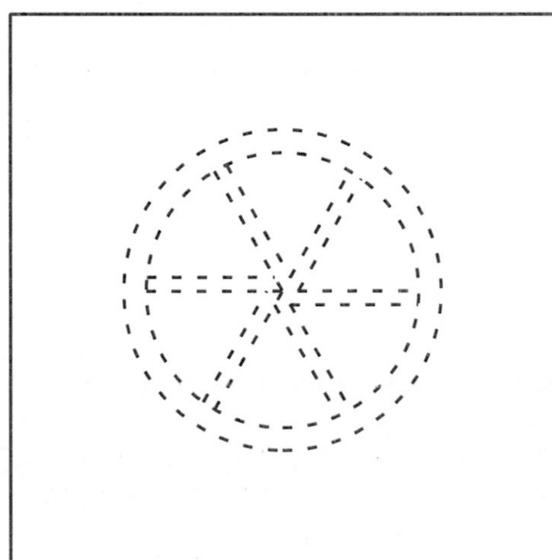

Figure 10-4.

The Hex Wheel dates from 1850 to 1860 and probably had the same symbolism as the Wheel. Draw two Concentric Circles. Using a protractor, mark the circles in 60° increments to draw the spokes of the wheel.

Star Hex (Figure 10-5)

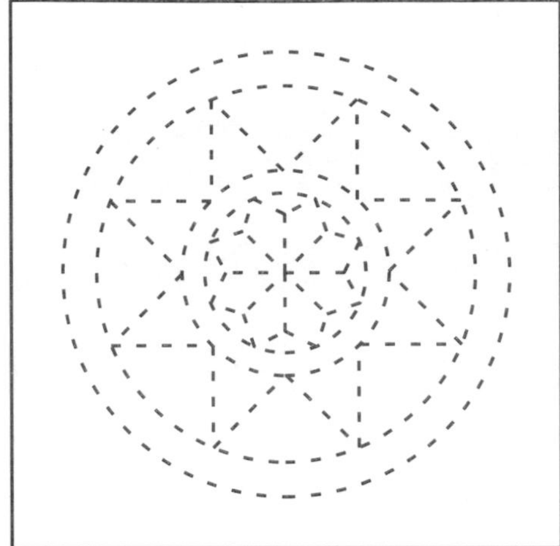

Figure 10-5.

The definition of hex is a spell or a charm, usually associated with witchcraft. To draw the Star Hex, the center is an Eight-Pointed Star and then two Concentric Circles. The star points in the outer circles can be drawn by marking the circle in 60° increments using a protractor.

Wheel Star (Figure 10-6)

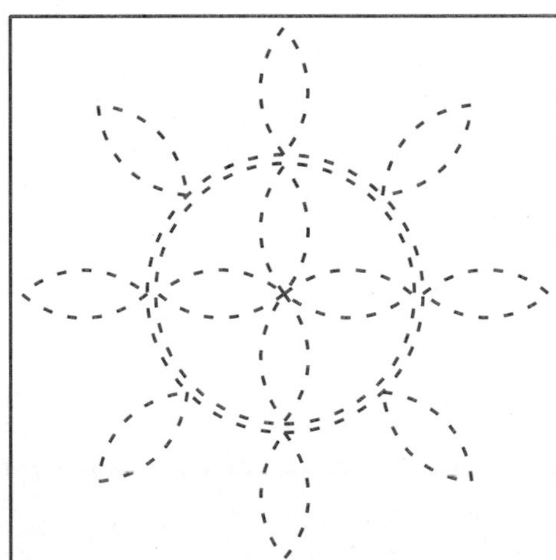

Figure 10-6.

The Wheel Star is double circles with Pumpkin Seeds (see p. 103). Draw the circles in a square. Divide the width of the square in fourths to find the length of the Pumpkin Seed. The four in the center are placed on the center lines. To find the placement of the eight Pumpkins Seeds around the outside of the circle, mark guide lines across the center and diagonally from corner to corner.

Hands (Figure 10-7)

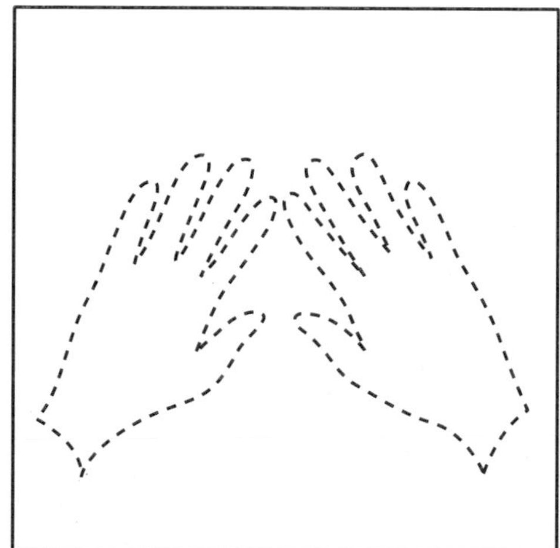

Figure 10-7.

Hands symbolize a pledge and were often used on bride's quilts. Draw around your own hand/hands or another person's hands to get this design.

Pipe Stem (Figure 10-8)

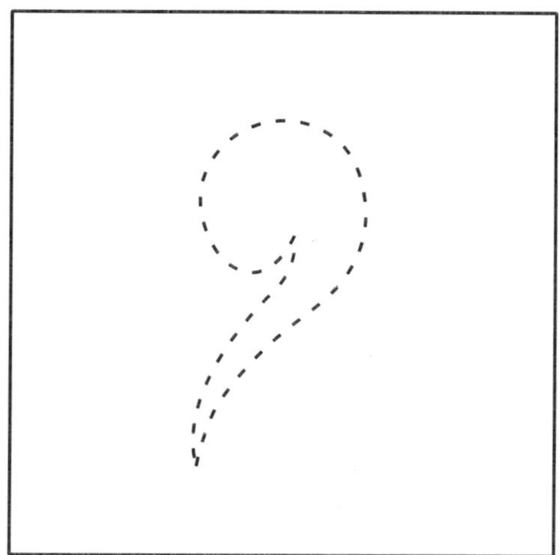

Figure 10-8.

This design also looks like a fat question mark. It can be arranged around a circle or end to end to make several different designs.

Anchor (Figure 10-9)

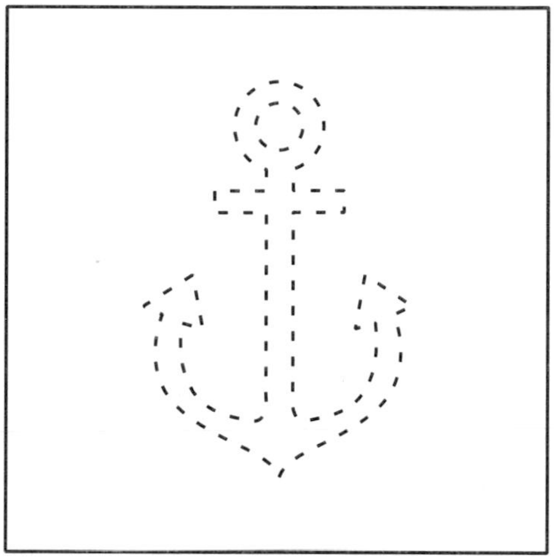

Figure 10-9.

The Anchor is considered to be a masculine design. It was used on quilts in the 1930's that had a nautical theme such as the Ships or Ocean Waves pieced patterns.

Teardrop (Figure 10-10)

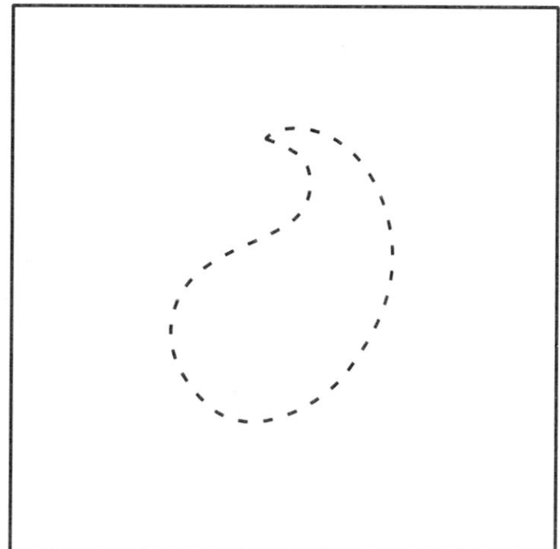

Figure 10-10.

The word teardrop conjures up a shape in most of our minds. Feather templates are often this shape. The example here is a version of a simple Teardrop. Use the Teardrop shape to create other designs or in narrow sashings or borders.

Cornucopia (Figure 10-11)

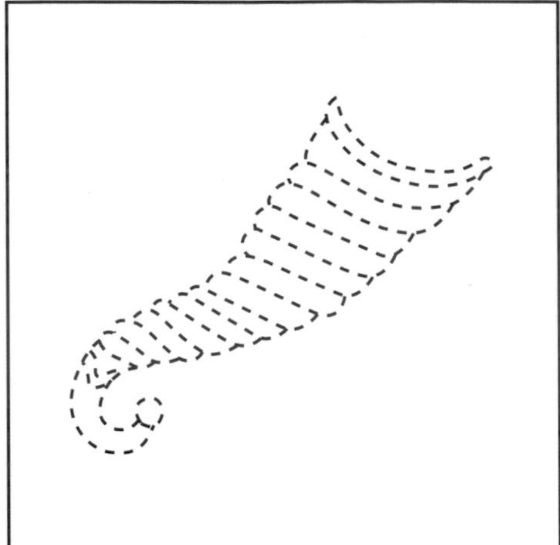

Figure 10-11.

The Cornucopia is a symbol of abundance. The design was used on quilts dated in the 1860's. It can be used in a plain setting block or in a central design in a whole cloth quilt.

Horn of Plenty (Figure 10-12)

Figure 10-12.

This is another name for the Cornucopia and in this example is shown overflowing with fruit and leaves.

Cherry Basket (Figure 10-13)

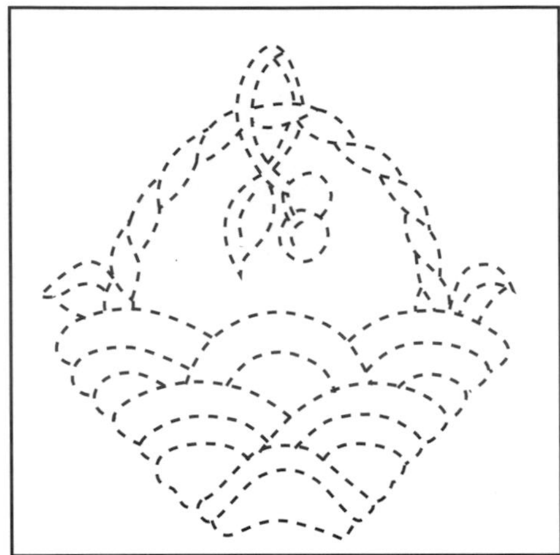

Figure 10-13.

The Cherry Basket and other basket designs are favorites for filling plain setting blocks.

President's Wreath (Figure 10-14)

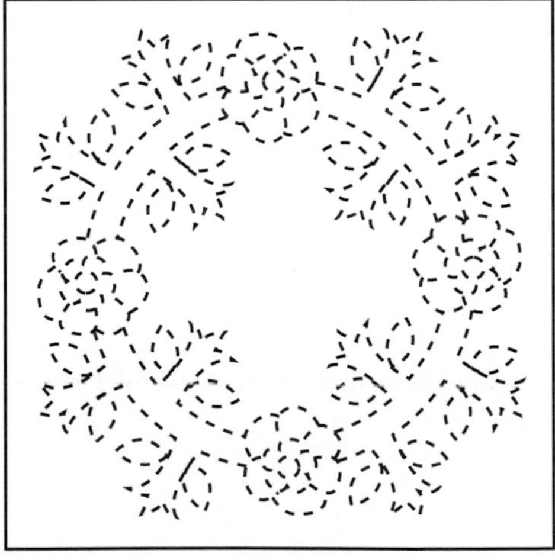

Figure 10-14.

This wreath design is representative of the many variations that quilter's have used in plain setting blocks when fancy quilting was desired. The wreaths are usually a combination of flowers and leaves placed in a circle.

Lyre (Figure 10-15)

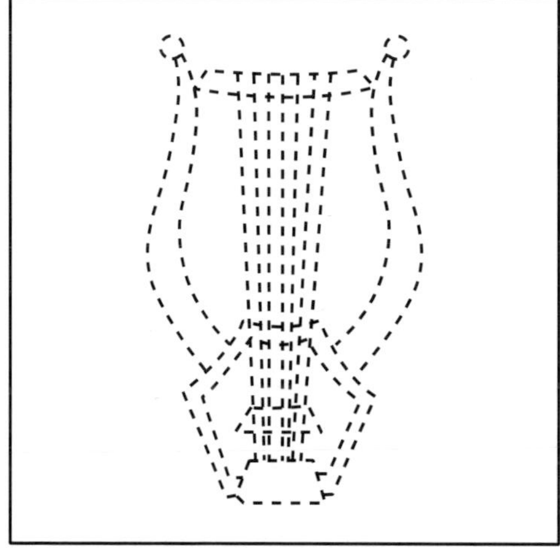

Figure 10-15.

The Lyre is a musical instrument from ancient Greece. It was used in the last part of the 1800's in plain setting blocks.

Harp (Figure 10-16)

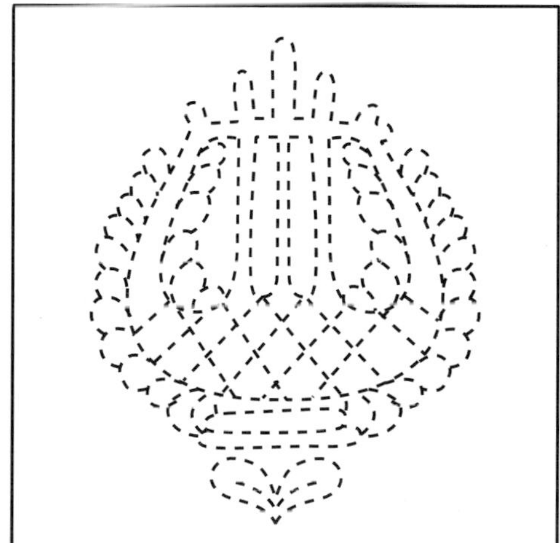

Figure 10-16.

The Harp is a musical instrument. It was used in plain setting blocks on quilts dating from the last quarter of the 1800's.

Bow (Figure 10-17)

Figure 10-17.

The Bow can be used in borders and in other designs. Make your own Bow design by tying a ribbon in a bow and photocopying it.

Amish Fancy (Figure 10-18)

Figure 10-18.

This design is a variation of the Scroll. It can be used in corners of pieced or plain setting blocks.

Five-Pointed Star (Figure 10-19)

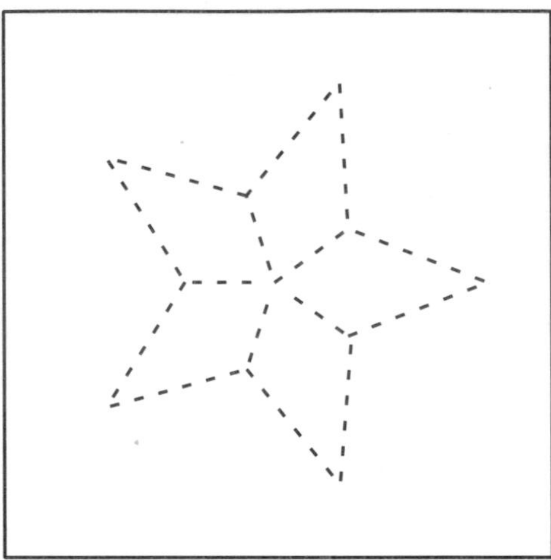

Figure 10-19.

The Five-Pointed Star is a patriotic symbol and can be found on quilts dating from the early 1800's. The Five-Pointed Star can be drawn using the Pentagon shape. Stars are quilting designs that are both representational and naturalistic.

Eight-Pointed Star (Figure 10-20)

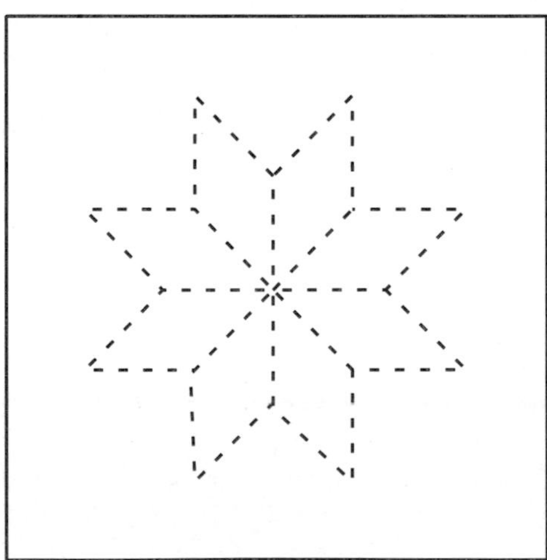

Figure 10-20.

The pieced pattern for the Eight-Pointed Star is probably where the design for quilting originated. The Amish used this design in the corner blocks of sashings. The Eight-Pointed Star has been used as a quilting design since at least the 1870's. The star is the symbol of fertility.

Eight-Pointed Star I (Figure 10-21)

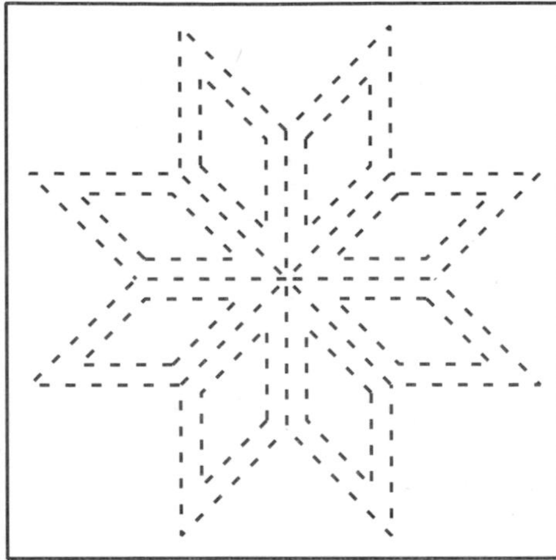

Figure 10-21.

This double lined Eight-Pointed Star was a favorite design used by the Amish. A pattern for the pieced block can be used for the design or can be drawn using a 45° diamond.

Rising Sun (Figure 10-22)

Figure 10-22.

The Rising Sun quilting design is the piecing lines of the pieced pattern.

There are many variations and most resemble Mariner's Compass designs. Use in plain setting blocks or in whole cloth quilt designs.

The following floral designs are representative of the multitude of quilting designs that have been inspired by flowers. The designs included here have been used over and over to

become a part of the designs for quilting that are now considered traditional. Use these designs alone or in combination with other designs to add elegance to your quilt.

Fleur-de-lis (Figure 10-23)

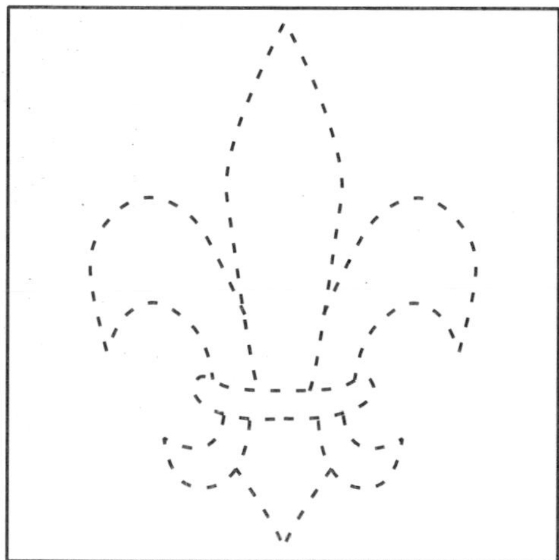

Figure 10-23.

The Fleur-de-lis resembles the floral segment of the iris tied with a band and is a symbol of the royal family of France. It can be repeated to form a border design or combined with other designs, such as a Swag.

Simple Flower-Amish (Figure 10-24)

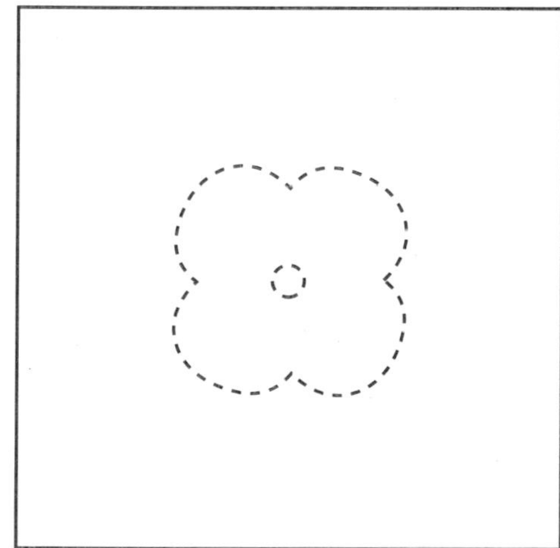

Figure 10-24.

This is a simple, almost childlike, design. Use in small setting squares in sashings or space them in a line in sashings or borders.

Floral (Figure 10-25)

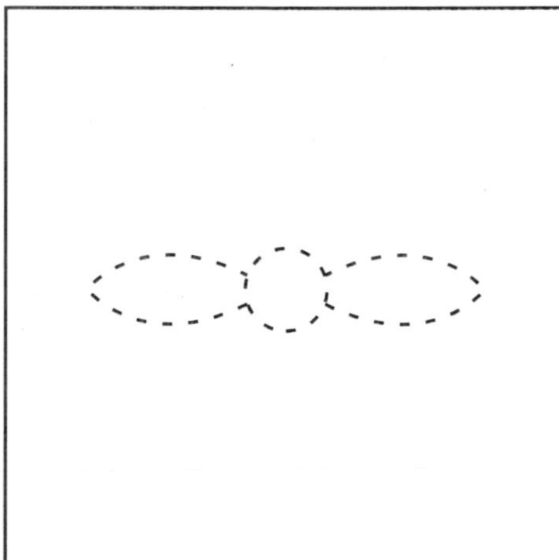

Figure 10-25.

Draw this design by drawing a circle with a Pumpkin Seed shape on each side. This Floral is often found in the melon shape piece in Double Wedding Ring quilts made after 1930.

Four Petal Flower (Figure 10-26)

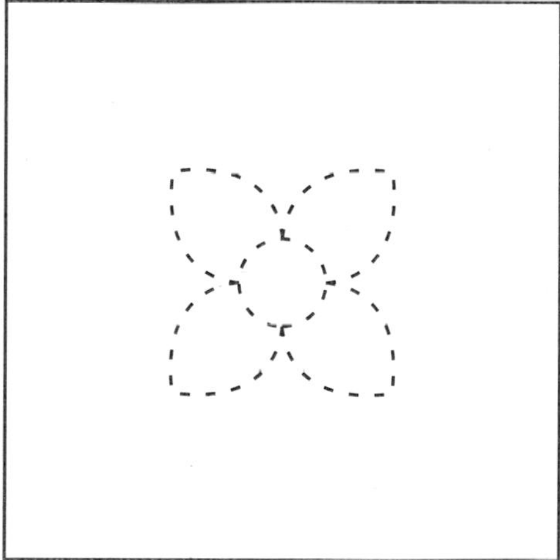

Figure 10-26.

Use four of the Ellipse shapes or the Pumpkin Seed shapes placed around a circle to draw this simple but effective flower. The design can be used in small squares alone or perhaps on a vine or in a bouquet with other floral designs.

Rosette (Figure 10-27)

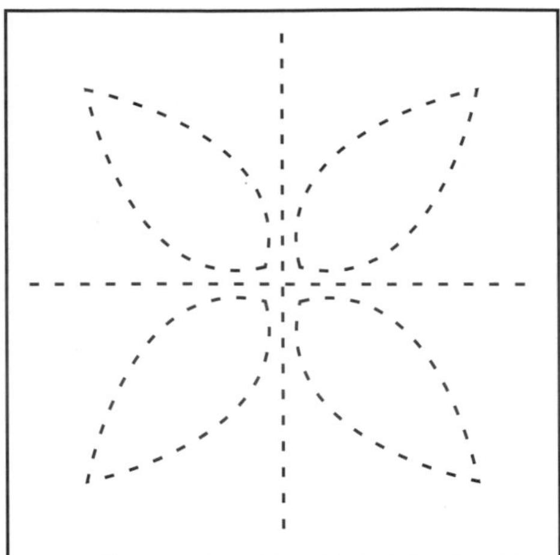

Figure 10-27.

Draw two lines that cross and place either the Ellipse, Pumpkin Seed, or Laurel Leaf shape in the corners. This design can be used where four blocks are pieced together and the corners of sashings and borders.

This simple design was found on a quilt dated 1825 – 1850 and was combined with the Trailing Leaf design along the block edge.

Amish Flower (Figure 10-28)

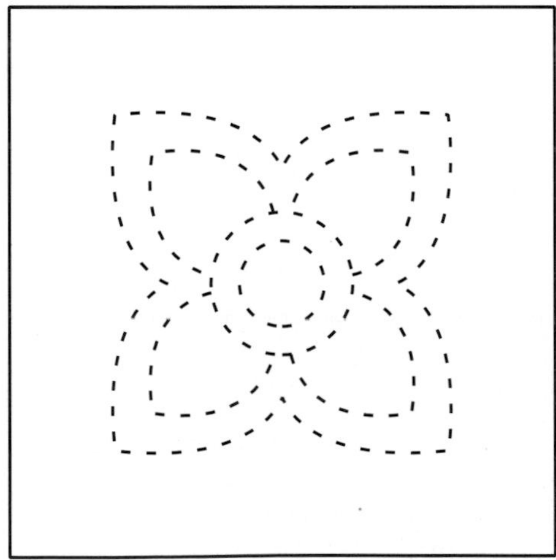

Figure 10-28.

This Amish design can be drawn in the same manner as the Four Petal Flower except two Concentric Circles are drawn for the flower center and then double line the petals.

Sunflower (Figure 10-29)

Figure 10-29.

Start with a square that is the size of the width of the desired Sunflower. Mark the square across the center vertically and horizontally and diagonally from corner to corner. These lines will give the placement for the petals of the Sunflower. Draw two Concentric Circles for the center. Using the Pumpkin Seed shape, draw petals around the circles by placing the Pumpkin Seed template on the lines (Figure 10-30). Double line only around the outside of the design.

Figure 10-30.

Pinwheel (Figure 10-31)

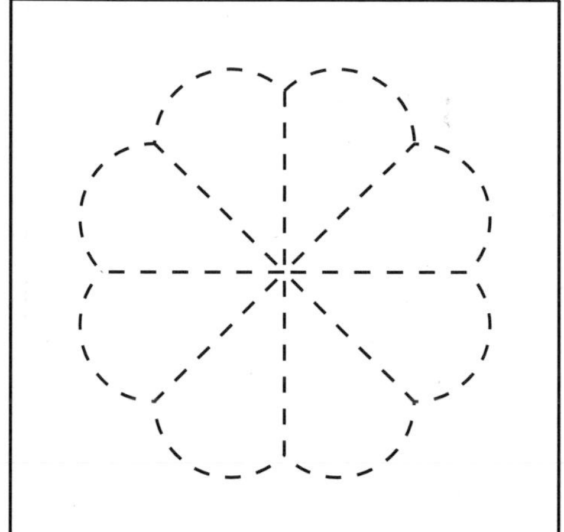

Figure 10-31.

Mark lines in a square as described for the Sunflower design. In the square, draw a circle in the size wanted for the design. This circle will be used as a guide line. Using a circular object, draw curves between the lines in the square (Figure 10-32). The curved lines should touch the circle guide.

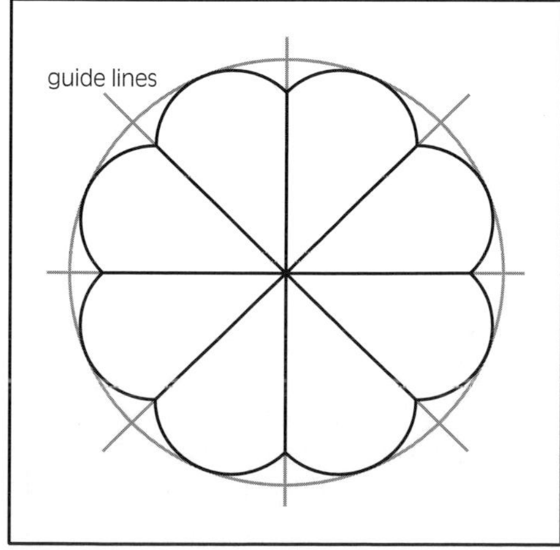

Figure 10-32.

Amish Rose (Figure 10-33)

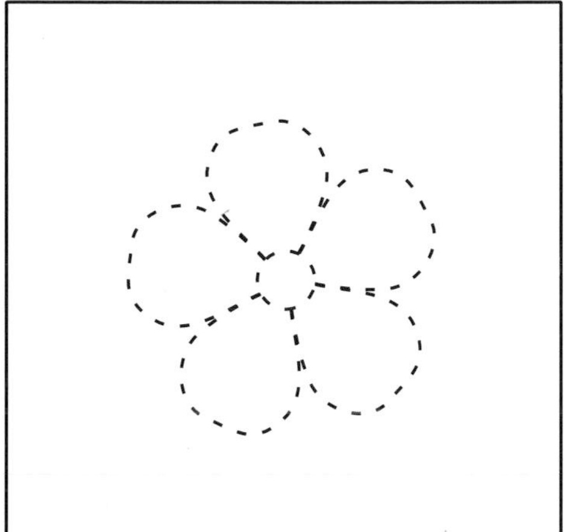

Figure 10-33.

This design is a five-petaled flower or a floral pentagon. The Amish Rose can be drawn by drawing a circle and marking the circle in 72° increments or follow the instructions for drawing a pentagon. Draw a small circle in the center. Draw each petal with a slight curve using the 72° marks for placement of the petals (Figure 10-34).

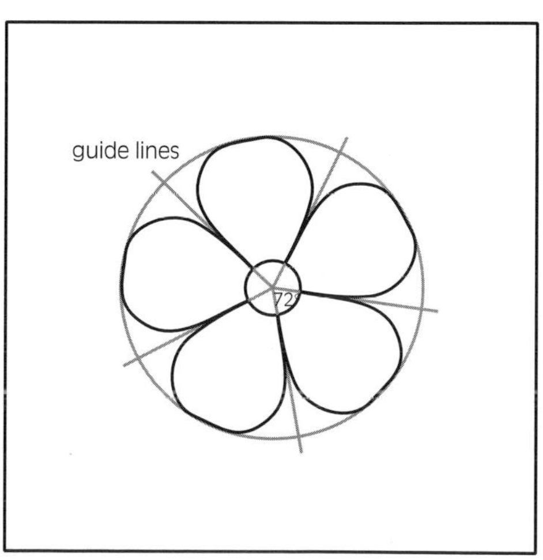

Figure 10-34.

Dog Rose (Figure 10-35)

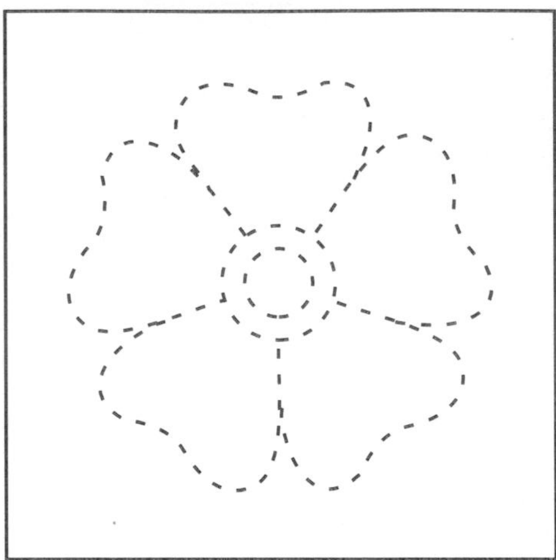

Figure 10-35.

The Dog Rose is an Old World rose that has pale-red flowers. It is drawn in the same way as the Amish Rose except each petal has a slight indentation in the curve and the center is two Concentric Circles. It very much resembles the flowers of the dogwood tree (Figure 10-36). The design can be varied by double or triple echo lines inside the petals.

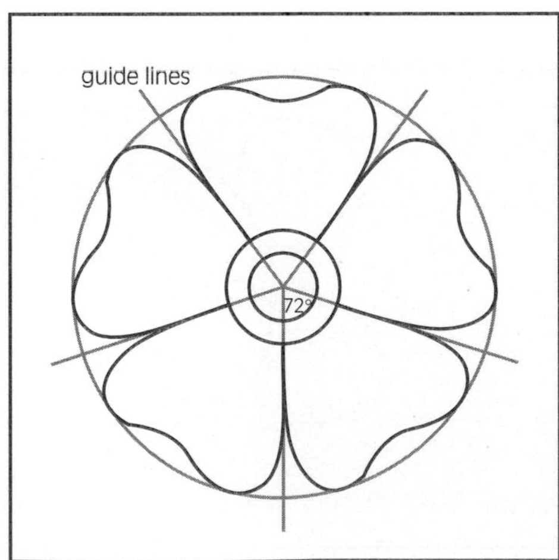

Figure 10-36.

Traditional Rose: also Pinwheel, Feather Rosette (Figure 10-37)

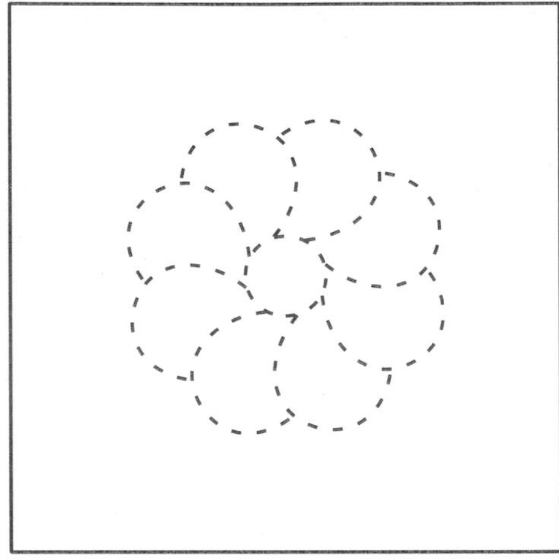

Figure 10-37.

Draw this design by following the instructions for drawing Feathers in Chapter 9, page 130. The Traditonal Rose has a larger circle for the center than does the Feather Rosette (Page 136). If the Traditional Rose is fairly large the center can be filled with Squares Crosshatching. Use this rose as a finial (a small, ornamental feature at the top of a design) with Swags for a good border design.

Four Flowers (Figure 10-38)

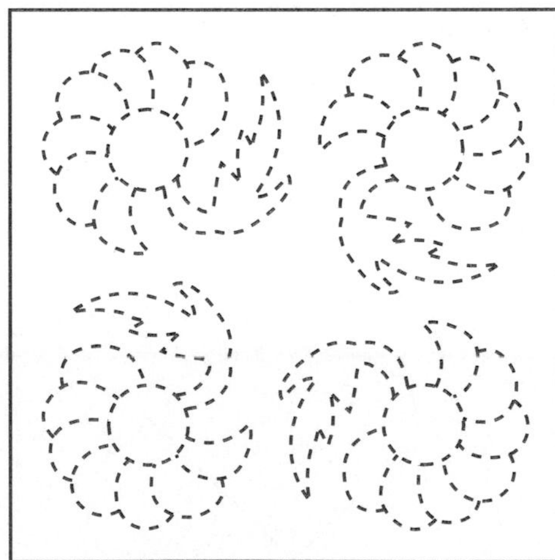

Figure 10-38.

The flowers in this design can be drawn by following the instructions for drawing Feathers in Chapter 9, page 130. Add a favorite leaf to the flowers that are placed in each of the four corners of a block. Use this design (or substitute another flower) in plain setting blocks.

Swirling Daisy (Figure 10-39)

Figure 10-39.

The Swirling Daisy is a design that has the Teardrop shape placed around a circle. Marking a square across the center and from corner to corner will give guide lines for placement of the teardrops. The teardrop (Figure 10-40) is the same shape that is often in commercial Feather template sets.

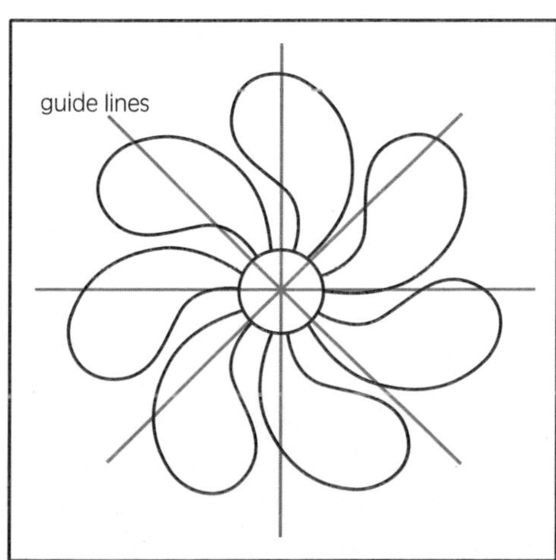

Figure 10-40.

Amish Sunflower (Figure 10-41)

Figure 10-41.

This design has two large concentric circles filled with a background filler design. The Sunflower shown has Squares Crosshatch in the center. The petals of the Sunflower are the Pumpkin Seed shape. They are placed around the circles in 45° increments or the same placement as the diamonds in an Eight-Pointed Star. This is a good design for plain setting blocks or in the corners of a border.

Thistle (Figure 10-42)

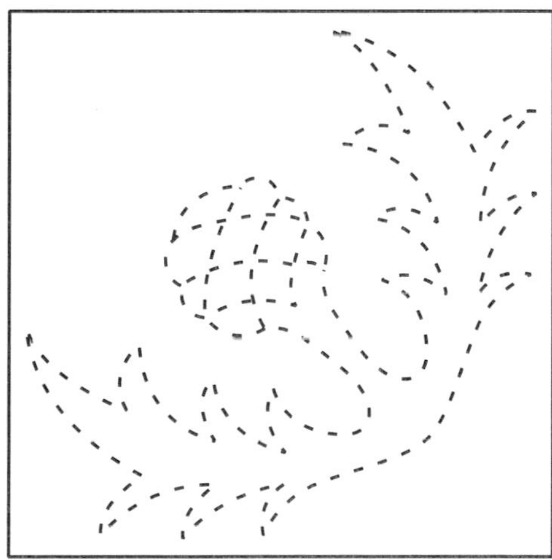

Figure 10-42.

The Thistle is a design that represents the many quilting designs that have been inspired by wild or garden flowers. Four of these placed in the corners of a square would make a good design for plain setting blocks.

Tulip (Figure 10-43)

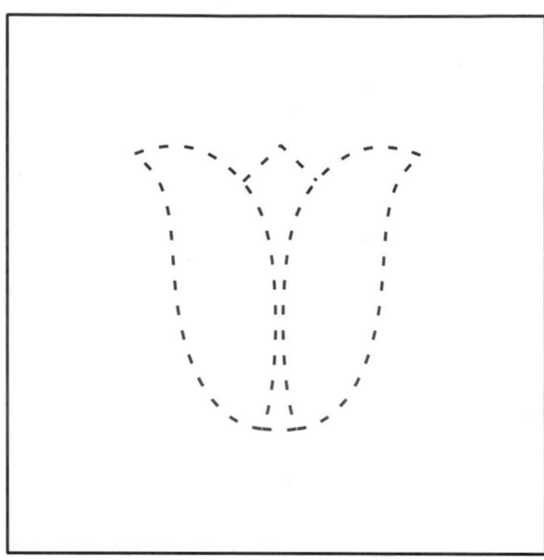

Figure 10-43.

The Tulip shown is just one example of the many variations of the tulip that have been used as quilting designs. The Tulip was and is a popular design on Amish quilts. It can be used alone,with leaves, on stems, in circles, in lines, or on vines.

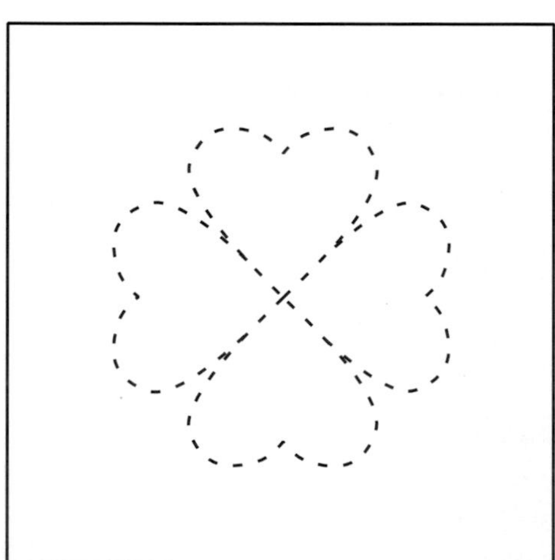

Figure 10-44.

Trumpet Vine (Figure 10-44)

This is a good example of a quilting design that can also be an appliqué pattern. It could be used in plain setting blocks to complement an appliquéd design.

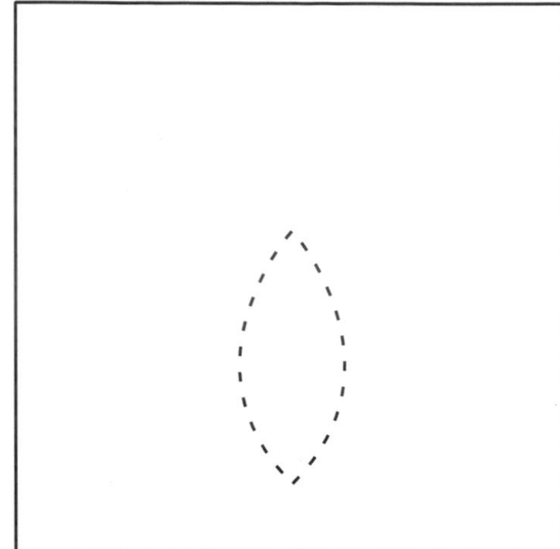

Figure 10-45.

Shamrock: also Four Leaf Clover (Figure 10-45)

The Shamrock is easily done by drawing four hearts with the points of the hearts to the center and touching. This design dates from the 1930's and has been popular on Irish Chain quilts. The Four Leaf Clover symbolizes good luck.

Laurel Leaf (Figure 10-46)

Figure 10-46.

Laurel symbolizes distinction, victory, or honor. The oldest dated quilt with the Laurel Leaf was made around 1800. It is the same leaf shape that is found in many appliqué patterns. It is nearly the same shape as the Pumpkin Seed except the bottom of the leaf is a little wider than the top. Use in any quilting design when a leaf shape is needed.

Laurel Leaves on Stem (Figure 10-47)

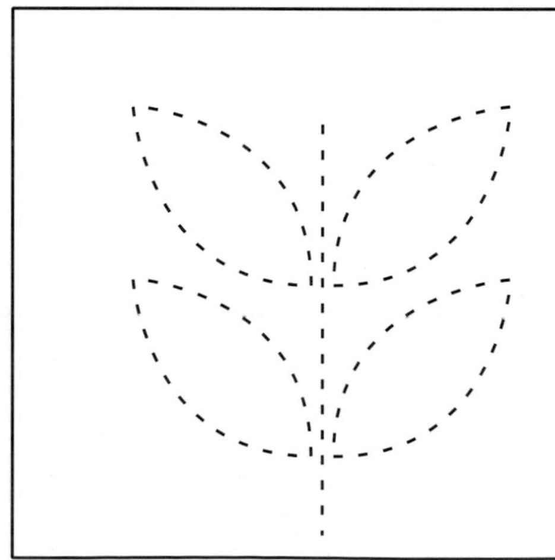

Figure 10-47.

Use the leaves as a design in sashings or borders. Draw a straight line with the leaves spaced evenly on each side of the line. This design can be drawn as you go by making a template of the Laurel Leaf.

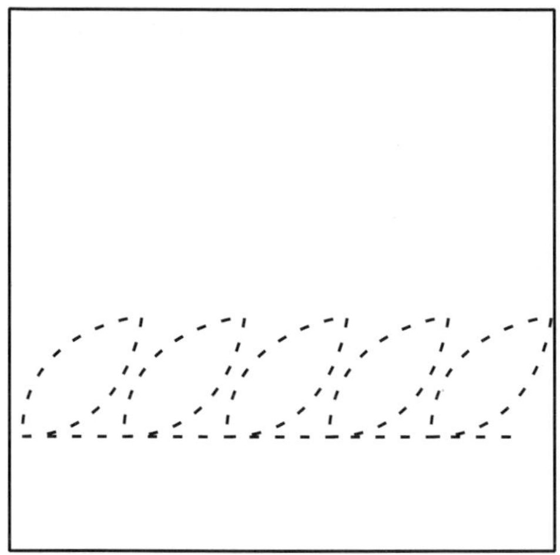

Figure 10-48.

Trailing Leaf Design (Figure 10-48)

This design is formed by placing the Laurel Leaf at a slight angle along the seam where two blocks have been sewn together. It was combined with the Rosette on a quilt from the early 1800's.

Laurel Leaf Border (Figure 10-49)

The Laurel Leaf Border design can be drawn by first making a template for a Laurel Leaf with a small leaf inside the larger leaf. Place the template end to end to make a string of leaves. Draw a leaf upright where the laurel leaves touch each other. The design was originally placed with the single leaves pointing up but, as shown, could certainly be placed with the leaves pointing to the outside of the quilt top. This design dates from 1840 to the present.

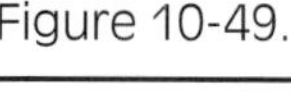

Figure 10-49.

Figure 10-50.

Laurel Leaves (Figure 10-50)

The placement of the Laurel Leaves on graceful curving stems gives the design the elegance of a Feathered design. Laurel Leaves was used on a broderie perse chintz quilt dated between 1825 and 1850.

Split Feather Leaf (Figure 10-51)

Figure 10-51.

Draw this design by first drawing a straight vertical line in the length needed for the area to be quilted. Use varying sizes of either the Laurel Leaf or the Pumpkin Seed shape to draw the leaves on each side of the stem or straight line. Draw a line down the center length of each leaf. Four of the Split Feather Leaf designs could be placed diagonally on a square to make a good design for a plain setting block.

Ivy Leaf (Figure 10-52)

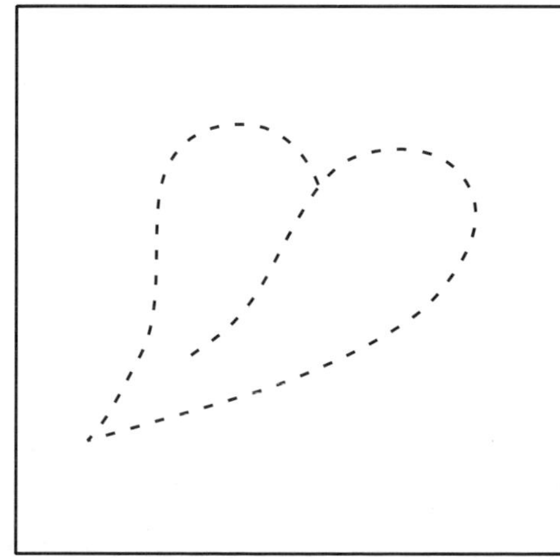

Figure 10-52.

The Ivy Leaf is usually somewhat heart shaped. Use along a Scrolling Vine in either sashings or in borders. A realistic Ivy Leaf can be drawn by drawing around a real leaf or photocopying a real one. Be sure the leaf is not from poison ivy!

Maple Leaf (Figure 10-53)

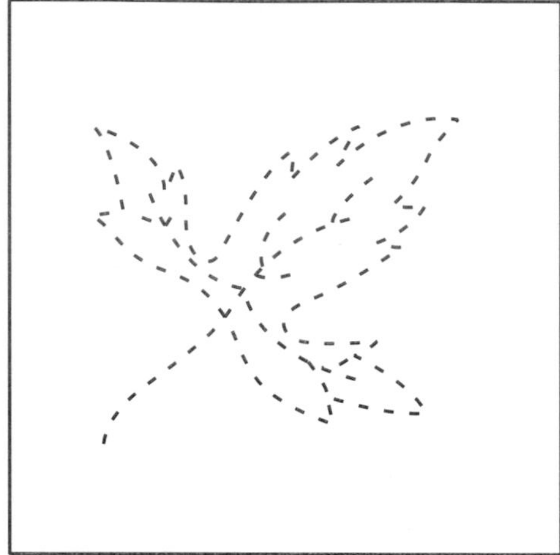

Figure 10-53.

There have been many variations of this leaf. For realism, copy a leaf from a maple tree.

Oak Leaf (Figure 10-54)

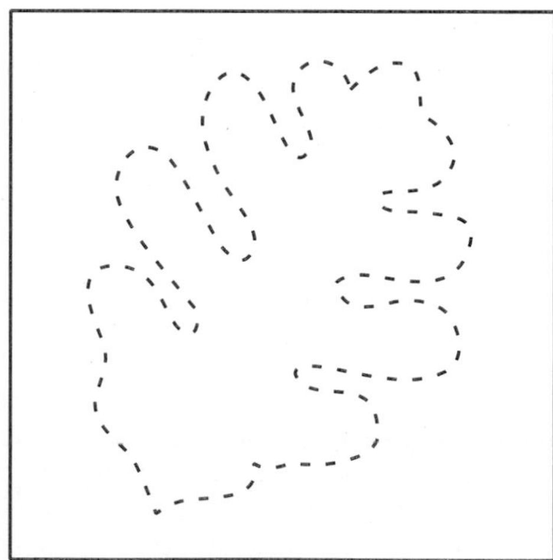

Figure 10-54.

Place the Oak Leaf diagonally on a square with the leaf stem to the center of the block for a design that can be used in a plain setting block. A real Oak Leaf can be photocopied or drawn around to make a template for the Oak Leaf design.

Oak Leaf and Acorn (Figure 10-55)

Figure 10-55.

A combination of the Oak Leaf and an Acorn makes a good design for a plain setting block. It seems appropriate for a scrap quilt and especially for someone who loves the outdoors.

Leaf Spray (Figure 10-56)

Figure 10-56.

The Leaf Spray is a design that can be used in combination with other designs when leaves are required. It can be drawn using the instructions for drawing a feathered design, see Chapter 9, p. 130. It could be used as a finial with Swags.

Acanthus (Figure 10-57)

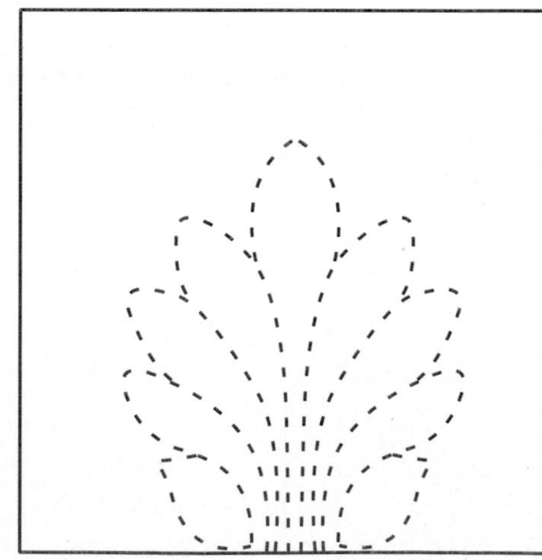

Figure 10-57.

Use the instructions for drawing Feathers to

draw this design (see Chapter 9, p. 130) but make the outside for the design more pointed where a feather would be curved. The Ancanthus design makes a good border design when placed side by side. It is any of several herbs from the Mediterranean belonging to the genus Acanthus. The design was familiar to Corinthian architecture.

Curled Leaf (Figure 10-58)

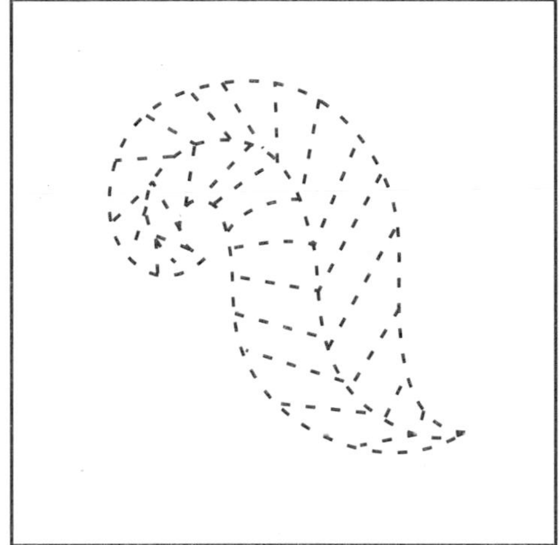

Figure 10-58.

The Curled Leaf is often used in pairs to fill a strip in a strippie or bar quilt. When used in pairs, have the tip of one leaf to the left and the tip of the other leaf reversed or to the right.

Grape Leaf (Figure 10-59)

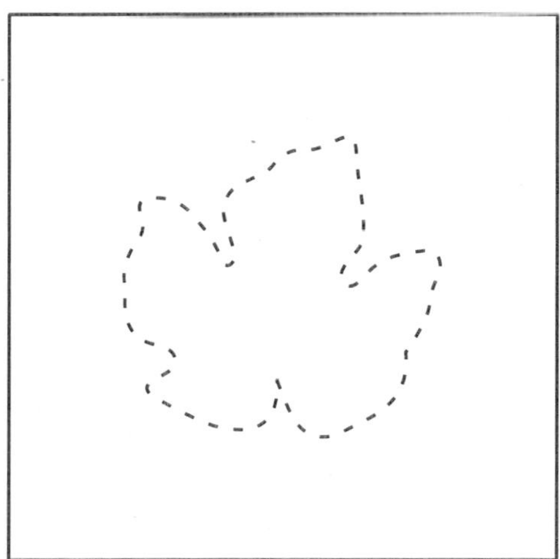

Figure 10-59.

Draw around a real Grape Leaf or use one similar to the one shown. The leaf could be used in sashings side by side or combined with grape clusters to make designs for plain setting blocks and for borders.

Grapes (Figure 10-60)

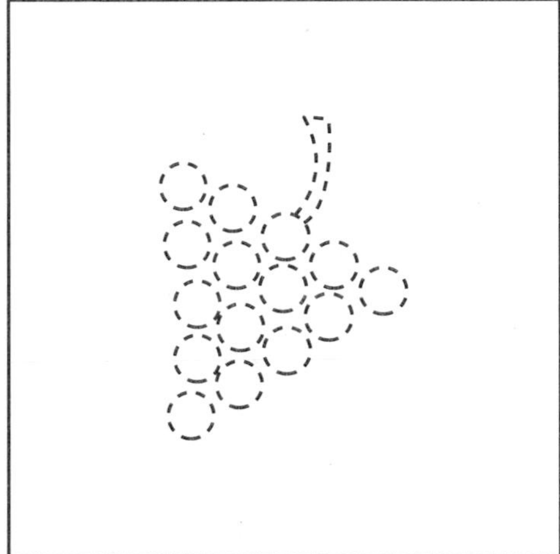

Figure 10-60.

The cluster of Grapes can be drawn by using a dime or a button to draw the circles that make up the cluster. Add a stem and combine with a Grape Leaf for a good design for a small block.

Grapes and Leaves (Figure 10-61)

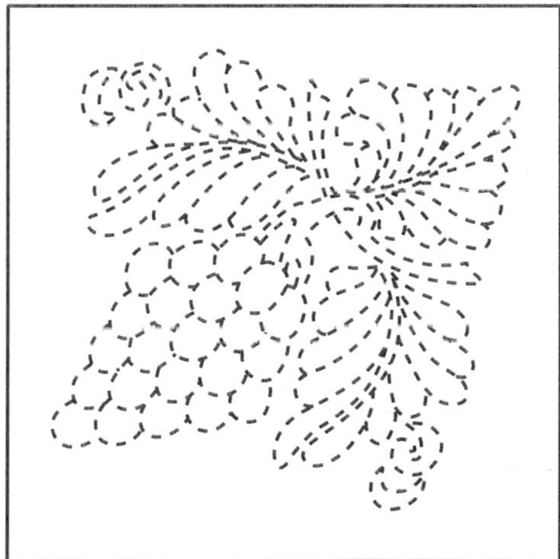

Figure 10-61.

The Grapes and the Leaves for this design can be drawn using the methods for drawing Feathers, see Chapter 9, p. 130. Four of these individual clusters would make a good design for plain setting blocks. Consider this design for a whole cloth quilt.

Vine with Grapes and Leaves (Figure 10-62)

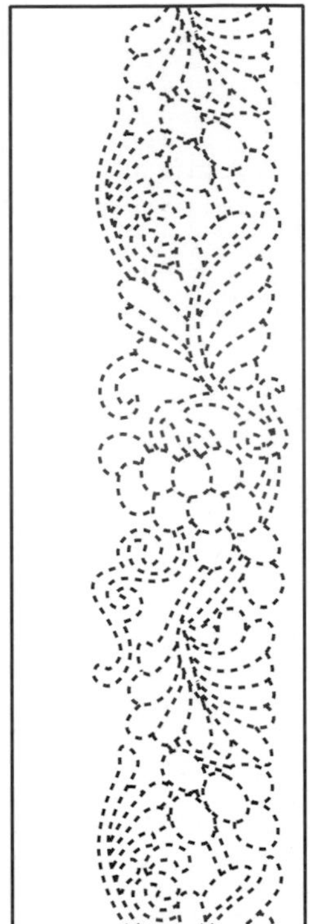

Figure 10-62.

This design is perfect for a border especially when the Grapes and Leaves design has been used elsewhere on the quilt.

Paisley II: also Welsh pear (Figure 10-63)

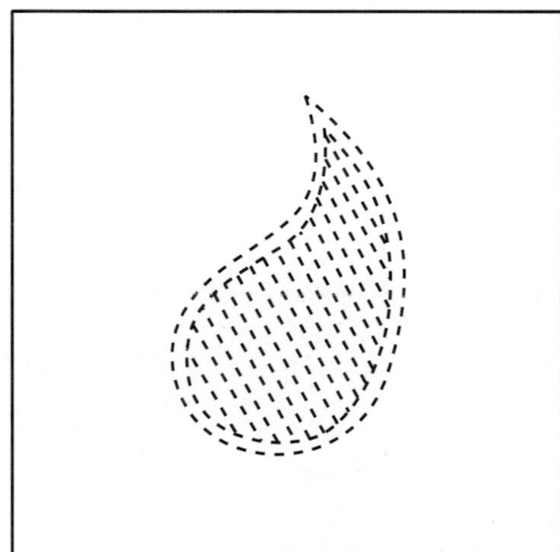

Figure 10-63.

Paisley is from the name of the Scottish city of Paisley where the design was woven into wool for shawls. The outside resembles a Teardrop and the center can be filled with a variety of designs. The design can also be feathered.

Use the Paisley in a border design.

Pomegranate: also Pomegranite (Figure 10-64)

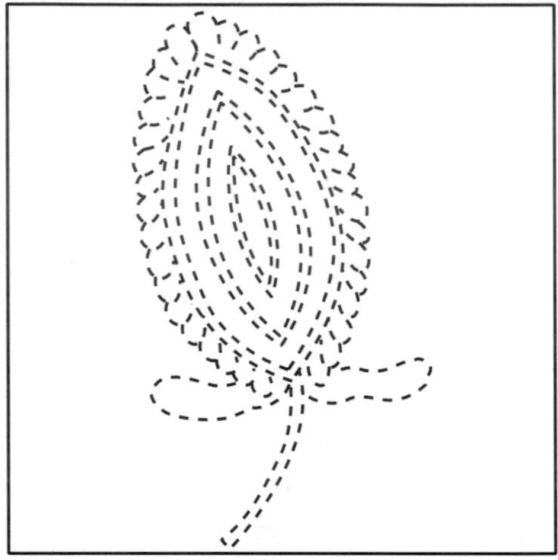

Figure 10-64.

This fancy design was used on quilts dating from 1830. The Pomegranate is a many seeded fruit and the center of the design for quilting was often filled with small Clamshells. Use the methods for drawing Feathers in Chapter 9, p. 130 to draw the outside edge of the Pomegranate.

Butterfly (Figure 10-65)

Figure 10-65.

There can be as many variations of the Butterfly as there are butterflies. Add the Butterfly as a quilting design in a floral appliquéd block. Four

quilts with a nautical theme.

Use the instructions for drawing a S
Vine in Chapter 7, page 101, to make a g
marking the Wave. This curving line
echoed over the area to be quilted.

Wrinkle Quilting (Figure 10-74)

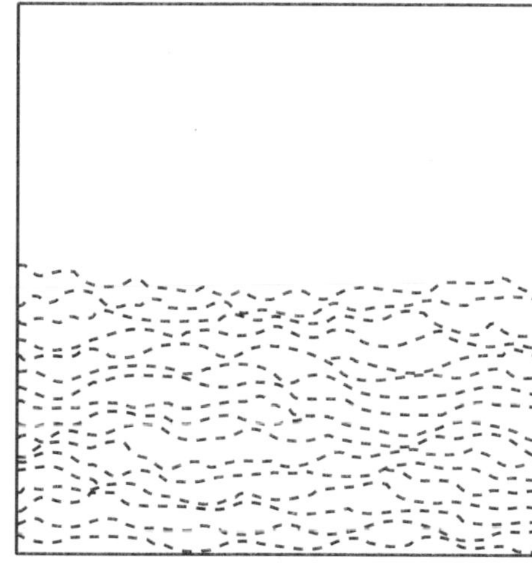

Figure 10-74.

Draw uneven wavy lines freehand t
the surface of the quilt. It can be used a
ground filler and is a good quilting design
on abstract designs.

*The following are a sampling of the pos
that can be attained from the combination c
more designs for quilting. The intent is to sp
imagination to the possibilities that come fr
ing the various designs. The names of the de
included so that you can use the individual
tions to reproduce these. Sometimes the c
tion was given a name and that will be listed*

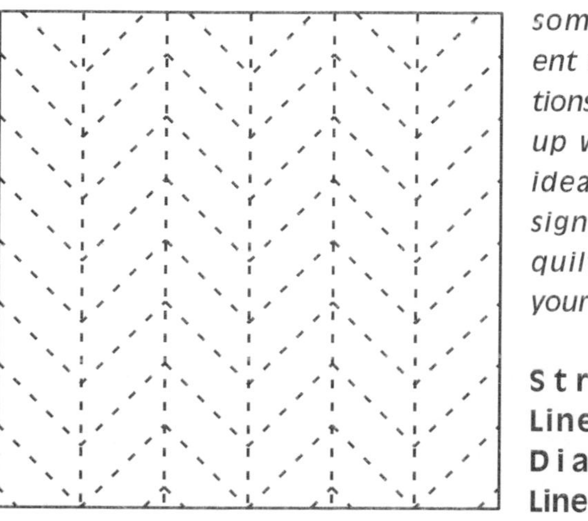

*some
ent c
tions
up wi
ideas
signir
quilti
your c*

**Stra
Lines
Diag
Lines**
10-75)

Figure 10-75.

butterflies would make a good design for a plain setting block.

Bird (Figure 10-66)

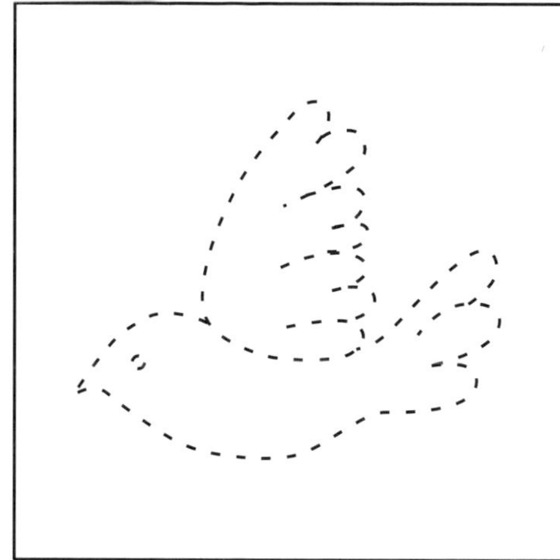

Figure 10-66.

This example of a Bird is a very simplified version.

Bird II (Figure 10-67)

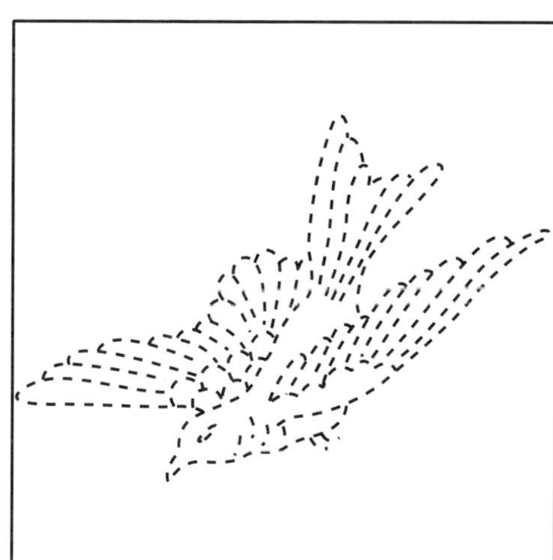

Figure 10-67.

This Bird has more details. Birds were often included in the quilting designs on bridal quilts. They symbolize gentleness and innocence.

Dove of Peace (Figure 10-68)

Figure 10-68.

The Dove is a symbol of peace and designs depicting the Dove were used on patriotic quilts and wedding quilts.

Eagle (Figure 10-69)

Figure 10-69.

Eagles were popular designs on patriotic quilts and on centennial and bicentennial quilts. It was a popular design on quilts made around the time of the Civil War. There are many variations of the Eagle as each quilt artist has drawn them a little differently. They can be dated at least back to the war of 1812.

Shell (Figure 10-70)

Figure 10-70.

The Shell makes a good border
the shells are placed side by side.

Snowflake (Figure 10-71)

Figure 10-71.

The variations that can be create
Snowflake are endless. This is just c
Make your own original Snowflake by
cutting paper. Use tracing paper as i
fold and easier to cut than heavier
square of paper the size needed for t
filled with the design. Fold the pap
make a rectangle. Fold the rectan
shaped pieces. Start cutting lines and s
folds being careful to leave paper
between sections to hold it all togethe
paper this way will give a design with si

The designs can be made mor
more intricate by folding the paper
rectangle, fold the rectangle agai

Leafy Scroll (Simple Scroll and Twisted Braid Template) (Figure 10-79)

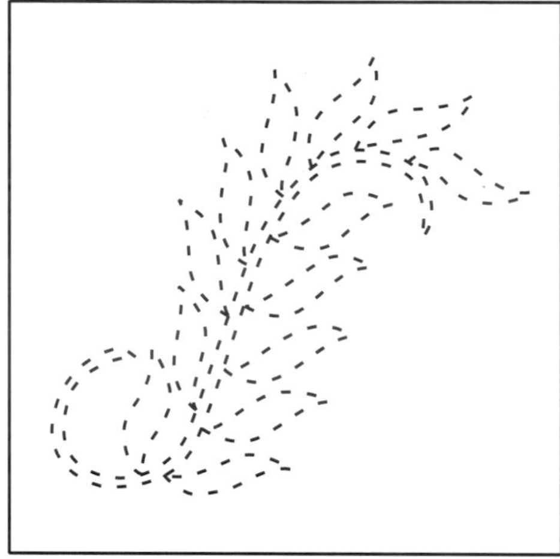

Figure 10-79.

Swirling Swastikas or Hexfeiss (Concentric Circles and Teardrops) (Figure 10-80)

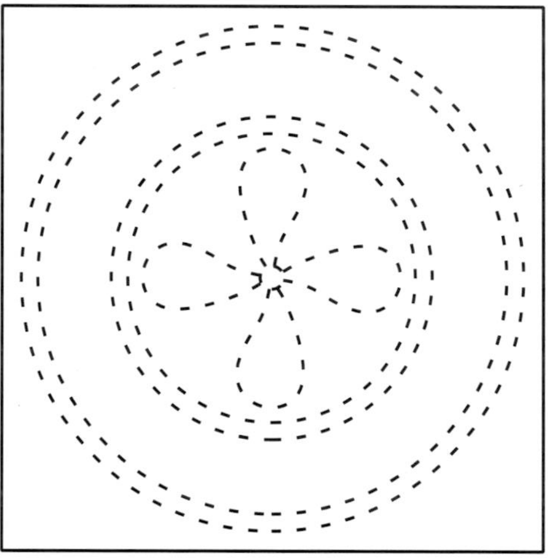

Figure 10-80.

Dahlia (Sunflower and Circle) (Figure 10-81)

Figure 10-81.

Sunflower and **Spirals** (Figure 10-82)

Figure 10-82.

Clamshell and **Echo** (Figure 10-83)

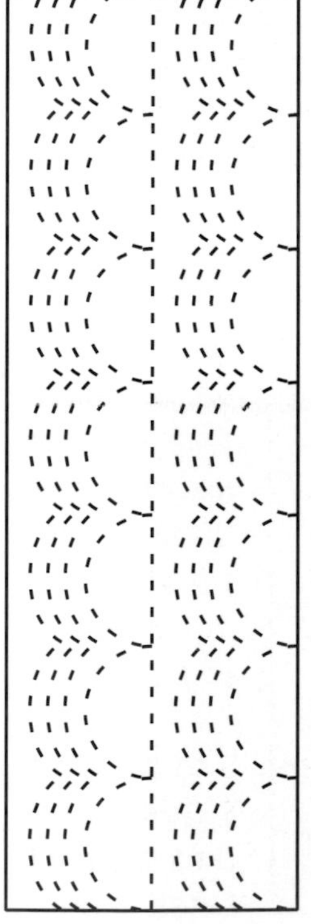

Figure 10-83.

Triangle Elbow and **Fan** (Figure 10-84)

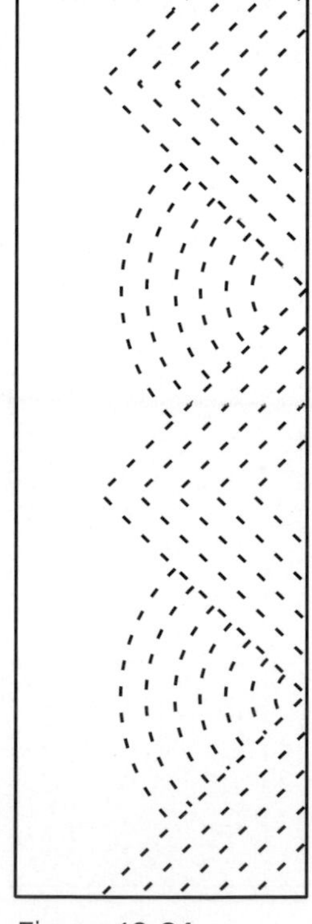

Figure 10-84.

Double Zig-zag and **Clamshells** (Figure 10-85)

Double Zig-zag and **Fan (From a Quilt Pattern)** (Figure 10-86)

Swag Variation and **Fan** (Figure 10-89)

Circles and **Straight Lines** (Figure 10-90)

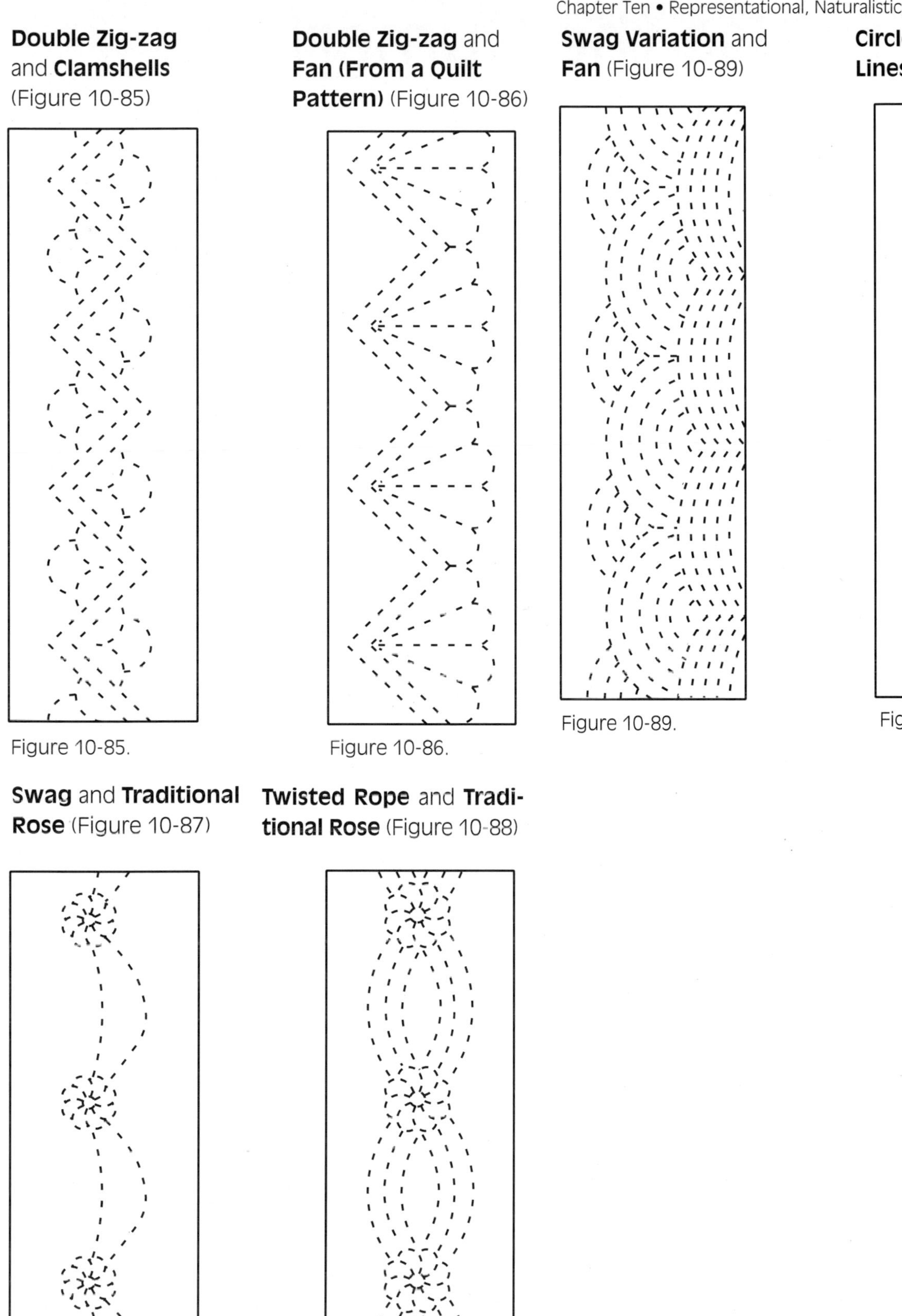

Figure 10-85.

Figure 10-86.

Figure 10-89.

Figure 10-90.

Swag and **Traditional Rose** (Figure 10-87)

Twisted Rope and **Traditional Rose** (Figure 10-88)

Figure 10-87.

Figure 10-88.

How to Use the Numerical Index of Designs for Quilting

Since I started my first quilt in 1968 and then later when I started teaching, I have been aware of the need for a comprehensive resource for the designs that are used for quilting. One of the most often asked questions from students in classes for piecing and appliqué is "How would you quilt this?" Often in attempting to answer this question, I would find it necessary to draw a sketch of the design. There seemed to be no common language for the designs for quilting that would give quilters a mental image.

As chairman of the Kentucky Quilt Registry, which is an on-going documentation project, I find that the need is great for the documentors to have a reference of quilting designs so that the recording of these designs is consistent.

The numerical index is a record of the traditional quilting designs that authors of books about quilting have mentioned either in sketches, in conjunction with photographs, or described in their text.

In my research for this book, I found that many of the designs have been given many different names. The names assigned to the designs are the names that have been used in books. When assigning names to each of the different designs for quilting, I used the name most frequently used in previously printed material or the name most commonly used today. In the instructional text, the assigned name to a quilting design is listed first and the other name/names, if any, that I found for each particular design are also listed.

In the instructions for drawing quilting designs, reference is made to the earliest dated quilt on which the design was found. This does not necessarily mean that quilting designs can be used for dating a quilt. It also does not mean that the design was not used earlier since my research covered only information written about quilting designs and often little or no reference to the designs for quilting was found. The Figure numbers refer to the illustration of the design in the instructional text of this book. Color photographs are denoted by Plate numbers.

The designs for quilting are indexed by catergories that have either a common design line or a common theme. For example, all of the designs that are formed from a diamond shape are grouped together. Under each catergory, the designs are then classed by similar shapes or images.

Each of the designs is numbered with a decimal system. The first numbers are the catergory divisions followed by a decimal and then the number of the design within the catergory. This numbering system is similar to the one in the ***Encyclopedia of Applique*** by Barbara Brackman.

When using this name and numbering system in documentation projects, it will often be necessary to record two or more names and numbers in order to give a mental image of a design which is actually a combination of designs. This index is a record of the basic traditional designs for quilting. Only the designs that appeared in print many times and therefore can now be considered traditional have been included. The combinations of the basic designs are as numerous as the numbers of quilters.

I wish I could say that every design for quilting is illustrated here but any image that can be drawn with a pencil can be quilted. Since there are obviously many quilting designs that are one-of-a-kind drawings by individual quilt artists, these designs have been considered to be original, one-of-a-kind designs and not traditional.

The quilter of today can use the Numerical Index of Designs for Quilting to find a quilting design to use for their quilt. In the numbering system of the designs, the Figure number indicates the chapter number where further instructions for drawing the design can be found. The second numbers are the numerical order in that particular chapter. By using the cross reference to the illustration, you can then find the instructions for drawing the quilting design in the instructional text of this book.

The designs for quilting are listed alphabetically in the index. If you know the name of a quilting design, you can find it by name in the Index.

GUIDE TO THE NUMERICAL INDEX OF DESIGNS FOR QUILTING

STRAIGHT LINE 01
GEOMETRIC 02
TRIANGLES 03
SQUARES 04
DIAGONAL LINE 05
DIAMONDS 06
FROM THE QUILT PATTERN 07
CIRCLES 08
OVALS 09
CRESCENTS 10
CURVES 11
ROPES 12
CABLES 13
HEARTS 14
FEATHERS 15
REPRESENTATIONAL 16
FLORAL 17
LEAVES 18
FRUIT 19
BUTTERFLIES 20
BIRDS 21
NATURALISTIC 22

Numerical Index of Designs for Quilting

01.01 Parallel Lines, Single; Figure 2-1; Plate 2-1, 2-4, 4-4, 5-1, 6-4, 7-1, 10-2

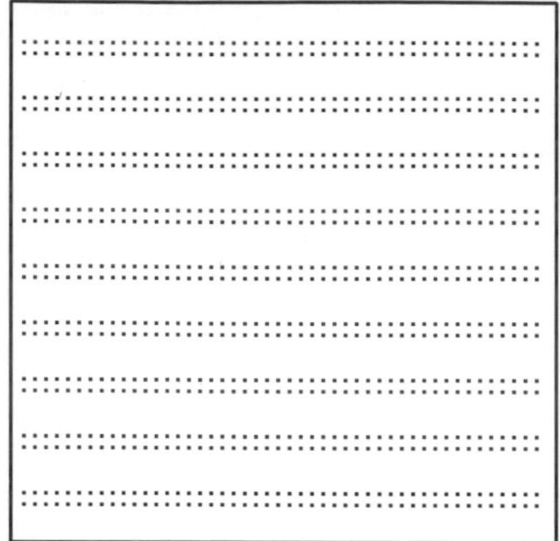
01.02 Parallel Lines, Double; Figure 2-4

01.03 Parallel Lines, Triple; Figure 2-7

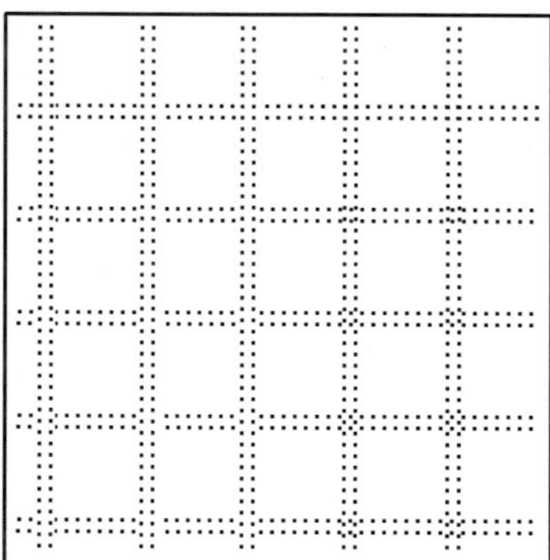
01.04 Bars; Figure 2-8

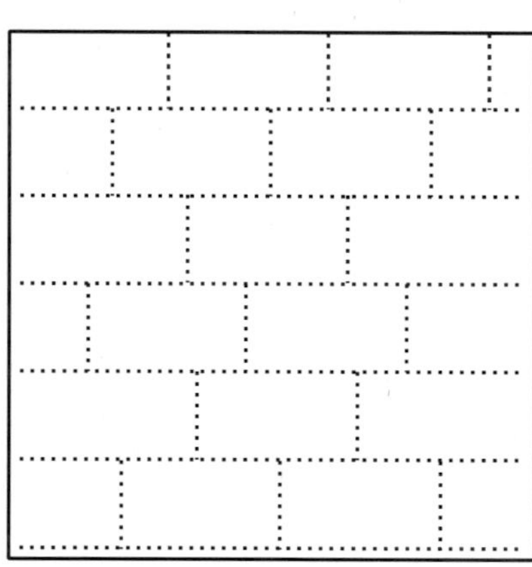
01.05 Bricks; Figure 2-12; Plate 2-3

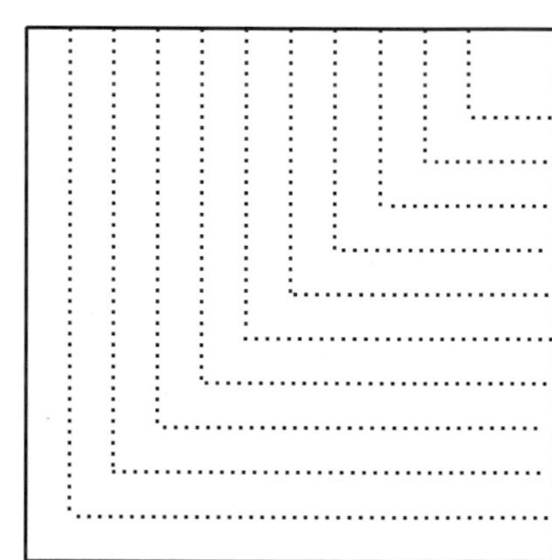
01.06 Elbow; Figure 2-15

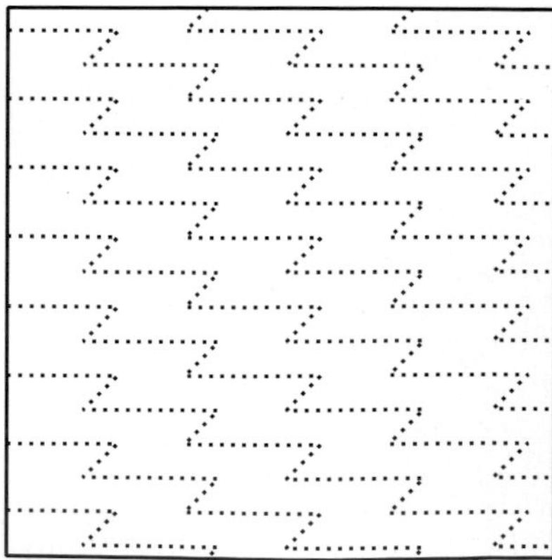
01.07 Zig-Zag; Figure 2-19; Plate 10-1

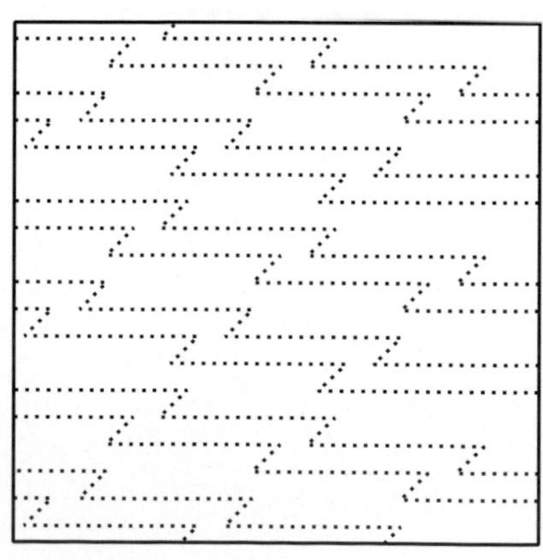
01.08 Elongated Z; Figure 2-24

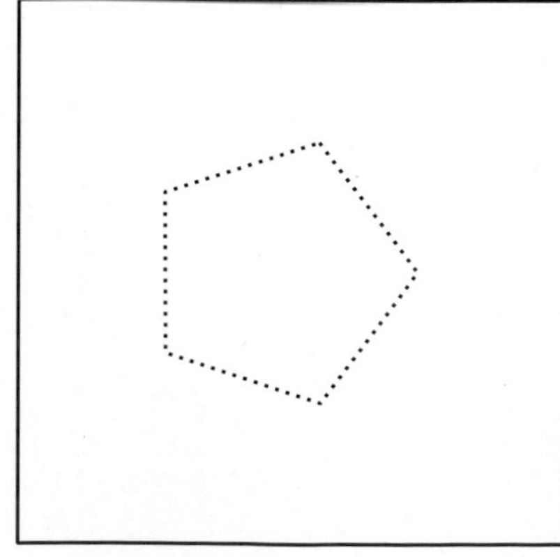
02-01 Pentagon; Figure 2-29

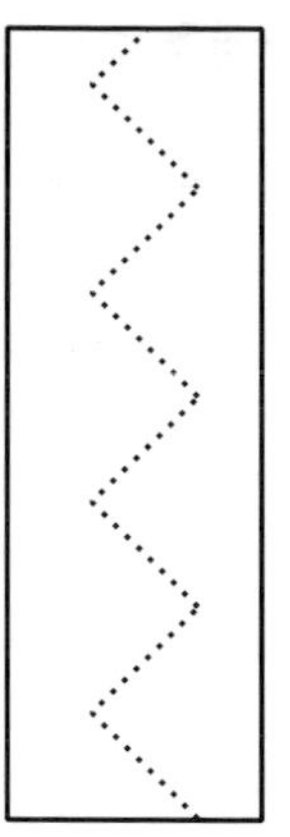
03.01 Sawtooth; Figure 2-33

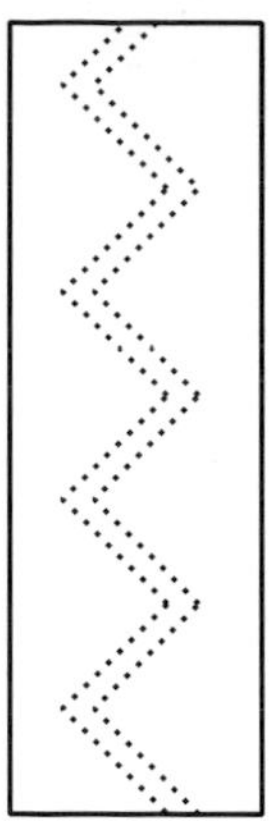
03-02 Double Zig-Zag; Figure 2-36

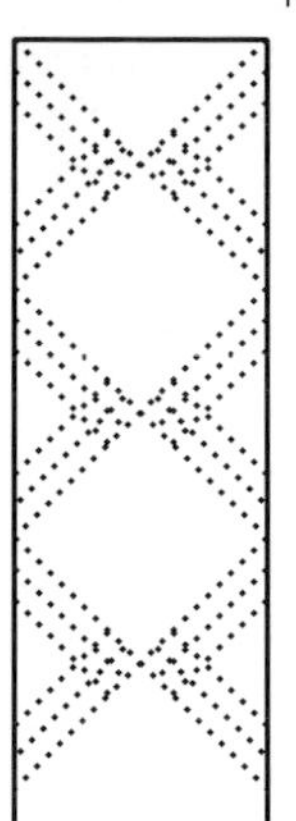
03.03 Amish Border Triangle; Figure 2-38

03.04 Zig-Zag II; Figure 2-42

03.05 Wave; Figure 2-46

03.06 Triangle Elbow; Figure 2-50

03.07 Tents; Figure 2-54; Plate 2-2, 2-1

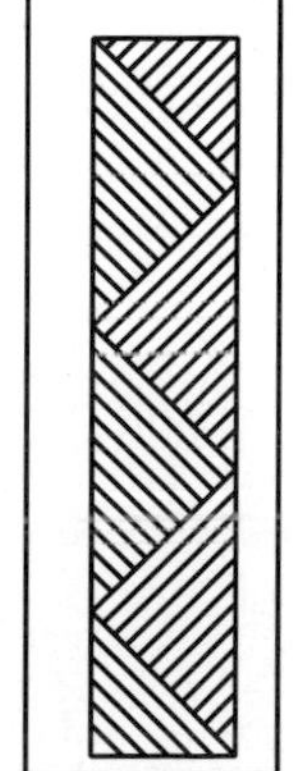
03.08 Triangles; Figure 2-59; Plate 7-3

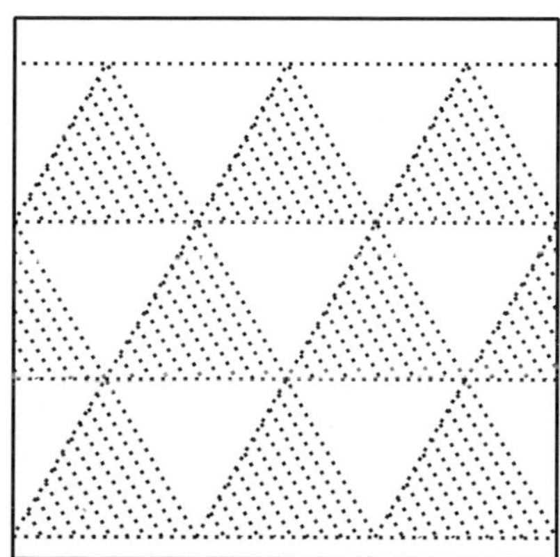
03.09 Equal-Sided Triangle; Figure 2-63

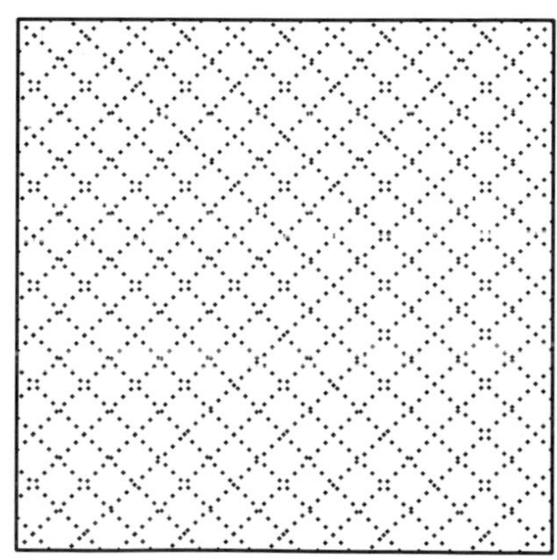
04.01 Squares Crosshatch; Figure 3-1; Plate 2-2, 2-4, 3-1, 3-2, 5-4, 6-3, 7-4, 10-1

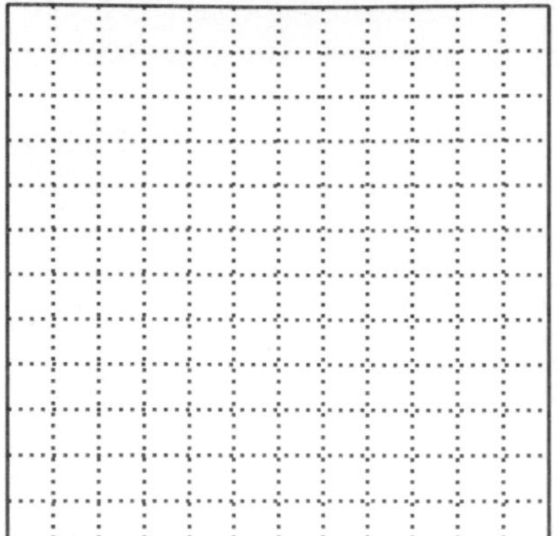

04.02 Checkerboard; Figure 3-4

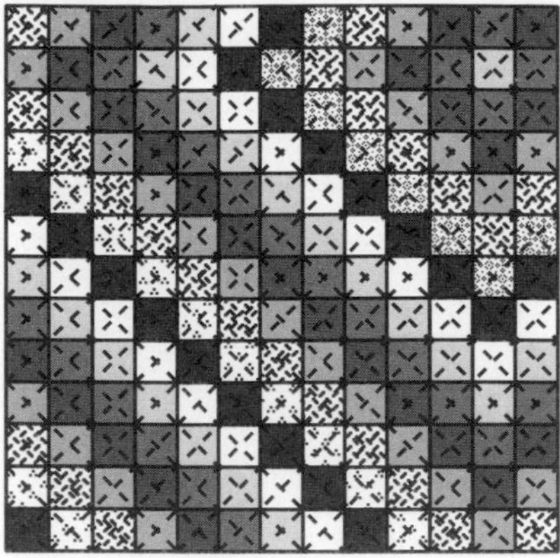

04.03 Crisscross; Figure 3-7

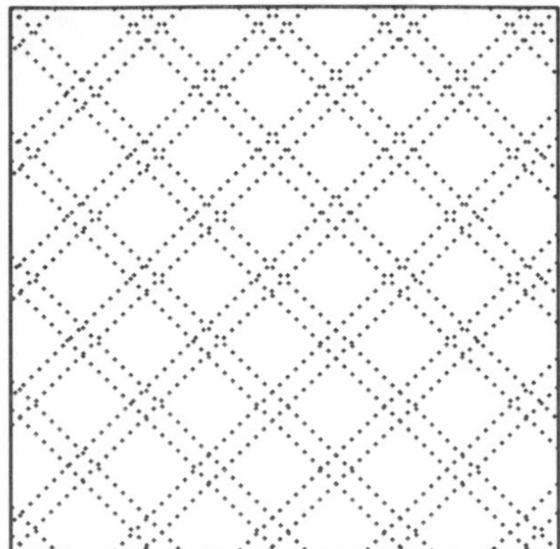

04.04 Plaid; Figure 3-10; Plate 3-3

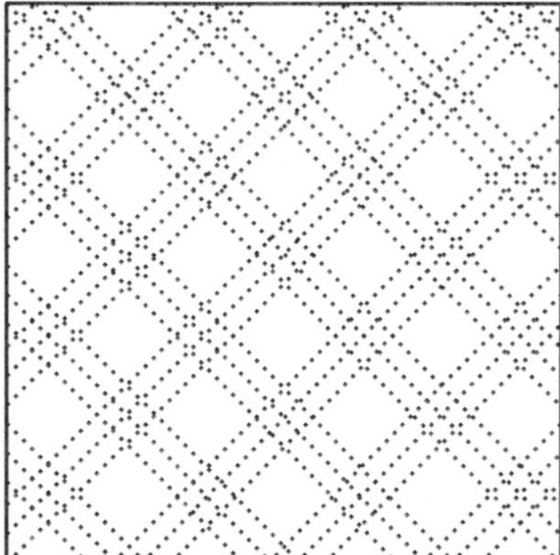

04.05 Triple Plaid; Figure 3-14; Plate 8-2

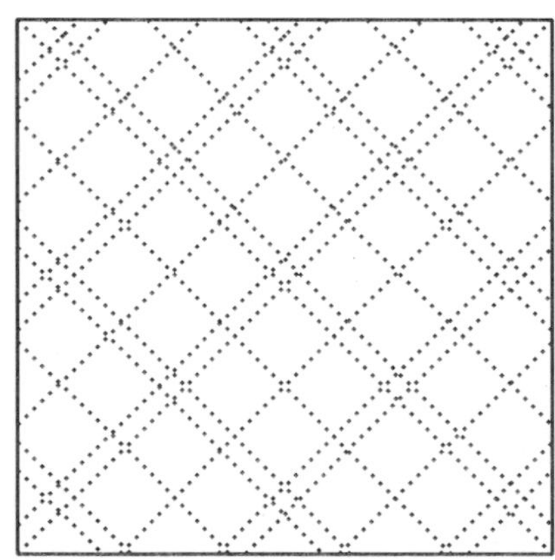

04.06 Broken Plaid; Figure 3-16

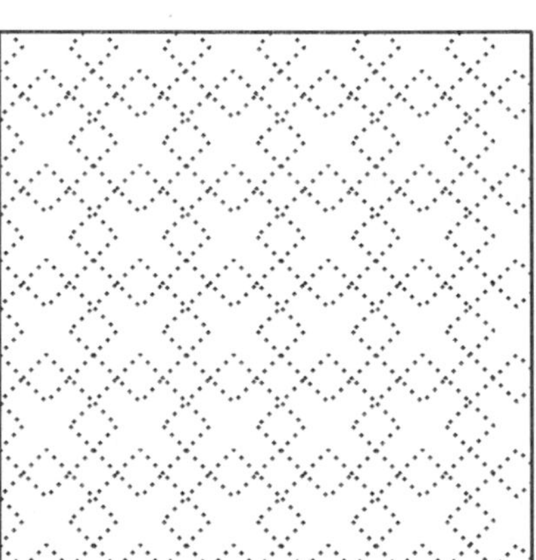

04.07 Crosses; Figure 3-18

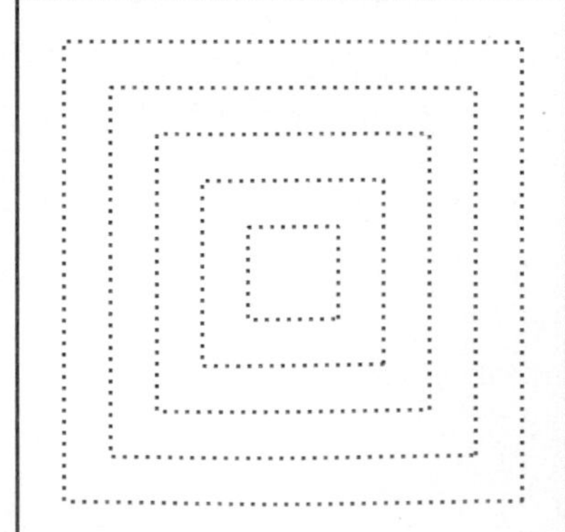

04.08 Concentric Squares; Figure 3-22; Plate 5-3

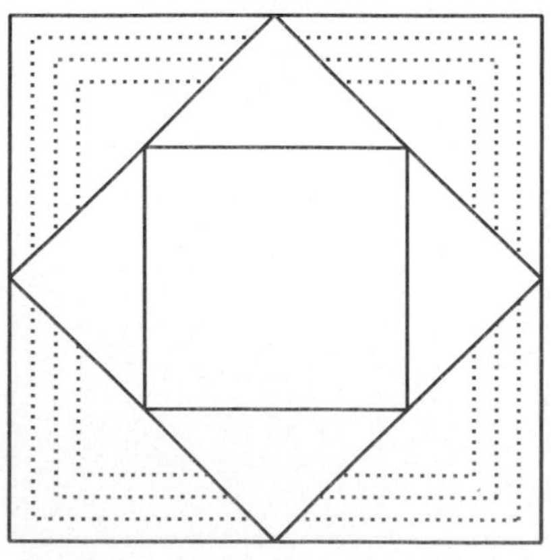

04.09 Concentric Squares Variation; Figure 3-24

04.10 Concentric Squares Variation I; Figure 3-25

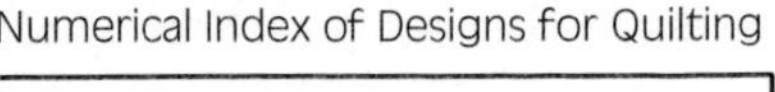

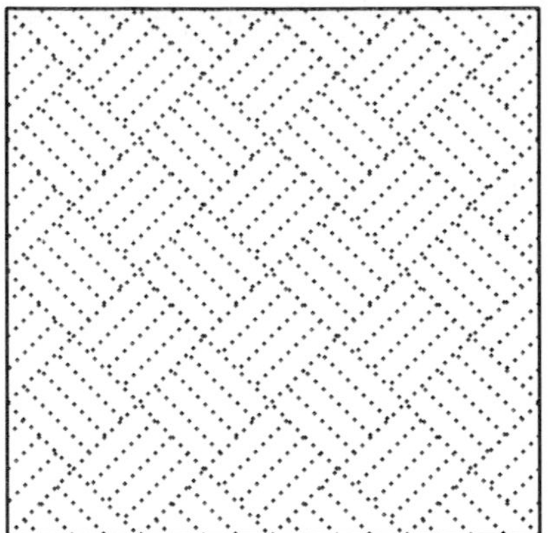

04.11 Weave Pattern; Figure 3-26

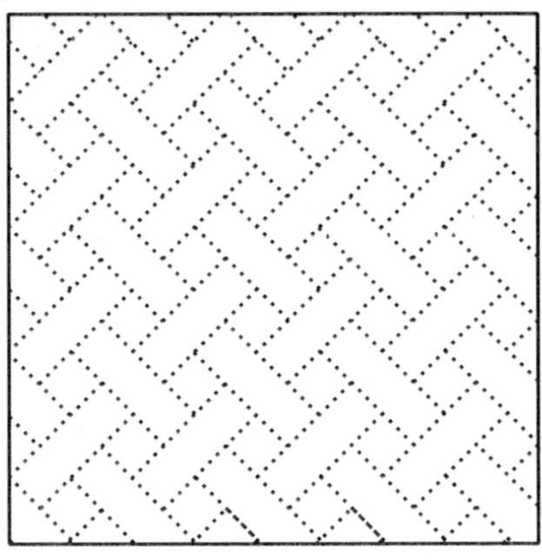

04-12 Basket Weave; Figure 3-31;; Plate 3-4, 10-4

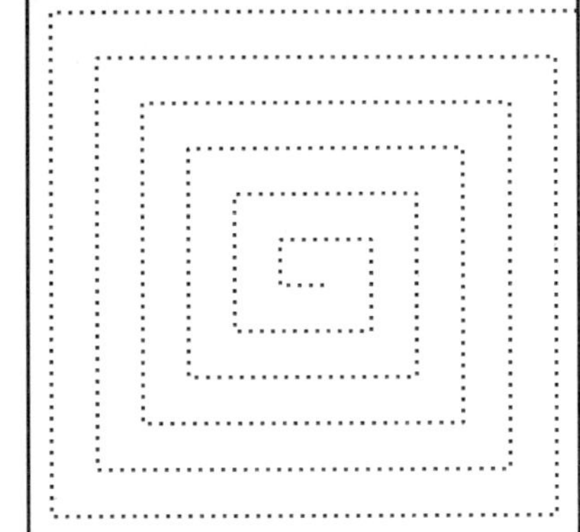

04.13 Inward-Spiraling Maze; Figure 3-35

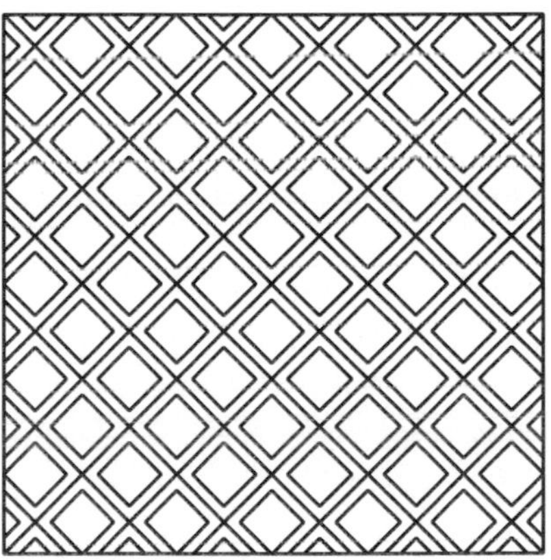

04.14 Square in a Square; Figure 3-37; Plate 3-1

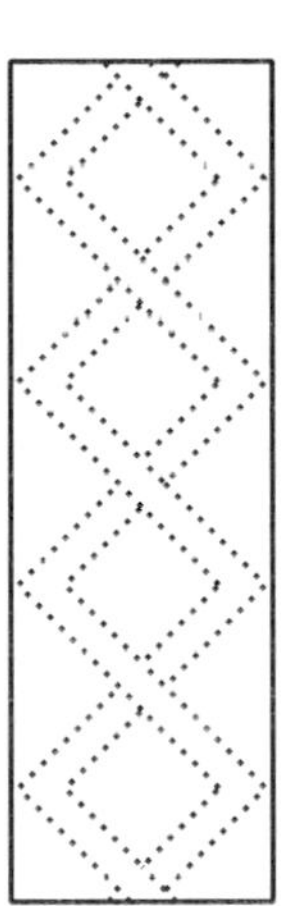

04.15 Linked Squares; Figure 3-40

04.16 Linked Squares II; Figure 3-45

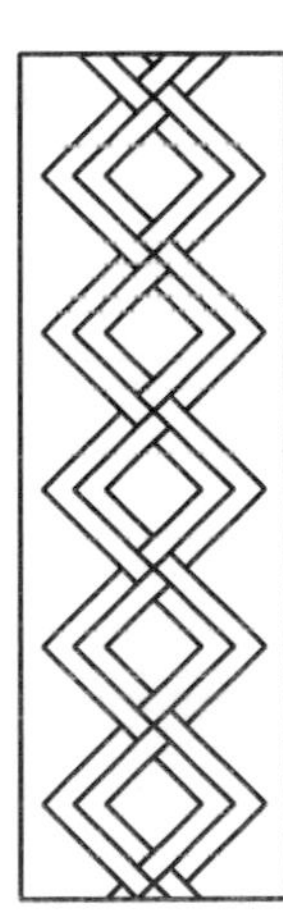

04.17 Woven Squares; Figure 3-48

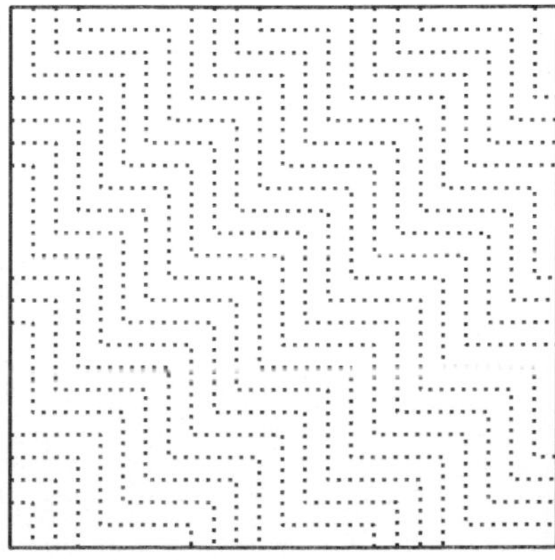

04.18 Herringbone; Figure 3-52

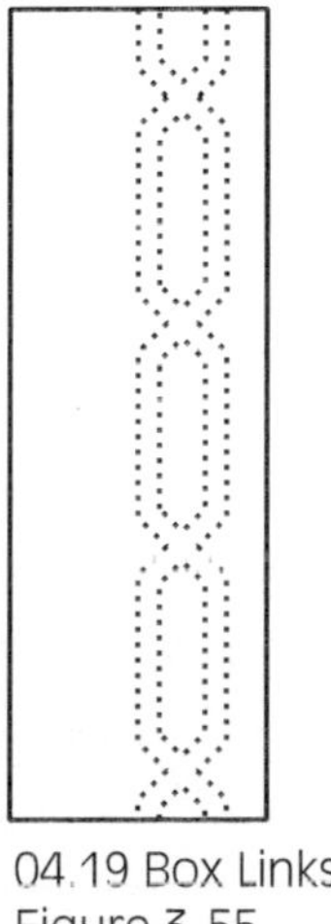

04.19 Box Links; Figure 3-55

04.20 Diamond-Set Squares; Figure 3-60

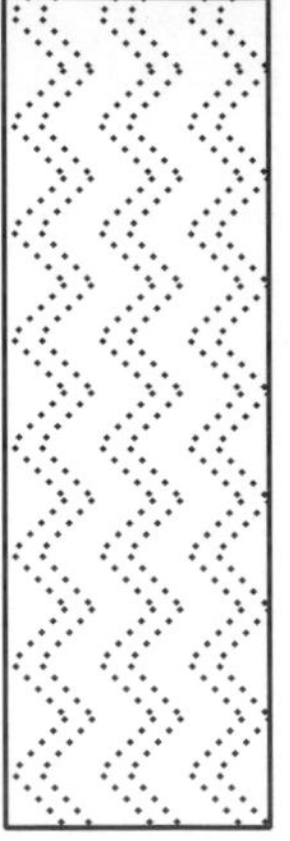

04.21 Double Chevron; Figure 4-55

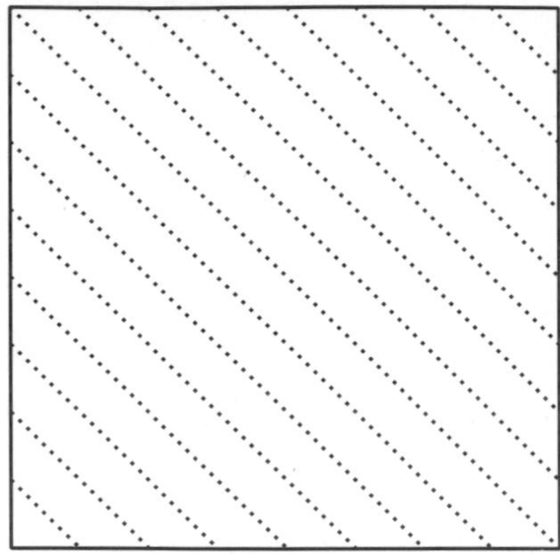

05.01 Diagonal Lines; Figure 4-1; Plate 2-2, 4-1, 4-2, 6-3, 8-4, 9-2

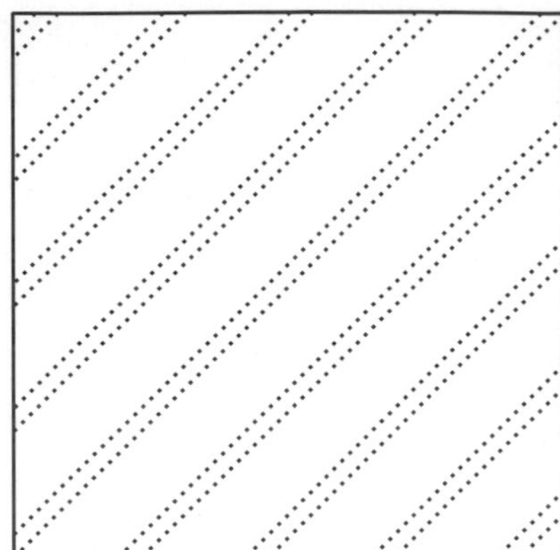

05.02 Double Diagonal Lines; Figure 4-3; Plate 3-3

05.03 Triple Diagonal Lines; Figure 4-6

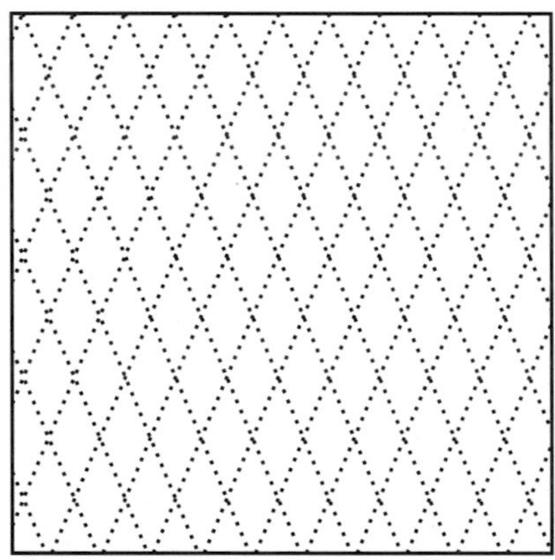

06.01 Diamond; Figure 4-8; Plate 4-3, 9-4

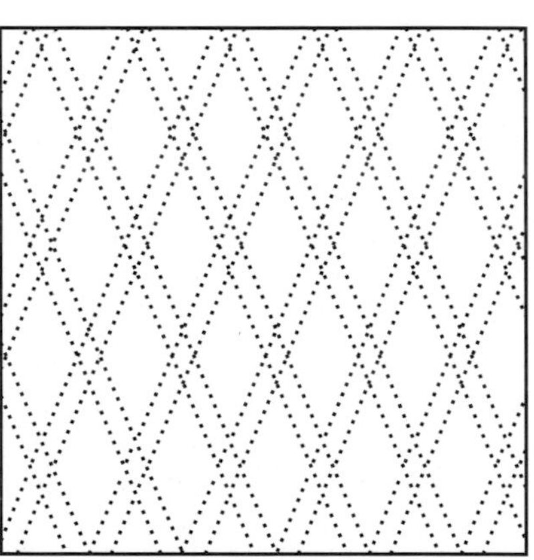

06.02 Double Line Diamond; Figure 4-12; Plate 4-4

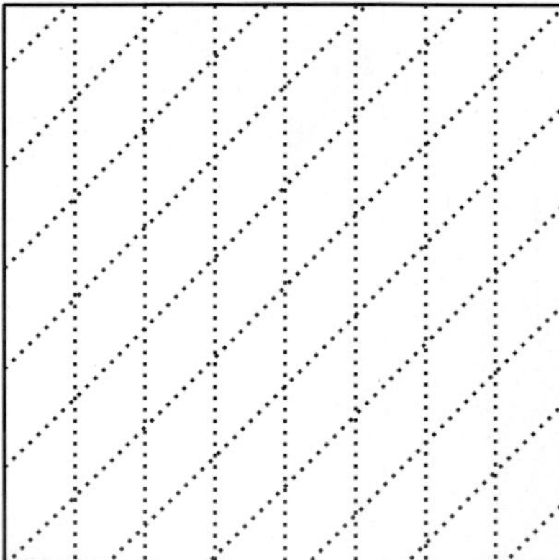

06.03 Hanging Diamonds; Figure4-14

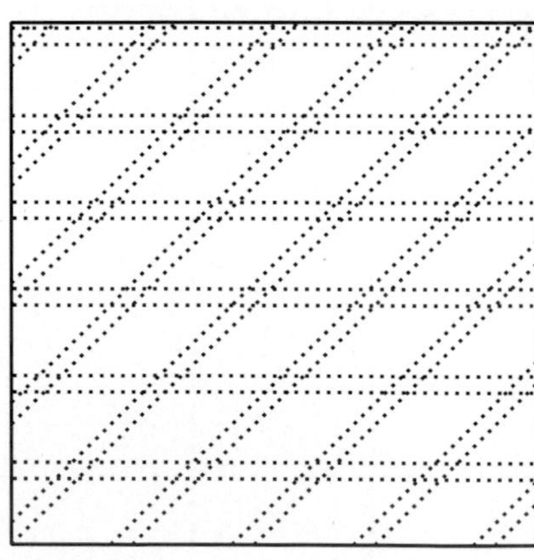

06.04 Double Hanging Diamond; Figure 4-17

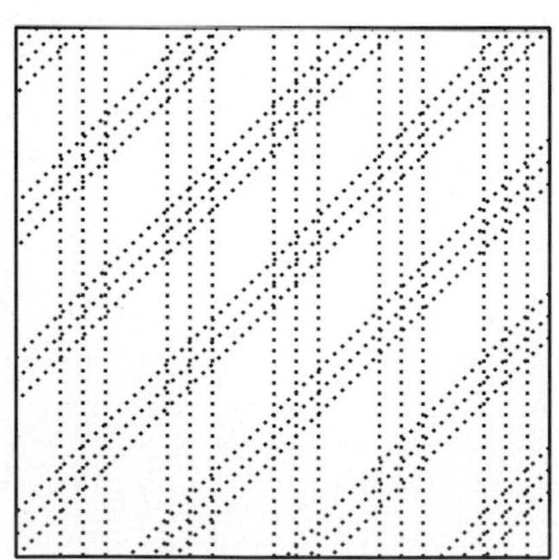

06.05 Triple Hanging Diamond; Figure 4-20

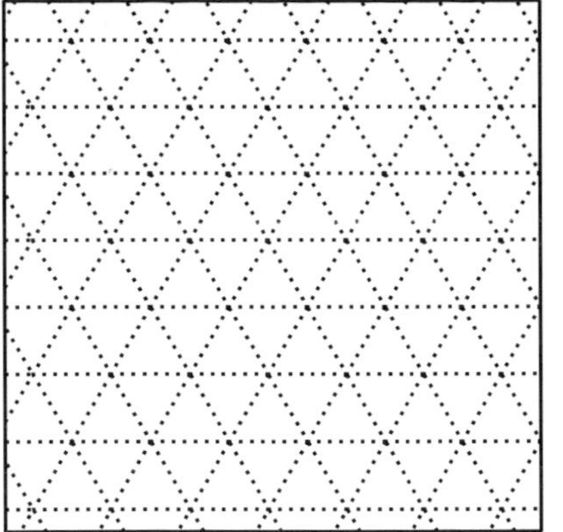

06.06 Diaper;
Figure 4-22

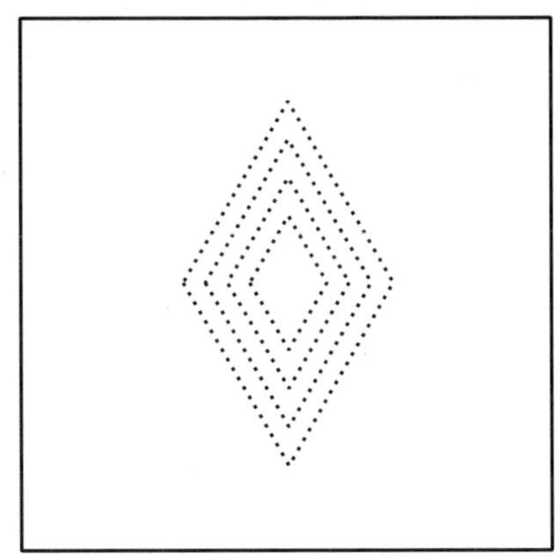

06.07 Concentric Diamonds;
Figure 4-26

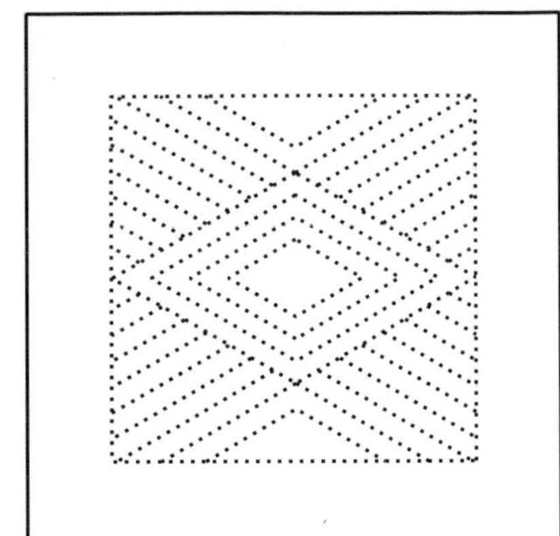

06.08 Concentric Diamonds with Diagonals; Figure 4-29

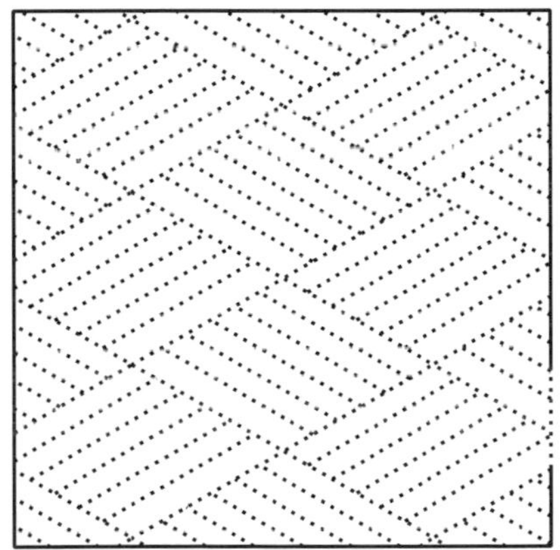

06.09 Diamond Weave;
Figure 4-30

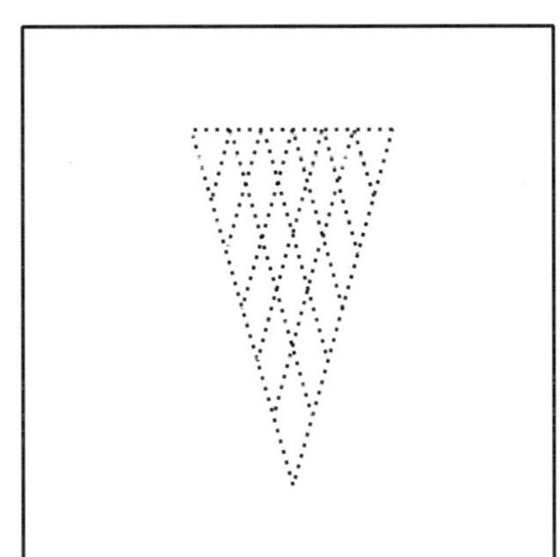

06.10 Long Diamond;
Figure 4-34

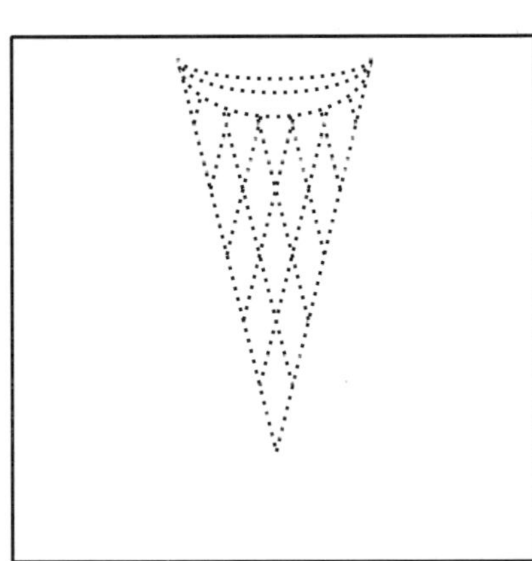

06.11 Long Diamond with Swag;
Figure 4-39; Plate 7-4

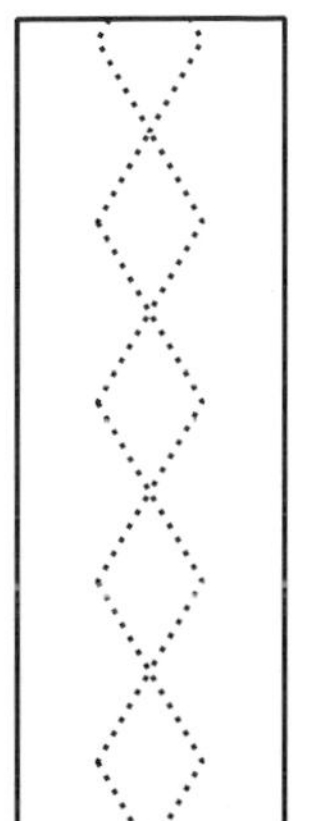

06.12 Running Diamond;
Figure 4-40

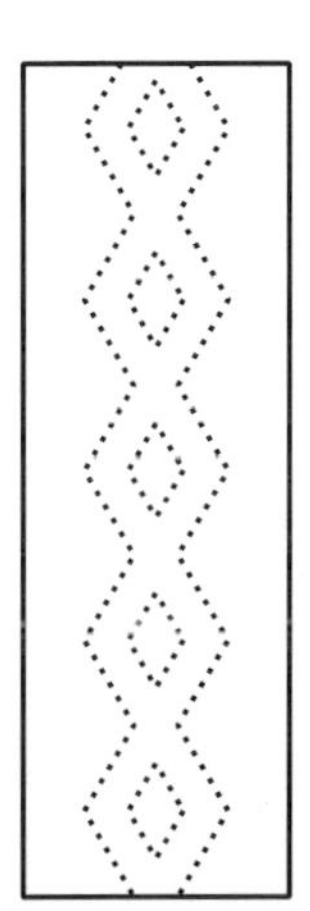

06.13 Running Double Diamond; Figure 4-43

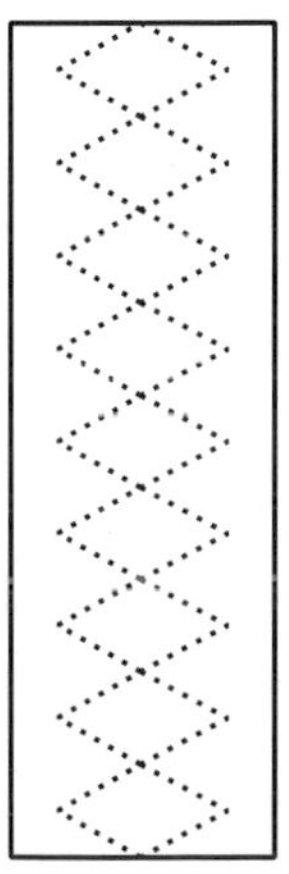

06.14 Standing Diamonds; Figure 4-46

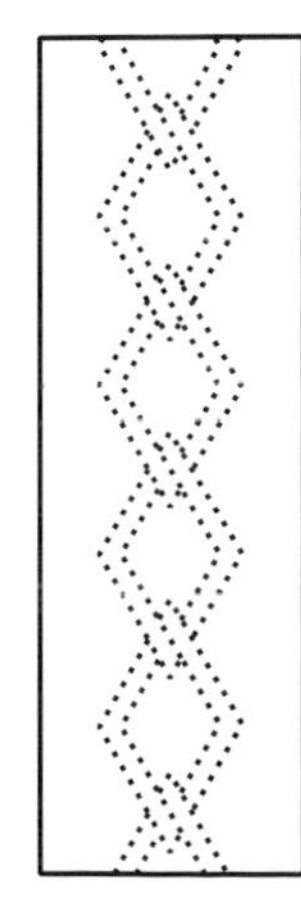

06.15 Interlaced Diamonds; Figure 4-48

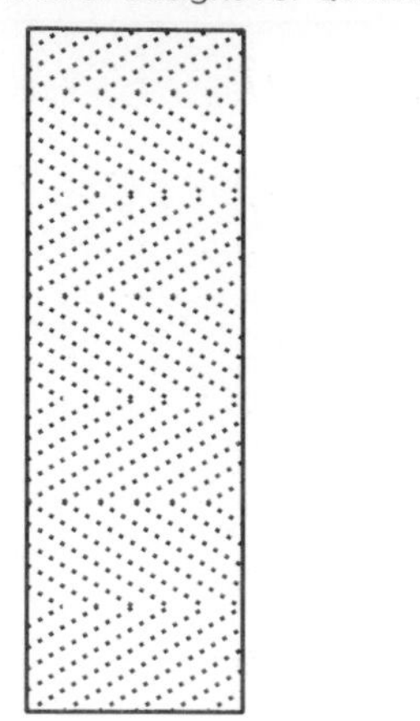

06-16 Pyramidal Pattern; Figure 4-51

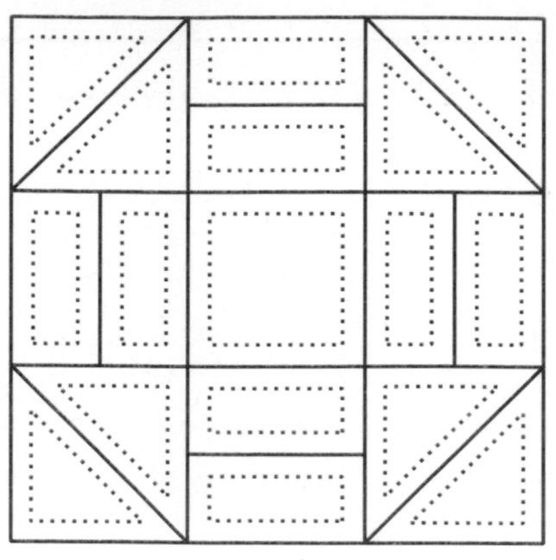

07.01 By the Piece; Figure 5-1; Plate 2-1, 4-3, 5-3, 5-4, 6-1, 6-3, 7-3, 8-1, 8-2

07.02 Outline Quilting; Figure 5-2; Plate 3-2, 3-4, 7-4, 8-2

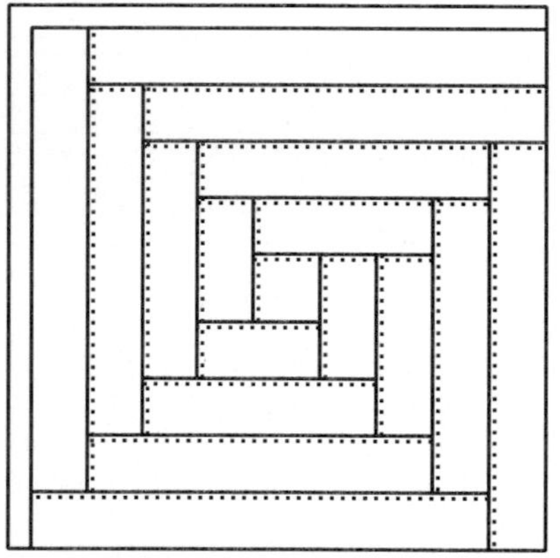

07.03 In the Ditch; Figure 5-3; Plate 4-3, 6-4, 7-1, 7-2, 10-2

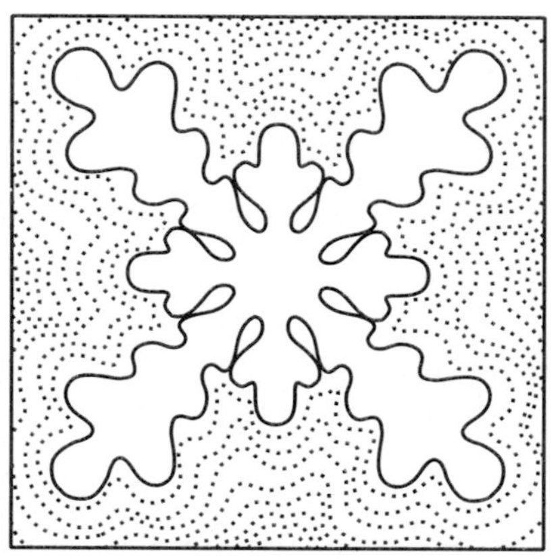

07.04 Echo; Figure 5-4; Plate 3-2, 4-2, 5-2, 5-3, 9-4

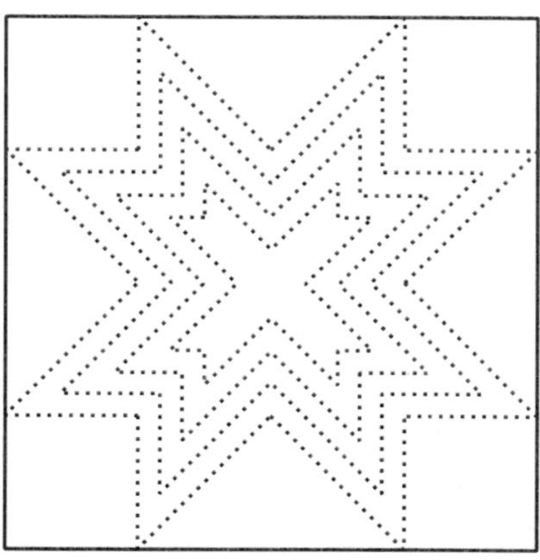

07.05 Concentric Design Line; Figure 5-6; Plate 5-3

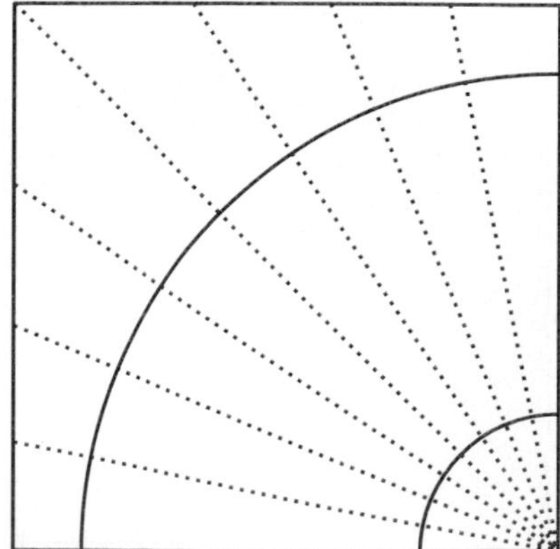

07.06 Radiating Lines; Figure 5-7; Plate 5-1

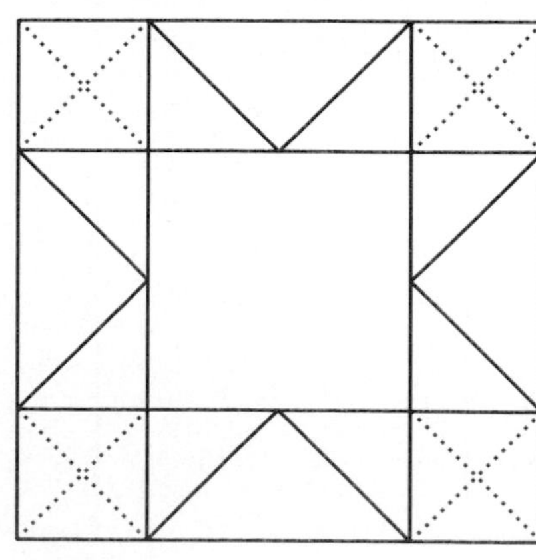

07.07 X's; Figure 5-8

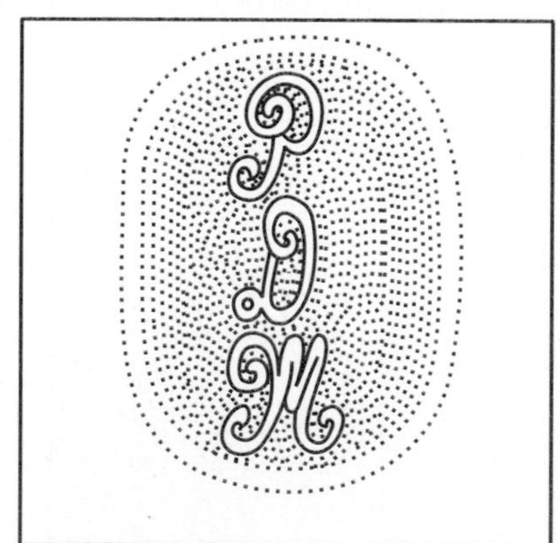

07.08 Stippling; Figure 5-9; Plate 9-3, 10-1

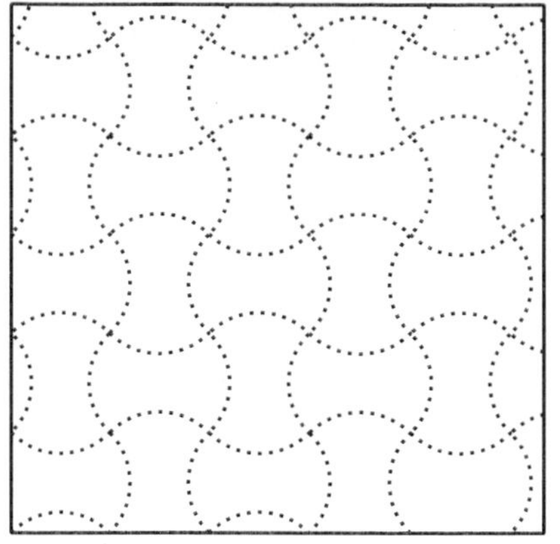

07.09 One-Patch Pieced Pattern; Figure 5-10

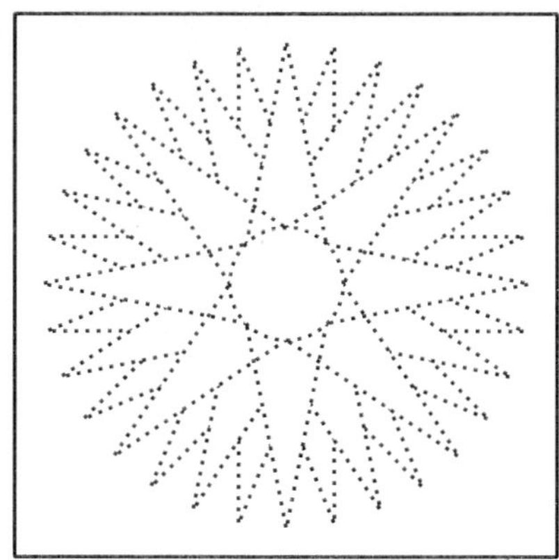

07.10 Traditional Pieced Pattern; Figure 5-12

07.11 Traditional Appliqué Pattern; Figure 5-13

08.01 Clamshell; Figure 6-1; Plate 6-4

08.02 Double Clamshell; Figure 6-5

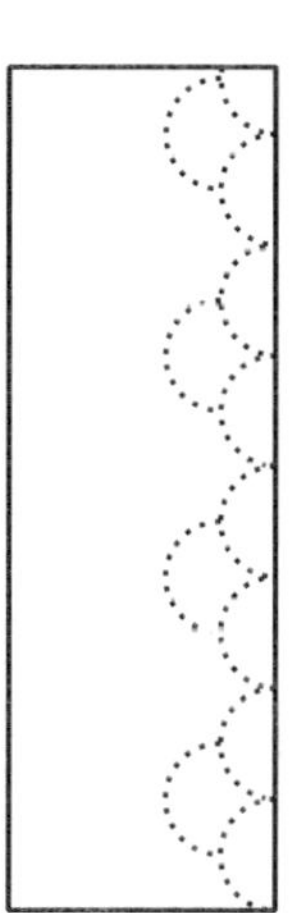

08.03 Scallops; Figure 6-8

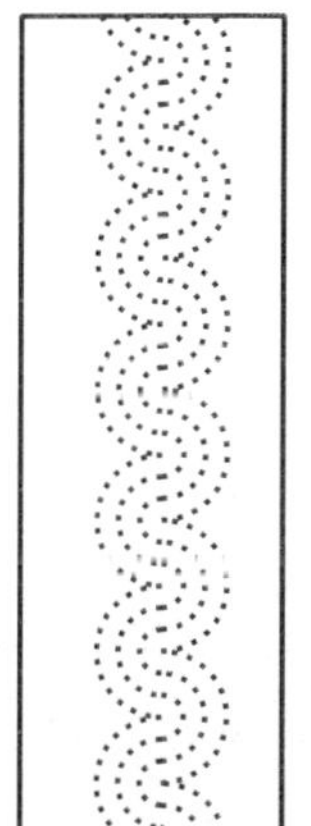

08.04 Half Moons; Figure 6-11

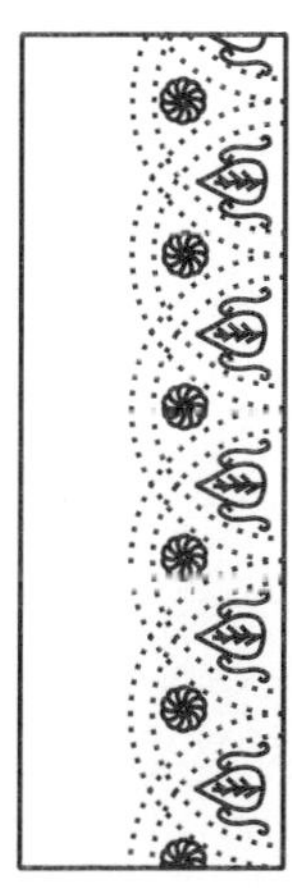

08.05 Church Window; Figure 6-14

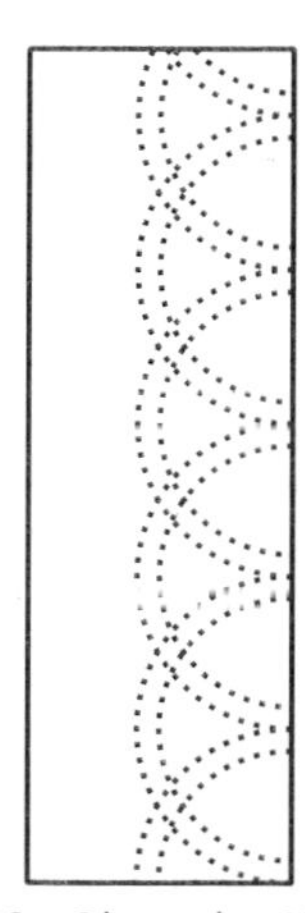

08.06 Church Window, Plain; Figure 6-17; Plate 8-2

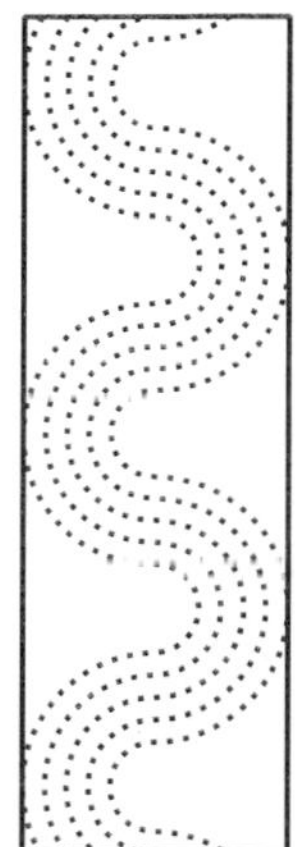

08.07 Ocean Wave Quilting; Figure 6-43

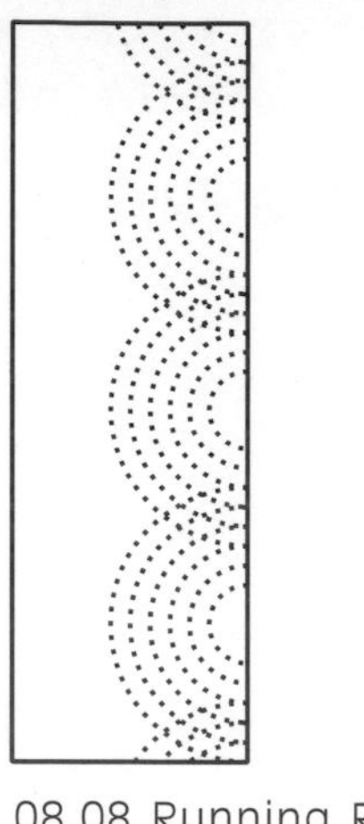

08.08 Running Rope Pattern; Figure 8-17

08.09 Teacup; Figure 6-18; Plate 6-1, 8-3

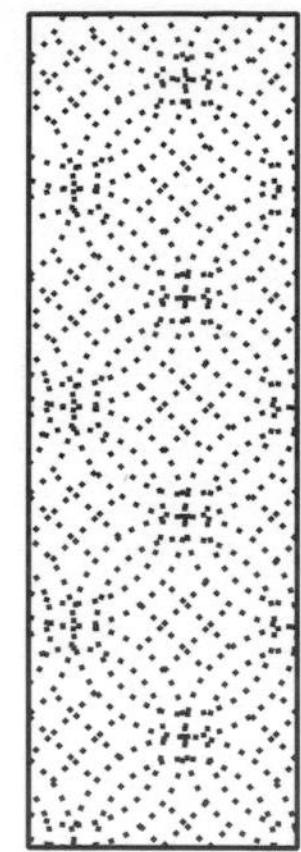

08.10 Overlapping Circles; Figure 6-22

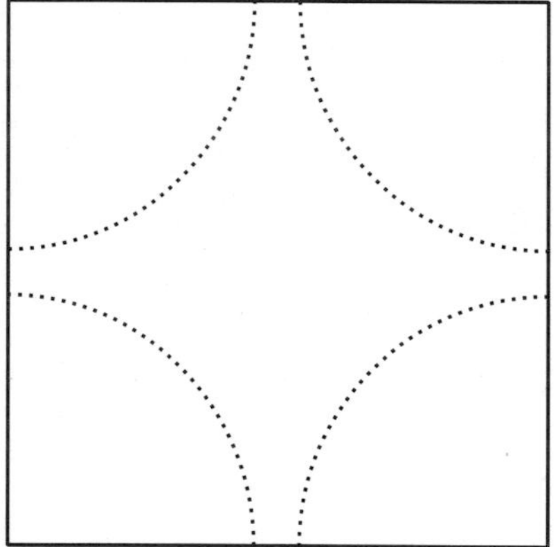

08.20 Simple Arcs; Figure 6-57

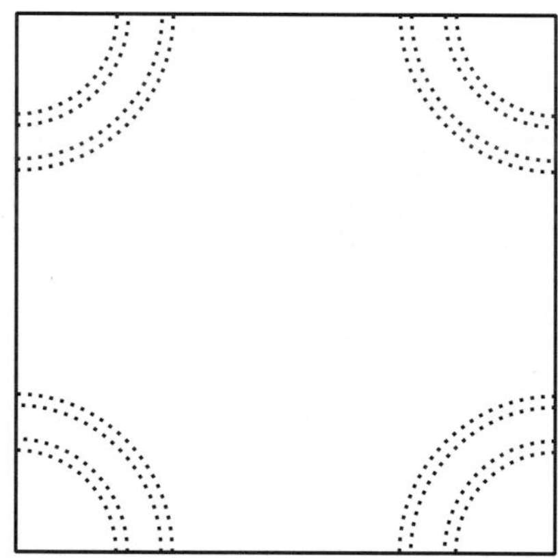

08.21 Arcs; Figure 6-55

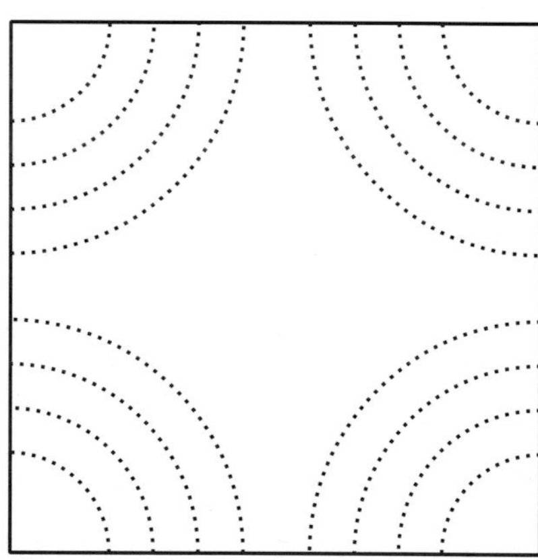

08.22 Concentric Fans; Figure 6-34

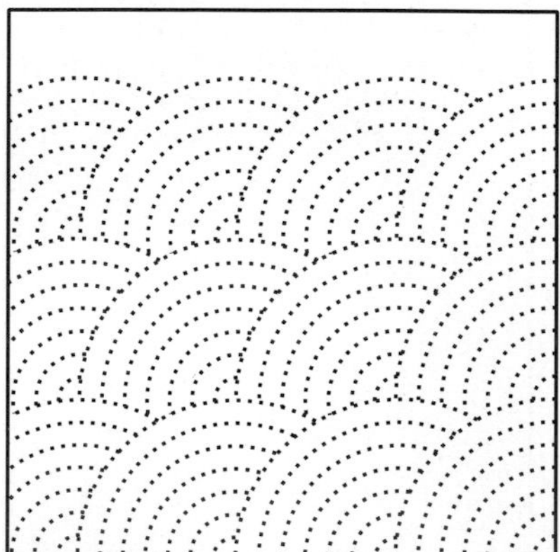

08.23 Fan; Figure 6-25; Plate 6-2

08.30 Circles; Figure 6-29

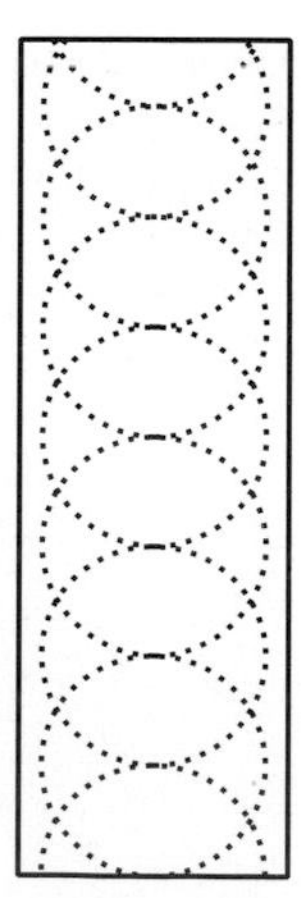

08.31 Circles Chain; Figure 6-30

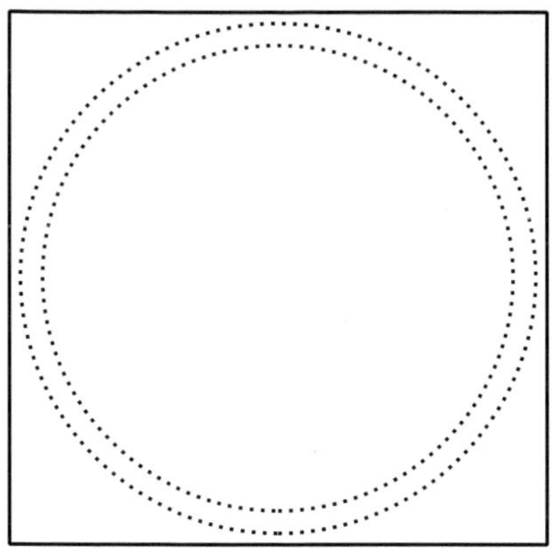

08.32 Circle in a Circle;
Figure 6-36

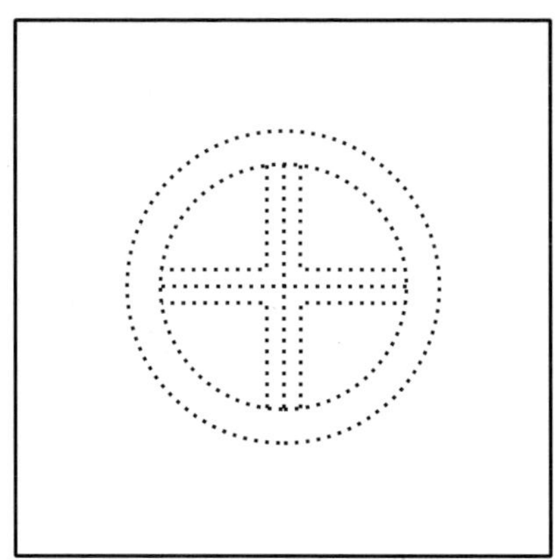

08.33 Cross-in-a-Cricle;
Figure 6-53

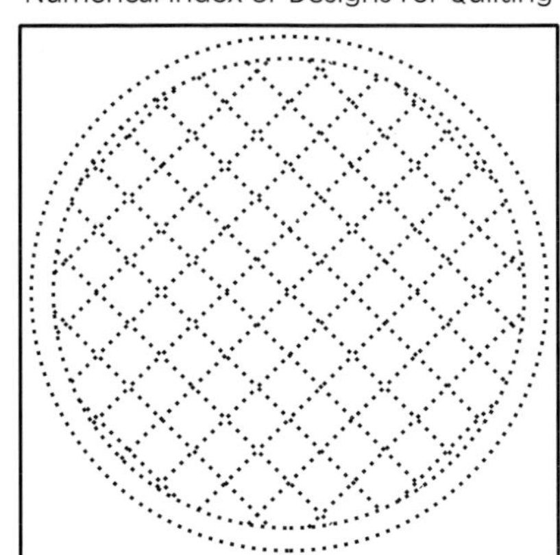

08.34 Circle in a Circle Variation;
Figure 6-37

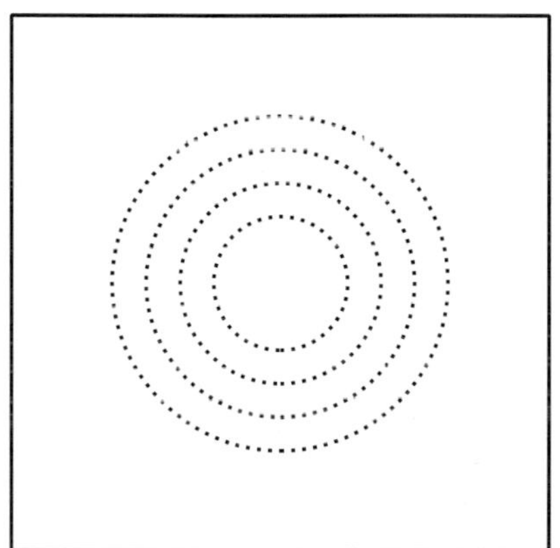

08.35 Concentric Circles;
Figure 6-32; Plate 6-3

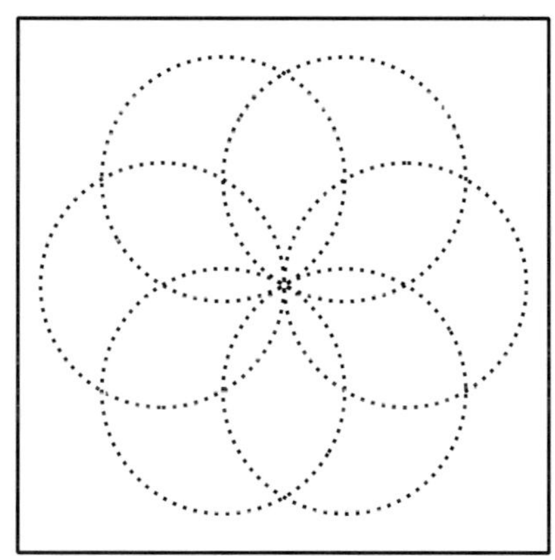

08.36 Floral Circles;
Figure 6-46

08.37 Star Flower;
Figure 6-49

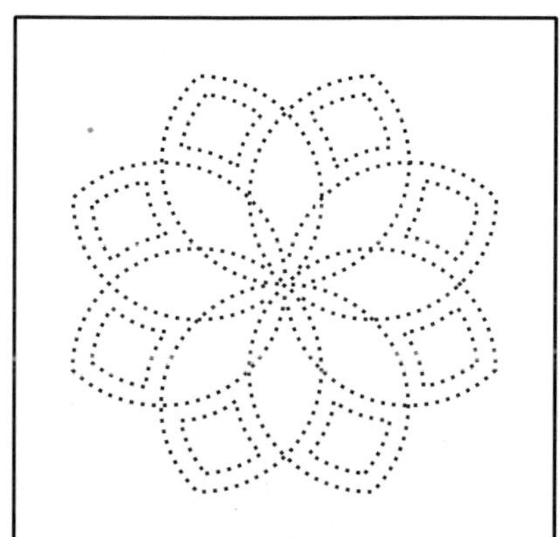

08.38 Star Flower Variation;
Figure 6-52

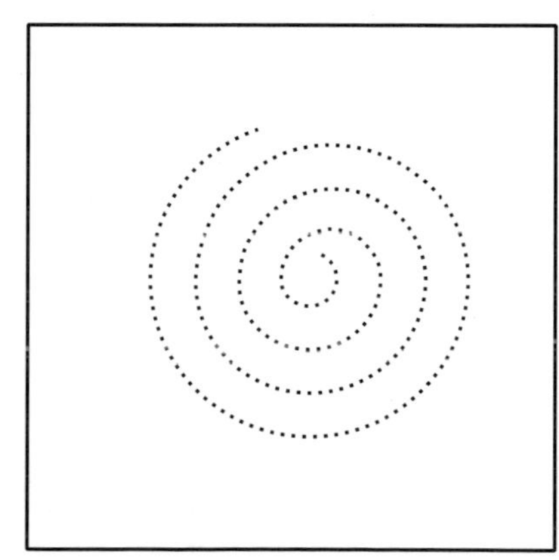

08.40 Spiral;
Figure 6-38; Plate 3-1

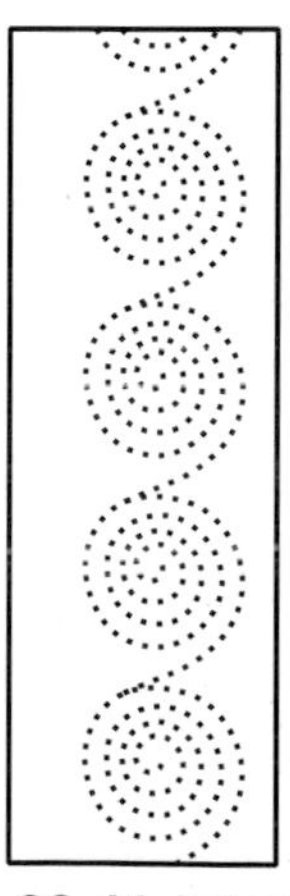

08.41 Interlocking
Swirl; Figure 6-40

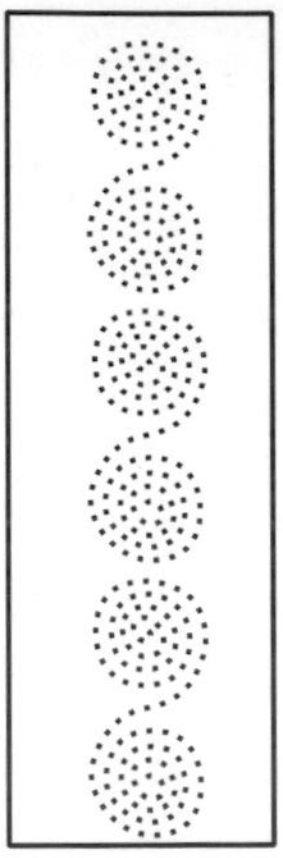

08.42 Scroll;
Figure 7-38

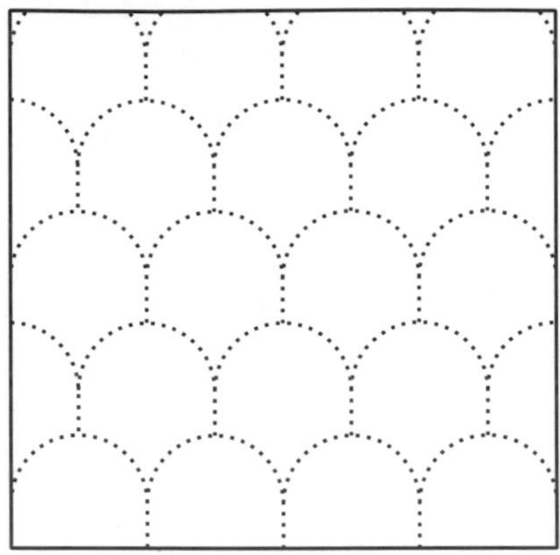

09.01 Ovals;
Figure 7-1; Plate 4-3

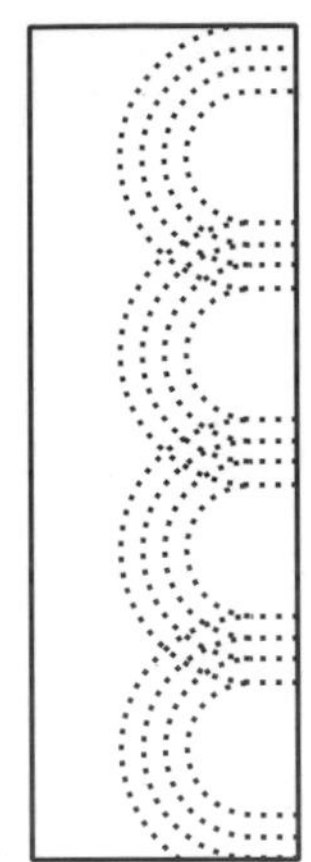

09.02 Gothic Fans;
Figure 7-5

09.03 Overlapping Ovals;
Figure 7-5

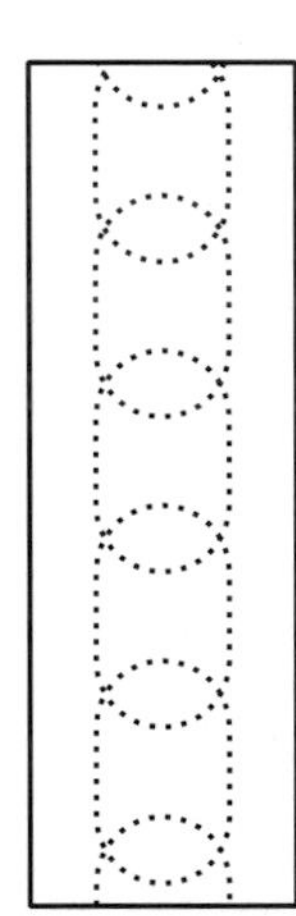

09.04 Oval Chain;
Figure 7-9

10.01 Crescent;
Figure 7-12

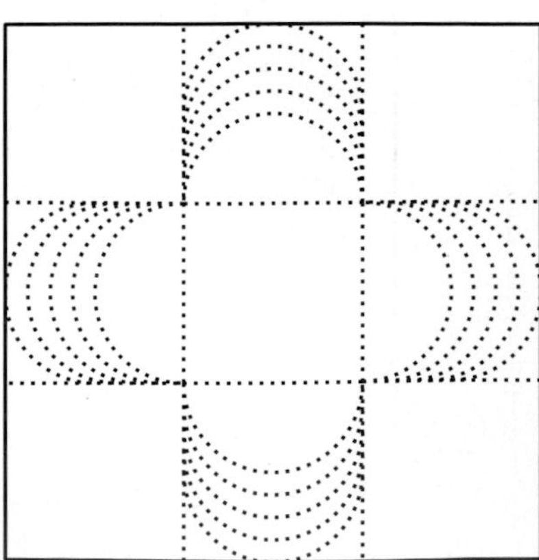

10.02 Radiating Curves;
Figure 7-16

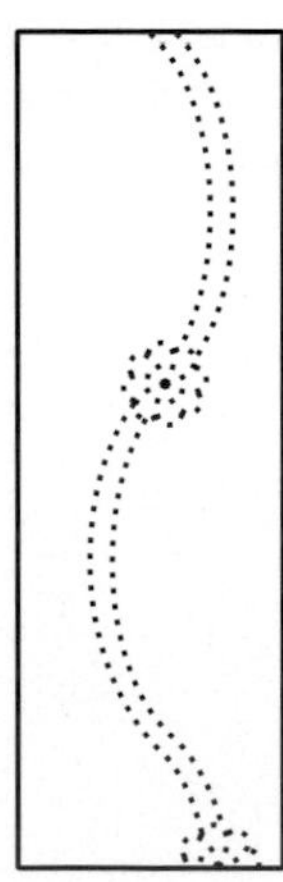

10.10 Scrolling Vine;
Figure 7-30; Plate 7-1

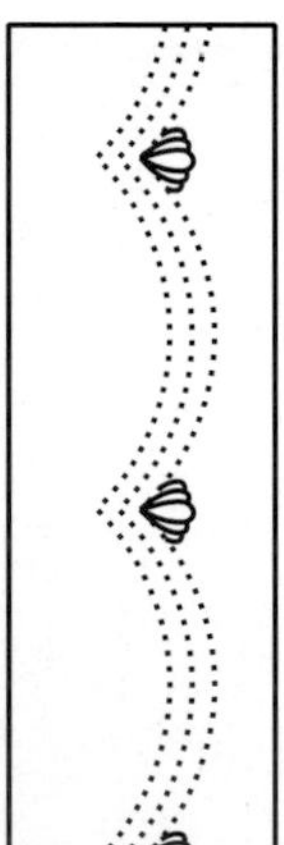

10.11 Swag Variation with Tassels;
Figure 7-23

11.01 Weave Variation; Figure 3-29

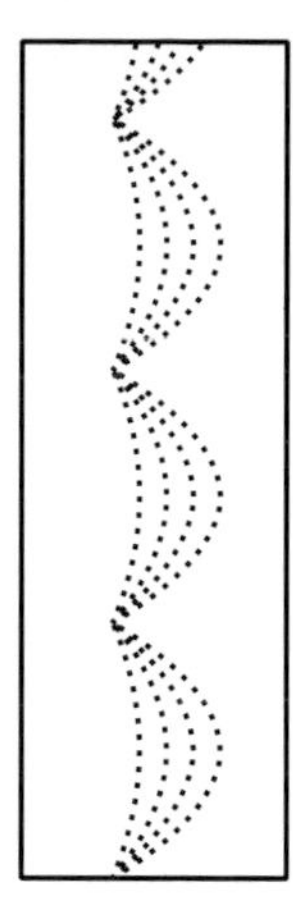
11.02 Swag; Figure 7-19; Plate 7-4, 10-3

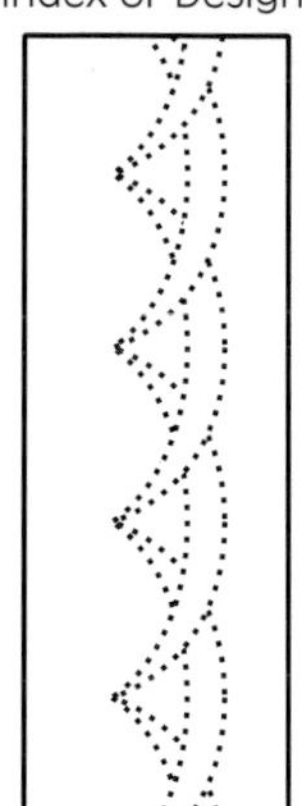
11.03 Overlapping Swags; Figure 7-26

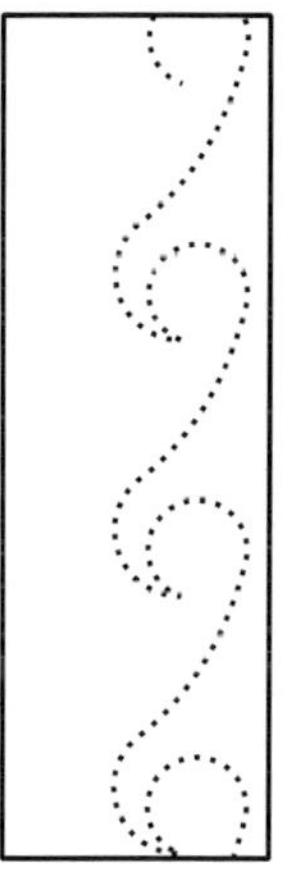
11.10 Simple Scroll; Figure 7-34; Plate 7-2

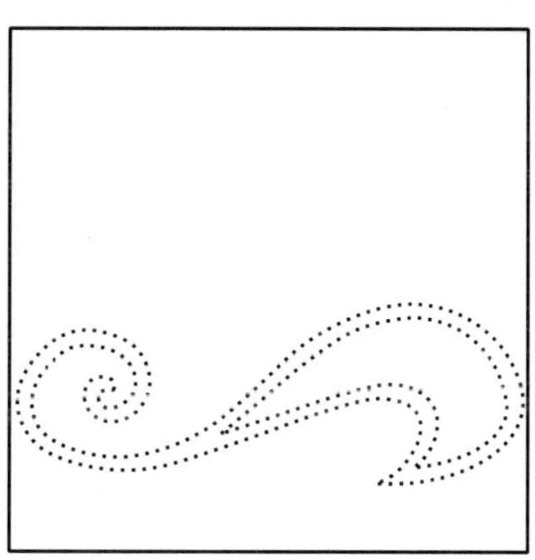
11.11 Scroll Variation; Figure 7-41

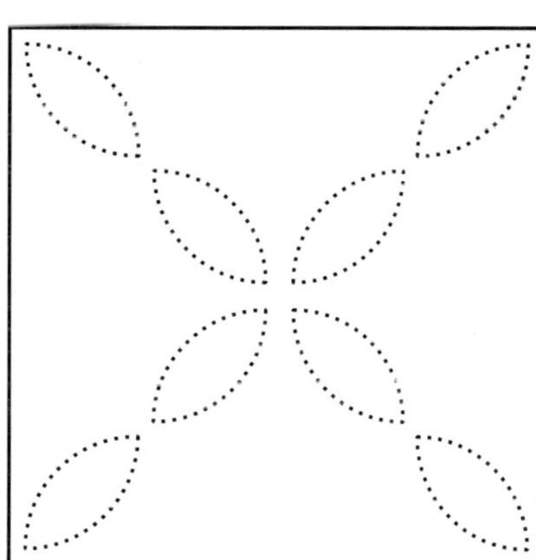
11.20 Pumpkin Seed; Figure 7-42

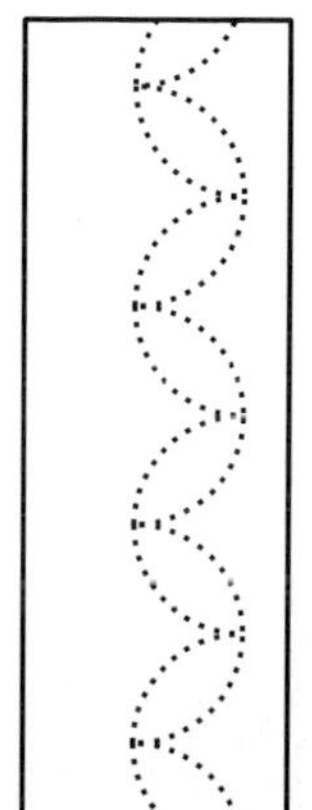
11.23 Pumpkin Seed Border I; Figure 46

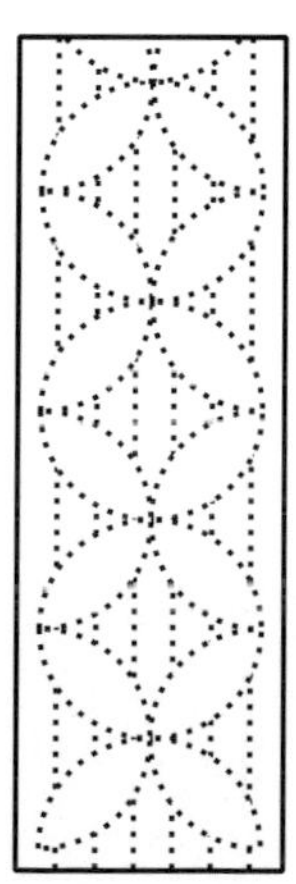
11.24 Pumpkin Seed Border II; Figure 7-47

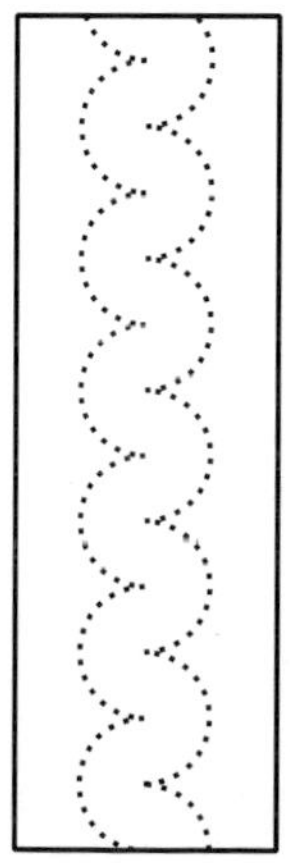
12.01 Clamshell Rope; Figure 8-1

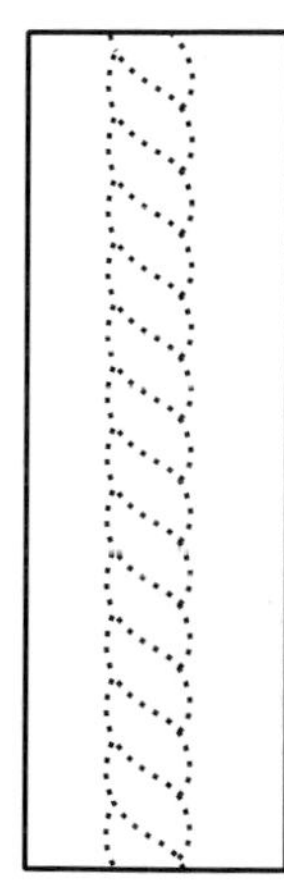
12.02 Rope; Figure 8-13; Plate 7-2

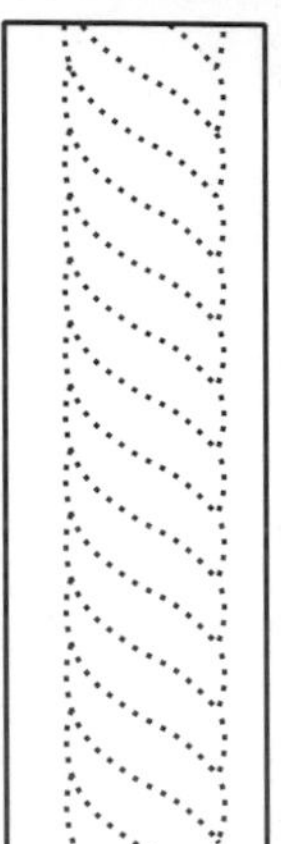
12.03 Twisted Braid; Figure 8-15

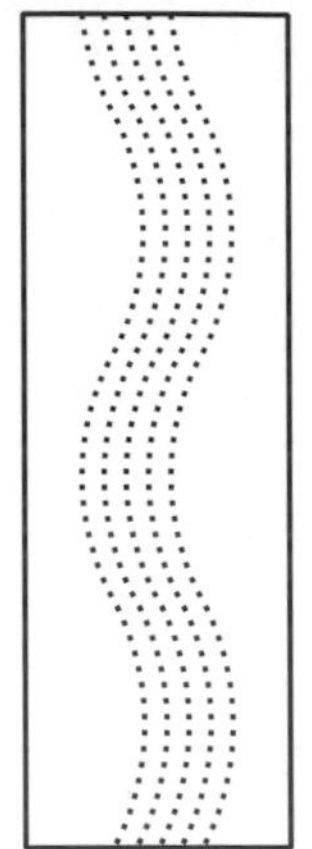
12.04 Running Rope II; Figure 8-20

12.05 Braided Rope; Figure 8-24

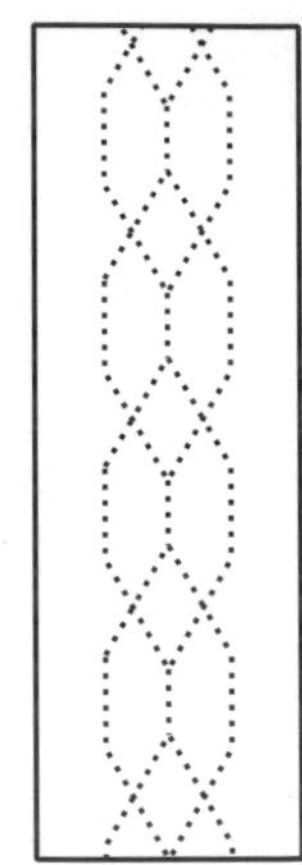
12.06 Diamond Rope; Figure 8-67

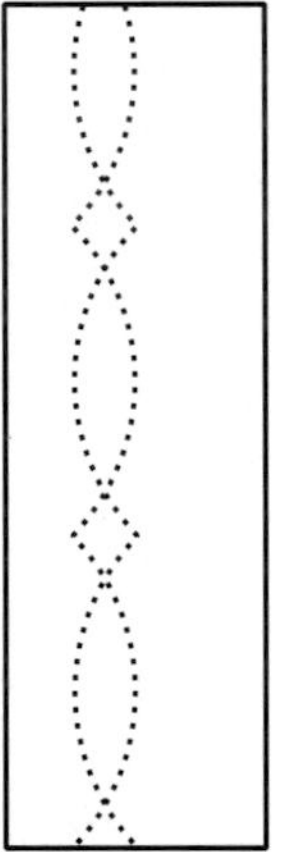
13.01 Diamond and Rope; Figure 8-3

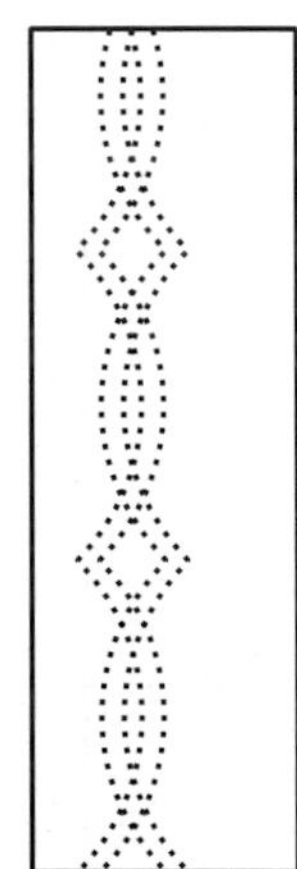
13.02 Double Diamond and Rope; Figure 8-7

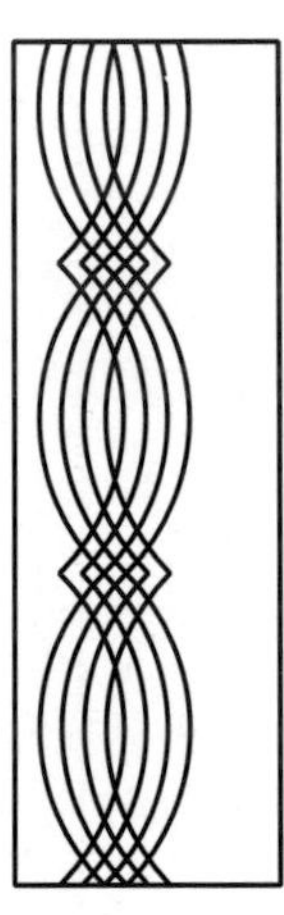
13.03 Diamond and Rope Cable; Figure 8-10

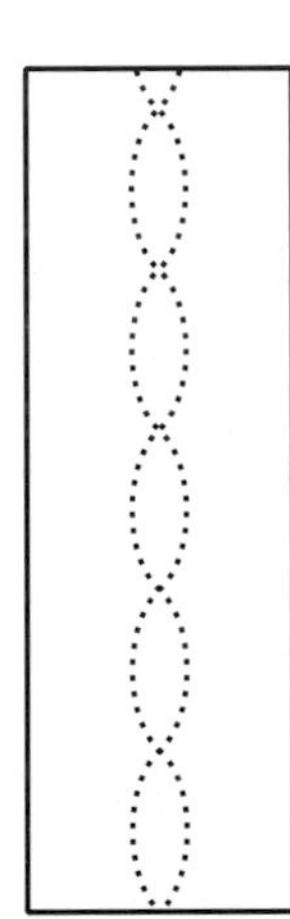
13.10 Single Cable-Pumpkin Seed; Figure 8-31

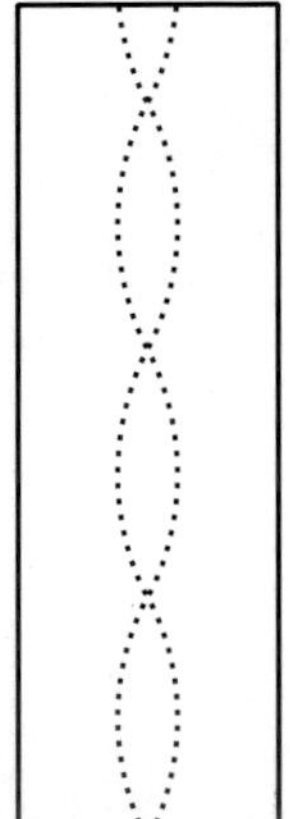
13.11 Running Single Cable; Figure 8-32

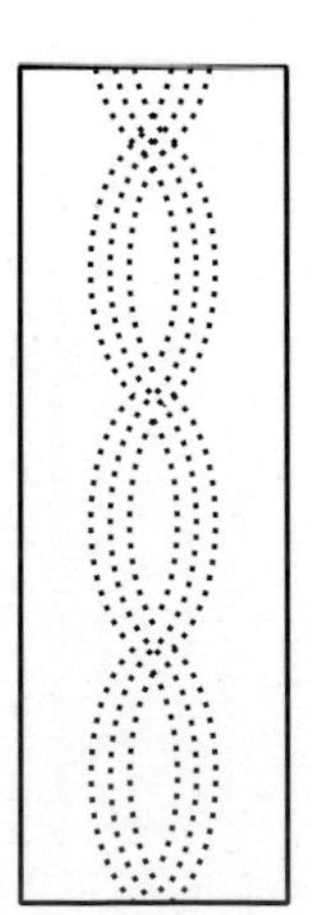
13.12 Twisted Rope; Figure 8-41

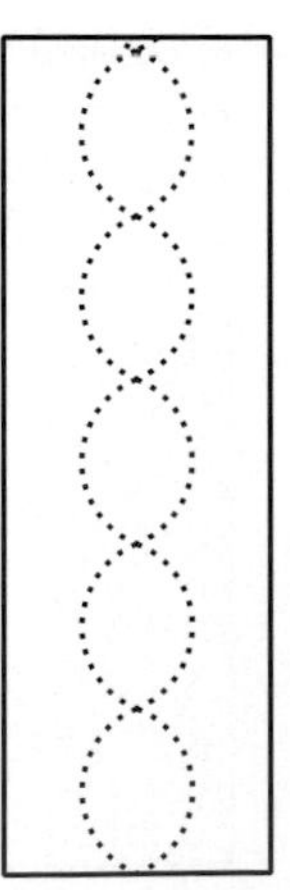
13.20 Single Cable; Figure 8-28

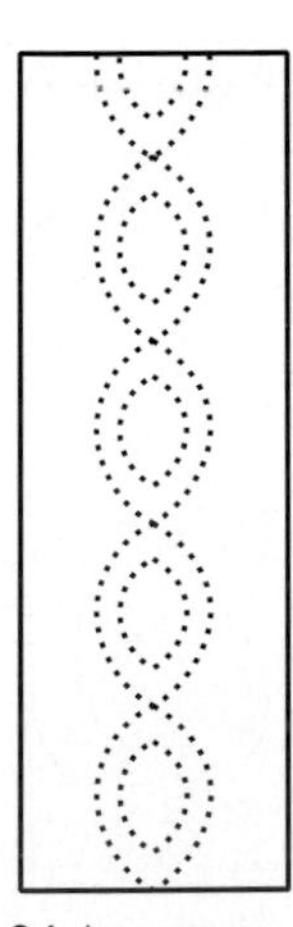
13.21 Lozenge; Figure 8-33

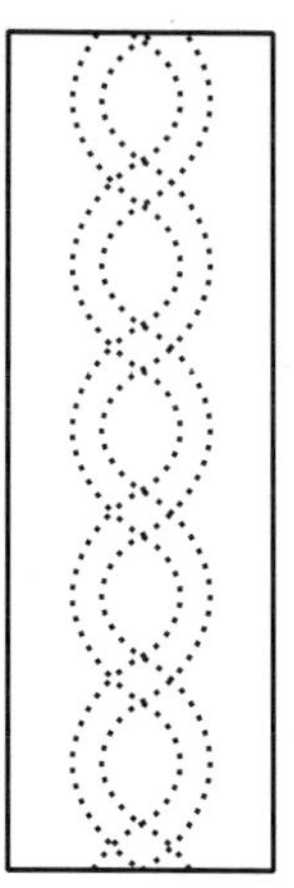
13.22 Double Cable; Figure 8-36; Plate 8-1

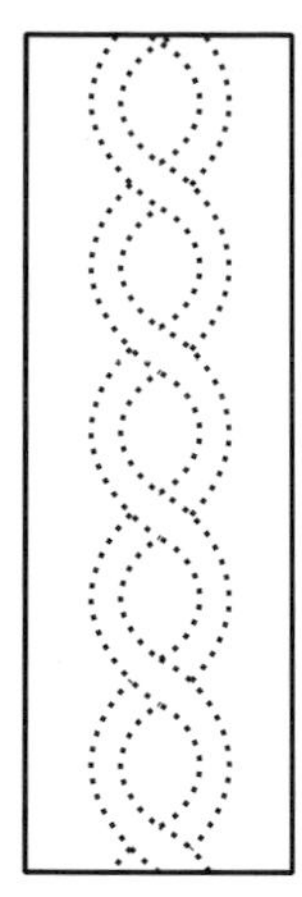
13.23 Double Cable Variation; Figure 8-38; Plate 8-4

13.24 Triple Cable; Figure 8-45; Plate 8-2, 8-3

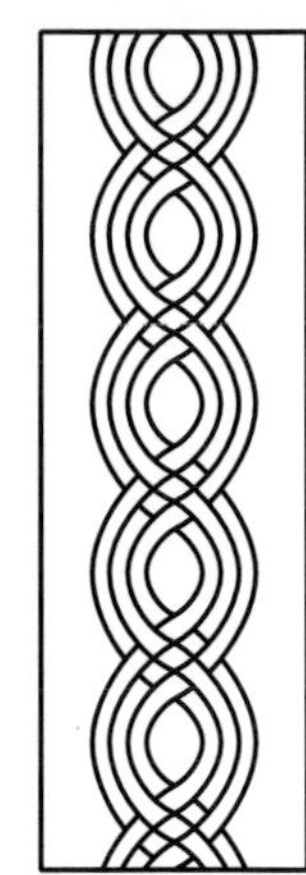
13.25 Braided Triple Cable; Figure 8-47

13.26 Chain Triple Cable; Figure 8-48

13.27 Twist Cable; Figure 8-49

13.28 Chain Twist; Figure 8-51

13.29 Twisted Rope Cable; Figure 8-52

13.30 Twisted Rope Cable Variation; Figure 8-53

13.31 Classical Cable; Figure 8-54

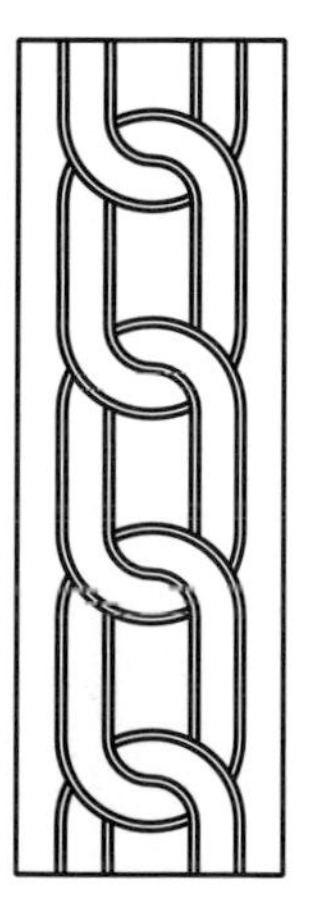
13.40 Chain Links; Figure 8-58

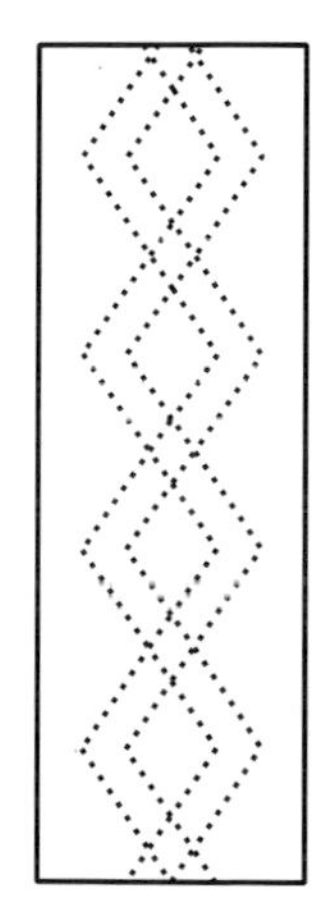
13.50 Diamond Cable; Figure 8-62

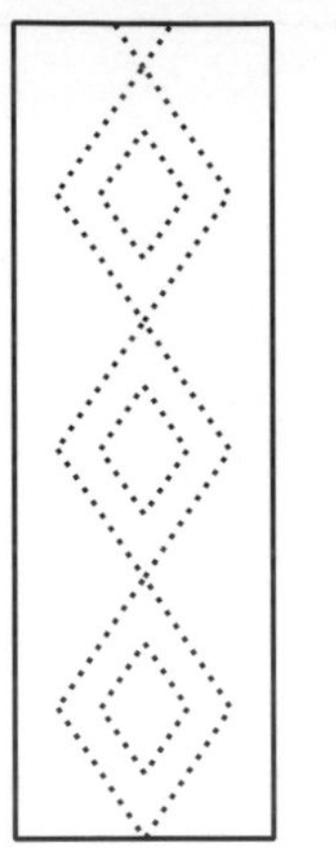
13.51 Diamond String; Figure 8-65

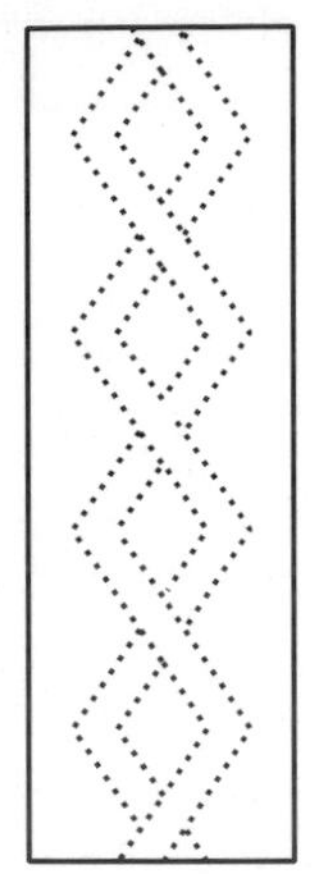
13.52 Weaving Diamond Cable; Figure 8-66

14.01 Heart; Figure 9-1; Plate 9-1

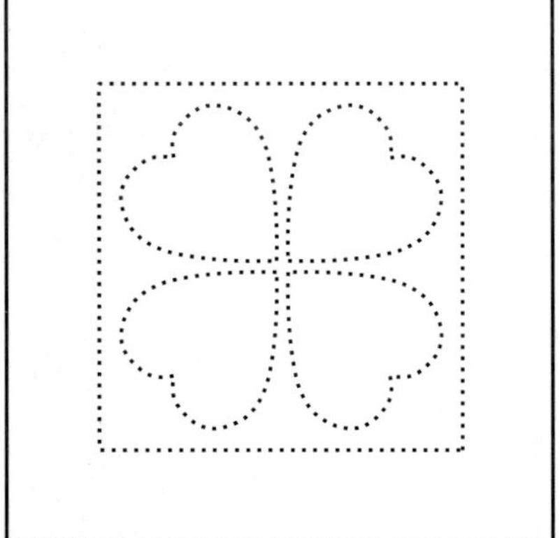
14.02 Heart Corner Design; Figure 9-6

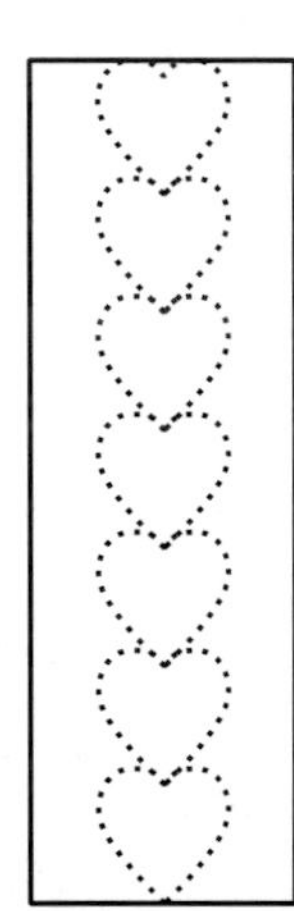
14.03 Heart String; Figure 9-8

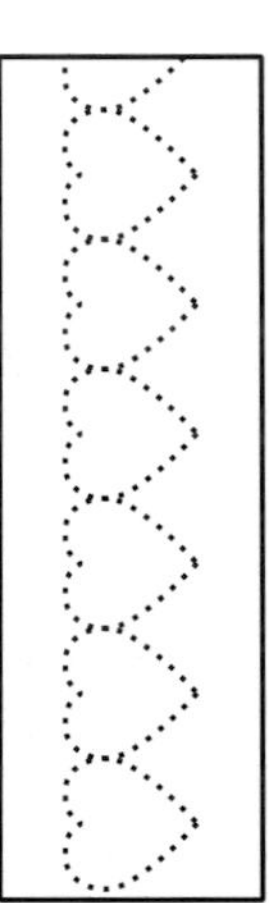
14.04 Line of Hearts; Figure 9-10

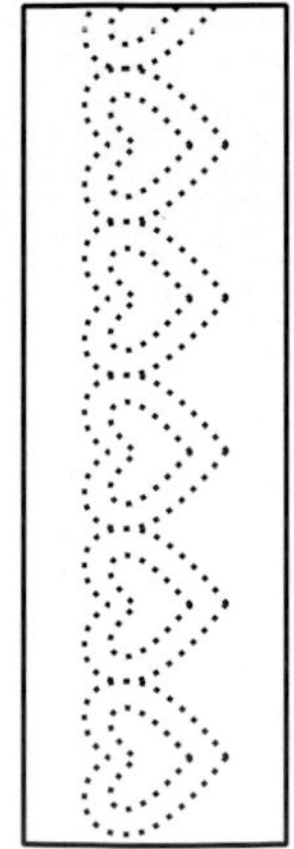
14.05 Line of Hearts Variation; Figure 9-13

14.06 Circle of Hearts; Figure 9-14

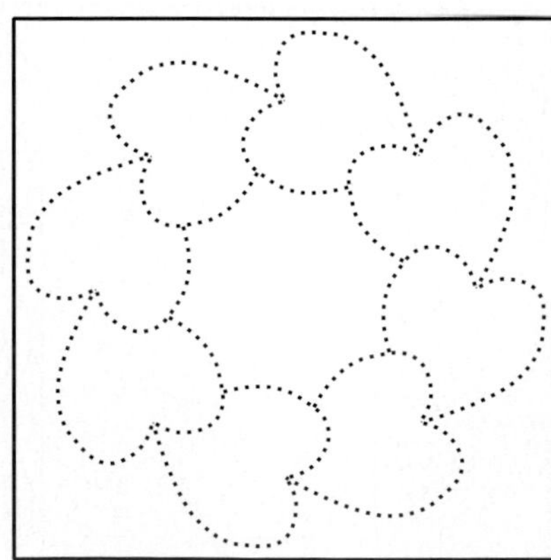
14.07 Heart Wreath; Figure 9-17

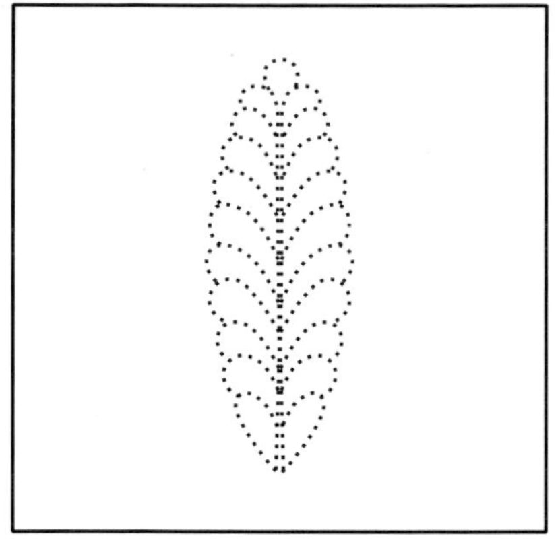

15.01 Straight Feather;
Figure 9-28; Plate 7-3

15.02 Ostrich Plume;
Figure 9-30; Plate 9-2, 9-3

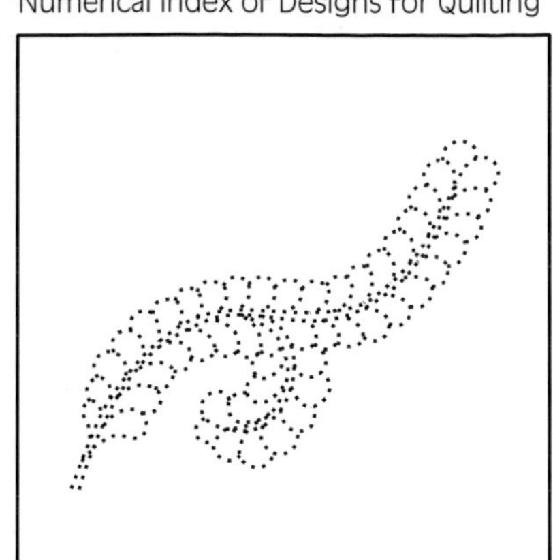

15.03 Feather Scroll;
Figure 9-32

15.04 Fiddlehead;
Figure 9-38; Plate 9-2

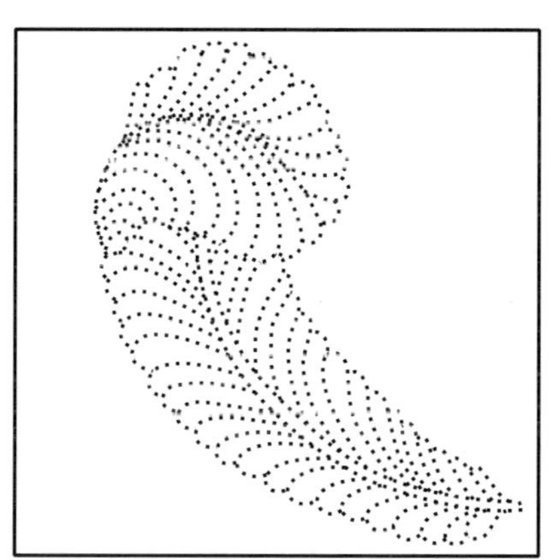

15.05 Princess Feather;
Figure 9-34; Plate 7-4

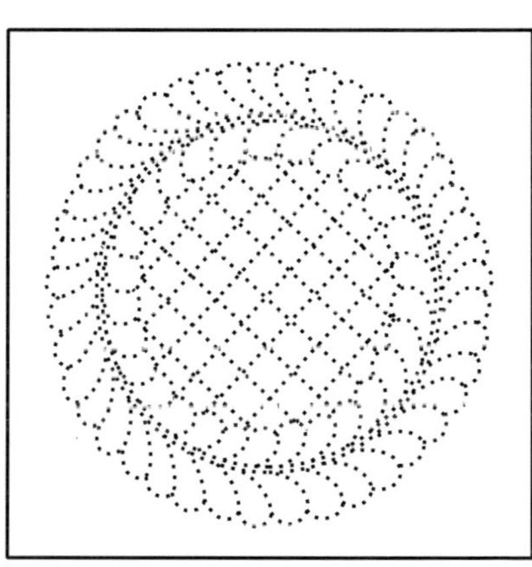

15.10 Feathered Circle;
Figure 9-42; Plate 7-3

15.11 Feathered Circle-in-a-Square;
Figure 9-50; Plate 2-4

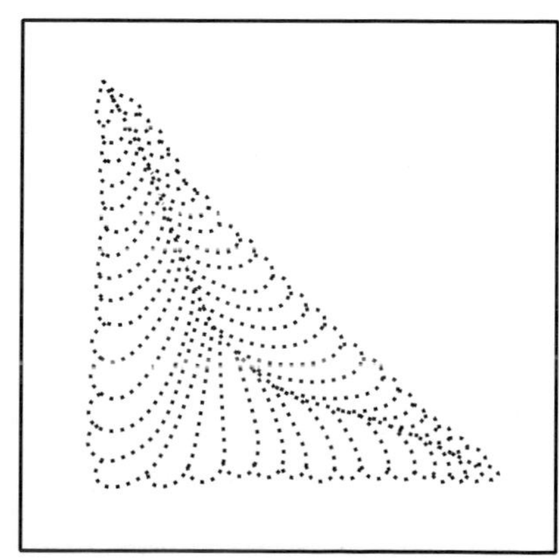

15.12 Feathered Triangle;
Figure 9-70

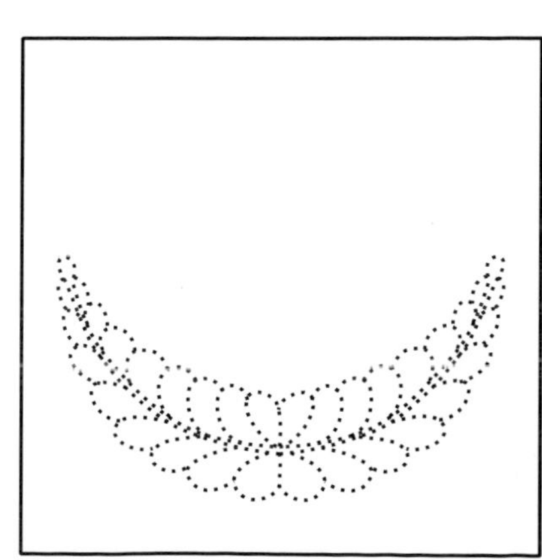

15.20 Feather Swag;
Figure 9-48; Plate 3-2

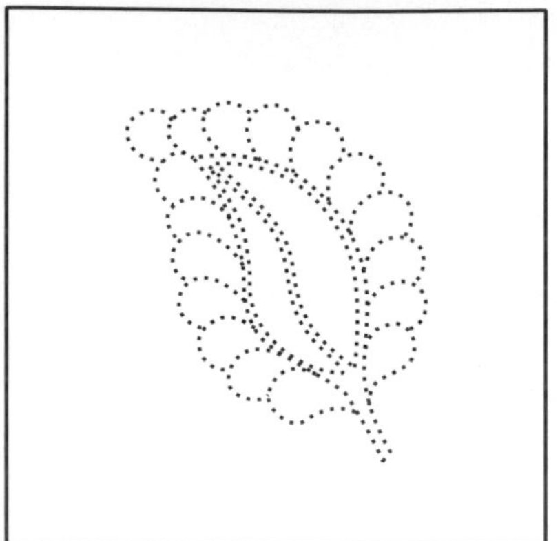

15.21 Paisley;
Figure 9-44; Plate 9-3

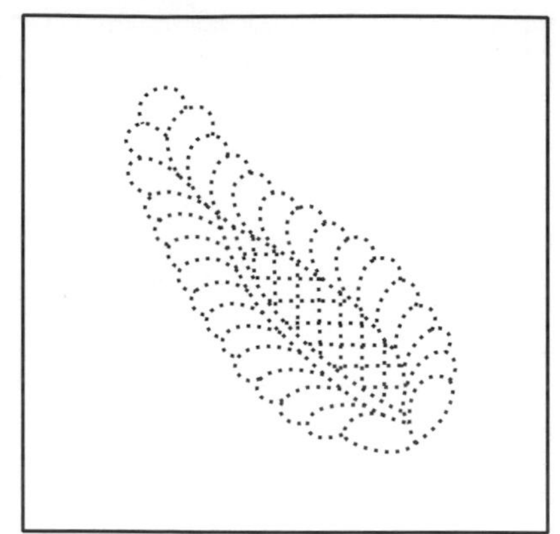

15.22 Lace Vein Feather;
Figure 9-46

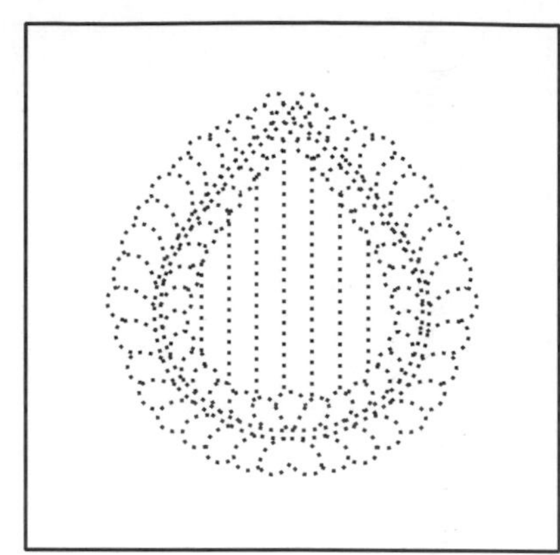

15.23 Feathered Harp;
Figure 9-52

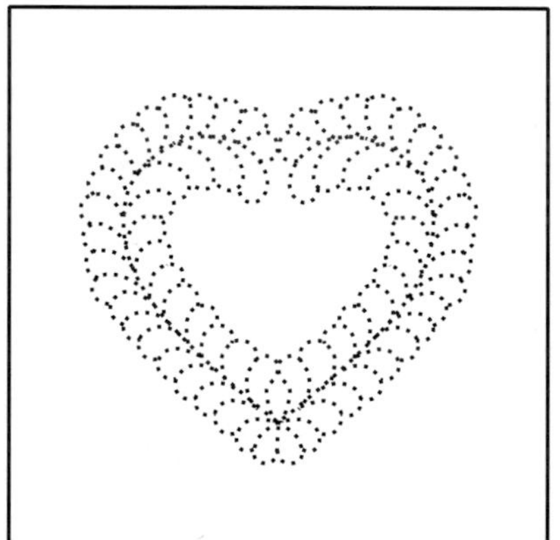

15.24 Feathered Heart;
Figure 9-54

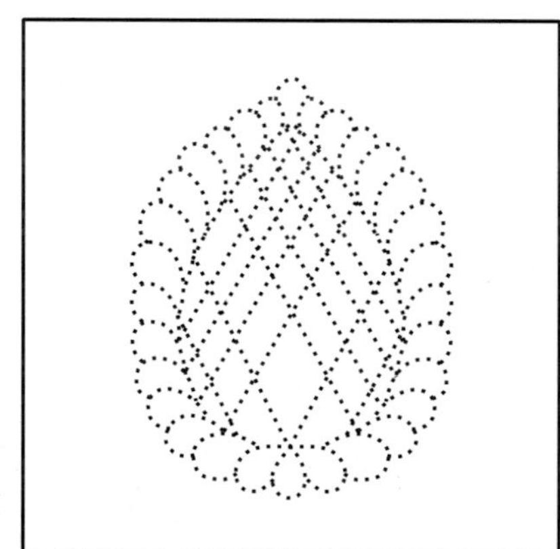

15.25 Feathered Pineapple;
Figure 9-56; Plate 9-4

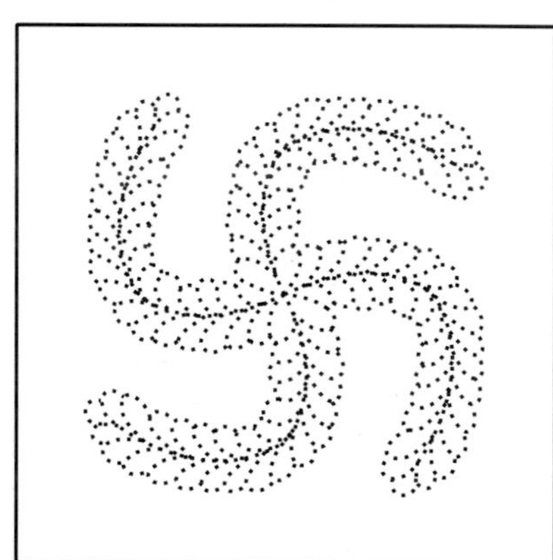

15.26 Plumed Swastika;
Figure 9-36

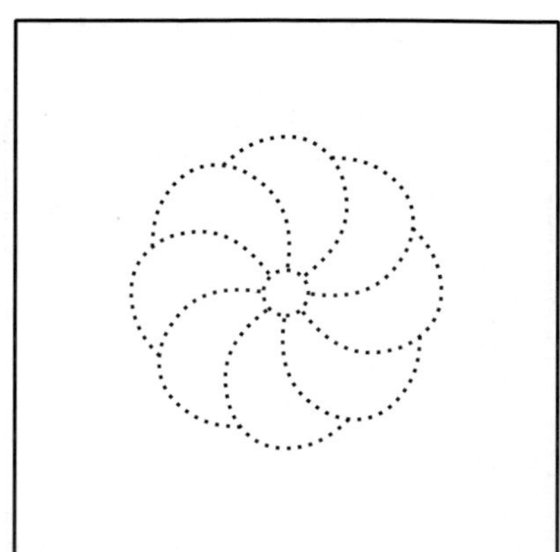

15.30 Feather Rosette;
Figure 9-40

15.31 Peacock Fan;
Figure 9-68

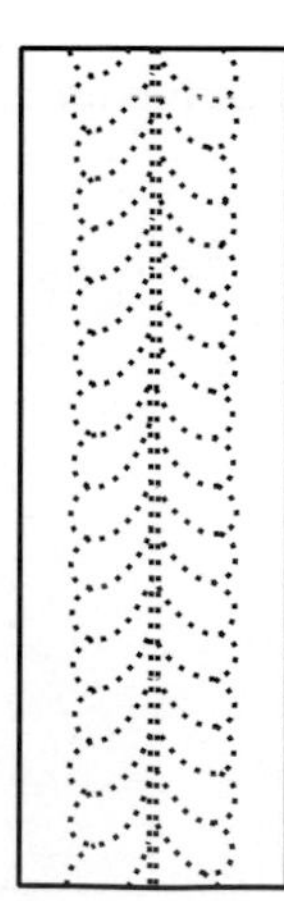

15.40 Feather Band;
Figure 9-19

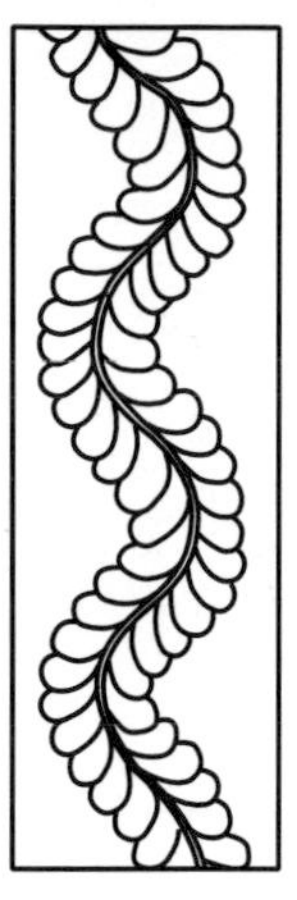
15.41 Feathered Vine; Figure 9-58; Plate 5-2

15.42 Feathered Cable; Figure 9-60

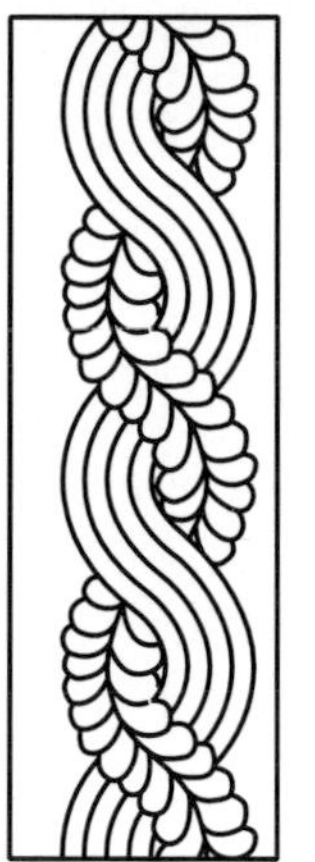
15.43 Feather Twist; Figure 9-62

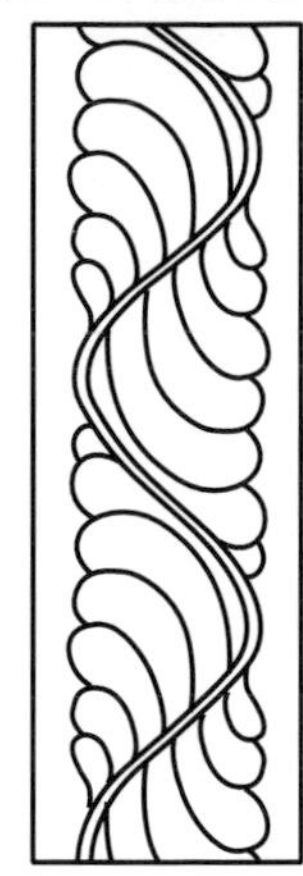
15.44 Finger Feather; Figure 9-64

15.45 Feathered Garland; Figure 9-66; Plate 8-1, 9-3

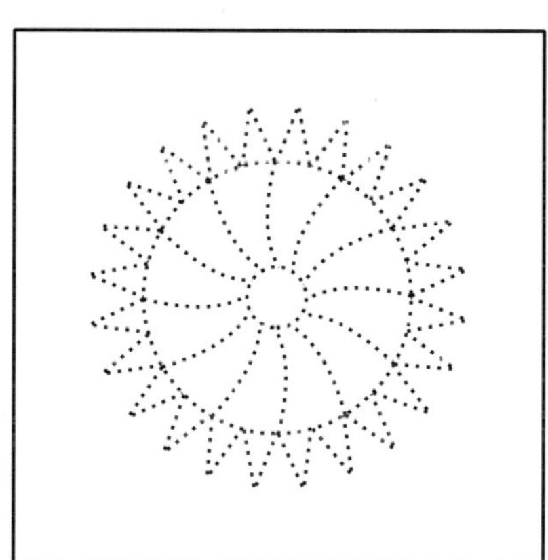
16.00 Rising Sun; Figure 10-22

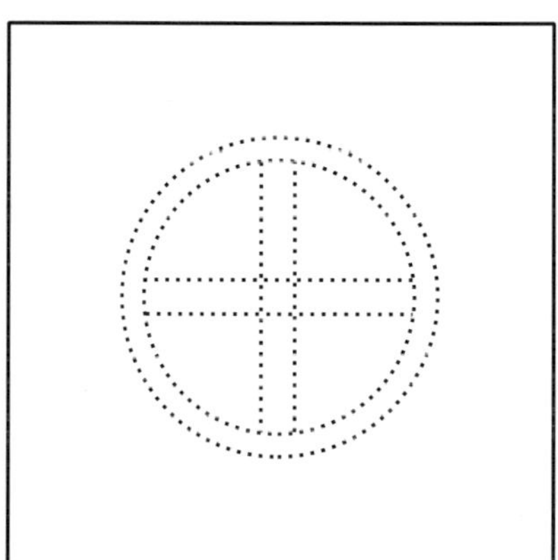
16.01 Wheel; Figure 10-3

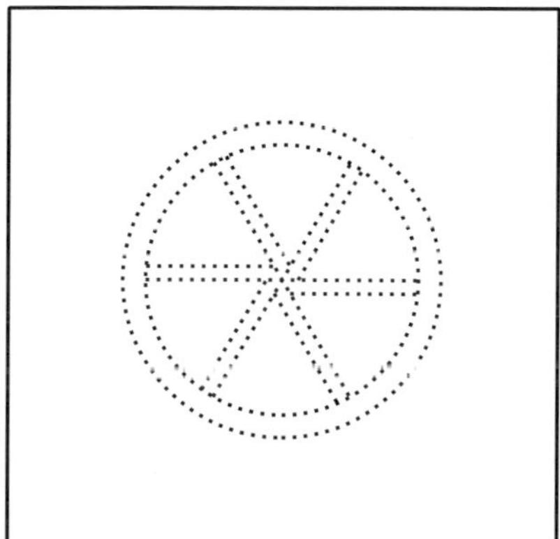
16.02 Hex Wheel; Figure 10-4

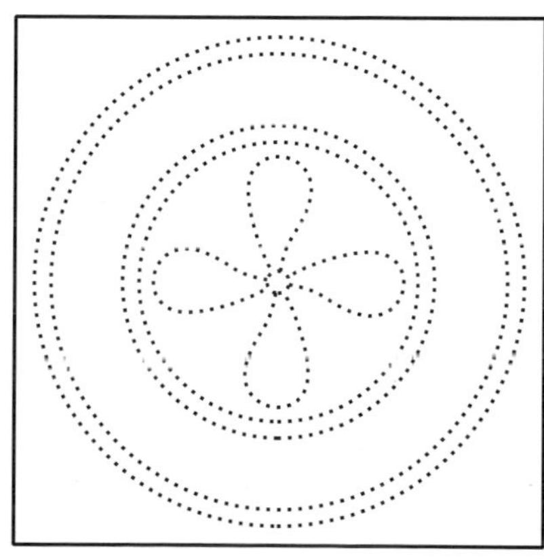
16.03 Swirling Swastikas or Hexfeiss; Figure 10-80

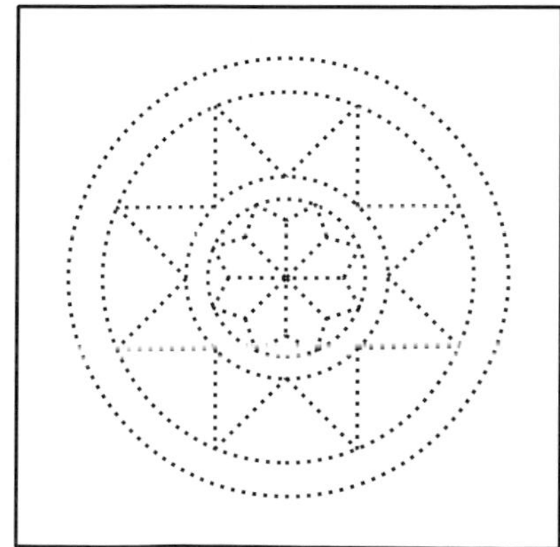
16.04 Star Hex; Figure 10-5

16.05 Wheel Star;
Figure 10-6

16.10 Bowtie;
Figure 10-76

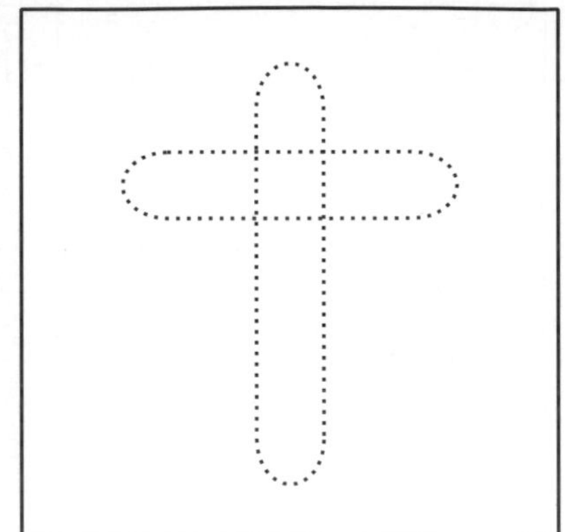

16.11 Cross;
Figure 10-1

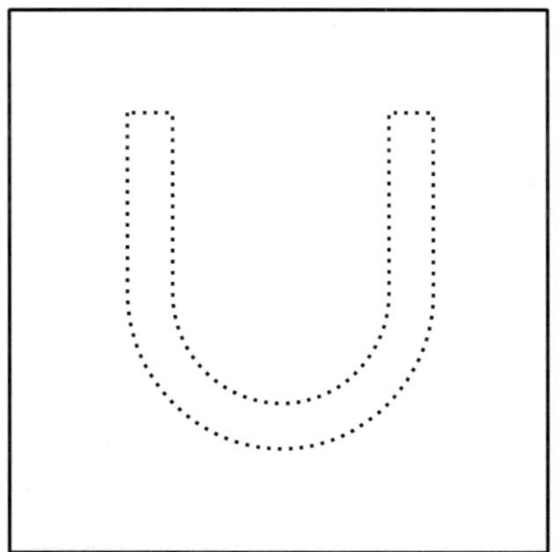

16.12 Horseshoe;
Figure 10-2

16.13 Pipe Stem;
Figure 10-8

16.14 Anchor;
Figure 10-9

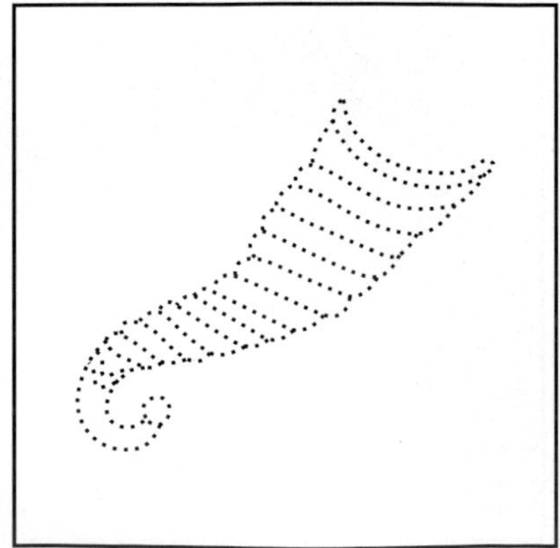

16.15 Cornucopia;
Figure 10-11

16.16 Horn of Plenty;
Figure 10-12

16.17 Cherry Basket;
Figure 10-13

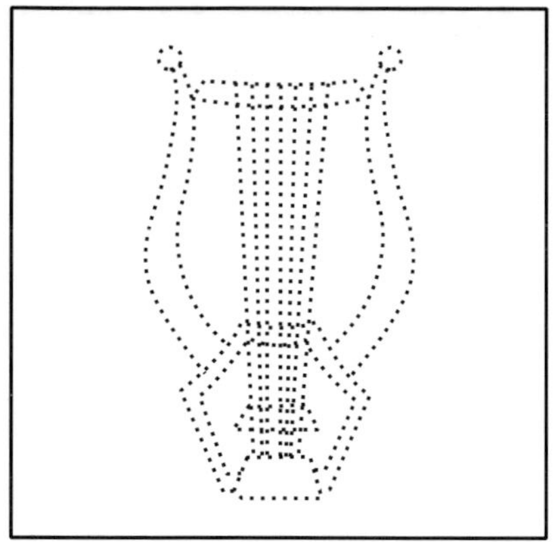
16.19 Lyre;
Figure 10-15

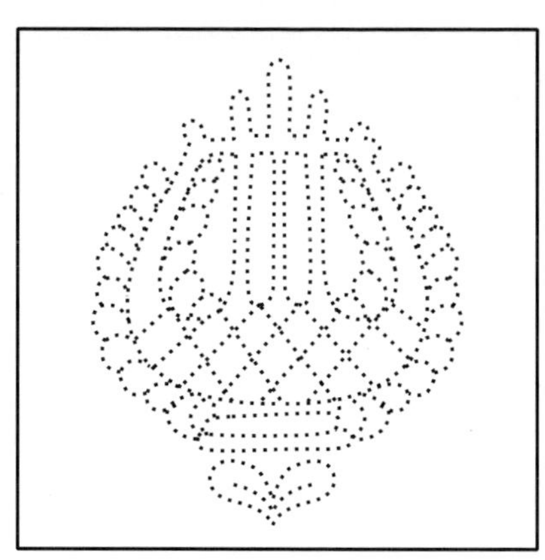
16.20 Harp;
Figure 10-16

16.20 Bow;
Figure 10-17; Plate 9-1

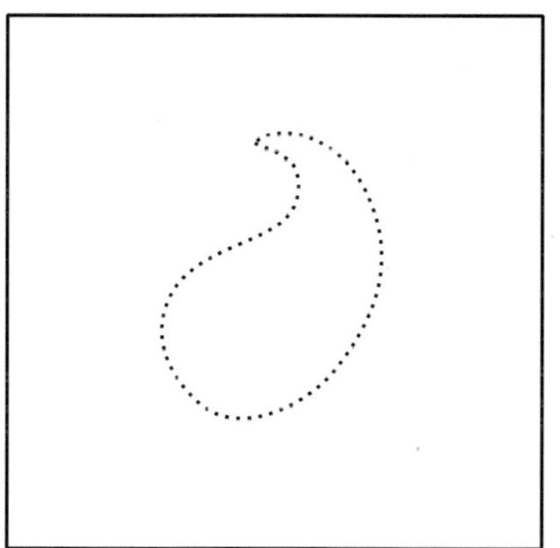
16.30 Teardrop;
Figure 10-10

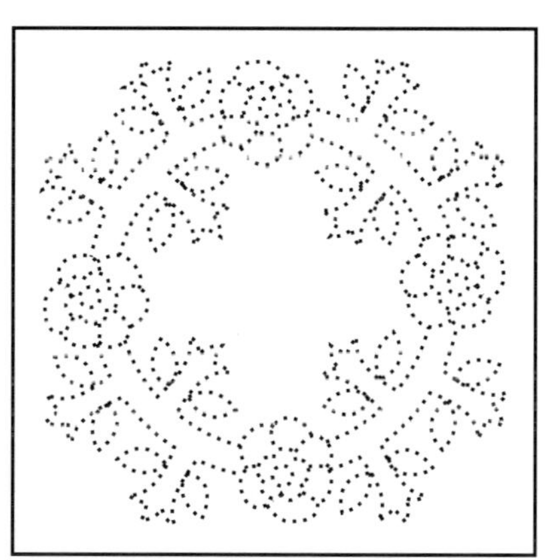
16.31 President's Wreath;
Figure 10-14

16.32 Amish Fancy;
Figure 10-18

16.40 Hands;
Figure 10-7

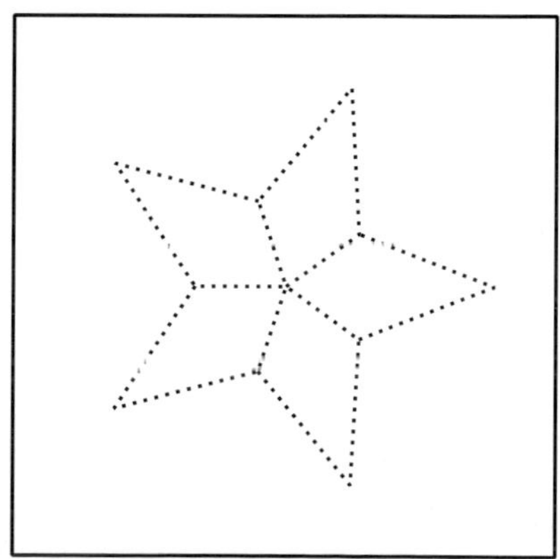
16.50 Five-Pointed Star;
Figure 10-19

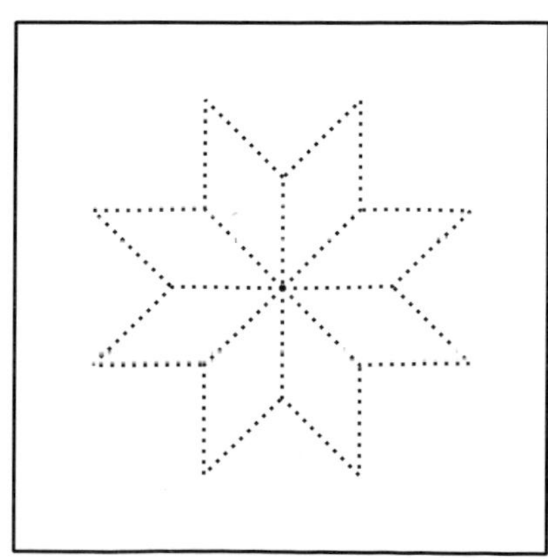
16.51 Eight-Pointed Star;
Figure 10-20

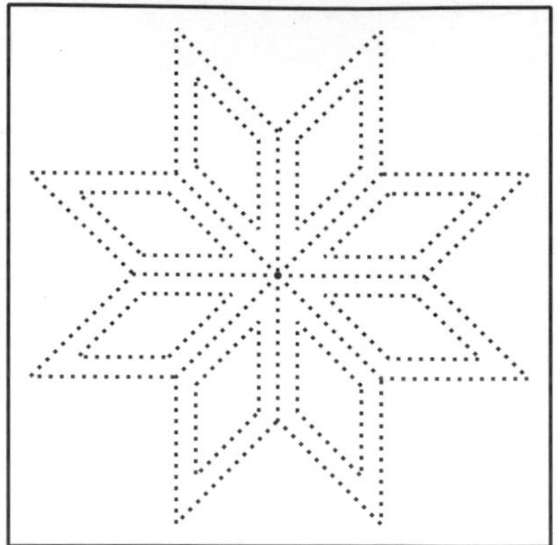

16.52 Eight-Pointed Star I;
Figure 10-21

17.01 Fleur-de-lis;
Figure 10-23

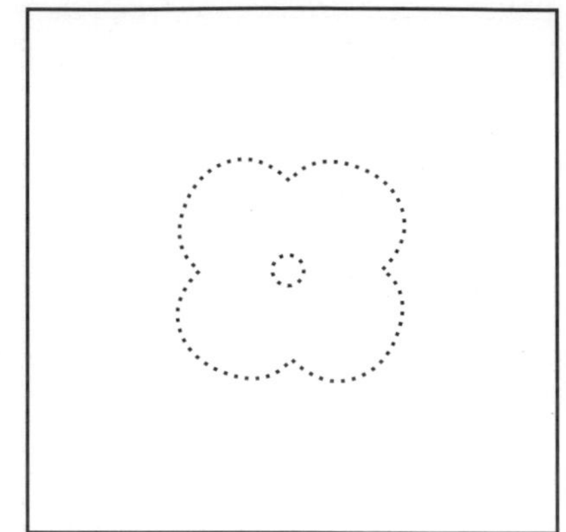

17.02 Simple Flower, Amish;
Figure 10-24

17.10 Floral;
Figure 10-25; Plate 10-1

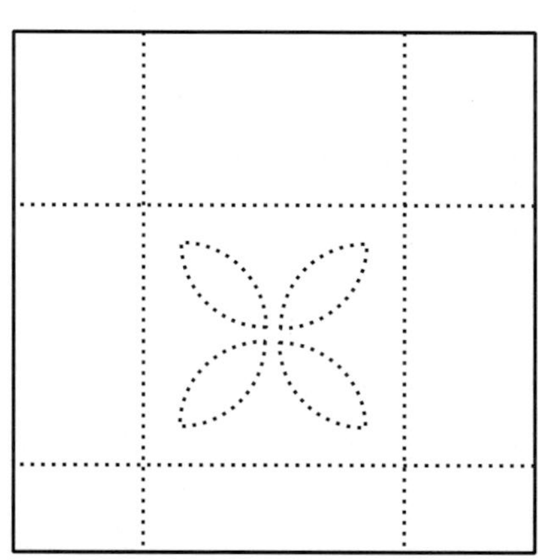

17.11 Simple Floral;
Figure 7-44

17.12 Four-Petaled Flower;
Figure 7-45; Plate 7-3

17.13 Four Petal Flower;
Figure 10-26

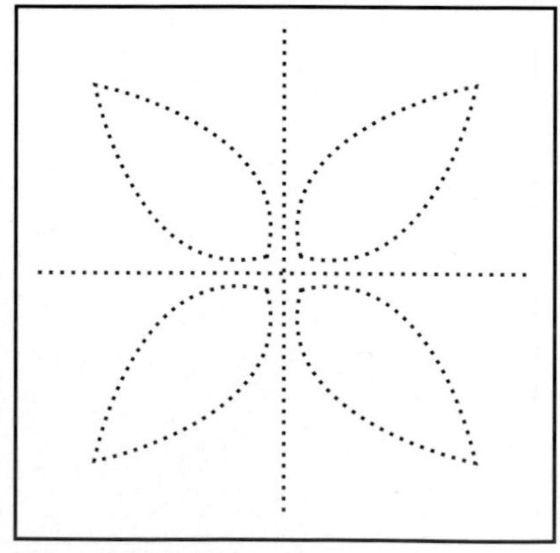

17.14 Rosette;
Figure 10-27

17.15 Amish Flower;
Figure 10-28

17.16 Sunflower;
Figure 10-29

17.17 Dahlia;
Figure 10-81

17.18 Amish Sunflower;
Figure 10-41

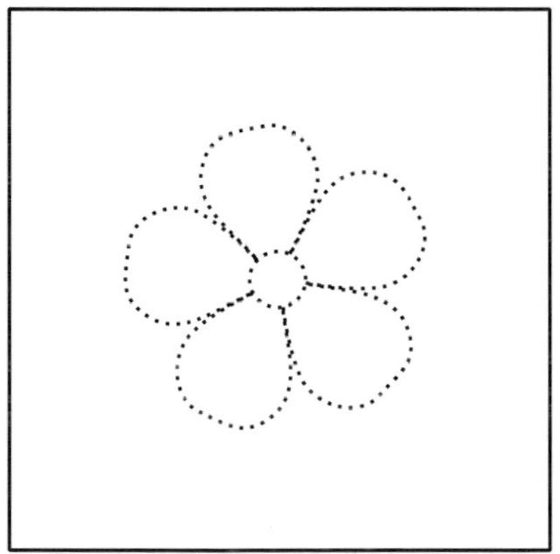
17.20 Amish Rose;
Figure 10-33

17.21 Dog Rose;
Figure 10-35; Plate 10-4

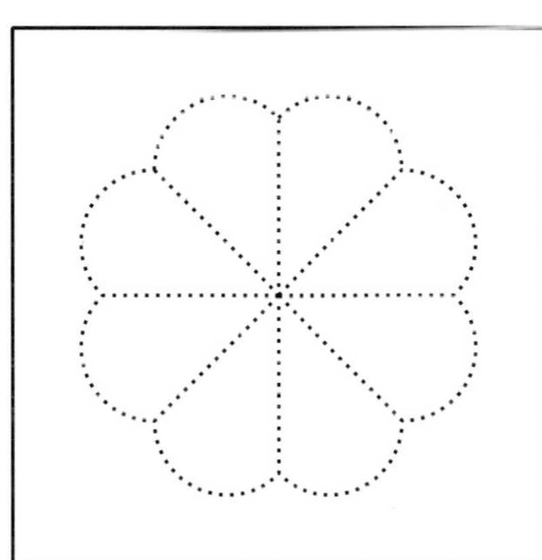
17.30 Pinwheel;
Figure 10-31

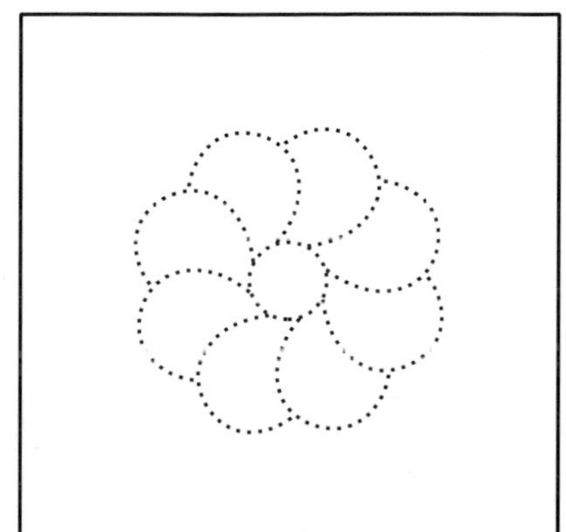
17.31 Traditional Rose;
Figure 10-37; Plate 8-4

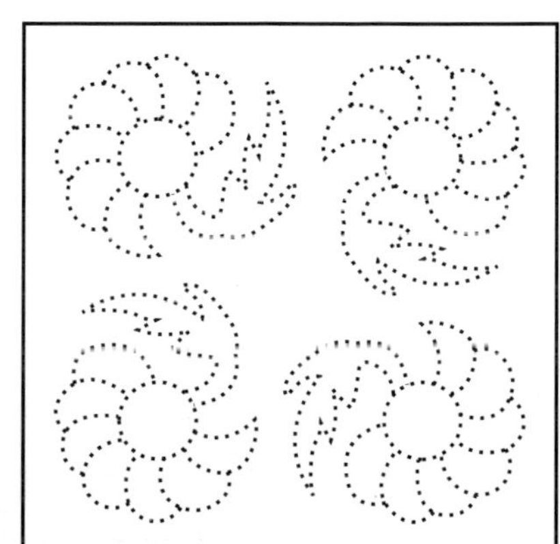
17.32 Four Flowers;
Figure 10-38

17.40 Swirling Daisy;
Figure 10-39

17.50 Thistle;
Figure 10-42

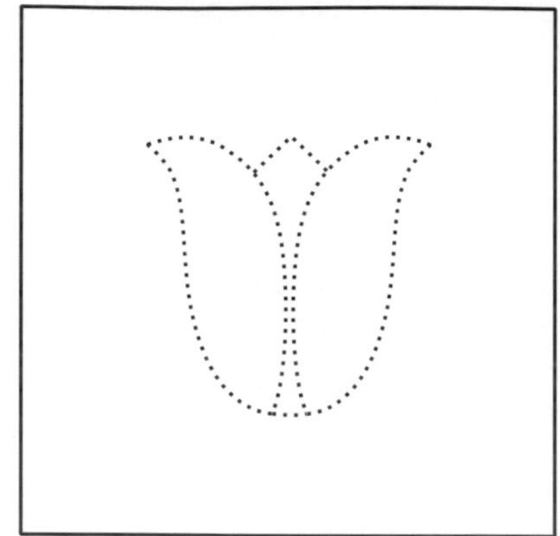

17.60 Tulip;
Figure 10-43; Plate 9-1

17.70 Trumpet Vine;
Figure 10-44

18.01 Shamrock;
Figure 10-45

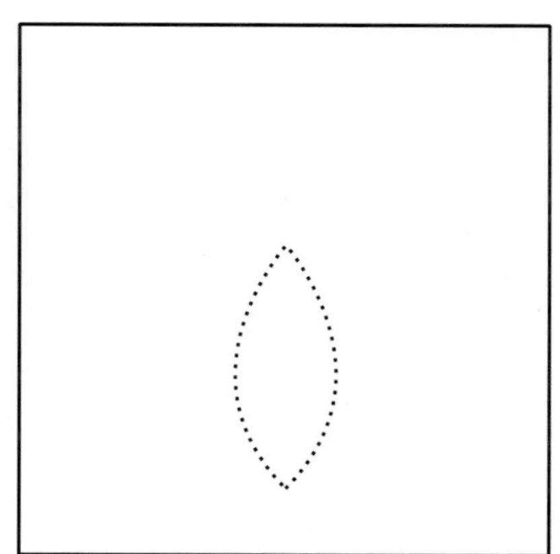

18.10 Laurel Leaf;
Figure 10-46; Plate 10-1

18.11 Laurel Leaves on Stem;
Figure 10-47

18.12 Trailing Leaf Design;
Figure 10-48

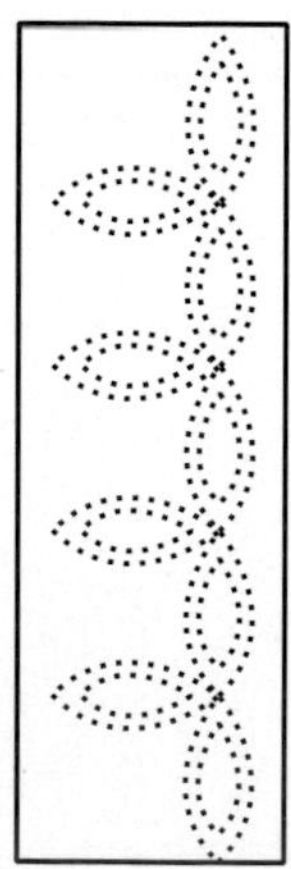

18.13 Laurel Leaf
Border; Figure 10-49

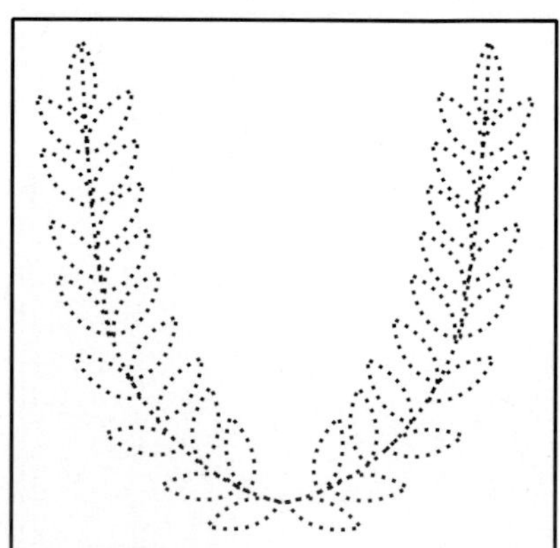

18.14 Laurel Leaves;
Figure 10-50

18.15 Split Feather Leaf;
Figure 10-51

18.20 Leafy Scroll;
Figure 10-79

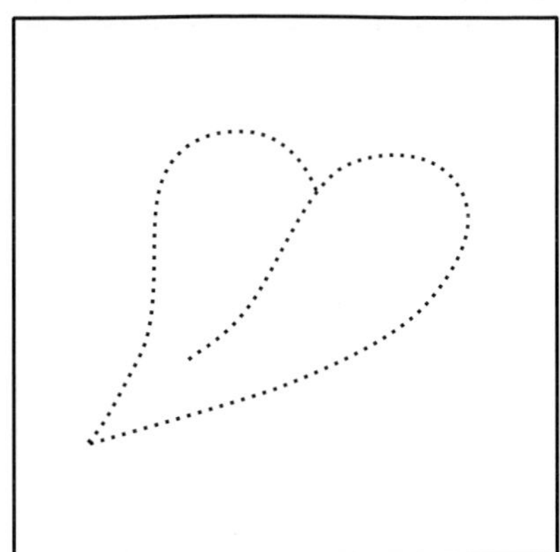

18.30 Ivy Leaf;
Figure 10-52

18.31 Maple Leaf;
Figure 10-53

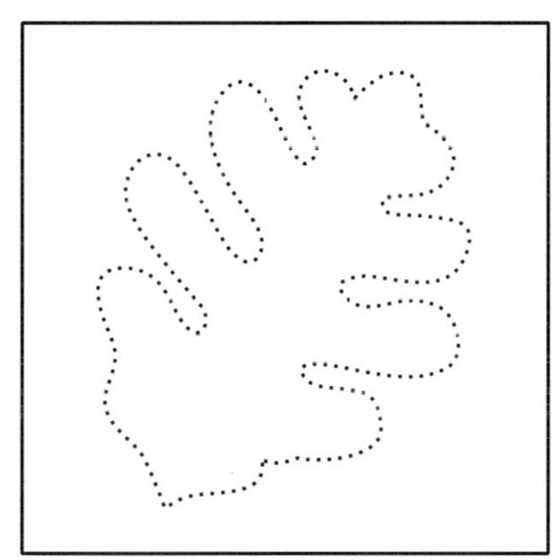

18.32 Oak Leaf;
Figure 10-54

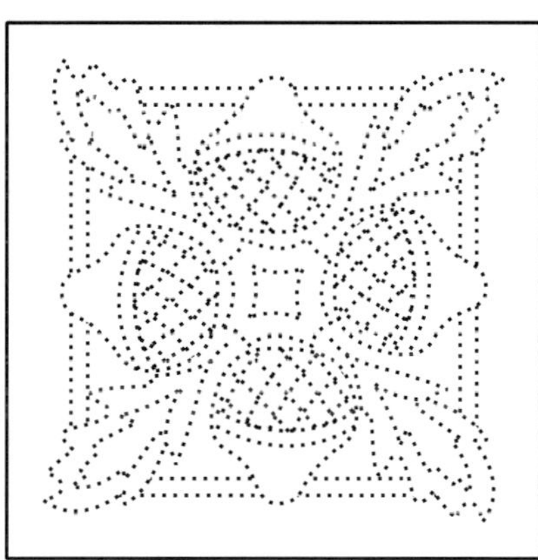

18.33 Oak Leaf and Acorn;
Figure 10-55

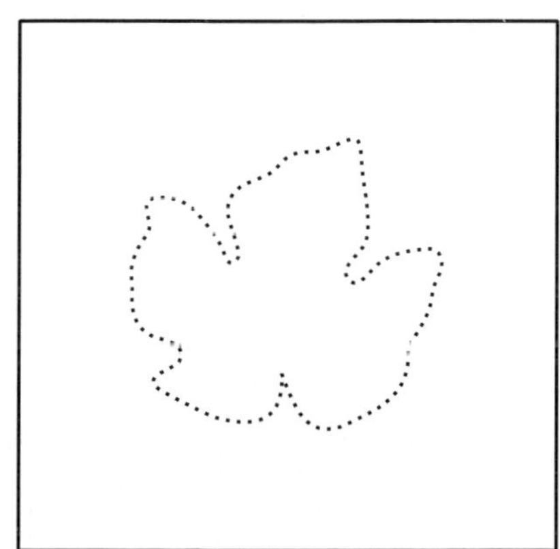

18.34 Grape Leaf;
Figure 10-59

18.40 Leaf Spray;
Figure 10-56

18.41 Acanthus;
Figure 10-57; Plate 10-3

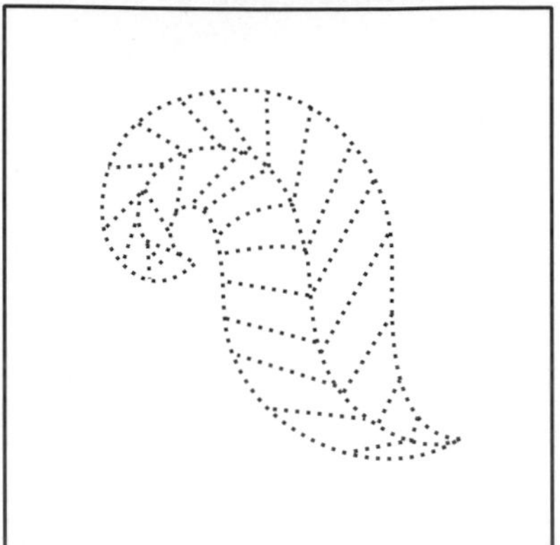

18.50 Curled Leaf;
Figure 10-58

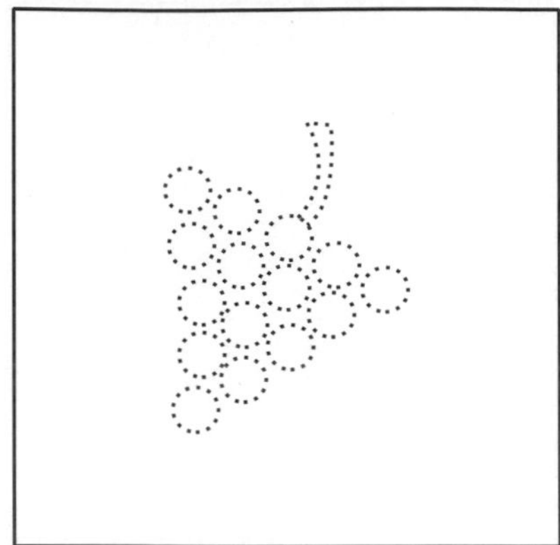

19.01 Grapes;
Figure 10-60

19.02 Grapes and Leaves;
Figure 10-61; Plate 3-3

19.03 Vine with Grapes
and Leaves; Figure 10-62

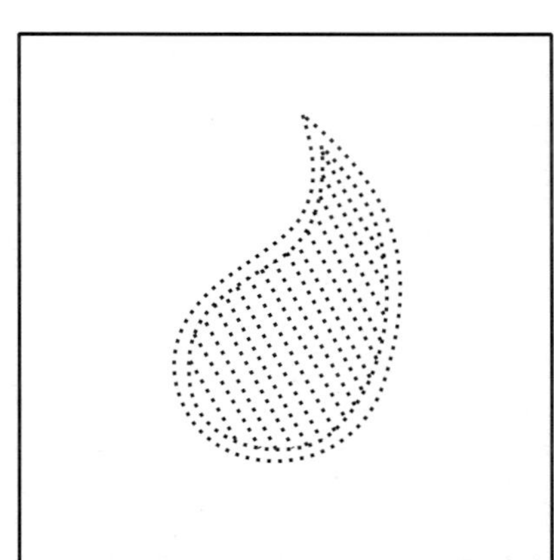

19.20 Paisley II;
Figure 10-63

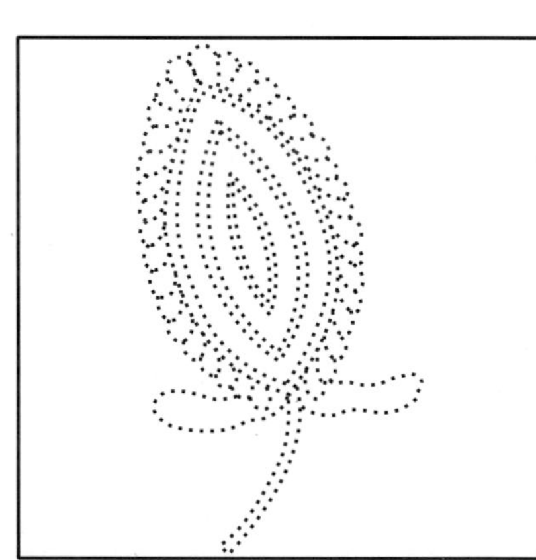

19.21 Pomegranate;
Figure 10-64

20.01 Butterfly;
Figure 10-65; Plate 8-4; 9-1

21.01 Bird;
Figure 10-66; Plate 10-4

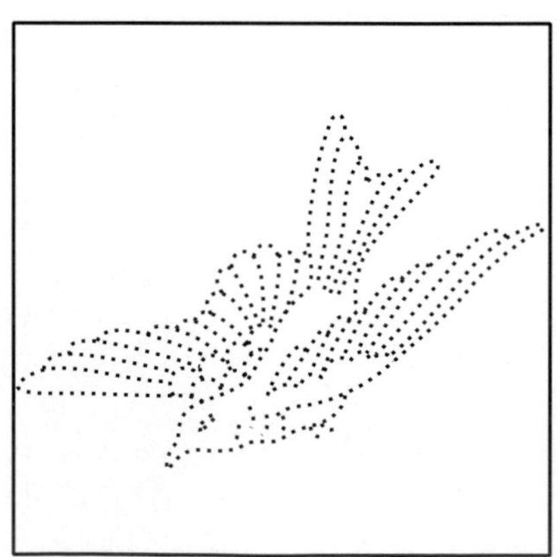

21.02 Bird II;
Figure 10-67

21.03 Dove of Peace;
Figure 10-68

21.04 Eagle;
Figure 10-69

22.01 Shell;
Figure 10-70

22.10 Snowflake;
Figure 10-71

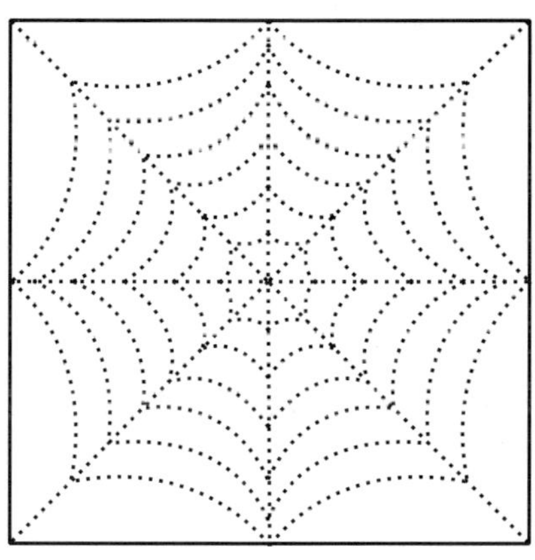

22.20 Spiderweb;
Figure 10-72

22.30 Waves;
Figure 10-73; Plate 10-2

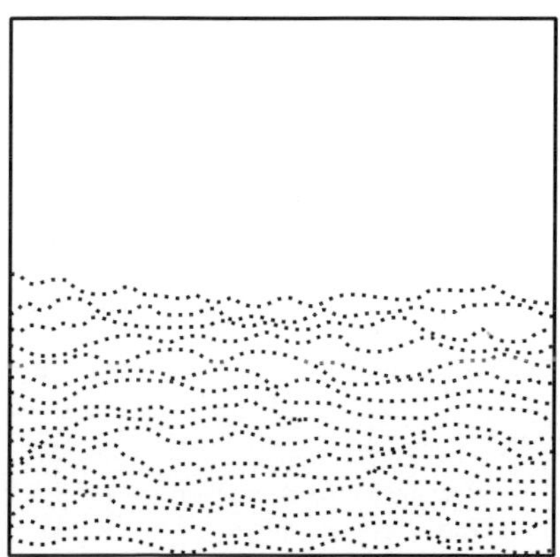

22.31 Wrinkle Quilting;
Figure 10-74

Alphabetical Index of Designs for Quilting

Acanthus **144,** 158, *191*
Amish Border Triangle 24, *169*
Amish Fancy 149, *187*
Amish Feathers 142
Amish Flower 152, *188*
Amish Rose 153, *189*
Amish Sunflower 155, *189*
Anchor 147, *186*
Arcs 91, *176*
Baptist Fan 82
Bars 15, 17, *168*
Basket Weave 40, *171*
Basketweave 28, 35, **144**
Bird **144,** 161, *192*
Bird II 161, *192*
Bow **124,** 149, *187*
Bowtie 163, *186*
Box 33
Box Links 47, *171*
Braid 110, 115
Braided Cable 117
Braided Rope 112, *180*
Braided Triple Cable 118, *181*
Bricks **14,** 18, *168*
Broken Plaid 36, *170*
Bunched 72
Butterfly **106, 124,** 160, *192*
By the Piece ... **14, 50, 68,** 69, **76, 92, 106,** *174*
Cable **14,** 115, 118
Chain 115, 117, 118
Chain Links 121, *181*
Chain Quilting 80
Chain Triple Cable 118, *181*
Chain Twist 119, *181*
Channel 15
Checkerboard 17, 33, *170*
Cherry Basket 148, *186*
Chevron 46, 66
Church Window, Filled 79, *175*
Church Window, Plain **106,** *175*
Circle in a Circle 85, *177*
Circle in a Circle Variation 85, *177*
Circle Marking Template 82
Circle of Feathered Swirls 137
Circle of Hearts 128, *182*
Circles 83, *176*
Circles and Straight Lines 165
Circles Chain 83, *176*
Clam 74
Clamshell 74, **76,** 82, *175*
Clamshell and Echo 164
Clamshell Rope 105, *179*
Classical Cable 119, *181*
Clouds in Triangle 75
Concentric Arcs 82
Concentric Circles **76,** 84, 86, *177*
Concentric Design Lines **68,** 71, *174*
Concentric Diamonds 58, *173*
Concentric Diamonds with Diagonals .59, *173*
Concentric Fans 85, *176*
Concentric Lozenge 38
Concentric Ridges 70
Concentric Rings 84
Concentric Squares 18, 38, **68,** *170*
Concentric Squares Variation 38, *170*
Concentric Squares Variation I 39, *170*
Continuous Scroll 142
Continuous Vine Feathers 140
Contour Quilting 70
Cornucopia 148, *186*
Crescent 96, *178*
Crisscross 34, *170*
Cross 145, *186*
Cross Bar Quilting 31
Cross-diamond Pattern 53
Cross-in-a-Circle 90, *177*
Crossed Diagonals 31
Crosses 37, *170*
Crown 137
Curled Leaf 159, *192*
Curved Feathers 135
Dahlia 164, *189*
Demilunes 78
Diagonal Background 51
Diagonal Crosshatching 51
Diagonal Herringbone 51
Diagonal Lines **14, 50,** 51, **76, 106, 124,** *172*
Diagonal Parallel 51
Diagonal Pipe Line 51
Diagonal Waffle 33
Diamond 31, 33, **50,** 53, **124,** *172*
Diamond and Rope 107, *180*
Diamond and Rope Cable 108, *180*
Diamond Cable 122, *181*
Diamond Chain 64
Diamond Cross-hatching 53
Diamond Rope 123, *180*
Diamond String 122, *182*
Diamond Weave 60, *173*
Diamond-Set Squares 48, *171*
Diaper 57, *173*
Ditch Quilting 70
Dog Rose **144,** 154, *189*
Double Cable **106,** 115, 116, *181*
Double Cable Variation **106,** 116, *181*
Double Chevron 66, *172*
Double Clamshell 75, *175*
Double Crosshatch 17
Double Crosshatching 35
Double Diagonal Lines **32,** 52, *172*
Double Diamond and Rope 107, *180*
Double Diamonds 35
Double Hanging Diamond 56, *172*
Double Line Crosshatching 35, 54
Double Line Diamond **50,** 54, *172*
Double Line Squares 35
Double Parallel 52
Double Zig-zag 23, *169*
Double Zig-zag and Clamshells 165
Double Zig-zag and Fan 165
Dove of Peace 161, *193*
Eagle 161, *193*
Echo **32, 50, 68,** 70, **124,** *174*
Eight Row Cable 119
Eight-Pointed Star 150, *187*
Eight-Pointed Star I 150, *188*
Elbow 18, 38, 82, *168*
Ellipse 103
Elongated Z 20, *168*
Equal-Sided Triangle 29, *169*
Fan **76,** 82, **106,** *176*
Feather Band 130, *184*
Feather Circle 137
Feather Hammock 138
Feather Rosette 136, 154, *184*
Feather Scroll 134, 142, *183*
Feather Swag **32,** 138, *183*
Feather Tendrils 135
Feather Twist 141, *185*
Feather Variations **124**
Feather Vines 140
Feathered Cable 141, *185*
Feathered Circle **92,** 137, *183*
Feathered Circle-in-a-Square 139, *183*
Feathered Garland **106, 124,** 142, *185*
Feathered Harp 139, *184*
Feathered Heart 139, *184*
Feathered Lyre 139
Feathered Pineapple **124,** 140, *184*
Feathered Square Variation **14**
Feathered Triangle 143, *183*
Feathered Vine **68,** 140, *185*
Feathered Wreath 137
Feathers **50**
Fiddlehead **124,** 136, *183*
Finger Feather 142, *185*
Finial 154
Five-Pointed Star 150, *187*
Five-Strand Cable 118
Fleur-de-lis 151, *188*
Floral **144,** 151, *188*
Floral Circles 88, *177*
Following Top Design 70
Four Flowers 154, *189*
Four Leaf Clover 156
Four Petal Flower 151, *188*
Four-Petaled Flower **92,** 104, *188*
Freehand 70
Gothic Fans 94, *178*
Grape Leaf 159, *191*
Grapes 159, *192*
Grapes and Leaves **32,** 159, *192*
Grid 31
Ground Pattern 31
Half Moons 78, *175*
Hands 147, *187*
Hanging Diamonds 55, *172*
Harp 149, *187*
Heart **124,** *182*
Heart Corner Design 126, *182*
Heart String 127, *182*
Heart Wreath 129, *182*
Hearts **124**
Herringbone 46, 66, *171*
Hex Wheel 146, *185*
Hexfeiss 164, *185*
Horn of Plenty 148, *186*
Horseshoe 145, *186*
In the Ditch **50,** 70, **76, 92, 144,** *174*
Interlaced Diamonds 64, *173*
Interlocking Circles 80
Interlocking Diamonds 64
Interlocking Ovals 95
Interlocking Squares 37

Key
Roman = Instructional Text
Bold = Plate Numbers
Italic = Numerical Index of Designs

Interlocking Swirl 86, *177*
Inward-Spiraling Maze 41, *171*
Ivy Leaf 157, *191*
Lace Vein Feather 138, *184*
Laurel Leaf 156, *190*
Laurel Leaf Border 157, *190*
Laurel Leaves 157, *190*
Laurel Leaves on Stem 156, *190*
Leaf Spray 158, *191*
Leafy Scroll 164, *191*
Leaves **144**
Lemon Peel 80, 81
Line of Hearts 128, *182*
Line of Hearts Variation 128, *182*
Lined Hammock 98
Linked Squares 43, *171*
Linked Squares II 44, *171*
Long Diamond **32,** 61, **92,** *173*
Long Diamond with Swag 62, *173*
Lozenge 53, 95, 113, 115, *180*
Lyre 149, *187*
Maple Leaf 158, *191*
Meandering 72, **124, 144**
Melon 103
Methodist Fan 82
Multiple Line Cable 117
Oak Leaf 158, *191*
Oak Leaf and Acorn 158, *191*
Ocean Wave Quilting 87, *175*
One-Patch Pieced Pattern 72, *175*
Orange Peel 80, 81, 103
Ostrich Feather 134
Ostrich Plume **124,** 134, *183*
Outline Quilting **32,** 69, **92, 106,** *174*
Outline the Piece 69
Oval Chain 95, *178*
Ovals **50,** 93, *178*
Overlapping Circles 81, *176*
Overlapping Ovals 94, *178*
Overlapping Shells 74
Overlapping Swags 100, *179*
Paisley **124,** 137, *184*
Paisley II, ...160, *192*
Paper Folding 12
Parallel Lines, Double 16, 52, **76,** *168*
Parallel Lines, Single .**14,** 15, **50, 68, 92, 144,** *168*
Parallel Lines, Triple 16, *168*
Parallel Triangles 25
Peacock Fan 82, 143, *184*
Pentagon 21, *168*
Pineapple 140
Pinwheel 153, 154, *189*
Pipe Stem 147, *186*
Plaid 17, **32,** 35, *170*
Plait 118
Plumed Swastika 135, *184*
Pomegranate 160, *192*
Pomegranite 160
President's Wreath 148, *187*
Pressed Quilting 72
Prince's Feather 135
Princess Feather **32, 92,** 135, *183*
Princess Feather Plume 135
Pumpkin Seed 103, *179*
Pumpkin Seed Border I 104, *179*
Pumpkin Seed Border II 104, *179*
Pyramidal Pattern 65, *174*
Radiating Curves 97, *178*
Radiating Lines **68,** 71, *174*
Rainbow 82
Rays of Quilting 71
Relief Quilting 69
Ripple 72
Rising Sun 150, *185*
Rope **92,** 109, 115, 118, *179*
Rose **76**
Rosette 152, *188*
Running Diamond 62, *173*
Running Double Diamond 63, *173*
Running Feather 141
Running Rope II 111, *180*
Running Rope Pattern 111, *176*
Running Single Cable ....114 , *180*
Sawtooth 22, *169*
Scalloped Chain 115
Scallops 77, *175*
Scroll 102, *178*
Scroll Variation 103, *179*
Scrolled Frame 102
Scrolling Vine **92,** 101, *178*
Self Quilting 69
Shamrock 156, *190*
Shell 74, 82, 162, *193*
Shell Variation 93
Shells 77
Simple Arcs 91, *176*
Simple Chevron 25
Simple Floral 104, *188*
Simple Flower, Amish 151, *188*
Simple Grid 31
Simple Plaid 35
Simple Scroll **92,** 101, *179*
Single Cable 113, 115, *180*
Single Cable-Pumpkin Seed 114, *180*
Snail-Creep 86
Snowflake 162, *193*
Spiderweb 162, *193*
Spiral **32,** 86, *177*
Split Feather Leaf 157, *191*
Spool 73
Square in a Square **32,** 42, *171*
Squares 31, 33
Squares Crosshatch **14,** 31, **32, 68, 76, 92, 144,** *169*
Squares Crosshatching 31
Standing Diamonds 64, *173*
Star Flower 89, *177*
Star Flower Variation 90, *177*
Star Hex 146, *185*
Steps 46
Stippling 72, *174*
Straight Feather **92,** 130, 133, *183*
Straight Lines and Diagonal Lines 165
Straight Parallel Lines 15
Straight Plume 130, 133
Streak of Lightning 19
Sunflower 152, *189*
Sunflower and Spirals 164
Swag **32, 92,** 98, **144,** *179*
Swag and Traditional Rose 165
Swag Variation and Fan 165
Swag Variation with Tassels 99, *178*
Swirling Daisy 155, *189*
Swirling Swastikas 164, *185*
Teacup **76,** 80, **106,** *176*
Teardrop 147, *187*
Teardrop and Elbow 163
Teardrop and Ellipse 163
Tents **14,** 27, *169*
Thimble Quilting 74
Thistle 155, *190*
Traditional Applique Pattern 72, *175*
Traditional Pieced Pattern 72, 73, *175*
Traditional Rose **106,** 154, *189*
Trailing Leaf Design 157, *190*
Triangle Elbow 26, *169*
Triangle Elbow and Fan 164
Triangles 28, **92,** *169*
Triple Cable **106,** 117, *181*
Triple Diagonal Lines 53, *172*
Triple Hanging Diamonds 57, *172*
Triple Plaid 36, **106,** *170*
Triple Rodding 53
Trumpet Vine 156, *190*
Tulip **124,** 156, *190*
Twist 115
Twist Cable 118, *181*
Twisted Braid 110, *180*
Twisted Rope 110, 116, *180*
Twisted Rope and Traditional Rose 165
Twisted Rope Cable 119, *181*
Twisted Rope Cable Variation 119, *181*
Undulating Feather 141
Urns **144**
Vermicelli 72
Vine with Grapes and Leaves 160, *192*
Waffle Quilting 31
Wall Sweep 82
Wave 25, 26, 82, *169*
Wave Quilting 101
Waves **144,** 162, *193*
Weave Pattern 39, *171*
Weave Variation 40, *179*
Weaving Diamond Cable 123, *182*
Welsh Pear 160
Wheel 146, *185*
Wheel Star 146, *186*
Wine Glass 80
Worm 115, 117, 118
Woven Squares 45, *171*
Wrinkle Quilting 163, *193*
X's 72, *174*
Zig-Zag 19, 20, 22, 28, **144,** *168*
Zig-Zag Border Design 23
Zig-Zag II 25, *169*

Key
Roman = Instructional Text
Bold = Plate Numbers
Italic = Numerical Index of Designs

Bibliography

Atkins, Jacqueline M. & Phyllis A. Tepper. ***New York Beauties: Quilts from the Empire State***. New York: Dutton Studio Books, 1992.

Bowman, Doris M. ***The Smithsonian Treasury American Quilts***. New York: Gramercy Book, a Random House Company; Smithsonian Institution, 1991.

Brackman, Barbara...et. al. ***KANSAS Quilts & Quilters***. Lawrence, Kansas: University Press of Kansas, 1993.

Brackman, Barbara. ***Clues in the Calico***. USA: EPM Publications, Inc., 1989.

Bullard, Lacy Folmar & Betty Jo Shiell. ***Chintz Quilts: Unfading Glory***. Tallahassee, Florida: Serendipity Publishers, 1983.

Carlson, Linda Giesler. ***Roots, Feathers & Blooms***. Paducah, Kentucky: American Quilter's Society, 1994.

Chandler, Elizabeth & Joanne Donahue. ***Quilting Designs from Grandma's Attic***. Evansville, Indiana: Lizanne Publishing Company, 1994.

Cleland, Lee. ***Quilting Makes the Quilt***. Bothell, Washington: That Patchwork Place, Inc., 1994.

Cochran, Rachel...et. al. (The Heritage Quilt Project of New Jersey). ***New Jersey Quilts 1777 to 1950***. Paducah, Kentucky: American Quilter's Society, 1992.

Colby, Averil. ***Patchworks Quilts***. Denmark: Charles Scribner's Sons, 1965.

—-. ***Quilting.*** New York: Charles Scribner's Sons, 1971.

Cory, Pepper. ***Quilting Designs from the Amish***. N.p.: Pepper Cory, 1985.

—-. ***Quilting Designs from Antique Quilts***. Lafayette, California: C & T Publishing, 1987.

Crews, Patricia Cox and Ronald C. Naugle, eds. ***Nebraska Quilts & Quiltmakers***. Lincoln, Nebraska: University of Nebraska Press, 1991.

Cross, Mary Bywater. ***Treasures in the Trunk***. Nashville, Tennessee: Rutledge Hill Press, 1993.

Eanes, Ellen Fickling ...et. al. ***North Carolina Quilts*** Chapel Hill, North Carolina: The University of North Carolina Press, 1988.

Elbert, E. Duane & Rachel Kamm Elbert. ***History From the Heart: Quilt Paths Across Illinois***. Nashville, Tennessee: Rutledge Hill Press, 1993.

Fall, Cheryl. ***Treasury of Quilting Patterns***. New York: Sterling Publishing Company, 1994.

Finley, Ruth E. ***Old Patchwork Quilts and the Women Who Made Them***. Ruth E. Finley, 1929; McLean, Virginia: EPM Publications, 1992.

Fons, Marianne. ***Fine Feathers***. Lafayette, California: C & T Publishing, 1988.

Frager, Dorothy. ***The Quilting Primer.*** Pennsylvania: Chilton Company, 1974.

Gammel, Alice I. ***Polly Prindle's Book of American Patchwork Quilts***. New York: Grosset & Dunlap, 1973.

Hall, Carrie A. & Rose G. Kretsinger. ***The Romance of the Patchwork Quilt***. The Caxton Printers, Ltd.; 1935, Mrs. L. G. Paxton, 1963; New York: Dover Publications, 1988.

Hargrave, Harriet. ***Heirloom Machine Quilting.*** Lafayette, California: C & T Publishing, 1990.

Hassel, Carla J. ***You Can Be a Super Quilter!***. Des Moines, Iowa: Wallace-Homestead Book Company, 1980.

Ickis, Marguerite. ***The Standard Book of Quilt Making and Collecting***. Greysone Press, 1949; New York, New York: Dover Publications, Inc., 1959.

Indiana Quilt Registry Project, Inc., ***The. Quilts of Indiana.*** Indiana: Indiana University Press, 1991.

Jenkins, Susan & Linda Seward. ***The American Quilt Story***. Emmaus, Pennsylvania: Rodale Press, 1991.

Kentucky Quilt Project, Inc., The. ***Kentucky Quilts 1800-1900***. Louisville, Kentucky: The Kentucky Quilt Project, Inc., 1982.

Lasansky, Jeanette. ***In the Heart of Pennsylvania***. Lewisburg, Pennsylvania: Oral Traditions Project of the Union County Historical Society, 1985.

Laury, Jean Ray & The California Heritage Quilt Project. ***Ho For California! Pioneer Women and Their Quilts***. New York, New York: E. P. Dutton, 1990.

Lawther, Gail. ***The Complete Quilting Course***. London: Quarto Publishing, 1992.

Marston, Gwen & Joe Cunningham. ***Quilting with Style.*** Paducah, Kentucky: American Quilter's Society, 1993.

—-. ***Amish Quilting Pattern***s. New York: Dover Publications, 1987.

Martin, Nancy J. ***Threads of Time***. Bothell, Washington: That Patchwork Place, Inc., 1990.

McCall's Needlework & Crafts Publications, eds. ***The McCall's Book of Quilts***. New York, New York: Simon & Schuster, 1975.

McKim, Ruby. ***One Hundred and One Patchwork Patterns***. McKim Studios, 1931; New York: Dover Publications, 1962.

Orlofsky, Patsy & Myron. ***Quilts in America***. McGraw-Hill Book Company, 1974. Abbeville Press, Inc., 1992.

Osler, Dorothy. ***Quilting.*** London: Ferry House Merehurst, Ltd., 1991.

Pfeffer, Susanna. ***Quilt Masterpieces***. Hugh Lauter Levin Associates, Inc., 1988; New York: Park Lane, 1990.

Ramsey, Bets & Merikay Waldvogel. ***The Quilts of Tennessee***. Nashville, Tennessee: Rutledge Hill Press, Inc., 1986.

Regan, Jennifer. ***American Quilts***. New York: Gallery Books, 1989.

Safford, Carleton & Robert Bishop. ***America's Quilts and Coverlets***. New York: E. P. Dutton & Company, Inc., 1972.

Schorsch, Anita. ***Plain & Fancy: Country Quilts of the Pennsylvania-Germans***. New York: Sterling Publishing Company, Inc., 1992.

Spencer Museum of Art. ***American Patchwork Quilt***. Lawrence, Kansas: The University of Kansas, 1987.

Tribuno, Bertha Reth. ***Heritage Quilts and Quilting Designs II.*** Cedar Rapids, Iowa: Bertha Reth Tribuno & Dorathy Franson, 1985.

Tribuno, Bertha Reth and Dorathy Franson, ed. ***Heritage Quilting Designs***. Cedar Rapids, Iowa: n.p., 1981.

Twelker, Nancyann Johnson. ***Women & Their Quilts - A Washington State Centennial Tribute***. Bothell, Washington: That Patchwork Place, Inc., 1988.

Waldvogel, Merikay. ***Soft Covers For Hard Times: Quiltmaking & The Great Depression.*** Nashville, Tennessee: Rutledge Hill Press, 1990.

Webster, Marie D. ***Quilts Their Story and How to Make Them***. Santa Barbara, California: Practical Patchwork, 1990.

Wigginton, Eliot and Margie Bennett, eds. ***Foxfire 9.*** New York: Anchor Books, 1986.

Woodard, Thomas K. & Blanche Greenstein. ***Crib Quilts and Other Small Wonders.*** New York: E. P. Dutton, 1981.

About the Author

Phyllis D. Miller has been making quilts since the summer of 1968. She has made numerous quilts and wallhangings since that beginning. Her quilts have been exhibited and won awards on the local, state, and national levels.

Phyllis graduated from Berea College, Berea, Kentucky, in 1963 with a B. S. degree in business administration. She is well known in the quilt world as a teacher and for her organizational abilities.

She is an active supporter and member of the Kentucky Heritage Quilt Society and is currently the museum and archives committee chairman. In this capacity, she oversees the Kentucky Quilt Registry which is an on-going documentation project. Her duties in this position include training volunteers to register the quilts of Kentucky at Quilt Registry days that are held in the counties of the state. She is past president of the Kentucky Heritage Quilt Society and was the editor of the KHQS newletter. She is the founder of the Kentucky Heritage Appliqué Society, a KHQS auxiliary group.

Phyllis feels that one of her most rewarding accomplishments was starting Quilter's Day Out in Kentucky so that quilters would have one day each year when they could be together. This was a way to bring a statewide organization to the quilters. This day of celebration was later declared National Quilting Day by the National Quilting Association and is now celebrated around the world.

She is a member of the National Quilting Association and is a past first vice president and assistant treasurer. She was president and treasurer of the Murray Quilt Lovers and is a member of the Paducah Quilt 'n Sew On group.

Phyllis's favorite parts of quilting are designing the quilt and choosing an appropriate design for the quilting of the piece. She promotes using creative and innovative quilting designs to make every quilt unique. She makes both traditional and contemporary quilts often combining both ideas in one quilt.

AQS Books on Quilts

This is only a partial listing of the books on quilts that are available from the American Quilter's Society. AQS books are known the world over for their timely topics, clear writing, beautiful color photographs, and accurate illustrations and patterns. Most of the following books are available from your local bookseller, quilt shop, or public library. If you are unable to locate certain titles in your area, you may order by mail from the AMERICAN QUILTER'S SOCIETY, P.O. Box 3290, Paducah, KY 42002-3290. Customers with Visa or MasterCard may phone in orders from 7:00–4:00 CST, Monday–Friday, Toll Free 1-800-626-5420. Add $2.00 for postage for the first book ordered and $0.40 for each additional book. Include item number, title, and price when ordering. Allow 14 to 21 days for delivery.

2282 **Adapting Architectural Details for Quilts,** Carol Wagner $12.95
1907 **American Beauties: Rose & Tulip Quilts,** Marston & Cunningham $14.95
4543 **American Quilt Blocks: 50 Patterns for 50 States,** Beth Summers $18.95
4696 **Amish Kinder Komforts** Betty Havig $14.95
2121 **Appliqué Designs: My Mother Taught Me to Sew,** Faye Anderson $12.95
3790 **Appliqué Patterns from Native American Beadwork Designs,** Dr. Joyce Mori $14.95
2122 **The Art of Hand Appliqué,** Laura Lee Fritz $14.95
2099 **Ask Helen: More About Quilting Designs,** Helen Squire $14.95
2207 **Award-Winning Quilts: 1985-1987** $24.95
2354 **Award-Winning Quilts: 1988-1989** $24.95
3425 **Award-Winning Quilts: 1990-1991** $24.95
3791 **Award-Winning Quilts: 1992-1993** $24.95
4593 **Blossoms by the Sea: Making Ribbon Flowers for Quilts,** Faye Labanaris $24.95
4697 **Caryl Bryer Fallert: A Spectrum of Quilts, 1983-1995,** Caryl Bryer Fallert $24.95
3926 **Celtic Style Floral Appliqué** Scarlett Rose $14.95
2208 **Classic Basket Quilts,** Elizabeth Porter & Marianne Fons $16.95
2355 **Creative Machine Art,** Sharee Dawn Roberts $24.95
1820 **Dear Helen, Can You Tell Me?...** Helen Squire $12.95
3870 **Double Wedding Ring Quilts: New Quilts from an Old Favorite** $14.95
3399 **Dye Painting!** Ann Johnston $19.95
2030 **Dyeing & Overdyeing of Cotton Fabrics,** Judy Mercer Tescher $9.95
3468 **Encyclopedia of Pieced Quilt Patterns,** compiled by Barbara Brackman $34.95
3846 **Fabric Postcards** Judi Warren $22.95
4594 **Firm Foundations: Techniques & Quilt Blocks for Precision Piecing,** Jane Hall & Dixie Haywood $18.95
2356 **Flavor Quilts for Kids to Make** Jennifer Amor $12.95
2381 **From Basics to Binding: A Complete Guide to Making Quilts,** Karen Kay Buckley $16.95
4526 **Gatherings: America's Quilt Heritage,** Kathlyn F. Sullivan $34.95
2097 **Heirloom Miniatures,** Tina M. Gravatt $9.95
4628 **Helen's Guide to quilting in the 21st century,** Helen Squire $16.95
2120 **The Ins and Outs: Perfecting the Quilting Stitch,** Patricia J. Morris $9.95
1906 **Irish Chain Quilts: A Workbook of Irish Chains** Joyce B. Peaden $14.95
3784 **Jacobean Appliqué: Book I, "Exotica,"** Patricia B. Campbell & Mimi Ayars, Ph.D $18.95
4544 **Jacobean Appliqué: Book II, "Romantica,"** Patricia B. Campbell & Mimi Ayars, Ph.D $18.95
3904 **The Judge's Task: How Award-Winning Quilts Are Selected,** Patricia J. Morris $19.95
4523 **Log Cabin Quilts: New Quilts from an Old Favorite** $14.95
4545 **Log Cabin with a Twist,** Barbara T. Kaempfer $18.95
4598 **Love to Quilt: Men's Vests,** Alexandra Capadalis Dupré $14.95
4753 **Love to Quilt: Historical Penny Squares,** Willa Baranowski $12.95
2206 **Marbling Fabrics for Quilts** Kathy Fawcett& Carol Shoaf $12.95
4514 **Mola Techniques for Today's Quilters,** Charlotte Patera $18.95
3330 **More Projects and Patterns: A Second Collection of Favorite Quilts,** Judy Florence $18.95
1981 **Nancy Crow: Quilts and Influences,** Nancy Crow $29.95
3331 **Nancy Crow: Work in Transition,** Nancy Crow $12.95
3332 **New Jersey Quilts – 1777 to 1950: Contributions to an American Tradition,** The Heritage Quilt Project of New Jersey $29.95
3927 **New Patterns from Old Architecture,** Carol Wagner $12.95
2153 **No Dragons on My Quilt,** Jean Ray Laury $12.95
4598 **Ohio Star Quilts: New Quilts from an Old Favorite** $16.95
3469 **Old Favorites in Miniature,** Tina Gravatt $15.95
4515 **Paint and Patches: Painting on Fabrics with Pigment,** Vicki L. Johnson $18.95
3333 **A Patchwork of Pieces: An Anthology of Early Quilt Stories 1845-1940,** complied by Cuesta Ray Benberry and Carol Pinney Crabb $14.95
4513 **Plaited Patchwork,** Shari Cole $19.95
3928 **Precision Patchwork for Scrap Quilts,** Jeannette Tousley Muir $12.95
4779 **Protecting Your Quilts: A Guide for Quilt Owners, Second Edition** $6.95
4542 **A Quilted Christmas,** edited by Bonnie Browning $18.95
2380 **Quilter's Registry,** Lynne Fritz $9.95
3467 **Quilting Patterns from Native American Designs,** Dr. Joyce Mori $12.95
3470 **Quilting with Style: Principles for Great Pattern Design,** Marston & Cunningham $24.95
2284 **Quiltmaker's Guide: Basics & Beyond,** Carol Doak $19.95
2257 **Quilts: The Permanent Collection – MAQS** $9.95
3793 **Quilts: The Permanent Collection – MAQS, Volume II** $9.95
3789 **Roots, Feathers & Blooms: 4-Block Quilts, Their History & Patterns, Book I,** Linda Carlson $16.95
4512 **Sampler Quilt Blocks from Native American Designs,** Dr. Joyce Mori $14.95
3796 **Seasons of the Heart & Home: Quilts for a Winter's Day,** Jan Patek $18.95
3761 **Seasons of the Heart & Home: Quilts for Summer Days,** Jan Patek $18.95
2357 **Sensational Scrap Quilts,** Darra Duffy Williamson $24.95
3375 **Show Me Helen...How to Use Quilting Designs,** Helen Squire $15.95
1790 **Somewhere in Between: Quilts and Quilters of Illinois,** Rita Barrow Barber $14.95
3794 **Spike & Zola: Patterns Designed for Laughter...and Appliqué, Painting, or Stenciling,** Donna French Collins $9.95
3929 **The Stori Book of Embellishing,** Mary Stori $16.95
3903 **Straight Stitch Machine Appliqué,** Letty Martin $16.95
3792 **Striplate Piecing: Piecing Circle Designs with Speed and Accuracy,** Debra Wagner $24.95
3930 **Tessellations & Variations: Creating One-Patch and Two-Patch Quilts,** Barbara Ann Caron $14.95
3788 **Three-Dimensional Appliqué and Embroidery Embellishment: Techniques for Today's Album Quilt,** Anita Shackelford $24.95
4596 **Ties, Ties, Ties: Traditional Quilts from Neckties,** Janet B. Elwin $19.95
3931 **Time-Span Quilts: New Quilts from Old Tops,** Becky Herdle $16.95
2029 **A Treasury of Quilting Designs,** Linda Goodmon Emery $14.95
3847 **Tricks with Chintz: Using Large Prints to Add New Magic to Traditional Quilt Blocks,** Nancy S. Breland $14.95
2286 **Wonderful Wearables: A Celebration of Creative Clothing,** Virginia Avery $24.95

DATE